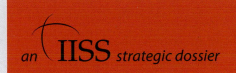

an IISS *strategic dossier*

Russia's Military Modernisation

published by

The International Institute for Strategic Studies
ARUNDEL HOUSE | 6 TEMPLE PLACE | LONDON | WC2R 2PG | UK

an **IISS** *strategic dossier*

Russia's Military Modernisation

The International Institute for Strategic Studies

ARUNDEL HOUSE | 6 TEMPLE PLACE | LONDON | WC2R 2PG | UK

DIRECTOR-GENERAL AND CHIEF EXECUTIVE **Dr John Chipman**
EDITORS **Douglas Barrie, James Hackett**
ASSOCIATE EDITOR **Nicholas Payne**
CONTRIBUTORS **Douglas Barrie, Charles K. Bartles, Piotr Butowski, Nick Childs, Richard Connolly, Julian Cooper, Keir Giles, James Hackett, Anton Lavrov, Roger N. McDermott, Andrew Monaghan, Alexey Ramm, Dmitry Stefanovich, Brian Weeden**
RESEARCH SUPPORT **Henry Boyd, Fenella McGerty, Michael Tong, Tom Waldwyn**
EDITORIAL **Sara Hussain, Jill Lally, Michael Marsden**
GRAPHICS COORDINATOR **Nick Fargher**
DESIGN AND PRODUCTION **John Buck, Kelly Verity**

This publication has been prepared by the Director-General and Chief Executive of the Institute and his staff. It incorporates commissioned contributions from recognised subject experts, which were reviewed by a range of experts in the field. The IISS would like to thank the various individuals who contributed their expertise to the compilation of this dossier. The responsibility for the contents is ours alone. The views expressed herein do not, and indeed cannot, represent a consensus of views among the worldwide membership of the Institute as a whole.

First published September 2020 by the International Institute for Strategic Studies.

COVER IMAGES: Top: (l–r) Monument in Victory Square during Russia's Victory Day, 2020 (Roman Pimenov/TASS/Getty Images); RS-24 intercontinental ballistic-missile system at the rehearsal of Russia's Victory Day military parade, 2019 (Mikhail Metzel/TASS/Getty Images); Russian Su-35 combat aircraft shadowing a US Navy P-8A maritime-patrol aircraft over the Mediterranean Sea, 2020 (Jonathan Nelson/US Navy/Zuma Press/PA Images); Centre: *Delfin*-class nuclear-powered ballistic-missile submarine in the Barents Sea, 2018 (Lev Fedoseyev/TASS/Getty Images); Bottom: (l–r) Defense Minister Sergei Shoigu and President Vladimir Putin at Russia's Navy Day, 2019 (Mikhail Metzel/TASS/Getty Images); T-80 main battle tank at an Eastern Military District firing range, 2020 (Yuri Smityuk/TASS via Getty Images); *Borey*-class nuclear-powered ballistic-missile submarine in the White Sea, 2018 (Oleg Kuleshov/TASS/PA Images).

Printed and bound in the UK by Hobbs the Printers Ltd.

British Library Cataloguing in Publication Data
A catalogue record for this book is available from the British Library

Library of Congress Cataloging in Publication Data
A catalog record for this book has been requested

ISBN 978-0-367-69811-9

About The International Institute for Strategic Studies

The International Institute for Strategic Studies is an independent centre for research, information and debate on the problems of conflict, however caused, that have, or potentially have, an important military content. The Council and Staff of the Institute are international and its membership is drawn from over 100 countries. The Institute is independent and it alone decides what activities to conduct. It owes no allegiance to any government, any group of governments or any political or other organisation. The IISS stresses rigorous research with a forward-looking policy orientation that can improve wider public understanding of international security problems and influence the development of sounder public policy.

Contents

Common abbreviations

AAM	air-to-air missile	**div**	division	**MRL**	multiple-rocket launcher	
AB	airborne	**EW**	electronic warfare	**NBC**	nuclear, biological, chemical	
ABM	anti-ballistic missile	**FFG**	frigate with anti-ship missiles	**PPP**	purchasing-power parity	
AEW	airborne early warning	**FFGHM**	frigate with anti-ship and surface-to-air missiles and a hangar	**PSOH**	offshore patrol ship with hangar	
AFV	armoured fighting vehicle					
AIP	air-independent propulsion	**FGA**	fighter/ground attack	**R&D**	research and development	
APC	armoured personnel carrier	**FLD**	full-load displacement	**recce**	reconnaissance	
arty	artillery	**FS**	corvette	**regt**	regiment	
ASW	anti-submarine warfare	**FSG**	corvette with anti-ship missiles	**SAM**	surface-to-air missile	
atk	attack			**SF**	special forces	
bde	brigade	**FSGM**	corvette with anti-ship and surface-to-air missiles	**SOF**	special-operations forces	
BMD	ballistic-missile defence			**SLBM**	submarine-launched ballistic missile	
bn	battalion/billion	**ftr**	fighter			
C2	command and control	**GLCM**	ground-launched cruise missile	**SP**	self-propelled	
C4ISR	command, control, communications, computers, intelligence, surveillance and reconnaissance	**hel**	helicopter	**SRBM**	short-range ballistic missile	
		HGV	hypersonic glide vehicle	**SSBN**	nuclear-powered ballistic-missile submarine	
		ICBM	intercontinental ballistic missile	**SSGN**	nuclear-powered guided-missile submarine	
CG	cruiser with anti-ship missiles	**IFV**	infantry fighting vehicle	**SSK**	attack submarine	
CGHMN	nuclear-powered cruiser with anti-ship and surface-to-air missiles and a hangar	**ISR**	intelligence, surveillance and reconnaissance	**SSM**	surface-to-surface missile	
				SSN	nuclear-powered attack submarine	
CGN	nuclear-powered cruiser with anti-ship missiles	**LACM**	land-attack cruise missile	**sqn**	squadron	
		LHD	amphibious assault ship	**TEL**	transporter-erector-launcher	
CIWS	close-in weapons system	**MBT**	main battle tank	**UAV**	uninhabited aerial vehicle	
CV	aircraft carrier	**MIRV**	multiple independently targetable re-entry vehicle	**UUV**	uninhabited underwater vehicle	
DDG	destroyer with anti-ship missiles					
		mod	modified/modification	**VLS**	vertical launch system	

Glossary of terms

Aerospace Defence Forces	*Voyska vozdushno-kosmicheskoy oborony*	VVKO
Aerospace Forces	*Vozdushno-kosmicheskie sily*	VKS
Air Base	*Aviabaza*	-
Air Defence Forces	*Voyska protivovozdushnoy oborony*	PVO
Air Defence Forces of the Ground Forces	*Protivo vozdushnaya oborona sukhoputnye voyska*	PVO SV
Air Force	*Voyenno-vozdushnye sily*	VVS
Airborne Forces	*Vozdushno-desantnye voyska*	VDV
Army Aviation	*Armeyskaya aviatsiya*	AA
Automated command-and-control systems	*avtomatizirovannaya sistema upravleniya*	-
Battalion tactical group	*Batal'onnaya takticheskaya gruppa*	BTG
Future Air Complex of Long-range Interception	*Perspektivnyy aviatsionnyy kompleks dalnego perekhvata*	PAK-DP
Future Aviation Complex Front-line Aviation	*Perspektivnyy aviatsionnyy kompleks frontovoi aviatsii*	PAK-FA
Future Aviation Complex Long-Range Aviation	*Perspektivnyy aviatsionnyy kompleks dal'ney aviatsii*	PAK-DA
General Staff	*General'nyy Shtab*	-
Ground Forces	*Sukhoputnye voyska*	SV
Information confrontation/ struggle	*informatsionnoe protivoborstvo*	-
information superiority	*informatsionnoe prevoskhodstvo*	-
Joint Strategic Command	*Ob'yedinennoe strategicheskoe komandovanie*	OSK

Main Directorate of the General Staff	*Glavnoe upravlenie General'nogo shtaba*	-
Military district	*Voyennyy okrug*	MD
Military Intelligence Directorate	*Glavnoe razvedyvatel'noe upravlenie*	GRU
Motor rifle	*Motornaya vintovka*	MR
National Defence Management Centre	*Natsional'nyy tsentr upravleniya oboronoy*	NDMC/ NTsUO
Naval Infantry	*Morskaya pekhota*	MP
Navy	*Voyenno-morskoy flot*	VMF
New Look	*Novy Oblik*	-
Space Forces	*Kosmicheskie voyska*	KV
State Armament Programme	*Gosudarstvennaya programma vooruzheniya*	SAP/GPV
State Defence Order	*Gosudarstvennyy oboronnyy zakaz*	SDO/GOZ
Strategic Rocket Forces	*Raketnye voyska strategicheskogo naznacheniya*	RSVN
Unified System for Command and Control at the Tactical Level	*Yedinoy sistemy upravleniya takticheskogo zvena*	YeSU-TZ

Note: While US alphanumeric designators now include a two-letter country identifier – in the case of Russia, 'RS' – this volume uses the still more widely publicly used previous approach; for example, 'SS-N-30' not 'RS-SS-N-30'.

Introduction

In the Western popular imagination at least, the United States and its allies emerged victorious in the Cold War against the communist Soviet Union. Russia did experience severe economic and political turbulence in the immediate post-Soviet era, but Moscow did not necessarily see itself as having been defeated. Rather, the Russian political elite's view is increasingly that the country was betrayed by those in the West who had assured that Russia would benefit from free-market economics, but instead expanded the reach of an alliance (NATO) that had been established with the single purpose of containing Moscow, while the new economy concentrated wealth in the hands of a few. Analysis of the misunderstandings and the missed opportunities of the late 1980s and early 1990s falls outside the scope of this study, but Moscow's view of these events continues to influence and shape its security policies and its armed forces, the capabilities of which were degraded severely by the turmoil of the 1990s.

This IISS Strategic Dossier examines how Russia's armed forces have fared in the three decades since the end of the Soviet Union. There is particular focus on the most recent defence reforms and military-modernisation ambitions. However, what becomes clear is that modernisation, in this case, does not just mean introducing new capabilities. Many of Moscow's plans to improve its armed forces have depended on upgrading existing equipment and, in some cases, simply introducing into service capabilities that were planned decades earlier. But they are improving. As such, the conclusions of this publication are also valuable when considering the nature and extent of any challenge that Moscow's more capable armed forces pose to European security.

Soviet no more

The Soviet Union's armed forces entered the 1980s with ambitious research and development and acquisition goals, but by the end of the decade the fall of the Berlin Wall presaged the collapse of the USSR only two years later, in 1991. Instead of introducing a range of advanced weapons across the armed services during the 1990s, the rump of the

Key takeaways

RUSSIA'S MILITARY-MODERNISATION EFFORTS SINCE 2008 HAVE PROVIDED MOSCOW WITH A CREDIBLE MILITARY TOOL FOR PURSUING NATIONAL POLICY GOALS

- All arms of the armed forces are now more capable than at any time since the end of the Soviet Union.

- Modernisation has taken place on a Russian, not a Soviet scale – Moscow's military is a fraction of the size of that of the Soviet Union. Russia's overall military posture remains fundamentally defensive, but is combined with below-the-threshold activities to unbalance rivals.

- The size and nature of Russia's armed forces militate toward planning for a quick campaign and decisive outcome.

RUSSIA'S ARMED FORCES HAVE BENEFITED SIGNIFICANTLY FROM MORE THAN A DECADE OF SUSTAINED INVESTMENT FUNDING. CONTINUITY, HOWEVER, IS NOT GUARANTEED

- Sustaining defence investment during the 2020s poses a challenge. Near-term cuts have been proposed by the Finance Ministry in response to COVID-19, and wider economic performance issues could put pressure on further military expenditure.

- Russia's capacity to fully reinvigorate its defence research and technology base and its capacity to then exploit developments are problems that could constrain Moscow's ambitions.

- Defence-technology relationships with China could prove key in some technology areas, but this will be dependent on the wider geostrategic relationship between the two.

NUCLEAR FORCES CONTINUE TO BE VIEWED AS THE ULTIMATE GUARANTOR OF RUSSIAN SECURITY

- Russia will sustain the nuclear triad, and land-based systems remain the priority.

- Novel strategic weapons are intended as a counter to the perceived threat of US ballistic-missile defences, and as possible bargaining chips in any future arms-control talks.

GROUND FORCES ARE NOW BETTER TRAINED AND EQUIPPED, AND MORE READILY DEPLOYABLE

- Improvements in extended-range fire support, but ambitious armour programmes delayed.

- Airborne Forces provide a rapid-reaction force.

NAVAL FORCES NOW PROVIDE FAR GREATER CONVENTIONAL FIREPOWER

- Widespread introduction of dual-capable land-attack cruise missiles improves naval utility.

- Sub-surface-fleet development lagging behind schedule, but remains the focus.

AEROSPACE FORCES CAPABILITIES ARE MARKEDLY IMPROVED

- Introduction of new-build combat aircraft provides the Air Force with genuine multi-role platforms.

- But a next-generation multi-role combat aircraft is nearly a decade late.

RUSSIA'S MILITARY-MODERNISATION PROGRAMME IS BASED PREDOMINANTLY ON UPGRADES RATHER THAN NEW PLATFORMS AND WEAPONS

- New platform and weapon developments have repeatedly failed to meet schedules because of overly optimistic time frames and technical problems.

- The Russian armed forces will continue to depend on upgraded systems throughout the 2020s, with new platforms and weapons being introduced only at a modest pace.

- The recapitalisation of Russia's military capabilities is a key driver of military-policy and -capability planning in many European states.

Soviet Union's armed forces was instead faced with a fight to sustain even a modest capability. Structured force reductions introduced by Soviet leader Mikhail Gorbachev in 1988, intended to cut 500,000 personnel as part of his wider effort to begin to shift emphasis from a military-focused to a civil economy, were overtaken by events in the USSR's final chaotic two years. For the armed forces, however, this heralded worse to come. In the 1990s, only Russia's strategic missile forces received enough funding to remain credible, as the conventional elements of the armed forces struggled to manage the impact of the collapse of the USSR and the end of the Warsaw Pact, Moscow's 36-year-old military alliance designed to counter NATO.[1]

NATO expansion and US ballistic-missile-defence goals were fault lines along which the US–Russia relationship fractured.[2] What for NATO member states was clearly the sovereign right of a nation to seek Alliance membership was viewed from Moscow as a betrayal of assurances it felt were given during the discussions over German reunification in 1990.[3] More recently, this has been compounded by Russia's demand for a sphere of influence in the post-Soviet space, part of which contains now Alliance members.

From Washington's perspective, ballistic-missile defence was aimed at the defeat of a handful of intercontinental ballistic missiles from a rogue state. However, Moscow saw it as the beginning of a threat to its deterrent forces, a view reinforced by the United States' 2001 decision to withdraw from the Anti-Ballistic Missile Treaty and its pursuit of ballistic-missile defence in Europe, however limited these capabilities are in reality.[4]

Russia's view of NATO expansion, merited or not, was made clear by then-president Boris Yeltsin in 1998, who said it was a 'serious mistake' with 'serious consequences'.[5] However, from a European perspective, Moscow had ample opportunity to avoid confrontation.

Having extracted the Soviet Union from a protracted war in Afghanistan, Gorbachev said, idealistically, in 1989 that the 'use of force … has become historically obsolete'.[6] Three decades later, Russia had annexed foreign territory, fought wars with former parts of the USSR and embarked on a successful expeditionary operation to support the Syrian regime in a civil war.

Far from being 'historically obsolete', by 2018 President Vladimir Putin was lauding the armed forces and telling the Federal Assembly that Russia possesses a 'modern high-technology army'.[7] He chided those international 'partners' who considered it 'impossible in the foreseeable historical perspective for our country to revive its

INSPECTING THE TROOPS
Russia's then minister of defence Anatoly Serdyukov during the May 2008 Victory Day parade. CREDIT: Dmitry Beliakov/Bloomberg/Getty Images

economy, industry, defence industry and Armed Forces to levels supporting the necessary strategic potential'.[8]

Examining the extent to which Putin's boast of 'a modern high-technology army' is justified is a founding question of this dossier. Nevertheless, without Putin and his political associates, it is at the very least debatable whether Russia's armed forces would have recovered to the extent they have from the vicissitudes of the 1990s.

Reform efforts

Reform of the armed forces had been on the agenda during the 1980s, even before Gorbachev's proposed cuts. **Chapter One** charts the thinking within the senior Soviet ranks in the 1980s over potential approaches to restructuring the armed forces, through the thwarted reform efforts of the 1990s, up to and including the 2008 New Look modernisation programme. The groundwork for the New Look had been completed under defence minister Sergei Ivanov (incumbent 2001–07). In 2006, Ivanov outlined planned cuts in conscript numbers, the thinning of the senior ranks and moving to a larger percentage of professional soldiers. All of these were to be implemented as part of the 2008 New Look programme, though

by Anatoly Serdyukov, who replaced Ivanov as defence minister in February 2007. Irrespective of previous reform efforts, the conflict with Georgia had shown that Russia still lacked the capacity to rapidly deploy enough combat-ready units even for a small war. However, unlike previous reform efforts, New Look benefited from adequate funding for many of its goals, and from the backing of Russia's political leaders.

Strategic forces

Throughout the 1990s, only Russia's nuclear forces received anything resembling the required funding to sustain a modicum of credibility. **Chapter Two** examines the development of Russia's nuclear deterrent since the end of the USSR. Irrespective of the end of the Cold War, there was little question that Russia would remain a major nuclear power, even if several of the weapon systems planned or in development during the 1980s fell into abeyance. If anything, during the 1990s, as its conventional armed forces were hollowed out through a lack of investment and associated cuts in personnel and inventory, Moscow's nuclear systems took on even greater importance. The perceived vulnerability to conventional warfare was

reflected in the Soviet Union's declared position of 'no first use' of nuclear weapons being dropped in 1993.

Land-based systems have continued to remain the largest part of Moscow's nuclear triad, with the shift from silo-based to mobile systems ongoing. Nuclear-powered ballistic-missile submarines (SSBNs) provide the second element of the deterrent, despite the difficulties Russia has had in introducing a new submarine-launched ballistic missile into the inventory. The air-launched element of Russia's strategic forces today remains arguably the weakest, in that it is dependent on a small number of modern bomber aircraft, supported by a turbo-prop-powered bomber that has its origin in the 1950s.

Along with investing in 'traditional' nuclear delivery systems, Moscow is also pursuing several 'novel' systems, including nuclear-powered cruise missiles and 'torpedoes', and is in the early stages of introducing a hypersonic boost-glide system into its nuclear inventory.

Ground Forces

Russia's Ground Forces are today smaller and more capable than they were in the mid-1990s. Elements of these forces are held at a high state of readiness and

SOVIET ARMY TANKS
Tanks near the Kremlin during the abortive coup attempt against then Soviet president Mikhail Gorbachev, August 1991. CREDIT: Dima Tanin/ AFP/Getty Images

have had recent combat experience. The Airborne Forces and reorganised Special Forces are also seen as a key component of Russia's high-readiness capability. **Chapter Three** assesses the organisational changes that have reshaped these forces since the end of the Soviet Union. Tracing the origins of the reforms in late-Soviet military thinking, it also evaluates the lessons that Russia's military leaders derived from reform efforts, including the post-2008 New Look, and how these were reshaped by experimentation and, as time went on, lessons from operations.

The decision in 2008 to wholly change formations by transitioning to a brigade structure was designed to generate units capable of more independent self-sustaining missions of the sort that were anticipated on Russia's periphery. However, lessons arising from trials, from increased tensions with the West and with Ukraine (and the fighting there) contributed to Moscow's decision to reintroduce divisions. These forces' equipment has also changed, though perhaps not in so far-reaching a manner as anticipated in the middle of the last decade, when new designs like the T-14 main battle tank were first observed. The inventory of the Ground Forces, certainly the manoeuvre formations, will in the immediate future consist of some wholly new equipment types,

as well as a large number of modernised platforms, such as the T-72B3. But there has been particular progress in improving artillery and missile capabilities, with the replacement of the *Tochka*-U (SS-21B *Scarab*) short-range ballistic-missile system with the *Iskander*-M (SS-26 *Stone*) system and modernisation of self-propelled artillery systems. These hold the potential, when combined with new command-and-control systems and uninhabited aerial vehicles, to improve the ability of Russia's forces to find, fix and strike adversary formations at greater range than before. In common with the other services, these have also been tested on operations.

Naval forces

The US intelligence community assessed that by the mid-1990s the Soviet Navy would field 60–70 SSBNs, fewer but larger principal surface combatants and five or more aircraft carriers as part of a balanced fleet increasingly capable of addressing all maritime roles. As of 2020, the navy has a single aircraft carrier, now in refit, with no replacement as yet funded, 11 SSBNs and a surface-ship-building programme focused on platforms more suited to the littoral than the blue-water environment. **Chapter Four** considers developments

in the Russian Navy, and the gulf, often apparent, between the ambition and the reality of the service's goals and actual capabilities. Nevertheless, the navy retains considerable capabilities, even beside its SSBNs. The introduction, for example, of the 3M14 *Kalibr* (SS-N-30A *Sagaris*) land-attack cruise missile provides the navy with a notable power-projection weapon.

The navy retains vestiges of a blue-water role, relying predominantly on its larger, ageing Soviet-era surface platforms and more modern submarines. However, more recent additions to its surface fleet are better suited to defending the Russian littoral and its near waters, as well as supporting and protecting the submarine-based deterrent. While the navy was allocated the second-largest funding element after Russia's nuclear forces in the 2020 State Armament Programme (SAP), covering 2011–20, it has not fared as well in the follow-on 2027 SAP, covering 2018–27.

Aerospace Forces

Like the navy, several of the Aerospace Forces' goals in the 2020 SAP went unmet. Unlike for the navy, however, Russia's defence industry was better placed to provide interim solutions that have improved considerably the combat-air

ADMIRAL KUZNETSOV
The Russian aircraft carrier on fire while berthed in Murmansk, December 2019. CREDIT: Lev Fedoseyev/TASS/Getty Images

elements of the service. **Chapter Five** examines what is a smaller by far air force than that fielded by the Soviet Union at the end of the Cold War, but one which has benefited considerably from recent investments. Less successful, however, were some of the structural changes introduced by the 2008 New Look programme, several of which have been re-cast in the intervening years.

For the Soviet Air Force, the 1990s was to be a decade of recapitalisation, with new combat-aircraft types and major upgrades of existing designs to be introduced. Instead, the embryonic Russian Air Force struggled to maintain even a semblance of capability. Its performance in the first and second wars in Chechnya and in the short Georgia campaign exposed shortcomings in equipment and training. By the launch of the Syrian intervention in 2015, however, the service was benefiting from sustained investment from SAP 2020 and those positive elements of New Look. A new multi-role fighter, the Su-57 *Felon*, remains in development (albeit years behind the original schedule), while a modernised variant of the original Su-27 *Flanker* design, the Su-35S *Flanker* M, now provides the air force with its most capable fighter/ground-attack aircraft. In Long Range Aviation terms, as well as upgrading in-service types, the air force is returning the Tu-160 *Blackjack* to production. Meanwhile, the programme to develop a new long-range bomber to meet the service's PAK-DA requirement was part of SAP 2020, and continues to be funded in SAP 2027 alongside the new-build of an upgraded Tu-160. However, whether Russia can afford to run two expensive bomber projects in parallel and has the industrial capacity to do so is debatable.

Military decision-making and joint operations

The US was not alone in the early 1980s in considering the implications of the digital revolution for military operations. Similar thinking was being led by the Soviet

TU-160 *BLACKJACK*
United Aircraft Corporation President Yuri Slyusar and Deputy Minister of Defence Yuri Borisov sign a contract to put the Tu-160 *Blackjack* back into production while President Vladimir Putin looks on, January 2018. CREDIT: Lev Fedoseyev/TASS/Getty Images

Union's Marshal Nikolai Ogarkov. While the US went on to field an increasing array of digitally enabled weapons throughout the 1990s, any hope of Ogarkov's vision of a Russian revolution in military affairs was thwarted by the Soviet Union's collapse. **Chapter Six** assesses the impact of the 2008 New Look reforms on the Russian armed forces' decision-making structures, Russia's approach to joint operations and its increasing adoption of digital systems across the spectrum of military equipment. Nearly four decades after Ogarkov envisaged a 'reconnaissance strike complex', Russia's armed forces are putting in place a decision-making architecture and network-enabled capabilities and weapons to finally deliver such a capability. The 2008 reforms set in train an overhaul of the Russian military decision-making process, moving from what was mainly a paper-based process to a digital architecture. The development and adoption of command, control, communications, computers, intelligence, surveillance and reconnaissance (C4ISR) systems was emphasised as part of the modernisation programme.

A revised framework for military decision-making has emerged over the past decade as Moscow carried out a widespread structural reorganisation of the armed forces and its command-and-control systems. This is designed to improve efficiency and speed in command and control, as well as positioning the armed forces to conduct operations in an information-driven environment. A test-and-adjust approach has been adopted, including with systems trialled during joint-operations exercises. As with many large-scale computer-based developments, progress has not always been smooth.

Defence economics and industry

Defence expenditure is predicated upon, though not directly pegged to, wider economic performance. The travails of the Russian economy throughout the 1990s were reflected in the near collapse of defence expenditure. Even when sums were allocated, sometimes only a fraction of the amount would be forthcoming. **Chapter Seven** considers the arc of Russian defence expenditure since the end of the Soviet Union and examines how the country's domestic defence industry has had to navigate turbulent times.

Defence spending fell steeply in the early 1990s, a situation exacerbated by the 1998 financial crisis. It recovered somewhat during the early 2000s, with a notable further improvement for most of the 2010s.

The government's goal now is to secure a steady state of funding that will support the reform and modernisation progress made in the previous decade.

However, measuring Russian defence expenditure is not straightforward, as Moscow has unsurprisingly not adopted a NATO-standard approach to accounting for military-related expenditure. Nearly all military spending is included in the Federal Budget, though not all of it is included in the document's chapter on defence expenditure. Military housing infrastructure and pension costs, for example, are to be found elsewhere in the Federal Budget's 14 volumes.

After a difficult two decades, the defence industry has benefited from the sustained investment supported by SAP 2020. However, even before the impact of the COVID-19 pandemic, it was evident that the levels of procurement investment of the 2010s were not going to be replicated in the 2020s.

In addition, the sector is not homogeneous, and nor is the performance of its various elements. Maritime and land systems have fared less well than defence aerospace, though even here the accomplishments are far from uniform. While smaller by far than in the Soviet era, the defence industry is still significant, an important employer and a sector upon which some cities remain dependent.

Scope of the dossier

The intent of this dossier is to assess the impact of Russia's military-modernisation project using open-source material, to consider the extent to which Moscow's explicitly stated goals have been or are being met across all the military domains, and the capacity this confers on the Russian government to suggest, threaten the use of or wield military power in all its guises to meet its policy aims.

In the past decade, Russia has used many of the military tools it now has at its disposal, from 'below-the-threshold' information operations to traditional kinetic activity in Syria and eastern Ukraine. However, this dossier is not intended as an exhaustive study of all of Moscow's military and paramilitary organisations.

Instead, the dossier examines the impact of the 2008 New Look modernisation programme, which remains the most important of all post-Soviet military reforms, and weighs the successes and failures of this project just over a decade after it was launched. In concert, the current and recent SAPs are reviewed across all the military domains to measure their effectiveness. Particular attention is paid to the 2020 SAP, which was intended to implement 'modernisation' across all of Russia's armed services, to consider whether and the extent to which the programme's targets have been met and the implications for each of the armed services.

Notes

1 See, for example, Benjamin S. Lambeth, 'Russia's Air Power At The Crossroads', RAND, 1996, p. xv.

2 President Vladimir Putin, 'Speech and the Following Discussion at the Munich Conference on Security Policy', 10 February 2007, http://en.kremlin.ru/events/president/transcripts/24034; President Dmitry Medvedev, 'News conference following NATO–Russian Council Meeting', 20 November 2010, http://en.kremlin.ru/events/president/transcripts/9570.

3 Archie Brown, *The Human Factor, Gorbachev, Reagan and Thatcher, and the End of the Cold War* (Oxford: Oxford University Press, 2020), pp. 324–25; President of Russia, 'Speech and the Following Discussion at the Munich Conference on Security Policy', 10 February 2007, http://en.kremlin.ru/events/president/transcripts/24034.

4 Office of the Press Secretary, White House, 'ABM Treaty: US Withdrawal Statement', 13 December 2001, https://www.acq.osd.mil/tc/abm/ABM-withdrawal.htm.

5 TASS, 'Yeltsin views domestic, foreign policy issues in Austrian newspaper interview', 24 October 1998, BBC Monitoring, https://monitoring.bbc.co.uk/product/mom8q8hi.

6 Brown, *The Human Factor, Gorbachev, Reagan and Thatcher, and the end of the Cold War*, p. 237.

7 President Vladimir Putin, 'Presidential Address to the Federal Assembly', 1 March 2018, http://en.kremlin.ru/events/president/transcripts/messages/56957.

8 *Ibid.*

Russia's armed forces since the end of the Cold War

Military reform after 1991

The Russian armed forces faced critical challenges following the collapse of the Soviet Union in 1991. Over the following decade, the services had to confront the reality of a smaller establishment strength, with units and equipment allocated to newly independent republics of the former Soviet Union. They also had to deal with the legacy of the 1979–89 Afghanistan war, the damaging wars in Chechnya, the need to reshape Russia's defence organisations, and personnel and funding crises. Additionally, economic problems had serious implications for defence funding: budgets fell sharply and procurement atrophied. Service chiefs, meanwhile, were unable over the decade to establish balanced and well-trained forces equipped with modern weapons. Factors stemming from the Soviet legacy also helped stymie their ambitions, including a complicated deployment system that was designed to bring combat formations to readiness by mobilising a reserve component and a vast array of equipment – much held in store – intended to outfit these forces.[1] Indeed, these arrangements had ramifications. Then-president Boris Yeltsin's decision not to issue a mobilisation order in advance of the First Chechen War meant that Russia's formations sent there were in effect ad hoc and only brought up to strength by drafting in troops from disparate units.

There were fitful – and unsuccessful – attempts to initiate reforms during the 1990s, largely aiming to generate a combat-ready core within this overall structure. However, matters only began to improve in 2003 when the Ministry of Defence (MoD) formally introduced a contract-service initiative (though this was itself briefly reversed in 2009–10), and after 2007–08, when experiments began to improve command and control by activating strategic commands.[2] This coincided with the MoD being tasked with fundamental change in the wake of the August 2008 war with Georgia, which heralded the shift away from the mass-mobilisation model.

Key takeaways

NEW LOOK AIMS

The New Look programme was designed to transform armed forces that still reflected the Soviet-era mass-mobilisation army into a modern combat-ready force held at high readiness.

BITTER EXPERIENCE

Russia's experiences in the Chechen wars reinvigorated reform aspirations. In the first war, Russia's forces there were often understrength and it was difficult to deploy coherent units. The Second Chechen War saw a modest improvement, and performance in the 2008 Georgia war was a key impetus for reform.

REFORM ORIGINS

Although the reforms after 2008 finally led to fundamental change, some Russian military leaders – notably Marshal Nikolai Ogarkov – had long advocated reforms that would lead to restructured, more professional and higher-readiness formations.

COMMAND AND CONTROL IMPROVES

The reforms were also intended to streamline command and control. Military districts were reduced in number and in 2010 four strategic commands were created, rising to five in 2015. A fifth military district was due to be formed in 2021.

MANOEUVRE COMBAT POWER STILL VITAL

Russia has developed capabilities that enable actions short of war and has honed existing competencies in areas like electronic warfare. But armour and artillery modernisation, together with the moves to improve command and control, organisation and deployability, indicate that the ability to conduct rapid deep-strike operations remains an aspiration.

Personnel and the mass-mobilisation legacy

Russia's legacy mass-mobilisation system, in which the armed forces would be brought up to wartime strength by recalling reservists, meant that both Soviet-era military formations and, until 2008, their Russian successors effectively had two distinct tables of organisation and equipment (TOE).[3]

The wartime TOE set out the number of personnel and equipment required for a military operation, whereas its peacetime counterpart indicated the numbers intended for daily routines and combat training. Due to the different tasks required, these differed significantly in scale and composition. The plan was that units would in crisis or wartime be brought to strength with reservists, also gaining additional vehicles from equipment storage bases or from the civilian sector. These differential TOEs were seen not only in motor-rifle and tank divisions but also in the air force, air-defence formations and even in the Strategic Rocket Forces.[4]

Readiness, already challenged by the nature of the mobilisation model, was further tested by personnel shortages.[5] All battalions, regiments, brigades, divisions, armies and districts were short of personnel. These shortages resulted from troops leaving service, transferring to other postings or leaving for training courses – in these cases of 'current' shortages, posts remained vacant. Units also experienced 'temporary' personnel shortages, when soldiers were temporarily unable to perform their tasks, for instance due to a tour of duty, a spell in hospital or a period of leave.

If a unit were deployed on operations, it had to transition to its wartime TOE, rectifying its 'current' and 'temporary' personnel shortages and taking from storage additional equipment. Without mobilisation, it was difficult to compensate for these personnel shortages.

There were broader challenges facing Russia's service personnel in the 1990s, ranging from poor conditions and pay to the persistence of practices like *dedovshchína* ('hazing' or 'bullying') – and even the hiring of military personnel for labour.[6] (Authorities attempted to address practices like the latter through legislation after the mid-2000s.) Meanwhile, Russia's military formations were still dominated by conscripts. Conscription had a number of functions. It generated, each year, thousands of recruits arriving at reception centres and entering training, eventually to emerge on unit postings. It meant that there was, across society, a level of military experience that would be useful should mobilisation occur. Also, after contract-service initiatives began to be introduced after 1992, it was hoped that some conscripts would then decide to stay on as contractors, thus building up a more professional body of troops.[7]

However, challenges arose in the 1990s, as Russia experienced the results of declining birth rates. Between 1987 and 1999, live male births in Russia fell by around half, meaning that in time fewer young men were available to be called up – a challenge compounded by plans in 2008 to reduce the term of conscript service from two years to one.[8] Additionally, more modern and more technically complex military equipment required more experienced and generally longer-serving troops.

This was the Soviet-era legacy: the complex system of mobilisation deployment that, for many years, frustrated many of Russia's military leaders. And, despite the reform initiatives in the 1990s and from 2005–08, a qualified solution only emerged in 2008, when the mass-mobilisation principle came to an end and concerted effort began to generate contractor-staffed combat-ready formations.

Afghanistan: the Soviet-era mobilisation system in practice

The former Soviet army comprised several categories of formation. The most combat-ready were called Type-A units.[9] Documents indicate that these were to be staffed at 95–100% of their peacetime table of organisation and equipment (TOE), though this was only 70% of the wartime TOE. Military specialists presumed that such formations could be committed to combat on short notice without the remaining 30%.[10]

Lessons learned in Afghanistan proved such calculations overly optimistic. The motor-rifle and airborne divisions and brigades deployed there were all Type-A units. Although they would have been augmented up to the wartime TOE with reservists in case of war, the peacetime TOE of the 40th Army (which was re-formed for this mission) was deemed sufficient. It is possible that political factors lay behind this decision. Officially, the Soviet army was carrying out its 'international duty' to aid the communist government of the Democratic Republic of Afghanistan and assisting its people in maintaining national stability.[11] If, however, the 40th Army had adopted a wartime TOE, the Soviet Union would in effect have been acknowledging that it was at war. An additional problem was that forces there had to contend with high levels of both 'current' and 'temporary' personnel shortages.

Although there is little official information on the 40th Army's mobilisation readiness and staffing, a number of memoirs have been written by personnel involved in the conflict, referencing high casualties, poor conditions and long deployments (a tour of duty could last 24 months). Some motor-rifle companies, with a wartime TOE of 70 troops, would sometimes begin a mission in Afghanistan with only 30, while some motor-rifle battalions would only be able to dispatch on missions one company staffed to wartime TOE levels.[12]

The Soviet army had a system to compensate for these personnel shortages. Military commissariats mobilised reservists with similar military skills, but the system became effective only when there was a partial or a national mobilisation. In 1979, Soviet military leaders did indeed initiate a partial mobilisation in order to fully staff tank, motor-rifle and airborne divisions to be deployed in Afghanistan. The mobilisation lasted six months; the reservists were then dismissed and replaced by officers and soldiers transferred from other military districts.[13]

There were no more mobilisation orders throughout the campaign, and the Soviet army had no legal grounds by which it could activate its mechanism to bring units to strength. However, in 1984 the Turkestan and Central Asian military districts established a special reserve comprising lieutenants who had just

SOVIET PRESENCE IN AFGHANISTAN
Soviet soldiers on parade in Kabul in 1986, shortly before returning to the Soviet Union. The Soviet army withdrew in 1989. CREDIT: Daniel Janin/ AFP/Getty Images

graduated from military schools (some 200 men in each district) as well as non-commissioned officers (NCOs) fresh from training.[14] Afterwards, this decision came in for criticism: those in the district reserve had no combat training; there was also no time limit to this commitment; and replacements soon had to be found for NCOs because they served only a relatively short period in conscript service.

The Soviet army was more than two million strong at the time of the war in Afghanistan, but this force found it difficult to activate relatively few combined-arms and airborne divisions, independent battalions, and air-force regiments and squadrons: the MoD was, in effect, hamstrung by the mobilisation decisions taken by Soviet political leaders.

The Ogarkov legacy

Although it might appear that significant reductions in military formations were the only Russian military reforms of the early 1990s, military leaders at that time did attempt to begin a comprehensive military-reform process. Its main advocate was Marshal of the Soviet Union Nikolai Ogarkov.[15] Ogarkov was a former c hief of the General Staff (CGS, 1977–84) who, in January 1992, was appointed advisor

to the MoD. (In May the same year, Army General Pavel Grachev was appointed as Russia's first Minister of Defence.)

In the early 1980s, Ogarkov had conceived a complex reform of the Soviet army that would have involved phasing out its mobilisation deployment mechanism in favour of permanent-readiness formations. The idea was that the structure of these formations would not be governed by peacetime and wartime TOEs. There was also a plan to establish a professional training system for NCOs. Changes to the command system were considered, with military districts restructured as strategic commands and the establishment of an Aerospace Force.[16] Ogarkov was also notable for advocating

MARSHAL OGARKOV
Marshal of the Soviet Union Nikolai Ogarkov, pictured in 1983, was an advocate for armed-forces reform. CREDIT: Boris Kavashkin/Valentin Cheredintsev/TASS/Getty Images

inventory modernisation, higher readiness, changes to force structures and organisations as well as assessments of the future operating environment.[17] In the West, Ogarkov became more widely known as a spokesman on television after Korean Air Lines flight 007 was shot down by an Su-15 *Flagon* interceptor in September 1983. One year later, he was dismissed from his post as CGS and replaced by Marshal Sergei Akhromeyev, with his reform plans unrealised. And when he had a second chance to advocate for revolutionary change to the Russian military system, in 1992 after his advisory appointment, the economic situation hindered far-reaching change; instead, the MoD settled on what it called the Mobile Force.

The Mobile Force concept

The Mobile Force concept is relatively little-known in the history of post-Soviet military reforms. Marshal Ogarkov, in his role as advisor to the defence minister, was a proponent of the concept.[18] The plan was that there would be several stages towards establishing the Mobile Force. Because not all of these were accomplished, the effect the concept would have had on the army, had it been fully implemented, remains a source of speculation.

The Mobile Force was a revolutionary concept for Soviet and Russian military schools. It encompassed several motor-rifle brigades that were to be kept at the highest state of readiness, able to be committed to combat at short notice. Because the brigades were intended to be manned with 100% of their wartime TOE, they were not dependent on reservists when deploying to their area of operations. Because of this, it would in theory only take 24 hours to redeploy and field these brigades to their assigned regions. The main tasks envisaged for these brigades were: engaging in local wars and conflicts; assisting in national emergencies; and protecting the integrity of the Russian state.

The table of organisation and equipment of those mobile brigades was the same as the two Independent Army Corps (5th and 48th) – mobile operational forces that had been activated in the early 1980s. Instead of traditional regiments and divisions, these corps comprised independent tank and motor-rifle brigades, an air-assault regiment and a helicopter regiment. The brigades were tasked with continuous offensive operations, once enemy defences had been breached, with the intention that they manoeuvre into the enemy's rear, destroying advancing reserves and seizing important infrastructure.[19] Although it is believed that Marshal Ogarkov was the main proponent of the mobile army corps, some former members of the Soviet General Staff attribute the initiative to General Makhmut Gareev. In the late 1980s, both formations were reshaped as regular motor-rifle divisions.

It remains unclear how many were intended to be activated, though it may have been one mobile brigade per military district. In the end, three Mobile Force independent brigades were activated: the 74th (in Yurga, Kemerovo Region); the 131st (at Maikop, in the Republic of Adygea); and the 136th (in Buynaksk, in the Republic of Dagestan). The new brigades were drawn from motor-rifle divisions and included the following elements:

- one Brigade Command and Brigade Headquarters
- one Reconnaissance Company
- one Tank Battalion (comprising five tank companies)
- four Motor-rifle Battalions
- two Artillery Battalions (self-propelled howitzers)
- one Anti-Tank Battalion
- one MRL Battery
- one Communications Battalion
- one Repair and Recovery Battalion
- one Combat Service Support Battalion
- one Radiation Chemical and Bacteriological Protection Company
- one Electronic Warfare Company
- one Engineering Company
- one Medical Company

Except for a few combat-service-support components, all battalions and companies were self-sustaining formations. This was intended to increase their endurance on operations. For example, they operated combat repair teams and recovery vehicles for the maintenance and repair of damaged equipment. Each battalion also had mobile stores including rations, ammunition and spare parts. These self-sustaining military formations led to increased numbers of commissioned-officer positions in companies and, more importantly, in battalion staffs: a battalion commander had two new deputies, one for logistics and one for armaments (the latter tasked with maintenance and repair of weapons and military equipment).

The activation of three mobile brigades was to have been the first stage in establishing the Mobile Force. It is likely that the second stage would have seen them increase in number and be augmented with an army aviation component. Russian analysts understand that this would have included helicopter regiments and airlift squadrons as well as attack aircraft and tactical bombers.[20] Little is known about the third stage, although it may have encompassed the activation of a self-sustaining Army Corps – perhaps similar in organisational structure to the Soviet-era Army Corps. It may even have included an army aviation brigade.[21]

A self-sustained army aviation brigade would have comprised two or three helicopter regiments, an airlift squadron and a regiment of Su-25 attack aircraft. The first attempt to activate such a formation was made in the Far Eastern Military District in the late 1980s, though the experiment ended with the collapse of the Soviet Union. The General Staff and Air Force Command tried unsuccessfully to activate army aviation brigades in the early 1990s.[22] If Russia had been successful in implementing the Mobile Force concept, it is possible that by the mid-1990s the Russian army would have been able to field a number of mobile task forces, perhaps independent of the mass-mobilisation structure.

1991–93: further reform initiatives

As the Soviet Union ended, in 1991, its army comprised 32 tank divisions and 100 motor-rifle divisions.[23] The Russian army inherited much of this legacy and also had to relocate back to Russian territory numerous formations that had been stationed in the former Soviet republics and abroad. With the economy taking a downward turn, Russia's military leaders were unable to maintain these numbers but wanted nonetheless to retain some combat potential. As a result, the General Staff in 1992 introduced new classifications for military formations which were applied to the army, the Air Defence Force and the Air Force:

Type-A and -B units were to be at 70% of the wartime TOE; cadre (often mistakenly referred to as 'reduced') units were to be at no more than 5% of the wartime TOE; and Equipment Storage Bases were to be at 5–10% of the wartime TOE.

As of 1 January 1991, the Air Force had a significant establishment comprising 11 air-force armies, 25 air-force divisions and 129 air-force regiments. It was particularly hard hit by the collapse of the Soviet Union: more than 3,400 aircraft (including 2,500 combat aircraft) officially remained in former Soviet republics, some 35% of the Soviet Air Force. However, Russia inherited the majority of the advanced fourth-generation fighters (MiG-29 *Fulcrum*, MiG-31 *Foxhound*, Su-27 *Flanker*, Su-24M *Fencer* tactical bombers and Su-25 *Frogfoot* attack aircraft.[24] It became clear that the main challenge facing the force was a shortage of pilots – many of whom had resigned or retired, while the number and quality of lieutenants had decreased – as well as persistent fuel shortages that had a negative impact on active pilots.

At the time of the collapse of the Soviet Union, the Air Defence Force was on paper equally formidable, including two Air Defence Districts and more than a dozen Air Defence Armies. However, less than 20% of its anti-aircraft systems were the latest S-300s (SA-10 *Grumble*), with the national air-defence system instead relying heavily on systems such as the then-obsolete S-75 (SA-2 *Guideline*) and S-125 (SA-3 *Goa*). The Ministry of Defence decided to significantly reduce the number of air-defence troops by deactivating those divisions and regiments equipped with obsolete equipment. This, in turn, created large stocks of various equipment and anti-aircraft missiles.

In response, the General Staff, Air Defence and Air Force commands proposed that several equipment storage bases be established to store fixed- and rotary-wing aircraft, helicopters, auxiliary and air-defence equipment. Then, if necessary, Air Force Regiments, Air Defence and Radar Divisions could be fielded and equipped, with these bases comprising special facilities to store equipment and provide routine maintenance and repair.[25] However, their activation depended on reservists. In theory, this system eliminated the need to maintain a large army in peacetime, as this could be augmented by mobilisation deployments. However, while this process might have been acceptable for Air Defence forces, it was not suitable for the Air Force, which would have required the mobilisation of well-trained pilots ready for combat duty.

Failure of the Mobile Force reforms, and the First Chechen War

These reform plans were thwarted by the poor state of the Russian economy, which did not allow for sufficient funds to implement the full set of changes.[26] Moreover, the paradoxical decision was taken, probably at either the end of 1992 or the beginning of 1993, to transform the three mobile brigades into peacetime TOEs, which undermined the Mobile Force concept. Regardless of their organisational structure, the transition to a peacetime TOE effectively turned the brigades into regular formations. The First Chechen War soon illustrated this problem.

When Russian politicians decided to deploy troops to Chechnya, in 1994, they refused to order even a partial mobilisation, a move which seriously affected the operational readiness of the entire force. Without a decision by the government to mobilise reservists, several high-ranking military officials refused to take part in operations in Chechnya, including Colonel General Eduard Vorobyev, then the Deputy Commander-in-Chief of the Army for Combat Training.[27]

On 2 December 1994, units from the 131st Motor-rifle Brigade were redeployed to the village of Terskoye for assembly and preparation to move into Chechnya. The 131st provided two motor-rifle battalions, a tank battalion, a reconnaissance company and artillery batteries. This brigade was then fielded in its peacetime TOE, where a motor-rifle company comprised some 50–60 soldiers; actual manpower was even lower. Conversely, if mobilisation had been announced, the wartime TOE then in use meant the company would (in theory at least) have had 115 men.[28]

Another problem was that the formations engaged in hostilities were experiencing personnel shortages, particularly of NCOs, while a 1993 decision to gradually reduce the number of conscripts began to decrease the numbers of privates and sergeants.

As a result, and with a nod to Russia's experience in the 1979–89 Afghanistan war, military districts were authorised to augment their formations in Chechnya with soldiers from other units. For example, the 74th Motor-rifle Brigade of the Mobile Force (Siberian Military District) was reinforced by troops from the 85th and 122nd Motor-rifle Divisions. This brigade acquired a motor-rifle battalion from the 228th Motor-rifle Regiment of the Siberian Military District's 85th Motor-rifle Division (Novosibirsk). This battalion operated the then-latest BMP-3 infantry fighting vehicles. Also, the 74th Brigade's fourth motor-rifle battalion – which as a cadre unit was staffed to 5–10% of its strength – was effectively replaced by a battalion from the 228th Motor-rifle Regiment.[29]

The situation was particularly bad in the Northern Fleet, which deployed to Chechnya a battalion from the 61st Naval

Infantry Brigade. Because this unit, established on the basis of the 876th Air Assault Battalion, was not at full strength, various military personnel were recruited from throughout the Fleet. In one case, cargo-handling personnel from the Fleet's rocket and artillery weapons base were assigned to the battalion as riflemen.[30]

Personnel shortages dogged government forces throughout the First Chechen War. Although military districts worked hard to find troops to replenish the formations involved in the operation, combat readiness suffered. Moreover, the First Chechen War saw some mistakes of the Soviet intervention in Afghanistan repeated. The Russian army was more than one million strong and yet struggled to deploy coherent units. Strategy and tactics were found wanting and morale was poor; there were stories in the press of inadequately trained soldiers recruited from wherever they could be found and sent to the front. There remain unconfirmed reports that defence minister Pavel Grachev appealed to the government and to the president to conduct at least a partial mobilisation, but each time the appeal was turned down.[31]

Military reform between the wars: 1996–98

When the First Chechen War officially ended on 31 August 1996, the Russian army's reputation was tarnished and Pavel Grachev's career was nearing its end. He was replaced as defence minister by Igor Rodionov (promoted to General of the Army on 5 October 1996). However, the MoD had learned lessons. Firstly, it should not rely on mobilisation. From 1980–96, mobilisation was enacted only once, as a response to the Chernobyl nuclear disaster. In other cases, even in wartime, appeals for mobilisation were denied. Secondly, the poor economic situation meant that the MoD could not expect the government to pay for far-reaching changes and would instead have to use its own resources.

Towards an Aerospace Force

Continued economic problems prompted the MoD to consider reducing the number of units in, and the strength of, the armed services. In July 1997, president Yeltsin signed Decree 725 to merge the Air Force and the Air Defence Force.[32] The decision may have been primarily political and economic, but it was largely supported in the armed forces. The government hoped for budget savings by deactivating commands and formations, while military leaders considered the combined Air Force as the first step towards an Aerospace Force.

The Aerospace Force concept originated in the early 1980s. Marshal Nikolai Ogarkov, who advocated the change, proposed a step-by-step merger of the Air Force, Air Defence Force, Missile Defence Force and Space Force into a joint multi-role military service. The collapse of the Soviet Union did not kill off the idea, and it was studied and discussed throughout the 1990s.[33] Moreover, the merger finally solved a complex issue of inter-service coordination between the Air Force, the army and the Navy. Each military district activated an Air Force Army to command all Air Force formations, air-defence divisions and regiments, and radar installations within its territory.

Combat-ready formations

Assessments of the 1992–93 reforms indicated that the Mobile Force concept had, in general, proved its value. However, the MoD lacked the funds to generate new brigades at the wartime TOE level and instead introduced so-called 'combat-ready' formations.[34]

The idea was straightforward: active formations would provide personnel and equipment to raise regiments, brigades and divisions under the wartime TOE. For instance, two motor-rifle regiments and one artillery regiment provided personnel to help activate the 228th Motor-rifle Regiment as a combat-ready formation (within the Siberian Military District's 85th Motor-rifle Division (Novosibirsk)). However, the number of combat-ready formations depended on the district. In the North Caucasus Military District, the 19th and 20th Motor-rifle Divisions as well as the 131st, 136th and 205th Motor-rifle Brigades were reorganised as combat-ready formations, while the Siberian Military District fielded only one motor-rifle brigade and three motor-rifle regiments (each within a reduced division). All Airborne Divisions, Strategic Missile Regiments, Air Defence Regiments, and Air Force Regiments were restructured as combat-ready formations.

Defence minister Rodionov had been an advocate of the new reforms but was himself replaced, on 22 May 1997, by General of the Army Igor Sergeyev. (On 21 November the same year, Sergeyev was promoted to the rank of Marshal of the Russian Federation, so far the only Russian officer to hold this rank.) The reforms were supervised by Anatoly Kvashnin, chief of the General Staff. In December 1994, Kvashnin had taken over as acting commander of the Russian force in Chechnya and in February 1995, he was appointed commander of the North Caucasus Military District.

The activation of combat-ready formations, meanwhile, had a negative impact on overall army strength and led to the effective generation of 'paper formations' lacking personnel.[35] They also put an end

to the idea of Air Defence and Air Force Reserve Bases. Russia was preparing for a new engagement in the North Caucasus and decided to sacrifice the reserve-base concept. Moreover, there was not enough money to establish them.

Because the new combat-ready units incorporated most of the available army personnel, military leaders again reconsidered the classification of army units, and a new version was approved in 1998:[36]

- Constant Combat Readiness (95–100% of the wartime TOE);
- Reduced (up to 70% of the wartime TOE);
- Cadre (5–10% of the wartime TOE);
- Equipment Storage Bases (less than 5–10% of the wartime TOE).[37]

Equipment Storage Bases (BKhVT)[38]

These bases contained a hundred or more commissioned and non-commissioned officers tasked with maintenance and mobilisation procedures. On receiving a mobilisation order, each was supposed to deploy into a wartime division or a brigade, whereupon its active component would organise combat training for arriving reservists. However, with only limited numbers of personnel tasked with deploying a fully fledged formation, the General Staff only activated its BKhVTs if there was an imminent threat of war.[39]

The bases were organised from support formations. The Army's BKhVTs were developed from units including nuclear, biological and chemical (NBC) brigades and electronic warfare (EW) units. The Air Force's BKhVTs were organised from engineering, communications, NBC and EW units, while Air Defence Force BKhVTs originated in units including radio-engineering battalions and brigades and engineer units. Meanwhile, Navy BKhVTs were organised from Coast Guard units including engineering and communications formations.

The Equipment Storage Bases were controversial. Their limited personnel were not fully combat trained, and as such they were unable to provide the required

training to reservists. At the same time, the small number of personnel proved unable to maintain all the equipment the bases contained, which amounted to hundreds, if not thousands, of tanks, infantry fighting vehicles and artillery systems, as well as more complex equipment such as communications and EW systems. Moreover, these locations lacked all-weather parking and, over time, a significant proportion of the equipment stored outside became unserviceable. Several high-ranking General Staff officers have tried to explain the BKhVT concept.[40] As Russia's military leaders tried to preserve combat power without reducing formations, it was felt that BKhVTs were a reasonable compromise. They were non-deployable and required little funding and, should a military situation deteriorate, there was an opportunity, albeit a limited one, to deploy them into fullyfledged military formations.

Personnel problems in the combat-ready formations

This complex system of combat-ready regiments, brigades, divisions, cadre and reduced formations, and equipment storage bases was designed to achieve mobilisation deployment in wartime. In peacetime, the BKhVTs were the source of personnel for the combat-ready units. However, these combat-ready units soon faced another personnel challenge because of conscription. Firstly, the declining prestige of the armed forces saw many young men evade their two-year military service and, even when they were drafted, try to reduce their term of service. Secondly, Russia's demographic situation remained parlous, and many conscripts had poor health and physical fitness; indeed, many were dismissed for health reasons after only a few months.

As a result, the personnel strength of combat-ready formations remained unstable. It may have been the case that combat-ready units were at full strength after the spring and autumn drafts, but over time these figures fell – sometimes by as much as 20–30%.

The numerous cadre and reduced units, as well as BKhVTs, constantly transferred personnel to combat-ready units, helping to resolve personnel shortfalls. For example, the 122nd Motor-rifle Division (at Aleisk, in the Altai Territory) had one combat-ready motor-rifle regiment – the 382nd Motor-rifle Regiment. The other two motor-rifle regiments, a tank regiment, an artillery regiment and an anti-aircraft regiment were the sources of additional personnel for the 382nd.

At first glance, the system of units 'donating' troops seems sub-optimal. It prevented the development of well-balanced deployable formations independent of the type classification based on units' 'percentage of wartime TOE'.

However, the concept of combat-ready formations was introduced in a challenging period: a parlous economy led to a reduced defense budget, and there was concern that the First Chechen War would escalate into a more complex conflict. Given this, the combat-ready formations had an important function. They delivered trained and relatively well-armed and staffed units and did not depend on a political decision to mobilise. It can be said that these formations became the backbone of the Russian army that was to be created during further reforms.

The Second Chechen War: towards the Battalion Tactical Group (BTG)

The period from 1993–98 was particularly challenging for the Russian armed forces. Military expenditure hit its lowest point in 1998, at 2.85% of GDP. This had significant ramifications. There was insufficient funding for salaries, and there were shortages of fuel and lubricants. Exercise regimes also suffered, with consequent effects on military skills and readiness. By 1998, expenditure had been reduced by more than half over six years, though the Second Chechen War spurred a modest increase. The war began after Chechen fighters crossed into the Republic of Dagestan in August 1999 and launched attacks there. The militants returned to Chechnya after military action in Dagestan by federal troops and, the following month, government troops crossed the regional border in pursuit.[41]

The war was a test for combat-ready formations and for the BTG concept.[42] The main proponent of this concept is understood to have been Anatoly Kvashnin, then chief of the General Staff. Compared to the First Chechen War, there was a large combat-ready force, but the army introduced BTGs in order to reduce the number of personnel involved in hostilities.

The BTGs were intended to be drawn from combat-ready formations: one BTG per regiment, two BTGs per brigade. The first battalion-sized forces were activated in 1998, just before the Second Chechen War began. A BTG was either a motor-rifle or tank battalion augmented by an artillery battalion, a tank (or motor-rifle) company, an anti-aircraft and an anti-tank battery, and other combat-support elements. BTGs were formed not only in the army but also in airborne divisions and brigades and in the Navy's Coastal Force (marine brigades and regiments). If a BTG was part of a regiment incorporated in a motor-rifle (or tank) division, it was reinforced from other units in the division.

Their parent regiments and brigades remained at their permanent stations with the idea that they would replenish personnel shortages in their deployed BTGs. These parent divisions, regiments and brigades, however, had to make up their own shortages from reduced and cadre formations as well as from Equipment Storage Bases. In 2002 the army began to gradually withdraw. Of Russia's combat-ready forces, only the 74th Motor-rifle Brigade and the 205th Motor-rifle Brigade were deployed to Chechnya at full strength. The other combat-ready formations were employed in battalion tactical groups. After the main withdrawal, the 42nd Motor-rifle Division was permanently stationed in Chechnya.[43]

SECOND CHECHNYA INTERVENTION
Russian forces in the rubble of Grozny during the Second Chechen War, February 2000. CREDIT: Antoine Gyori/Sygma/Getty Images

From conscripts to volunteers

The Ministry of Defence (MoD) had long been aware that the use of conscripts significantly reduced combat readiness. In 2000, a proposal was submitted to staff all non-commissioned officer (NCO) positions in the combat-ready formations with volunteers. The plan was intended to accomplish several aims:

Firstly, to significantly improve the soldiers' military skills; secondly, to break the vicious cycle whereby units had to post personnel to other formations to make up their personnel strength; and thirdly, to address the negative public perception of military casualties. The first and second Chechen wars indicated that there was a greater public reaction to the death of conscripts than to that of professional soldiers. (Indeed, immediately after the first war ended, president Yeltsin signed a decree indicating that contract service would become the norm by 2000.)[44]

The contract-NCO initiative originated in the early 1990s. Russia's first defence minister, Pavel Grachev, said at the beginning of his term that the Russian army would become an all-volunteer force. However, professional NCOs tended to join units directly involved in hostilities. These contractors increased in number as a result of the First Chechen War, but resignations increased when a formation was withdrawn from Chechnya and its personnel lost their combat-related allowances, and after the war

ended. Additionally, pay and social benefits in peacetime were also proving problematic: in the 1990s a contractor's monthly wage was significantly lower than that of a commissioned officer or a warrant officer and only slightly exceeded the pay of a conscript. Although in 1999 political leaders decreed that contractors as well as conscripts could serve in conflict zones, which might have indicated an increase in contractor numbers there, conscripts were still engaged in combat in Chechnya until 2003.[45]

In that year – two years into Sergei Ivanov's term as defence minister (though he had been a senior official in the Federal Security Service, he was arguably the first civilian to hold the post) – Russia launched the programme on the 'Transition of permanent readiness units to professional service', the contract-service programme, with the ambition that all combat-ready formations be staffed with volunteers by 2006.[46] The project was piloted in an airborne regiment. When the recruitment campaign started, the MoD did offer better pay, but civilian wages were still more competitive.[47] Moreover, this coincided with a general improvement in living standards and civilian wages, stemming from an improvement in the economy. However, the issue of social benefits had not been resolved. Single men were accommodated in dormitories, but contractors with families had to rent apartments. For these personnel, the rent immediately outweighed any advantage over civilian wages. Moreover, commissioned officers and warrant officers could apply for a housing allowance but con-

tractors could not.[48] Factors like these had a negative impact on morale. Volunteers looking for a military career often resigned, while the army began to attract the wrong candidates, including those with alcohol and drug dependencies and other health problems. Some combat-ready regiments had to remove personnel and it was against this background that the MoD introduced an order preventing commanders from dismissing soldiers.

In 2006 the MoD adjusted the contract-service programme. Conscripts were now sent to combat-ready formations, and some brigades and divisions adopted a mixed-personnel structure with both conscripts and contractors. For example, the 41st Army (Novosibirsk) in the old Siberian (now Central) Military District had three combat-ready formations: two recruited volunteers (the 74th Motor-rifle Brigade and the 382nd Motor-rifle Regiment) and one (the 228th Motor-rifle Regiment) recruited conscripts. In the North Caucasus Military District the situation was different. There, the 42nd Motor-rifle Division (Chechnya) comprised contractors while the neighbouring 19th (Vladikavkaz, North Ossetia) and 20th (Volgograd Region) Motor-rifle Divisions encompassed mixed regiments staffed by both volunteers and conscripts.

The contract-service programme finally yielded positive results for the MoD in 2008 when it judged that the volunteers in the army, Airborne Force and the Navy's combat-ready formations had performed well in large-scale military exercises.[49]

High-level command before the Georgia war – anticipating Strategic Commands

In 2005, two years after formations had begun returning from Chechnya to their bases, Russian military leaders found that they were facing a management problem. There were too many commands and staffs with levels of control over combat-ready formations. For example, the 282nd Motor-rifle Regiment of the Siberian Military District (Borzya, then in Chita Region) was subordinate to its divisional command,

the 36th Army and to the Siberian Military District. At the same time, there were cases of cumbersome army, military-district and division staffs administering only a few regiments or even battalions; other subordinate units were either reduced and cadre formations or BKhVTs. Similar issues were seen in the other services. For example, the 14th Air Force and Air Defence Army (Novosibirsk) operated only one fighter regiment, while the Northern Fleet's 2nd Anti-Submarine Warfare Division had only three warships.[50]

In 2005 the MoD and the General Staff (then headed by Colonel General Yuri

Baluyevsky) redesigned the command-and-control system. The plan was to activate three Regional Commands in order to directly control all combat-ready formations and combined-arms armies.

Eastern Command was activated in Ulan-Ude in 2007.[51] In March and April 2008 its units conducted exercises with forces from the Siberian and Far Eastern military districts as well as from the Pacific Fleet. However, its operational concept meant that the Command coordinated with Military District staffs instead of issuing orders directly to the combined-arms armies, Air Force divisions, combat-ready formations and naval vessels, meaning that 'the Regional Command became yet another layer between the General Staff and Military District commands'.[52] The drills were deemed unsuccessful and it was concluded that simply imposing another command level – in addition to the existing structures – had not improved efficiency. The command-and-control system had proved too cumbersome and inefficient and Eastern Command was deactivated in May 2008.[53] A month later, Baluyevsky was replaced as CGS by Nikolai Makarov, but it is possible that lessons from the failed experiment with Eastern Command may have been useful in informing the next attempt to reform high-level command and control, after the war with Georgia. These reforms would see the command-and-control system slimmed down.

Georgia and the 'New Look'

After its five-day war with Georgia in August 2008, the result of long-simmering tensions over the Russian-backed breakaway provinces of Abkhazia and South Ossetia, Russia finally embarked on the long and complex reform of its Armed Forces. While there has not been an official announcement that this 'New Look' reform programme has been completed, two distinct stages of the reforms can be

discerned. These are popularly associated with the two individuals who have served in the post of defence minister during this period: Anatoly Serdyukov and Sergei Shoigu.

The performance of Russia's armed forces during the Georgia war exposed serious shortcomings. Notwithstanding its overall personnel strength, Russia lacked enough trained and combat-ready troops for this small conflict. The MoD's own figures for the year following the war identified only 17% of army units as combat ready. The figure was even lower for the air force, at 7%, while none of the country's air-defence units met the combat-readiness threshold.[54]

Georgia rapidly exposed weaknesses in command and control as well as tactics. Familiar problems persisted with an inadequate and overburdened command-and-control structure that still remained similar to that designed to bring to the field a mass-mobilisation army. At a crucial time, the two BTGs deployed by the 19th Motor-rifle Division were simultaneously commanded by the 19th

Division, the 58th Combined Arms Army, the North Caucasus Military District and even the General Staff. These formations were later augmented.

At the same time, the military equipment used in the war had been inherited from the Soviet Union and obsolescence proved a problem. For instance, the T-72 (and some T-62) tanks operated by units in the North Caucasus Military District were generally inferior to the modernised variants in Georgia's inventory, even if they were more numerous. For the air force, the war exposed shortcomings in equipment, tactics and personnel availability – front-line aircrews were in such short supply that staff from training bases were used for flight operations. Meanwhile, Georgia's air-defence capabilities complicated the task for Russia's air force, downing at least two Russian aircraft including – on the second day of hostilities – the sole Tu-22M3 *Backfire* C lost during the campaign. Friendly fire also accounted for some of the six Russian aviation losses, pointing to problems in command and control as well as air–ground liaison.[55]

Figure 1.1: **Proposed regional command structure, 2008**

REGIONAL COMMAND	CONSTITUENT FORMATIONS
Western Command	Baltic and Northern fleets, Air Force and Air Defence Special Operations Command
Southern Command	North Caucasus and Volga–Ural military districts, Caspian Military Flotilla and Black Sea Fleet
Eastern Command	Siberian and Far Eastern military districts, Pacific Fleet

Source: IISS

Figure 1.2: **Typical New Look independent motor-rifle brigade**

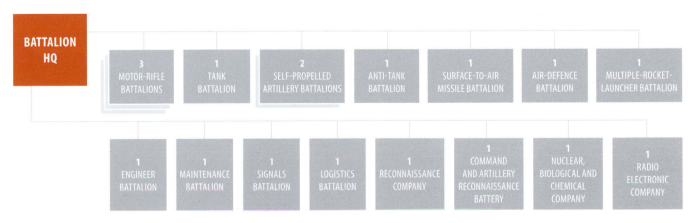

Source: 'Reform of the Russian Army', in *Russia's New Army* (Moscow: Centre for Analysis of Strategies and Technologies, 2011), p. 23.

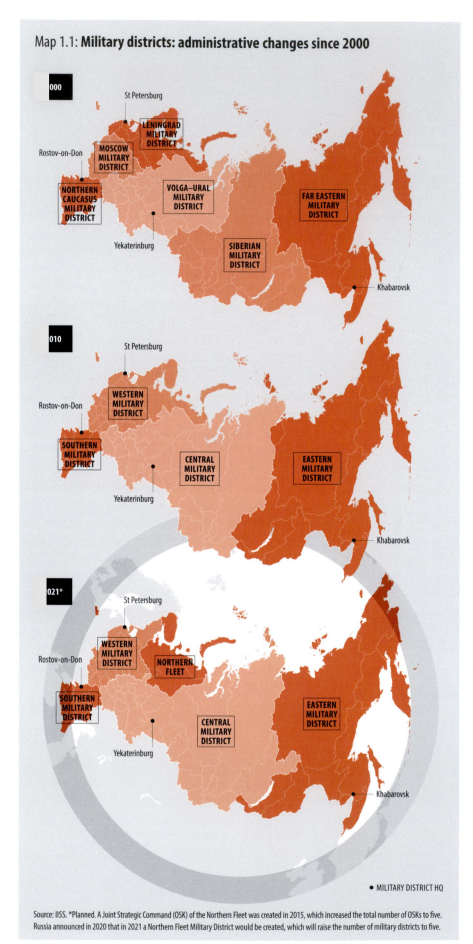

Map 1.1: **Military districts: administrative changes since 2000**

000

St Petersburg

Rostov-on-Don

LENINGRAD MILITARY DISTRICT

MOSCOW MILITARY DISTRICT

NORTHERN CAUCASUS MILITARY DISTRICT

VOLGA–URAL MILITARY DISTRICT

FAR EASTERN MILITARY DISTRICT

SIBERIAN MILITARY DISTRICT

Yekaterinburg

Khabarovsk

010

St Petersburg

Rostov-on-Don

WESTERN MILITARY DISTRICT

SOUTHERN MILITARY DISTRICT

CENTRAL MILITARY DISTRICT

EASTERN MILITARY DISTRICT

Yekaterinburg

Khabarovsk

021*

St Petersburg

Rostov-on-Don

WESTERN MILITARY DISTRICT

NORTHERN FLEET

SOUTHERN MILITARY DISTRICT

CENTRAL MILITARY DISTRICT

EASTERN MILITARY DISTRICT

Yekaterinburg

Khabarovsk

● MILITARY DISTRICT HQ

Source: IISS. *Planned. A Joint Strategic Command (OSK) of the Northern Fleet was created in 2015, which increased the total number of OSKs to five. Russia announced in 2020 that in 2021 a Northern Fleet Military District would be created, which will raise the number of military districts to five.

The exposure of military shortcomings raised serious questions about the armed forces' ability to address the challenges of modern warfare (and therefore support the aspirations of Russia's government). As a result, long-standing reform ambitions finally began to benefit from high-level political support, together with the necessary funds.[56]

President Dmitry Medvedev and prime minister Vladimir Putin entrusted the reform to the civilian team under defence minister Serdyukov, appointed in February 2007, and his first deputy and chief of the General Staff, General Makarov.[57] The choice of a civilian was deliberate. Serdyukov – perhaps more so than his predecessor Ivanov – lacked the baggage of service or institutional loyalty that might hinder far-reaching reform.[58] Given that the programme called for the dismissal of more than half of all active military officers, its popularity was perhaps bound to be somewhat limited within the army, and opposition from senior military personnel was inevitable. Reform plans were being generated a matter of months after Serdyukov took office, though they were not presented for another year. The essence of the plan, according to some Russian analysts, was to 'resurrect the idea of 'Mobile Forces' but on a much grander scale,' moving straight to an all-brigade structure.[59]

The ultimate goal of the New Look reforms, which were presented by Serdyukov during a meeting of the MoD Collegium on 14 October 2008, was to transform armed forces that still exhibited the characteristics of a Soviet-style mass-mobilisation army into a modern, combat-ready force held at high readiness. Experience had shown that the large number of officers in non-operational cadre units and headquarters – maintained in peacetime in order to support wartime expansion – were only of limited utility in peacetime and in local conflicts. By contrast, the New Look armed forces might well be smaller, but they would be permanently combat ready.

The reforms were opposed by some senior army personnel, and their implementation was also adversely affected by economic factors, particularly after the 2007–08 financial crisis led to a sharp drop in oil and gas prices. Any fall in revenues from Russia's principal exports was bound to have a deleterious effect on the economy and – while the country weathered the crisis – the damage to state finances was serious, with the banking system and the rouble also coming under pressure.[60] It meant that Serdyukov had to implement radical reforms while trying to avoid any significant increase in expenditure. The conflicting pressures meant that some short-term decisions were taken for economic rather than military reasons. One of the key cost-saving measures was to reduce the number of officers and contract personnel in favour of conscripts, running counter to the stated ambition to increase contract numbers in order to improve readiness. In combination with the reduction in conscript terms of service, this meant that overall personnel numbers were reduced to less than 850,000 by 2013.[61] And this at a time when Russia was still experiencing the effects of the 1990s demographic slump. As a result, in order to even attempt to fully staff the forces to which Russia aspired, the plans to reduce contract numbers were temporarily reversed.

High-level command and control had been subject to reform initiatives most recently under CGS Baluyevsky, and the Regional Command experiment was briefly trialled in 2008 in the form of Eastern Command. However, Serdyukov and Makarov's plan was that, instead of the additional layer of command that derived from the Regional Command initiative, Operational Strategic Commands (OSKs) would be created out of the military districts. In parallel to this, military districts were to be reduced from six to four. Makarov gave more detail in a speech on 8 June 2010. The military-district commander would control all forces – not just ground forces – within the district (bar those subordinated to the High Command, like the Airborne Forces (VDV) and Strategic Rocket Forces (RVSN)).[62] (OSKs would be rebadged as Joint Strategic

ZAPAD 2009
Defence minister Anatoly Serdyukov, president Dmitry Medvedev and chief of the General Staff Nikolai Makarov arrive in the Kaliningrad region to observe part of the *Zapad* 2009 military exercise. CREDIT: Konstantin Zavrazhin/Getty Images

Commands, perhaps to better reflect the objective to drive joint cooperation across the services, though the OSK–Military District convention was retained.)[63]

Another key aspect of the New Look was to restructure ground forces' command and control. This was originally structured according to military districts, armies, divisions and regiments, but now the headquarters of combined-arms armies or army corps would become Operational Commands, 'with a similar purpose of organizing and overseeing inter-branch operations' and with the brigade now the main unit of action.[64] Again, these would come under OSKs. Cutting the number of levels in the land forces' chain of command was intended not only to improve military efficiency, but also to allow for a reduction in high- and mid-level ranks. Meanwhile there were plans to replace some junior-officer posts by creating a core of professional sergeants: the idea was to have one lieutenant post per company,

WAR WITH GEORGIA
Russian troops on the move near Gori, Georgia, August 2008.
CREDIT: Cliff Volpe/Getty Images

Figure 1.3: Main objectives of the 'New Look' reform programme

OBJECTIVES

- Reduce military personnel from 1.35 million to 1m
- Disband cadre units and transition to a combat-ready army
- Halve the number of officers and increase the number of soldiers and sergeants
- Extensive structural reform:
  - Reduce the six military districts to four
  - Military districts to transform into Joint Strategic Commands
  - Transform armies, divisions and regiments into a unified brigade structure
  - Reorganise the Air Force and Air Defence forces, moving to 'Air Bases' for the Air Force (and transitioning the fleet into this

structure) and Aerospace Defence Brigades for the Air Defence forces.

- Merge 65 military higher-education institutions into ten combined universities
- Outsource rear support functions to civilian organisations, including equipment repair and catering
- Increase purchases of military equipment in order to replace obsolete hardware
- Increase the frequency and intensity of combat training
- Dispose of excess Ministry of Defence property and reduce the stockpile of surplus ammunition.

Source: IISS

Figure 1.4: Defence ministers, 1990–2020

NAME	ACTIVE YEAR
Sergei Shoigu	Nov 2012–present
Anatoly Serdyukov	Feb 2007–Nov 2012
Sergei Ivanov	Mar 2001–Feb 2007
Igor Sergeyev	May 1997–Mar 2001
Igor Rodionov	Jul 1996–May 1997
Pavel Grachev	May 1992–Jun 1996
Boris Yeltsin	Mar–May 1992
Evgeny Shaposhnikov	Aug–Dec 1991
Dmitry Yazov	May 1987–Aug 1991

Source: Russian Ministry of Defence

replacing three second-lieutenant platoon-commander positions with sergeants.[65] The decision was also taken to abolish the rank of warrant officer.

However, creating the new brigades proved problematic. One example of this was the aim to reorganise, by 2015, motor-rifle brigades into 'light', 'medium' and 'heavy' units based on their equipment, mainly whether they were predominantly composed of wheeled or tracked armour.[66] Tests of the new brigade concept began in 2010, but structural changes continued for several years.

Another far-reaching structural reform was enacted in the Air Force, as air armies, divisions and regiments were replaced with the Air Base (*Aviabaza*) concept, which combined aviation, maintenance and guard units. The difficulty in actually implementing this plan was reflected in the number of modifications to the concept that were manifest in the three years after its introduction. After 2009, each aviation regiment was reorganised into a separate air base. In the next phase of the reform, several of the former regiments deployed at satellite airfields were combined as one air base. In its final stage, air bases were further enlarged to include up to six or seven airfields, often separated from each other by hundreds of kilometres. Each air base could operate several types of aircraft and helicopters at once. The largest

of these bases, which were sometimes referred to as 'air wings', could have up to 150–200 fixed- and rotary-wing platforms attached, and it became apparent that effectively managing such large composite units with a smaller headquarters and a reduced number of officers was difficult.[67]

The New Look led to more limited change in the Navy, the Airborne Forces and the RVSN. The Airborne Forces are directly subordinate to the CGS and independent of the army; they retained a divisional and regimental structure, avoiding the transition to brigades.

Ensuring effective combat training proved difficult amid the reform process. For the first five years of the reform

CLASS-ONE *AVIABAZA*
The Tu-22 *Blinder* gate guard at Engels air base pictured in August 2008. Engels was to become one of seven class-one *aviabazy*. CREDIT: Wojtek Laski/Getty Images

programme, exercises in all service branches remained limited and fell short of effective combat training. CGS Makarov said – when explaining the factors motivating the transition to joint commands – that they would help in the organisation of combat training, 'which we simply have not had for the last 20 years and to which we have become unaccustomed'. There were, however, also unconfirmed comments from officers specifically about the deleterious effect on military training of the changes arising from the reform process.[68]

Similarly demanding was the need to quickly recapitalise equipment inventories. Russia's defence industry was unable to either complete development of new models or quickly increase production of available types due to a prolonged period of underinvestment. Instead, batches of equipment designed for export were put into service with minimal modifications. Serdyukov also looked to Europe as a source of military equipment, and as a spur to Russia's own industry. Notable projects included the purchase of two *Mistral*-class amphibious-assault ships from France as well as IVECO LMV *Lynx* armoured vehicles from Italy. Also, German firm Rheinmetall was contracted to deliver a new training facility in Russia.[69] This, like the *Mistral* deal, was halted after the 2014 seizure of Crimea. Technology transfer was a key objective, in order to aid the modernisation of Russia's defence industry – two further *Mistral*s were due to be constructed in Russia, which would have led to that shipbuilding sector becoming more familiar with Western shipbuilding methods. And the same could be said for the IVECO deal, though this did lead to the manufacture in Russia of some vehicles (with the *Lynx* vehicle called *Rys* in Russian service), though far fewer were built than the 3,000 that were originally intended to be manufactured under licence.[70] The need to flow-in new equipment as part of the New Look also led to the revival of a number of programmes that had begun in the late Soviet era but that were shelved by the early 1990s. These included some laser-weapons research and also the *Barguzin* rail-mobile intercontinental ballistic missile that was later to again be dropped.

The Serdyukov legacy

In November 2012, Serdyukov was sacked from his post, ostensibly because of a corruption scandal related to the MoD's property service agency, Oboronservis. Makarov too was sacked a few days later. Before being appointed as defence minister, Serdyukov's successor Sergei Shoigu had been Governor of the Moscow Region and, before that, in charge of the Ministry of Emergency Situations.

Although the Serdyukov years were marked by progress in implementing the New Look reforms, these remained incomplete on his departure. Furthermore, problems relating to the MoD's relationship with the defence industry, and indeed relating to the capabilities of the industry itself, remained unresolved.

As of 2020, few of the original structural reforms introduced in the first few years of the New Look now remain. Nearly all the elements of the Serdyukov–Makarov reforms were subsequently either modified substantially or abolished. Under Shoigu, the army has again been restructured, while the Aerospace Forces' Air Base approach was scrapped. Middle and senior rank numbers have been increased, and many of the military education and training establishments merged by Serdyukov were again separated.

However, their most important legacy was perhaps the idea that combat-ready armed forces should be held at a state of high readiness. A measure of its importance is that this aim has never been questioned, but instead has been further bolstered under Shoigu's tenure.

A less immediately apparent but important and lasting effect of

Figure 1.5: Chiefs of the General Staff, 1992–2020

NAME	ACTIVE YEAR
Valery Gerasimov	Nov 2012–present
Nikolai Makarov	Jun 2008–Nov 2012
Yuri Baluyevsky	Jul 2004–Jun 2008
Anatoly Kvashnin	Jun 1997–Jul 2004
Viktor Samsonov	Oct 1996–May 1997
Mikhail Kolesnikov	Dec 1992–Oct 1996
Viktor Dubynin	May–Nov 1992

Source: Russian Ministry of Defence

PUTIN MEETS WITH SHOIGU
President Vladimir Putin meeting with newly appointed Minister of Defence Sergei Shoigu, 6 November 2012. Putin had fired Shoigu's predecessor Anatoly Serdyukov earlier that day. CREDIT: Alexei Nikolsky/AFP/Getty Images

Serdyukov's reforms was the improvement in conscript conditions. The length of conscription was reduced in 2008 from 18 to 12 months (a year after it had been reduced from 24 months) and accommodations on military bases improved. Rations – something for which the Soviet and Russian armed forces had never been renowned – also improved. Conscripts were allowed to use mobile telephones, while non-governmental organisations, such as the Committee of Soldiers' Mothers – which had risen to prominence in its campaign against hazing – gained better access to military units. Measures like these improved the protection of conscripts from bullying and saw reports of criminality in the army fall in number. Military service increased in popularity and the number of those trying to evade the draft fell.

Although Serdyukov's New Look inevitably met challenges in implementation, it marked the period where combat readiness began to improve. In parallel, investments in research and development and in equipment acquisition began a sorely needed recapitalisation programme.

Enter Shoigu

Serdyukov's dismissal as defence minister came six months after Putin's return to the presidency in May 2012. His replacement Shoigu was a close associate of Putin and was understood to be viewed relatively positively by the public, particularly due to his period heading the emergencies ministry. Putin's reappointment also marked a return to reduced transparency.[71] This was only compounded in 2014 with the imposition of foreign sanctions following the annexation of Crimea and Russia's military involvement in the conflict in Ukraine.

Russia faced no direct military threat when Shoigu took office. Any prospect of renewed conflict with Georgia had receded and relations with the West – despite some friction – had yet to significantly deteriorate. Policy statements immediately after Putin's third presidential term began did not indicate major changes to military structures. The most significant announcements were of ambitions to ensure that equipment inventories comprised 70% 'modern' weaponry by 2020 (which was approved at the end of 2010, in the State

Armament Programme to 2020); that the military presence in the Arctic should be increased; and that the number of contract soldiers should increase by 50,000 annually over a five-year period.[72]

In his first months in office, Shoigu continued Serdyukov's 'humanisation' of military (particularly conscript) service and made only limited modifications and changes to the New Look:[73]

- The number of staff officers was to increase;
- Some of the dismissed mid-level and senior officers were to return to service;
- Some educational institutions that had been combined would be separated
- The plan to organise aviation into 'air bases' was to be revised;
- The sale of surplus MoD property was to end;
- Repair detachments were once again to be organic to units, with this function previously outsourced.

Although these steps may not have necessarily signalled the far-reaching changes that were to follow (especially after 2014 and the conflict in Ukraine), they contained indications that significant adjustments were possible. One was the reform of the 'Air Base' concept and another was the re-establishment in May 2013, from brigades, of two army divisions: the 2nd Motor-rifle Division and the 4th Tank Division.[74]

Early in his tenure, Shoigu oversaw the re-establishment or creation of new directorates within the General Staff. This included the Main Directorate of Combat Training, which had been closed in 2010 with training then designated a service responsibility,[75] as well as a Main Directorate for Scientific Research and the Support of Advanced Technology Research (Innovation), and centres for the development of uninhabited aerial vehicles (UAVs) and robotics. The directorates gave an early indication of the course that Shoigu would follow, particularly in relation to emphasis on training and improved weapons.

RUSSIAN FORCES IN CRIMEA
Crimea's Simferopol airport under the guard of then unidentified military personnel, March 2014. CREDIT: The Asahi Shimbun/Getty Images

The MoD continued the disposal of surplus military equipment and ammunition that had started under Serdyukov. In 2013, a tender was announced to scrap 422 aircraft and helicopters. In addition to obsolete and long-decommissioned weapons, the list included more than a hundred Sukhoi Su-24 *Fencer* attack aircraft, two dozen MiG-31 *Foxhound* A interceptors and several Tu-22M *Backfire* bombers. The nature of the list was indicative that a full-blown confrontation with Western states was still considered a relatively remote possibility. The disposal programme was only halted after relations with the West deteriorated.[76]

IMPROVING READINESS
Troops from the 83rd Air Assault Brigade during a combat-readiness check in Ussuriysk, October 2019. CREDIT: Yuri Smityuk/TASS/Getty Images

Combat training: a new priority

The most striking of the early initiatives were large-scale combat-readiness checks, or 'snap exercises' as they became known in the West. These were held at the level of an entire military district or branch of the armed forces. All personnel were put on alert, military units moved to training grounds and live-fire drills were carried out. The first of these was announced in February 2013, three months after Shoigu had taken office.[77]

Previously an unusual event for Russia, these became a means by which to audit the results of the reforms and to measure progress. (At the same time, routine exercises continued, with a degree of notification and understanding of the place, time and scenario.) Initial results were not encouraging. According to Shoigu, the first combat-readiness assessment in 2013 indicated that not a single army unit was able to reach even a 'satisfactory' grade (this being the lowest acceptable ranking).[78]

The outcome was that spending on combat training rose significantly, as did ammunition- and fuel-consumption rates.[79] This was a marked increase over the previous reform period. Surprise combat-readiness checks have since become an important element of combat training and are carried out four to six times per year at the level of a military district or service branch.[80] Although since 2019 these have become less frequent, snap checks on a smaller scale for individual military units have increased, reaching (officially) a thousand a year.[81] Nonetheless, it remains difficult to draw precise conclusions from these exercises about how effective they were in improving combat capability, as opposed to improvements in Russia's ability 'to move and sustain troops'. For this, Russia may have looked more to lessons from its military operations in Ukraine and particularly in Syria.[82]

Crimea: assessing the reforms

The military operation to annex Crimea in February–March 2014 was conducted less than a year and a half after the appointment of Shoigu as defence minister and of General Valery Gerasimov as CGS, and its success derives mainly from the reforms carried out by Serdyukov and Makarov.

A 'sudden check' of combat readiness was ordered by the MoD in late February 2014, and this turned out to be a useful cover for the large-scale Crimean operation, helping conceal intentions.[83] These exercises had by then become a common occurrence and the experience gained in previous drills proved useful.[84] However, the troops used came from the best units in the Southern Military District and the Black Sea Fleet and were mainly detachments of special forces, airborne troops and marines. Nonetheless, the presence of conscripts in some of the units employed meant that they still could not deploy in their entirety. Regular army units were little used since they remained far behind the elite units in terms of training.

The Crimea operation did not provide the Russian army with any profound combat lessons, though the continuing impact of the mix of contract and conscript personnel could have heralded a renewed push to make rapid-reaction units, and indeed BTGs, contractor staffed. The operation was accomplished without effective resistance and was smaller in scale than Russia's largest annual exercise. The few attempts at resistance by Ukraine's armed forces were dealt with by the Special Operations Forces without fatalities.

The subsequent fighting in eastern Ukraine, where Russian units involved mainly came from the Ground Forces, also had the desired outcome from Moscow's perspective. Nonetheless, Russia's military leadership apparently still regarded its troops' fighting qualities as insufficient, and this helped spur the next stage of the reform.

Russia and future conflict

Russia has long used military instruments as a tool of national policy, whether in peacekeeping roles in the Balkans and across the former Soviet space, or in Kosovo with the 'dash to Pristina', or in war-fighting roles in Chechnya and in Georgia in 2008. Nevertheless, its repeated deployment of military force during the 2010s, first in Ukraine, then in Syria and subsequently further afield, for instance in Libya, has consistently surprised transatlantic leaders.

Moscow's actions, particularly the annexation of Crimea, have generated much speculation about how Russian ways of war were evolving, and indeed that its leadership was 'reinventing war'. Some of the more prominent of these analyses argued that Russia was waging a form of 'hybrid war', as the result of a retrospective reading of a 2013 article signed by General Valery Gerasimov, then newly appointed as Russia's chief of the General Staff. Entitled 'The Value of Science Is in the Foresight: New Challenges Demand Rethinking in the Forms and Methods of Carrying out Combat

Operations', this piece appeared in the 27 February 2013 edition of the *Military Industrial Courier*. Commentators introduced a range of catchy epithets – some coined by Western authors, others picked from the discussion among Russian sources – such as 'war in the grey zone', 'non-linear war' or 'new generation war', generally labelled as the so-called 'Gerasimov doctrine'. These views have remained prominent, updated with 'new' or '2.0' following another speech by Gerasimov in March 2019.[85]

This emphasis derives from Western strategists' judgement that Russia is obliged to compete in indirect, asymmetric ways since it could not hope to win a direct conventional confrontation with NATO states. According to General Sir Nick Carter, the United Kingdom's chief of defence staff, speaking in 2018, countries like China and Russia had been studying Western states' strengths and weaknesses and had become 'masters at exploiting the seams between peace and war'. Moscow would operate below the threshold of conventional war, weaponising a range of tools to pose a strategic challenge. These tools include, but are not limited to, energy supplies, corruption, assassination, disinformation and propaganda,

and the use of proxies, including private military companies (PMCs).[86] Importantly, though, this is understood as a new Russian way of war that corresponds to 'measures short of war', and a preference for the manipulation of adversaries, avoiding military violence. Some even suggest that the Russian military sees the very nature of war changing, with a shift away from the use of force towards a broader definition of what war is, including political subversion and information war.[87]

Yet there is no formulation in the Russian debate that resembles the 'Gerasimov doctrine'. Moreover, giving too much weight to terms such as 'new generation war' hinders an accurate understanding of Russian views of contemporary conflict. These views do reflect a changing security environment and non-conventional capacities, but they also reflect significant continued focus on the use of combat power.

Russian debate on future conflict

There was some discussion in Russia in 2013 about 'new generation war', but since then Russian practitioners and observers have tended to use the term 'new type' warfare.[88] This is an important distinction in Russian military theory, given the extensive and long-running debates about the changing character of war, including the idea of 'sixth generation' warfare referenced by Major-General Vladimir Slipchenko following *Operation Desert Storm* in 1991.[89] However, even though the term 'hybrid warfare' does exist in the Russian debate, it is used in reference to Western forms of war and how contemporary warfare more generally is evolving, not as some form of particularly Russian reinvention of war. Gerasimov himself noted, again in the *Military Industrial Courier* but in March 2017, that while 'so-called hybrid methods' are an important feature of international competition, it is 'premature' to classify 'hybrid warfare' as a type of military conflict, as US theorists do.[90]

Indeed, rather than implementing 'measures short of war', there is evidence that Russia's leaders have sought to enhance national readiness, as illustrated by the many exercises that bring together all elements of the state and move the country onto a war footing.[91] These exercises – including the *Vostok*, *Tsentr*, *Kavkaz* and *Zapad* series of strategic-level drills – seek to

TSENTR 2019
Russian President Vladimir Putin watches part of the *Tsentr* 2019 military exercise at Donguz training area, September 2019.
CREDIT: Alexei Nikolsky/TASS/Getty Images

prepare Russia for fighting in a large-scale war. If it is the case that, as one observer has put it, these exercises prepare Russia to conduct increasingly sophisticated inter-service operations and to wage 'big war fighting operations with big formations', it is important to highlight their reach across the state apparatus: these exercises seek to prepare the whole of the Russian state for war.[92]

On the one hand, military exercises are often coordinated with internal security exercises. Interior troops and riot-control forces practise controlling mass demonstrations and coordinate with military forces and other state organs to seal Russia's borders and protect strategically important infrastructure. On the other, large military exercises include other state entities, including the ministries of Health, Transport, Communications, Industry and Trade, and Finance, as well as the Central Bank of Russia and the Bank of Russia. The exercises seek to weave together civilian and military authority and rehearse the coordination of activity at the federal, regional and local levels. This has on occasion revealed flaws in the system, with consequent requests from the Ministry of Defence (MoD) that civilian authorities should attend further mobilisation education and rehearsal. Here, the role of the National Defence Management Centre (NDMC), built and opened in 2014, is significant. The centre is intended to fulfil the function of a wartime supreme command centre, centralising the controls of the military machine and the nation's economy in the waging of war. It is the main coordination point during exercises (and deployments), seeking to bring together ministries, agencies and departments from across the whole state to this end.

Furthermore, as is evident from the battlefields in Ukraine and Syria, while it may be considered preferable to achieve aims non-violently, this remains a theoretical ideal and the considerable weight of combat firepower is still a prominent feature of Russian conceptions of war fighting. Indeed, the scale of Russia's combat deployment has regularly been announced by the Russian leadership, particularly with reference to operations in Syria. It is more appropriate to think, therefore, not in terms of Russian 'measures short of war', but perhaps instead in terms of Russian 'measures of war'.

Continuity and change

Contemporary Russian views of conflict reflect both established and novel factors. They are the consequence of the blending of tradition – including Russia's history and its political, military and social structures inherited from the former Soviet Union – and the results of the extensive military-modernisation and -reform process ongoing since the late 2000s. This has been characterised by a thoroughgoing, decade-long re-equipment programme, including organisational reform and increased exercises (including the reintroduction of 'snap tests'), interlaced with experience gained from foreign deployments.

An essential element in Russia's conception of contemporary conflict is the traditional importance of military science and the attempt to understand the changing character of war – and indeed to be able to forecast where and in what form war might in future occur – as well as to prepare the range of military structures and methods, such as doctrine and tactics, needed to employ the relevant forces. A range of organisations are involved in these processes of strategic analysis, forecasting and military science. The Scientific Council of the National Security Council and the NDMC are both involved in strategic analysis and forecasting. The NDMC is equipped with a supercomputer for this purpose, allowing the examination of material from past wars to assess continuity and change and to forecast how future wars might evolve.

In terms of the development and dissemination of military science more specifically, there are a number of organisations across the General Staff Military Academy, including the Centre for Military-Strategic Research, and the MoD, which oversees a number of Central Scientific-Research Institutes. These latter institutes have areas of specific priority, including nuclear weapons, command and control and the automation of information and communications, and procurement. The work of these institutes is supplemented by nongovernmental professional organisations such as the Academy of Military Sciences and civilian academic institutions.[93]

Indeed, this emphasis on military science runs throughout not only Gerasimov's 2013 article, but also some of those signed by him subsequently, as well as those by other senior figures.[94] This points to the ongoing influence of prominent historical Russian and Soviet military thinkers, as well as Russian history, particularly the Second World War, known in Russia as the Great Patriotic War. Nonetheless, there is foreign influence too, not only through Clausewitzian tradition, but also because Russia is actively seeking contemporary experience and expertise from abroad. For instance, between 2010 and 2012, Russian scientific teams were tasked with exploring foreign approaches to defence innovation and the exploitation of emerging technologies, in order to provide an assessment and recommendations drawing on leading international examples.[95]

The intellectual foundation provided by military science underpins a range of practical results, including the creation of new units and the establishment of links to non-state organisations. Gerasimov has noted, for example, that the conflicts at the end of the twentieth century and the start of the twenty-first differ in the balance of participants and weaponry used, as well as in the different types of forces and methods employed, such as 'joint teams of private military companies … and armed formations from the opposition' within a state.[96] He reiterated this view in 2019, stating that 'wars are expanding and their contents significantly changing' and include attempts to destabilise the internal security of a state, including through the active use of the 'protest potential of a fifth column'. The number of participants is therefore increasing to include not only armed forces, but also various non-state groups, PMCs and 'self-proclaimed quasi states'.[97]

This illustrates the view in Moscow that there are blurred lines between both peace and war and indeed between front lines and rear areas. It has led Russia's leadership to emphasise the need for effective territorial defence, in turn leading to shifts in the Russian security and defence landscape. The establishment in 2016 of the National Guard, also known as Rosgvardia, is an important example. The National Guard brings together Russia's interior troops and a range of other specialist forces, including riot police, and its remit ranges from the management of civil disobedience and protest to protecting strategic sites and addressing the potential challenge of well-armed insurgent forces.

Moscow's assessment that non-state groups with various roles are a feature of war is not new; it has sought to enhance its capacity by employing such groups to its own advantage, to enhance domestic security and to expand Russian influence abroad. In this respect, the activities of Russian PMCs in sub-Saharan Africa and Syria have received much attention. But the (re-) emergence of other non-state groups is also noteworthy in illustrating Moscow's attempt to enhance Russian territorial defence. Indeed, a number of paramilitary, militia-type organisations – including the Cossacks and other military-patriotic and sporting clubs – have emerged to play a role in forging patriotic social consensus, law enforcement, and martial-arts and military-style youth-training activities, such as urban warfare, anti-protest training and the control of public spaces. Taken together, non-state groups like these offer Moscow a number of advantages. They are useful as a comparatively cost-effective and flexible tool, potentially applicable in a range of contingencies, and for their deployability, including to trouble spots abroad, combined with plausible deniability.

Nonetheless, the armed forces remain central to contemporary Russian conceptions of conflict. As Gerasimov has often noted, while the principle of warfare may have evolved to include non-military measures, the armed forces retain a 'decisive role'. This is not only because military force can be used when goals cannot be achieved by non-military means, but because Russia's opponents are seen as preparing to wage war using precision-guided munitions. For this reason, Gerasimov said in 2019, Russia's armed forces 'must be ready to conduct wars and armed conflicts of a new type using classical … methods of action'. Indeed, Gerasimov has underlined this during his tenure as chief of the General Staff, repeatedly emphasising that military actions are becoming more dynamic and that new possibilities in command and control have strengthened the role of mobile, mixed groups of forces acting in a single information space. This offers the grounds to develop groups of forces for a 'strategy of limited action', in which Russia generates self-sufficient, highly mobile formations and a 'unified system of integrated forces', as well as the means to detect targets and deliver military strikes in real time.

Russian views of warfare have evolved considerably even since the Russia–Georgia war of 2008, with important consequences for force development and posture. The Russian defence and security landscape is changing in response, and the shifting balance between military and non-military resources to achieve political ends is often referenced by senior officials. But at the same time, the role of the armed forces in ensuring Russian security is being reinforced. As such, conventional combat will remain a central element in Russia's contemporary conception of conflict, with an emphasis on long-range precision strike and massed artillery fire, enhanced by new technology developments, including uninhabited systems and better command and control, and exploited by high-mobility forces.

This is in large part because the Russian state continues to see the international environment in terms that require such capabilities: security continues to permeate Moscow's thinking. This is reflected in Russian forecasting and Russian official strategic-planning documents which the leadership is currently in the throes of updating. The Security Council's forecasting into the 2030s suggests a pessimistic outlook,[98] perhaps offering insight into the foundations of the new National Security Strategy and the Concept of Public Security for Russia to 2030, which are being prepared for publication in 2020.[99]

Thinking again about large-scale conflict

The annexation of Crimea and the resulting conflict in eastern Ukraine put Russia and Ukraine on the brink of state-on-state conventional war. While tensions between Moscow and Kyiv have reduced, as of 2020 the risk of escalation remained. The conflict with Ukraine, but more importantly from Moscow's perspective the continued deterioration in relations with NATO nations, again meant some of the original tenets of the New Look had to be revisited. The pledge by NATO states to increase defence spending, resulting from concerns over renewed Russian assertiveness and its aggression in Ukraine, reinforced Moscow's worries over the risk of direct confrontation with the Alliance. This was apparent in the December 2014 update to Russia's Military Doctrine. For the first time, the doctrine labelled NATO as the country's main military threat.[100]

Military reform after 2014
- Reorienting the armed forces to the possibility of participation in a major conventional war
- Reviving divisional-level structures in the army
- Accelerating the procurement of conventional weapons
- Further improving combat training
- Modifying command and control at the strategic and operational levels
- Creating Russia's Aerospace Forces

The further reforms launched in 2014 and 2015 were all aimed at increasing the armed forces' ability to engage in a peer-on-peer war. In the Ground Forces, the brigade fell out of favour and there was a return to divisions and regiments intended to better structure them for large-scale warfare. For instance, the command structures established by Serdyukov were judged as inadequate in light of the Ukraine conflict. This mainly came about when regiments and BTGs, comprising significant numbers of troops and equipment, were deployed in the field in 2014 but faced sustainment difficulties because there was not adequate organic combat-service support; they also suffered command-and-control problems.[101] Assessing the combat power of the new units is difficult. For instance, a typical combined-arms army might consist of only two to three divisions, making it more closely equivalent in strength to a corps.

A further effect of the conflict in Ukraine was that it led to significant changes in Russia's deployments of ground forces on its western border. Previously this was viewed as requiring relatively little military attention: before 2014 there were no large army units deployed in these areas up to Moscow and the Volga region. The situation changed following the fighting in Ukraine and the prospect, from Russia's perspective, that Ukraine might at some point join NATO, irrespective of the lack of enthusiasm for this outcome within the Alliance.

Russia has since deployed a full-fledged combined-arms army to cover 2,000 km of its border, with units relocated from other parts of the country, while other units were newly formed. The infrastructure to support long-term garrisoning in the region was also built. One role of the Western Military District's 20th Combined Arms Army was to guard de facto Russian protectorates established by Moscow-supported separatists in eastern Ukraine. Its local military dominance has blocked Ukraine from trying to restore control over these 'people's republics' by using military force. According to Ukrainian intelligence estimates, the 'combat potential' of the Russian armed forces at the border had increased significantly since 2014 as a result of the deployments.[102]

A further step to improving combat readiness in some units, particularly in the army, has been a reassessment of the principle of mixed staffing of units with both contract and conscript personnel. By 2019 the Ground Forces, Airborne Forces and marines were able, according to Shoigu, to field 136 BTGs with contract personnel. Within regiments or brigades it is normal for two of the three battalions to be made up

of contract soldiers, with the third formed mainly of conscripts. Such a system sustains troops' core combat readiness regardless of the annual conscription cycle and it is also intended to mean that only professionals can be deployed to combat operations.[103]

Equipment recapitalisation

A key target, after Shoigu became defence minister in 2012, was that 70% of the armed forces' equipment inventory would be 'modern' by 2020. The MoD has never publicly discussed what equipment meets this criterion and how, but it can be taken to encompass new-build and upgraded combat platforms and weapons purchased or modernised in the post-Soviet period. Modernised examples include the T-72B3 main battle tank and the MiG-31BM *Foxhound* C interceptor. Equipment modernisation began under Serdyukov but gained greater traction under Shoigu. All the services have seen new equipment arrive, though the army's equipment-modernisation programme has so far been the least successful.

Despite the MoD's efforts, the volume of 'modern' weaponry in the Ground Forces was under 50% by the end of 2019.[104] This is significantly lower than the progress seen in the Aerospace Forces (VKS) or the RVSN.

Russia's authorities set out the volume of armaments to be procured by each service arm, by each type of system, in the State Armament Programme (SAP). This classified document is usually a rolling ten-year document, renewed every five years. It also details new weapons due for development in the next ten years. The current SAP, for the 2018–27 period, is believed to prioritise aerospace and maritime projects. Within this SAP, it is estimated that VKS projects comprise 35%, the Navy 30%, the Ground Forces 17%, the RVSN 10% and the VDV 8%.[105] Costs associated with naval and air elements of the strategic deterrent forces are included in the service budgets. Expenditure on the RVSN is counted separately from the army. As such, there is not a direct comparison of the share of the armed services, though it is evident that the conventional ground forces are lagging. That said, one key area of progress for the Ground Forces was the completion of the rearmament of its missile brigades. All units operating the 120-km-range 9K79-1 *Tochka*-U (SS-21 *Scarab*) have now been re-equipped with the (at least) 500-km-range 9K720 *Iskander*-M (SS-26 *Stone*).[106] The introduction of extended-range conventional power-projection systems in the Ground Forces has been mirrored in the Navy and Aerospace Forces.

Figure 1.6: **Brigade to division conversions, 2013–18**

YEAR	BRIGADE	DIVISION
2013	4th Tank Brigade	4th Tank Division
	5th Motor-rifle Brigade	2nd Motor-rifle Division
2016	9th Motor-rifle Brigade	3rd Motor-rifle Division
	23rd Motor-rifle Brigade	3rd Motor-rifle Division
	33rd Mountain Motor-rifle Brigade	150th Motor-rifle Division
	28th Motor-rifle Brigade	144th Motor-rifle Division
	7th Tank Brigade	90th Tank Division
	32nd Motor-rifle Brigade	90th Tank Division
	8th Mountain Motor-rifle Brigade	42nd Motor-rifle Division
	17th Motor-rifle Brigade	42nd Motor-rifle Division
	18th Motor-rifle Brigade	42nd Motor-rifle Division
2018	59th Motor-rifle Brigade	127th Motor-rifle Division
	70th Motor-rifle Brigade	127th Motor-rifle Division

Source: IISS

Changes in the Aerospace Forces

Significant reforms to the Air Force did not start immediately after Shoigu took control of the MoD. However, one year later, amendments to key structural changes under the New Look that had proven unsuccessful began to be made. Then-air-force chief Viktor Bondarev began to move in December 2013 away from the Air Base structure in favour of a return to Air and Air Defence armies and divisions, with associated battalions and regiments. Likewise, in 2014–15, Air Defence brigades once again became Air Defence divisions and regiments.[107]

More significant was the 2015 merger of the Air Force and the Space Forces to form the Aerospace Forces. This brought together fixed-wing aviation, army aviation helicopters, long-range air-defence systems, the strategic missile defences around Moscow, military space-launch sites and space vehicles. The VKS benefited from the influx of new equipment resulting from SAP 2020, with more than 400 new combat aircraft and 700 helicopters delivered along with upgrades to in-service types.[108] At the same time,

the VKS is benefiting from the lessons of the Syria operation. Improving the types and stock levels of air-launched guided weapons is a priority for the 2027 SAP, which superseded the 2020 programme in 2018.[109]

The VKS's long-range bombers are also increasingly seen as a means of power projection. New-build and upgrade projects are being undertaken to support this objective, including restarting Tu-160 production and the development of a new bomber design to meet the PAK-DA (*Perspektivnyy aviatsionnyy kompleks dalney aviatsii*) requirement. While the VKS has only a single Tu-160 squadron, aircraft have been deployed as far afield as Venezuela and South Africa. In part these were combat-readiness tests and a demonstration of capabilities. Ground-based air defence remains a focus of investment. The S-400 (SA-21 *Growler*) long-range surface-to-air missile system now equips 26 regiments, while preparations are under way for the production of the S-500 air and missile defence system. (The medium-range S-350 (SA-28) began to enter the inventory in 2020.)[110]

Maritime transformation?

Ostensibly, the renewal of the navy has been a priority of the three most recent SAPs, but results have so far been mixed. Delays to surface-ship construction mean that Russia has yet to compensate for the large numbers of Soviet-era ships that have been decommissioned. Even the construction of modern advanced vessels such as the Project 22350 *Admiral Gorshkov*-class frigate has proved difficult. However, SAP 2027 does not include a follow-on aircraft carrier to the *Admiral Kuznetsov*, nor a new large destroyer, while ageing surface ships and submarines continue to be withdrawn.

There has been more success in the construction of submarines and surface ships of corvette size and smaller. This, however, is not enough to meet the navy's ambitions to return to being a blue-water global player, instead giving it improved littoral capability.[111] The navy has also recently gained a long-range land-attack capability, which has been demonstrated in the Syria operation. The Novator 3M14 (SS-N-30A *Sagaris*) land-attack cruise missile (LACM) is being widely adopted. But this alone will not stop the navy falling

FOXHOUND MISSILE ARMAMENT
A MiG-31BM *Foxhound* C being armed with R-73 (AA-11 *Archer*) air-to-air missiles at Tsentralnaya Uglovaya air base, October 2018. CREDIT: Yuri Smityuk/TASS/Getty Images

further behind US maritime capability since new hulls are needed. Measures including the distribution of LACM strike power to more varied platforms are being pursued in order to mitigate the problems related to shipbuilding throughput. At the same time, China's continuing naval growth has been noted in Moscow. While it may be possible for Russia to generate a squadron to conduct out-of-area operations, as in the eastern Mediterranean in 2013, the lack of overseas basing facilities – excepting Tartus in Syria – combines with the lack of platforms to complicate any ambition for an expanded global footprint.

The Northern Fleet remains the navy's most powerful combat force in terms of the number of large ships and ballistic-missile submarines. Its strategic role is to control the Northern Sea Route and the Atlantic sea lines of communication. This was reflected in the plan (realised in presidential decree number 374 on 5 June 2020, with effect from 1 January 2021) that the Northern Fleet transform into an independent and fifth military district (while still retaining its name).[112]

The annexation of Crimea increased the importance of the Black Sea Fleet,

Figure 1.7: **Key military officials, 2020**

APPOINTMENT	NAME
Minister of Defence	Sergei Shoigu
Chief of General Staff	Valery Gerasimov
Commander, Aerospace Forces (VKS) (*Vozdushno-kosmicheskie sily*)	Sergei Surovikin
Commander, Strategic Rocket Forces (RVSN) (*Raketnye voyska strategicheskogo naznacheniya*)	Sergei Karakayev
Commander, Ground Forces (SV) (*Sukhoputnye voyska*)	Oleg Salyukov
Commander, Airborne Forces (VDV) (*Vozdushnodesantnye voyska*)	Andrei Serdyukov
Commander in Chief, Navy (VMF) (*Voyenno-morskoy flot*)	Nikolai Yevmenov

Source: IISS

headquartered in Sevastopol and seen as Russia's best location for deploying forces to the Mediterranean Sea, the Middle East, eastern Africa and the Indian Ocean. By mid-2019 the Black Sea Fleet had the largest single fleet of 3M14-capable platforms. Additional surface combatants will be added to the fleet in the next few years.[113] In the years after it annexed Crimea, Russia has bolstered as a deterrent the forces deployed there. An army corps, subordinate to the Black Sea Fleet, has been established on the peninsula, and a composite aviation division has been deployed. The peninsula's air defences were reinforced with S-400 (SA-21 *Growler*) battalions and the *Pantsir*-S1 (SA-22

Greyhound) point-defence system, as well as additional air-surveillance radars.[114]

Naval aviation is being renewed more quickly than the surface and sub-surface inventory. The Su-30SM *Flanker* H multi-role fighter has been introduced along with the MiG-29KR. UAV units have also been formed, equipped with *Orlan* 10 and *Forpost* UAVs. Nonetheless, the navy currently remains a tool to protect Russia's littoral, as well as providing additional means to support land operations. While the plan is that two large amphibious-assault ships will be completed, a reinvigorated and far-reaching surface-ship construction programme will be required to fully meet naval ambitions.

RUSSIA'S MEDITERRANEAN ACCESS
Russian Navy frigate *Admiral Gorshkov* in the eastern Bosporus, May 2019.
CREDIT: Yuri Smityuk/TASS/Getty Images

Intervention in Syria

For the past five years Moscow has deployed its military power in support of the government of President Bashar al-Assad, arguably turning the tide in Syria's civil war. At the peak of the deployment, up to 70 aircraft and helicopters, dozens of light UAVs and a ground contingent were deployed. Special-operations and artillery forces conducted tactical reconnaissance, supported Syrian government troops and tested new weapons. It is estimated that between 5,000 and 7,000 Russian personnel were deployed in the country at any one time.

Despite its limited scale, the operation has for Russia been a valuable test of its military reforms and existing and new equipment. For the first time since the end of the Soviet Union, Russia's Aerospace Forces have participated in a sustained military conflict. Aircraft and weapons acquired as part of the New Look programme have been tested in combat, as have tactics and a large number of personnel. Moreover, because Russia's intervention has so far lasted five years, this has enabled the armed forces to trial and implement a number of modifications.

A key lesson was putting into practice new approaches to command, control, communications, computers, intelligence, surveillance and reconnaissance, which had been introduced under Serdyukov. Russia has practised

a conventional high-technology war in Syria, even if some of its weapons – such as unguided bombs – were distinctly low tech. The Joint Headquarters deployed at the Hmeimim air base collected real-time data from satellites, reconnaissance aircraft, UAVs, ground intelligence teams and the information gained from allies. It controlled all of Russia's military assets in the region. If anything, this comprised a small-scale version of the military-region construct envisioned by the 2008 reforms. As such, it was no surprise that many of the commanders in Syria would later be appointed as military-region commanders.

Syria also provided Russia with the opportunity to gather intelligence on how the US and its allies operated in the region, and on the performance of some of their primary weapons systems. Unlike in Georgia, however, Russia's combat experience in Syria has not resulted in any readjustment to the reform programme, nor any significant structural changes to the armed forces. This would suggest that the change of direction to the original New Look, implemented by Shoigu, continues to hold.

Improvements achieved, but work remains

The reforms have been under way for more than a decade. While their effect

has on occasion been inconsistent, there has been considerable improvement to Russia's armed forces.

The benefits of a decade of reform

- Within the army, a permanent combat-ready professional core has been created
- Military hardware has been renewed
- Significant improvement has been made in combat training
- Command-and-control improvements have been implemented at all levels
- The Armed Forces have gained limited but useful combat experience
- Power-projection capabilities have increased

It is possible that by the end of 2020, Russia may have reviewed progress to date on the reform programme, as the changes implemented by Shoigu and Gerasimov near completion. Both the targets on the 'modern' proportion of Russia's weapons and for contract personnel are due to be achieved in 2020. Also, classified and public strategy documents are due for review, including the Arctic Doctrine, Maritime Doctrine, Military Doctrine and National Security Strategy. As such, it is possible that further long-term goals for the Russian armed forces may be made public toward the end of 2020 or early in 2021.

RUSSIA IN SYRIA
An Su-35S combat aircraft at Hmeimim air base in Syria, April 2018.
CREDIT: Marina Lystseva/TASS/Getty Images

Information and influence tools in Russian strategy

Russian military and civilian leaders have studied the importance of information activities in confrontations between states and their proxies and agents, from before the arrival of the internet and evolving with the spread of mass connectivity.[115] Developing views and changes in emphasis have been notable in the period since Moscow annexed Crimea in early 2014, with shifting judgements as to the overall importance and role of information activities in war.

In the immediate aftermath of seizing Crimea, information activities took on yet greater prominence. However, more recently this has been moderated, with the role of armed force again being stressed. Indeed, five years after Crimea, senior Russian military officers were giving renewed weight to the decisive role of armed force, with the role of information relegated to introducing war-winning technologies for employment during combat.

Russian military thought holds that while information warfare has been conducted in all wars, since the advent first of digitisation and then ever-increasing connectivity, information operations have become increasingly important. The argument has been made since the 1990s that information superiority (*informatsionnoe prevoskhodstvo*), at any level from international politics down to tactical war fighting, will be central to the outcome of wars.[116] This superiority has technological, systemic and psychological aspects: it is based not only on the capability to acquire more information, to process it faster and to make decisions more efficiently, and to deny the adversary those capabilities, but also the ability to manipulate the adversary while still nominally at peace.[117]

Developments in Russian thinking about the contribution of information warfare go to the heart of how wars are won; whether this is by physically destroying the enemy or by rendering the enemy unable to fight. For the latter purpose, the use of information operations against adversary populations and societies is part of an unbroken tradition in the institutional culture of Russia's military, intelligence and political leadership that reaches back to before the Soviet era.[118] However, from the early 2000s, electronic warfare (EW) specialists began to argue that EW combined with computer attacks, disinformation and kinetic strikes could provide information superiority in the initial phase of war.[119] By 2011, some Russian military analysts argued that the role of information operations had increased dramatically and that 'under today's conditions, means of information influence have reached a level of development such that they are capable of resolving strategic tasks'.[120]

Information superiority in practice

Cross-domain effects are implicit in Russian concepts of information warfare, which emphasise an integrated approach across all methods of information transmission, whether traditional or online.[121] Activities include both 'information-psychological' and 'information-technical' operations. This latter category includes technical attacks on information processing or delivery systems, whether through computer network operations, EW or other technical means. Future wars are to be 'resolved by a skilful combination of military, non-military, and special nonviolent measures delivered … by taking advantage of information superiority'.[122] A key attraction of this approach is that information effects can be delivered simultaneously to the entire depth of enemy territory: there are no rear areas.

In order to deliver effects across the whole of the information spectrum, Russia enlists not only government agencies but also a wide range of non-state and quasi-state organisations and individuals. Little is publicly known about the formal division of responsibilities between the various branches of the Russian security and intelligence apparatus in information activities although here, just as in the physical domain of warfare, Russia benefits from obscuring the dividing line between state and non-state actors.[123] Over and above outsourcing of information activities to 'troll farms', Russia appears routinely to source technology, expertise and intelligence from cyber-crime groups within its near abroad, which is believed to substantially enhance its cyber capabilities.[124]

Influence on adversary social or political processes plays an important role. Information superiority leveraged against populations and political leaders can 'achieve as a minimum an increase in the amount of time available for taking command decisions and lengthening the operational cycle; by means of influence on the mass consciousness of the population – directing people so that the population of the victim country is induced to support the aggressor, acting against its own interests'.[125] Information campaigns for subversion or political interference can therefore have aims as ambitious as a change in government or as modest as causing a single decision to be made to the benefit of the adversary, since the most effective way of causing or preventing movement or action by the armed forces of a given country is by causing the country's own chain of command or political leadership to issue a legitimate order.

Hostile information activities directed at adversary populations, societies and political structures are undertaken on a permanent basis.[126] Information confrontation or struggle (*informatsionnoe protivoborstvo*) is a constant campaign waged against the adversary during peacetime, primarily through psychological means. With the onset of overt hostilities, the nature of information warfare expands to include specific and focused actions aimed at achieving military advantage in, for instance, EW, intelligence, communications, command and control (C2), and means to protect C2 assets from the enemy.[127]

Russia's current understanding of warfare, and in particular the blurred line between peace and war, demands of Russia itself a whole-of-government approach with networked and integrated communications to manage conflict. The National Defence Management Centre in Moscow is intended to facilitate this. By combining 49 military, police, economic, infrastructure and other authorities under the stewardship of the General Staff, the centre is intended to improve Russia's speed of information exchange and hence reaction times.[128] Automated C2 systems (*avtomatizirovannaya sistema upravleniya*) have been introduced to facilitate protected high-speed communications with the management centre, with the intent of connecting all levels of C2, from the strategic to the tactical.[129] The result of operational use in Syria, according to one study, is that 'the high command has discovered

... the technical feasibility of tight control over tactical situations in far-away theatres from ... the National Defense Control Center'.[130]

Lessons from Crimea

Until 2014, information activities were seen consistently as an enabler for kinetic activities, and as a precursor for armed conflict. Information and psychological warfare would serve to 'lay much of the groundwork for victory' and for achieving 'strategic and political goals and in the defeat of an enemy's armed forces (and the capture of his territory, destruction of his economic potential, and overthrow of his political system)'.[131]

For some Russian military analysts, this view changed after the seizure of Crimea provided a case study of information dominance facilitating geopolitical gain. After gradually establishing control over traditional media in the days leading up to the operation to take the peninsula, Russian troops took over the Simferopol Internet Exchange Point and telecommunications cable connections to the mainland.[132] Together with the deployment of electronic-warfare capabilities, these operations gave Russia complete control of the Crimean information space, contributing greatly to preventing resistance to the takeover from the civilian population and isolated Ukrainian garrisons unable to communicate with their headquarters.

The effects on Russian military thinking were considerable. Demonstration of the power of information control led some to argue that information activities alone could potentially replace the need for full-scale armed conflict altogether, and could 'enable the opposing side to be deprived of its actual sovereignty without the state's territory being seized'.[133] In this context traditional roles would be reversed, and information activities would become the enabled rather than the enabler. With information the centre of gravity, kinetic actions that did take place would be designed to create information effects rather than the reverse.

Another of Crimea's lessons was increased interest in the vulnerabilities of civilian telecommunications nodes in order to create cyber and information effects; the reverse of the more commonly considered scenario where cyber vulnerabilities are exploited for damaging physical effect.[134] The seizure of Crimea demonstrated that advanced cyber capabilities were not needed in order to achieve total control of an internet and telecommunications network if it was possible to gain physical control of network infrastructure. This recognition may be driving the intense pattern of activity by Russian military and government agencies directed at civilian subsea cables, communications satellites, fibre-optic links and more.[135] The aim – as

also demonstrated by cyber campaigns aimed at permanently disabling home and small-office internet connections on demand – is to deny governments the ability to communicate with their citizens in time of conflict and deny populations access to outside information, emulating the situation in Crimea.[136]

However, keynote speeches in 2019 by Chief of General Staff Valery Gerasimov and Minister of Defence Sergei Shoigu once more emphasised the primacy of conventional operations, with information primarily mentioned in the context of essential communications infrastructure.[137] Information warfare – and non-military exercise of national strategy in general – were conspicuous by their absence. Indeed, with 2020 set as the target year for completing much of Russia's modernisation and military-reorganisation programmes – and the end date for multiple strategic-planning documents – one possible explanation for this further shift is that Russia no longer feels the need to rely as much on information activities, perhaps because it is now more confident in the capabilities of its conventional forces. However, these speeches may also be an indication that Russia views both information activities and kinetic force as key elements of its flexible 'toolkit' for securing optimum political and military outcomes.

Notes

1 Aleksey Gayday, 'Reform of the Russian Army', in Mikhail Barabanov (ed.), *Russia's New Army* (Moscow: Centre for Analysis of Strategies and Technologies, 2011), pp. 9–32, http://periscope2.ru/wp-content/uploads/2011/12/Russias-New-Army.pdf.

2 *Ibid*, p. 17. The 2003 initiative was termed the transition of permanent readiness units to professional service.

3 'Shtaty Voinskikh Chastey', Prizyvnik Forum, 17 August 2010, https://www.prizyvnik.info/entries/3503-shtatyi_voinskih_chastey.

4 By way of example, the 10th Rocket Division – with rail-mobile missile systems centred on

the SS-24 *Scalpel* – was in the 1980s intended to be dispatched to designated patrol areas on receiving a combat alert. Reservists would be mobilised in those patrol areas and these troops would then join the train at rendezvous points established by the division command, so bringing the unit up to its wartime TOE. Stanislav Yuryevich Ivanov, 'Zheleznodorozhnyy raketonosec ili prosto BZhRK', Kostroma, 2013.

5 'Vremennyy nekomplekt lichnogo sostava opredeleniye', Portal po bezopasnosti, https://sivcomsks.com/vremennyy-nekomplekt-lichnogo-sostava-opredelenie/.

6 Keir Giles, 'Military Service in Russia:

No New Model Army', Conflict Studies Research Centre, Russian Series no. 07/18, May 2007, https://www.files.ethz.ch/isn/94469/07_May_17.pdf.

7 Gayday, 'Reform of the Russian Army'; M.J. Orr, 'Manpower Problems of the Russian Armed Forces', Conflict Studies Research Centre, February 2002, https://www.files.ethz.ch/isn/96472/02_Feb_3.pdf.

8 IISS, *The Military Balance 2012* (Abingdon: Routledge for the IISS, 2012), p. 184; Keir Giles, 'Where Have All the Soldiers Gone: Russia's Military Plans Versus Demographic Reality', Conflict Studies Research Centre, Russian Series 06/47, October 2006, https://

www.files.ethz.ch/isn/94460/06_Oct_3.pdf.

9 V.I. Fes'kov, K.A. Kalashnikov and V.I. Golikov, *Sovetskaya Armiya v gody 'kholodnoy voyny' 1945–1991* (Tomsk: Tomsk University, 2004), pp. 27–8, http://militera.lib.ru/h/o/pdf/feskov_vi02.pdf.

10 See Mikhail Barabanov (ed.), 'Reform of the Ground Forces', in *Russia's New Army* (Moscow: Centre for Analysis of Strategies and Technologies, 2010).

11 See, for instance, Simon Saradzhyan, 'Lessons for Leaders: What Afghanistan Taught Russian and Soviet Strategists', Russia Matters, Belfer Center, 28 February 2019, https://www.russiamatters.org/analysis/lessons-leaders-what-afghanistan-taught-russian-and-soviet-strategists.

12 Author's estimates.

13 Vladimir Sazhin, '39 let vvodu sovetskikh voysk v Afganistan. Kak eto bylo', International Affairs, 25 December 2018, https://interaffairs.ru/news/show/21332.

14 Andrey Klimnyuk, *Moy Afgan. Zapiski okopnogo ofitsera* (Ridero, 2016), https://www.litres.ru/andrey-klimnuk/moy-afgan-zapiski-okopnogo-oficera/chitat-onlayn/.

15 Ministry of Defense of the Russian Federation, 'Nikolai Vesilievich Ogarkov, biography', https://structure.mil.ru/management/info.htm?id=11588255@SD_Employee; Michael Kofman, 'The Ogarkov Reforms: The Soviet Inheritance Behind Russia's Military Transformation', Russia Military Analysis, 11 July 2019, https://russian-militaryanalysis.wordpress.com/tag/nikolai-ogarkov/.

16 Pavel Ivanov, 'Po komande iz SSSR', *Voyenno-Promyshlennyy Kuryer*, 14 November 2017, https://www.vpk-news.ru/articles/39881.

17 Kofman, 'The Ogarkov Reforms'; 'USSR's Ogarkov provides Victory Day interview', *Krasnaya Zvezda*, 9 May 1984, https://www.cia.gov/library/readingroom/docs/CIA-RDP90T00155R000500030008-8.pdf; US Secretary of State, 'A Reordering of Soviet Military Priorities', 2 July 1984, https://www.cia.gov/library/readingroom/docs/CIA-RDP86B00420R000901750001-9.pdf; Mary C. FitzGerald, 'Marshal Ogarkov, On Modern War: 1977–1985', Center for Naval

Analyses, November 1986, https://apps.dtic.mil/dtic/tr/fulltext/u2/a176138.pdf; Dr Fritz Ermath, 'The Evolution of Soviet Doctrine', in *Power and Policy: Doctrine, the Alliance and Arms Control, Adelphi* 206 (London: IISS, 1986).

18 A.S. Iskrenko, 'Razvitiye poslevoyennykh otechestvennykh vzglyadov na rol' i mesto vidov i rodov voysk vooruzhennykh sil v reshenii problem voyennoy bezopasnosti gosudarstva: istoriya i sovremennost', *Bulletin of the Academy of Military Sciences*, no. 2, 2005, pp. 15–21, http://militaryarticle.ru/vestnik-akademii-voennykh-nauk/2005-vavn/10564-razvitie-poslevoennyh-otechest-vennyh-vzgljadov-na.

19 Igor Drogovoz, *Tankovyy mech strany Sovetov* (AST Harvest, 2002), https://arsenal-info.ru/b/book/1627328415/27; 'Gvardeyskiy armeyskiy korpus. Buryatskaya ASSR g.Kyakhta. 1983–1987 g.g.', Brotherhood of Zabvo forum, September 2012, http://zabvo.ru/e107_plugins/forum/forum_viewtopic.php?148905.last.

20 Air-assault forces from each military district would likely have formed the core of this group, together with marines, special mobile units from the ground forces, as well as transport and combat aircraft. See Iskrenko, 'Razvitiye poslevoyennykh otechestvennykh vzglyadov na rol' i mesto vidov i rodov voysk vooruzhennykh sil v reshenii problem voyennoy bezopasnosti gosudarstva: istoriya i sovremennost'.

21 Author interviews; Anatoly Tsynganok, 'SSSR - SNG - Rossiyskaya Federatsiya: stanovleniye novykh vooruzhennykh sil', *Nezavisimoye*, 8 September 2019, https://nvo.ng.ru/forces/2019-08-09/1_1056_ussr.html.

22 A. Chernyaev and A.A. Lande, *Armeyskaya aviatsiya na vertoletakh, 1948–2018* (Zhukovsky Academy of Sciences Publishing, 2018), pp. 117–18.

23 IISS, *The Military Balance 1991–92* (London: IISS, 2012), p. 30.

24 'Voyenno-vozdushnyye sily rossiyskoy federatsii', 100 Years of Russian Air Force, http://100letvvs.ru/?r=stolet&s=006&s=006-5.

25 'Bazy rezerva, khraneniya, utilizatsii aviatekhniki', Airforce forum, http://forums.airforce.ru/foto-video/2704-bazy-rezerva-

hraneniya-utilizacii-aviatehniki/.

26 Aleksey Gayday argues that economic and political challenges undermined the aspirations to fully implement the mobile forces concept. Gayday, 'Reform of the Russian Army', p. 12.

27 Nikolai Zenkovich, *Vysshiy generalitet v gody potryaseniy* (Olma Press, 2005), https://www.e-reading.club/chapter.php/145698/186/Zen%27kovich_-_Vysshiii_generalitet_v_gody_potryaseniii._Mirovaya_istoriya.html; Fred Hiatt, 'Russian General Assails Defense Minister on Chechnya', *Washington Post*, 27 January 1995, https://www.washingtonpost.com/archive/politics/1995/01/27/russian-general-assails-defense-minister-on-chechnya/4fd8fd54-ca68-43f1-b0ab-e6b97d8456c7/.

28 Pavel Milyukov and Konstantin Yauk, *Kalibr-10 Shturm Groznogo. Yanvar' 1995* (Rybinsk Printing House, 2010), pp. 9–21.

29 Vladislav Belogrud, *Tanki v boyakh za Groznyy* (Frontline illustration, 2008).

30 Alexey Ramm, 'Rezerv pora vernut' v story', *Voyenno-Promyshlennyy Kuryer*, 6 October 2014, https://vpk-news.ru/articles/22165.

31 Gayday, 'Reform of the Russian Army', p. 13.

32 President of the Russian Federation, 'O pervoocherednykh merakh po reformirovaniyu Vooruzhennykh Sil Rossiyskoy Federatsii i sovershenstvovaniyu ikh struktury', Decree no. 725c, 16 July 1997, http://www.consultant.ru/document/cons_doc_LAW_15179/.

33 See Pavel Ivanov, 'Po komande iz SSSR' and, for broader context, I.N. Vorobyov and V.A. Kiselev, 'O formirovanii voyennoy doktriny Rossiyskoy Federatsii', Academy of Military Sciences of the Russian Federation, http://www.avnrf.ru/index.php/publikatsii-otdelenij-avn/nauchnykh-otdelenij/voennogo-iskusstva/245-o-formirovanii-voennoj-doktriny-rossijskoj-federatsii-21-veka.

34 'Chast' postoyannoy gotovnosti', Mutual legal assistance forum, http://voensud.ru/problems-f11/topic2516.html.

35 In 1998, the 144th Guards Motor-Rifle Division was reorganised into the 4944th base for the storage of military equipment

(Equipment Storage Base) (*Baza khraneniya vooruzheniya i voyennoy tekhniki*, BKhVT). Regiments and battalions were reorganised into storage departments. For example, the engineer battalion became a 'paper formation' with no active military personnel. See 'V Smolenskoy oblasti budet sformirovana novaya motostrelkovaya diviziya', *Pervyy Smolenskiy*, 13 January 2016, http://1-smol. ru/10615-v-smolenskoj-oblasti-budet-sformirovana-novaya-motostrelkovaya-diviziya/.

36 'Aktual'nyye zadachi razvitiya vooruzhennykh sil rossiyskoy federatsii', *Krasnaya Zvezda*, 11 October 2003, http://old.redstar. ru/2003/10/11_10/3_01.html.

37 Gayday, 'Reform of the Russian Army', p. 14.

38 BKhVT, Baza khraneniya vooruzheniya i voyennoy tekhniki.

39 'Bazy khraneniya vooruzheniya i tekhniki', VIF2NE forum, 5 January 2001, http://www. vif2ne.org/nvk/forum/arhprint/53553.

40 Author interviews.

41 Dmitry Okunev, '"Ne povtorim oshibok": kak Basayev i Khattab vtorglis' v Dagestan', *Gazeta*, 7 August 2019, https://www.gazeta. ru/science/2019/08/07_a_12562051.shtml.

42 'Glavkom Sukhoputnykh voysk general Salyukov: "Gotovy vypolnit' lyubyye zadachi"', *Moskovsky Komsomolets* newspaper online, 30 September 2018, https://www.mk.ru/politics/2018/09/30/ glavkom-sukhoputnykh-voysk-general-salyukov-gotovy-vypolnit-lyubye-zadachi.html.

43 '42-ya gvardeyskaya motostrelkovaya diviziya', Bastion-Karpenko, 7 February 2018, http://bastion-karpenko.ru/42nd-msd/.

44 Igor Serebryany, 'Zachem Rossiya prodolzhayet proizvodstvo "pushechnogo myasa"', Reedus, 7 March 2019, https:// www.ridus.ru/news/294523.

45 President of the Russian Federation, 'Issues of military service, Decree N 1237', 16 September 1999, http://base.garant. ru/180912/Article 2, clause 3.

46 Government of the Russian Federation, 'Federal'naya tselevaya programma "Perekhod k komplektovaniyu voyennosluzhashchimi, prokhodyashchimi voyennuyu sluzhbu po kontraktu, ryada soyedineniy i voinskikh chastey na 2004 – 2007 gody"',

Kodeks, 29 December 2007, http://docs.cntd. ru/document/901872562.

47 On fluctuating pay rates, see 'Plan nabora kontraktnikov dlya sluzhby v vooruzhennykh silakh rossii vypolnen meneye chem napolovinu', 7ka, 21 July 2005, http://7ka.tv/ news/23213.

48 Minister of Defence of the Russian Federation, 'O poryadke obespecheniya zhilymi pomeshcheniyami v Vooruzhennykh Silakh Rossiyskoy Federatsii', Government of the Russian Federation, official internet portal, 7 June 2000, http://www.pravo.gov.ru/proxy/ips/?d ocbody=&prevDoc=102165756&backlink=1 &&nd=102131202.

49 See, for instance, 'Strategicheskoye ucheniye VS RF "Vostok-2008" zavershilos', RIA Novosti, 1 August 2008, https://ria. ru/20080801/115389092.html; 'V Sibiri startuyut voyennyye ucheniya "Vostok-2008"', *Vesti*, 26 July 2008, https://www.vesti.ru/ doc.html?id=196949; 'Desantirovaniye voyennoy tekhniki – ucheniya VDV', RIA Novosti, 25 July 2008, https://ria. ru/20080403/102893193.html; Alfiya Ibragimova, 'Masshtabnyye voyennyye ucheniya "Tsentr-2008" vstupayut v zavershayushchuyu stadiyu', Channel One, 26 September 2008, https://www.1tv.ru/ news/2008-09-26/182459-masshtabnye_ voennye_ucheniya_tsentr_2008_ vstupayut_v_zavershayuschuyu_stadiyu.

50 'Severnyy flot', *Kommersant*, 25 February 2008, https://www.kommersant.ru/ doc/856043.

51 'Regional'noye komandovaniye "Vostok" – Ulan-Ude', Puteshestvuy, 16 August 2018, http://safe-rgs.ru/4604-regionalnoe-komandovanie-vostok-ulan-ude.html; Greg Whisler, 'Strategic Command and Control in the Russian Armed Forces: Untangling the General Staff, Military Districts, and Service Main Commands (Part One)', *Journal of Slavic Military Studies*, vol. 32, no. 4, December 2019, https://www.tandfonline. com/doi/abs/10.1080/13518046.2019.1690188? af=R&journalCode=fslv20.

52 Gayday, 'Reform of the Russian Army', p. 19.

53 *Ibid*.

54 Ministry of Defence of the Russian

Federation, 'Speech by the Chief of the General Staff of the Armed Forces of the Russian Federation at a meeting of the Public Chamber of Russia', 17 November 2011, https://function.mil.ru/for_media/ press_conferences/detail.htm?id=10804648.

55 Anton Lavrov, 'Russian Air Losses in the Five Day War Against Georgia', in Ruslan Pukhov (ed.), *The Tanks of August* (Moscow: Centre for Analysis of Strategies and Technologies, 2010), pp. 104–5, http://www.cast.ru/files/ The_Tanks_of_August_sm_eng.pdf.

56 'Voyennaya reforma: na puti k novomu obliku rossiyskoy armii', Valdai Club, 19 July 2012, http://vid-1.rian.ru/ig/valdai/ Military_reform_eng.pdf.

57 'Novyy oblik armii ili 10 let reformam Serdyukova', Echo of Moscow, 28 September 2018, https://echo.msk.ru/blog/ planperemen/2286330-echo/.

58 Charles K. Bartles, 'Defense Reforms of Russian Defense Minister Anatolii Serdyukov', *Journal of Slavic Military Studies*, vol. 24, no. 1, 2011, pp. 55–80, https://www. tandfonline.com/doi/pdf/10.1080/13518046.2 011.549038.

59 Gayday, 'Reform of the Russian Army', p. 19; Mikhail Barabanov, 'Russian Military Reform up to the Georgian Conflict', in Colby Howard and Ruslan Pukhov (eds), *Brothers Armed: Military Aspects of the Crisis in Ukraine* (Moscow: Centre for Analysis of Strategies and Technologies, 2014), p. 87. Serdyukov's team was, in 2007, working on modest reforms including stocktaking and procurement, while a group of senior officers in parallel worked on military aspects.

60 Sergei Guriev and Aleh Tsyvinski, 'Challenges facing the Russian economy after the crisis', in Anders Åslund, Sergei Guriev and Andrew Kuchins (eds), *Russia after the Global Economic Crisis* (Washington DC: Peterson Institute for International Economics, 2010), pp. 9–38, https:// www.piie.com/publications/chapters_ preview/4976/01iie4976.pdf.

61 IISS, *The Military Balance 2013* (Abingdon: Routledge for the IISS, 2013), p. 225. There were a range of problems associated with the downsizing of personnel, including the provision of accommodation. See, for instance,

Bartles, 'Defense Reforms of Russian Defense Minister Anatolii Serdyukov'.

62 Greg Whisler, 'Strategic Command and Control in the Russian Armed Forces: Untangling the General Staff, Military Districts, and Service Main Commands (Part Two)', *Journal of Slavic Military Studies*, vol. 33, no. 1, March 2020, p. 95, https://www.tandfonline.com/doi/pdf/10.1080/1351804 6.2020.1723227?needAccess=true; Nikolai Makarov, 'Four operative strategic command centers to appear in Russian military districts (Part 2)', Interfax-AVN, 8 June 2010.

63 See, for instance, 'Two New Armies for the Central Military District', Russia Defense Policy, 14 August 2010, https://russiandefpolicy.com/tag/operational-strategic-command/; 'OSK Commanders Will Directly Control Navy and Air Forces', Russia Defense Policy, 8 June 2010, https://russiandefpolicy.com/2010/06/08/osk-commanders-will-directly-control-navy-and-air-forces/.

64 Whisler, 'Strategic Command and Control in the Russian Armed Forces: Untangling the General Staff, Military Districts, and Service Main Commands (Part Two)', p. 95.

65 More background on the decisions to reduce officer numbers can be found in V. Shlykov, 'Tayny blitskriga Serdyukova', *Rossiya v global'noy politike*, 27 December 2009, https://www.hse.ru/news/3797595/13386349.html.

66 Pukhov, Makienko and Barabanov, 'Voyennaya reforma: na puti k novomu obliku rossiyskoy armii', p. 22.

67 IISS, *The Military Balance 2012* (Abingdon: Routledge for the IISS, 2012), p. 186.

68 Bartles, 'Defense Reforms of Russian Defense Minister Anatolii Serdyukov', p. 75.

69 'Germany suspends Rheinmetall military contract with Russia', Deutsche Welle, 19 March 2014, https://www.dw.com/en/germany-suspends-rheinmetall-military-contract-with-russia/a-17508373; 'Russian Defense Ministry sues German company Rheinmetal for contract breach', TASS, 18 February 2015, https://tass.com/russia/778431.

70 Konstantin Bogdanov, 'Obyknovennyye priklyucheniya ital'yanskikh bronevikov v Rossii', RIA Novosti, 24 January 2013, https://ria.ru/20130124/919560586.html; 'Gen

Shamanov rejects Rys armoured vehicle made under Italian license', Interfax, 25 February 2012.

71 Ilya Kramnik, 'PR and his team: Achievements of Sergey Shoygu as Defense Minister', *Izvestia*, 24 September 2019, https://iz.ru/export/google/amp/924666. Moreover, information about the armed forces has increasingly been deemed classified, and there has been a reduction in the number of independent sources of military information about the state of the armed forces.

72 President of Russia, 'Executive Order on implementing plans for developing Armed Forces and modernising military-industrial complex', 7 May 2012, http://en.kremlin.ru/catalog/keywords/125/events/15242; President of Russia, 'Executive Order on further improvements to military service', 7 May 2012, http://en.kremlin.ru/catalog/keywords/125/events/15253.

73 'Sergey Shoygu: "Reforme armii nuzhen zdravyy smysl"', *Komsomolskaya Pravda*, 11 February 2013, https://www.tver.kp.ru/daily/26030/2947853/.

74 Mark Galeotti notes that the 2nd Guards Tank Division had been the first converted to a brigade. Mark Galeotti, *The Modern Russian Army, 1992–2016* (Oxford: Osprey Publishing, 2017), p. 28. Some Russian analysts have argued that the conversion of these two units back to divisions was designed to appeal to the military 'old guard' and that these divisions were not immediately fully staffed; nonetheless, they heralded the broader changes that were to come.

75 IISS, *The Military Balance 2014* (Abingdon: Routledge for the IISS, 2014), p. 161.

76 Alexey Mikhailov, 'Minoborony razrezhet na metall legendarnyye samolety i verto-lety', *Izvestia*, 15 May 2013, https://iz.ru/news/550212.

77 'Vnezapnyye proverki Vooruzhennykh sil Rossii', RIA Novosti, 14 June 2016, https://ria.ru/20160614/1447214070.html.

78 'Sergey Shoygu rasskazal, kak spasali rossi-yskuyu armiyu', *Moskovsky Komsomolets*, 22 September 2019, https://www.mk.ru/politics/2019/09/22/sergey-shoygu-rasskazal-kak-spasali-rossiyskuyu-armiyu.html.

79 'Obucheniye voyennosluzhashchikh v

RF stalo kachestvenneye – Shoygu', RIA Novosti, 6 November 2013, https://ria.ru/20131106/974971744.html.

80 Ministry of Defence of the Russian Federation, 'The main results of the activities of the Armed Forces of the Russian Federation since 2012', 2018.

81 *Ibid.*

82 Keir Giles, *Assessing Russia's Reorganized and Rearmed Military*, Carnegie Endowment for International Peace, 2017, p. 2, https://carnegieendowment.org/files/5.4.2017_Keir_Giles_RussiaMilitary.pdf.

83 Steve Gutterman, 'Putin puts troops in western Russia on alert in drill', Reuters, 26 February 2014, https://www.reuters.com/article/us-ukraine-crisis-russia-military/putin-puts-troops-in-western-russia-on-alert-in-drill-idUSBREA1P0RW20140226.

84 Michael Kofman et al., *Lessons from Russia's Operations in Crimea and Eastern Ukraine* (Santa Monica, CA: RAND Corporation, 2017), p. 16, https://www.rand.org/pubs/research_reports/RR1498.html.

85 Peter Pomerantsev, 'How Putin is Reinventing War', *Foreign Policy*, 5 May 2014, https://foreignpolicy.com/2014/05/05/how-putin-is-reinventing-warfare; Pavel Felgenhauer, 'A New Version of the "Gerasimov Doctrine"?', *Eurasia Daily Monitor*, vol. 16, no. 32, 7 March 2019, https://jamestown.org/program/a-new-version-of-the-gerasimov-doctrine/; Dmitry Stefanovich, 'What to Make of General Gerasimov's Latest "Doctrine"', *Moscow Times*, 28 March 2019, https://www.themoscowtimes.com/2019/03/28/what-to-make-of-general-gerasimovs-latest-doctrine-a64927.

86 Nick Carter, 'Annual Chief of the Defence Staff Lecture 2018', Royal United Services Institute, 11 December 2018, https://rusi.org/event/annual-chief-defence-staff-lecture-and-rusi-christmas-party-2018.

87 Rod Thornton, 'The Russian Military's New "Main Emphasis": Asymmetric Warfare', *RUSI Journal*, vol. 162, no. 4, October 2017, https://rusi.tandfonline.com/doi/pdf/10.1080/03071847.2017.1381401?needAccess=true; Oscar Jonsson, *The Russian Understanding of War: Blurring the Lines Between War and Peace*

(Washington DC: Georgetown University Press, 2019).

88 Timothy Thomas, 'The Evolving Nature of Russia's Way of War', *Military Review*, July–August 2017, https://www.armyupress.army.mil/Journals/Military-Review/English-Edition-Archives/July-August-2017/Thomas-Russias-Way-of-War/.

89 Vladimir Slipchenko, *Voyna budushchego* (Moscow: Moskovskii Obshchestvennyi Nauchnyi Fond, 1999).

90 Valery Gerasimov, 'Mir na granyakh voyny', *Voyenno-Promyshlennyy Kuryer* (*VPK*), no. 10, 13 March 2017, https://vpk-news.ru/articles/35591.

91 Valery Gerasimov, 'Vektory razvitiya voyennoi strategii', *Krasnaya Zvezda*, 4 March 2019, http://redstar.ru/vektory-razvitiya-voennoj-strategii/.

92 Johan Norberg, *Training to Fight: Russia's Major Military Exercises, 2011–2014* (Stockholm: FOI, 2015), p. 62, https://www.foi.se/report-summary?reportNo=FOI-R--4128--SE; Andrew Monaghan, *Power in Modern Russia* (Manchester: Manchester University Press, 2017).

93 For the work of the General Staff Academy, see http://vagsh.mil.ru/. For more detailed reflection on the roles of research institutes, see Anya Fink and Michael Kofman, *Russian Strategy for Escalation Management: Key Debates and Players in Military Thought* (Washington DC: Center for Naval Analysis, April 2020), https://www.cna.org/CNA_files/PDF/DIM-2020-U-026101-Final.pdf.

94 For instance, Valery Gerasimov, 'Tsennost nauki v predvidenii', *Voyenno-Promyshlennyy Kuryer* (*VPK*), 26 February 2013, https://vpk-news.ru/articles/14632; Gerasimov, 'Mir na granyakh voyny'; Gerasimov, 'Vektory razvitiya voyennoi strategii'.

95 Carl Scott, 'From Concept to Capability: The Russian Approach to Capability Development', CCW Research Paper, September 2018, https://static1.squarespace.com/static/55faab67e4b0914105347194/t/5ba245d921c67c53d0a04591/1537361372186/From+Concept+to+Capability+-+carl+scott.pdf.

96 Gerasimov, 'Mir na granyakh voyny'.

97 Gerasimov, 'Vektory razvitiya voyennoi strategii'.

98 Security Council of the Russian Federation, 'Statya Sekretarya Soveta Bezopasnosti Rossiyskoy Federatsii v Rossiyskoy gazete', 12 November 2019, http://www.scrf.gov.ru/news/allnews/2677/.

99 'Proyekt novoy Strategii natsionalnoy bezopasnosti Rossii podgotovyat v 2020 godu', TASS, 10 February 2020, https://tass.ru/politika/7726079; Security Council of the Russian Federation, 'Nachalas podgotovka proyekta Kontseptsii obshchestvennoy bezopasnosti v Rossiyskoy Federatsii do 2030 goda', 3 March 2020, http://www.scrf.gov.ru/news/allnews/2747/.

100 'Novyye ugrozy i yadernyy otvet: chto izmenilos' v voyennoy doktrine Rossii', *Zvezda*, 30 December 2014, https://tvzvezda.ru/news/forces/content/201412301322-5los.htm.

101 Aleksey Ramm, 'The Russian Army: Organization and Modernization', CNA occasional paper, October 2019, https://www.cna.org/CNA_files/PDF/IOP-2019-U-021801-Final.pdf; see the discussion on p. 10.

102 'Razvedka: Rossiya razvorachivayet dve armii vozle granitsy s Ukrainoy', Focus, 2 March 2020, https://focus.ua/ukraine/451243-razvedka_rossiia_razvorachivaet_dve_armii_vozle_granitsy_s_ukrainoi.

103 'Sukhoputnyye voyska dobilis' bol'shikh uspekhov, no yest' i nedostatki', *Vedomosti*, 11 March 2019, https://www.vedomosti.ru/politics/articles/2019/03/11/796128-suhoputnie-voiska-nedostatkami.

104 IISS assessments of 'modern' ground-forces equipment includes platforms that entered service after 1989–90 and upgraded under SAP 2020. So, for the ground forces' manoeuvre forces this includes T-72B3/B3M; T-80U/BV; T-80BVM; T-90/T-90A; T-90M; BMP-3/-3M; BTR-82A/-82AM. The Russian MoD's figures for the proportion of 'modern' ground-forces equipment are higher, though it remains difficult to reconcile the stated percentages against assessed inventories because the Russian MoD has not precisely defined what constitutes 'modern' equipment in this context (even if their definition too can be taken to encompass new-build and upgraded combat platforms and weapons purchased

or modernised in the post-Soviet period). See, for instance, 'Vo vseoruzhii: rossiyskaya armiya prodolzhayet obnovleniye', Rostec, 23 March 2020, https://rostec.ru/news/vo-vseoruzhii-rossiyskaya-armiya-prodolzhaet-obnovlenie.

105 Based on Viktor Murakhovsky's data, 27 April 2020, https://www.facebook.com/photo.php?fbid=3689242037816261.

106 Roger McDermott, 'Russia's Iskander Missile System and the Collapse of the INF Treaty', *Eurasia Daily Monitor*, vol. 17, no. 7, 22 January 2020, https://jamestown.org/program/russias-iskander-missile-system-and-the-collapse-of-the-inf-treaty/.

107 'V YUVO obrazovana 1-ya gvardeyskaya aviadiviziya', 10 December 2013, http://stat.mil.ru/et/news/more.htm?id=11876736@egNews; 'Analiz Sostoyaniya Vozdushno-Kosmicheskikh Sil Rosii, Perspektivy Razviti', 1 January 2019, https://vm.ric.mil.ru/Stati/item/177258/.

108 Viktor Khudoleev, 'My gordimsya nashimi lotchikami!', *Krasnaya Zvezda*, 18 March 2019, http://redstar.ru/my-gordimsya-nashimi-lyotchikami.

109 'Russian State Armaments Program to Focus on Precision Weaponry – Defense Official', TASS, 23 November 2017, http://tass.com/defense/977195; 'Ambitsioznyye Zadachi Nuzhno Stavit' Pered Soboy Vsegda', 1 December 2018, http://army.ric.mil.ru/Stati/item/156804/.

110 Anton Valagin, 'Pod Peterburgom razvernuto rekordnoye kolichestvo sistem S-400', *Rossiyskaya Gazeta*, 26 February 2020, https://rg.ru/2020/02/26/reg-szfo/pod-peterburgom-razvernuto-rekordnoe-kolichestvo-sistem-s-400.html. Technically, the SA-28 might still be termed SA-X-28 until it officially enters service.

111 Michael B. Petersen, 'Strategic Deterrence, Critical Infrastructure, and the Aspiration–Modernization Gap in the Russian Navy', Report of the CSIS Russia and Eurasia Program, April 2020, pp. 30–7, https://csis-website-prod.s3.amazonaws.com/s3fs-public/publication/200430_Mankoff_Russian%20Military_web_v3_UPDATED%20FINAL.pdf.

112 'Minoborony predlagayet uzakonit' status

Severnogo flota kak otdel'nogo voyennogo okruga', TASS, 7 August 2019, https://tass.ru/armiya-i-opk/6741637; Government of Russia, 'Decree of the President of the Russian Federation of 05.06.2020 No. 374: On the military-administrative division of the Russian Federation', 5 June 2020, http://publication.pravo.gov.ru/Document/View/0001202006050025.

113 Dmitry Boltenkov and Roman Krezul, 'S pritselom na yug: kakim stanet Chernomorskiy flot posle pereosnash-cheniya', Izvestia, 16 May 2020, https://iz.ru/1011772/dmitrii-boltenkov-roman-kretcul/s-pritcelom-na-iug-kakim-stanet-chernomorskiiflot-posle-pereosnashcheniia.

114 Michael Sheldon, 'PutinAtWar: Recent Military Developments on Fortress Crimea', Atlantic Council's Digital Forensic Research Lab, 9 January 2019, https://medium.com/dfrlab/putinatwar-recent-military-develop-ments-on-fortress-crimea-d3727b7c4e2a.

115 Juha Kukkola, 'Digital Soviet Union: The Russian national segment of the Internet as a closed national network shaped by strategic cultural ideas', National Defence University (Finland), Research Publication no. 40, 2020, https://www.doria.fi/bitstream/handle/10024/177157/Kukkola_Digital%20Soviet%20Union_finalnet.pdf; Keir Giles, 'Handbook of Russian Information Warfare', NATO Defense College, Fellowship Monograph 9, 2016, http://www.ndc.nato.int/news/news.php?icode=995.

116 V.M. Lisovoy, 'O zakonakh razvitiya vooruzhennoy bor'by i nekotorykh tendentsiyakh v oblasti oborony', Voyennaya Mysl', no. 5, 1993.

117 Voyennaya Akademiya General'nogo Shtaba, 'Slovar' terminov i opredeleniy v oblasti informatsionnoy bezopasnosti', (Moscow: Voyeninform, 2008).

118 Bilyana Lilly and Joe Cheravitch, 'The Past, Present, and Future of Russia's Cyber Strategy and Forces', in T. Jančárková et al. (eds), 20/20 Vision: The Next Decade 2020 (Tallinn: NATO Cooperative Cyber Defence Centre of Excellence, 2020), https://www.ccdcoe.org/uploads/2020/05/CyCon_2020_8_Lilly_Cheravitch.pdf.

119 Mary C. FitzGerald, 'Russian Views on IW, EW, and Command and Control: Implications for the 21st Century', Command & Control, Research & Technology Symposium (CCRTS), 1999, http://www.dodccrp.org/events/1999_CCRTS/pdf_files/track_5/089fitzg.pdf.

120 S.G. Chekinov and S.A. Bogdanov, 'Vliyaniye nepryamykh deystviy na kharakter sovremennoy voyny', Voyennaya Mysl', no. 6, 2011, pp. 3–13.

121 Vilma Luoma-aho and Katerina Tsetsura, 'Influence Mechanisms of Strategic Communication of Russia', in Georgij Alafuzoff, et al., Govorit Moskva – Moskova puhuu: Venäjän strategisen viestinnän erity-ispiirteet (Helsinki: Valtioneuvoston kanslia, 2020), pp. 176–96, http://julkaisut.valtioneu-vosto.fi/bitstream/handle/10024/162201/VNTEAS_2020_16.pdf.

122 S.G. Chekinov and S.A. Bogdanov, 'Prognozirovaniye kharaktera i soderzhaniya voyn budushchego: problemy i suzhdeniya', Voyennaya Mysl', no. 10, 2015, pp. 44–5.

123 Andrew Foxall, 'Putin's Cyberwar: Russia's Statecraft in the Fifth Domain', The Henry Jackson Society, Russia Studies Centre Policy Paper no. 9 (2016), http://henryjackson-society.org/wp-content/uploads/2018/06/Putins-Cyberwar.pdf.

124 Cory Bennett, 'Kremlin's ties to Russian cyber gangs sow US concerns', Hill, 11 October 2015, http://thehill.com/policy/cybersecurity/256573-kremlins-ties-russian-cyber-gangs-sow-us-concerns.

125 Yu. Kuleshov, B.B. Zhutdiev and D.A. Fedorov, 'Informatsionno-psikhologicheskoye protivoborstvo v sovremennykh usloviyakh: teoriya i prak-tika', Vestnik Akademii Voyennykh Nauk, no. 1 (46), 2014, p. 106, http://www.avnrf.ru/attachments/article/639/AVN-1(46)_001-184_print.pdf.

126 V. Kvachkov, Spetsnaz Rossii (Moscow: Voyennaya Literatura, 2004), http://militera.lib.ru/science/kvachkov_vv/index.html.

127 Kukkola, 'Digital Soviet Union: The Russian national segment of the Internet as a closed national network shaped by strategic cultural ideas', p. 114.

128 Keir Giles, 'Russia's "New" Tools for Confronting the West: Continuity and Innovation in Moscow's Exercise of Power', Chatham House, March 2016, https://www.chathamhouse.org/sites/default/files/publications/2016-03-russia-new-tools-giles.pdf.

129 Roger McDermott, 'Russian Military Introduces New Automated Command-and-Control Systems', The Jamestown Foundation, Eurasia Daily Monitor, vol. 16, no. 86, 11 June 2019, https://jamestown.org/program/russian-military-introduces-new-automated-command-and-control-systems/.

130 Pavel Baev, 'Transformation of Russian Strategic Culture: Impacts from Local Wars and Global Confrontation', Russie. Nei.Visions, no. 118, Institut Français des Relations Internationales, June 2020, https://www.ifri.org/sites/default/files/atoms/files/baev_russian_strategic_culture_2020.pdf.

131 Chekinov and Bogdanov, 'Prognozirovaniye kharaktera i soderzhaniya voyn budush-chego: problemy i suzhdeniya', pp. 44–5; V. Slipchenko, 'Informatsionnyy resurs i infor-matsionnoye protivoborstvo', Armeyskiy sbornik, October 2013, p. 52.

132 Shane Harris, 'Hack Attack: Russia's first targets in Ukraine: its cell phones and Internet lines', Foreign Policy, 3 March 2014, http://foreignpolicy.com/2014/03/03/hack-attack/.

133 A.V. Kartapolov, 'Uroki voyennykh konf-liktov, perspektivy razvitiya sredstv i sposobov ikh vedeniya. Pryamyye i nepryamyye destviya v sovremennykh mezhdunarodnykh konfliktakh', Vestnik Akademii Voyennykh Nauk, no. 2, 2015, pp. 28–9, http://www.avnrf.ru/index.php/zhurnal-qvoennyj-vestnikq/arkhiv-nomerov/737-vestnik-avn-2-2015; Valery Gerasimov, 'Po opytu Sirii', Voyenno-promyshlennyy kuryer, 7 March 2016, https://vpk-news.ru/articles/29579

134 Owen Matthews, 'Russia's Greatest Weapon May Be Its Hackers', Newsweek, 7 May 2015, http://www.newsweek.com/2015/05/15/russias-greatest-weapon-may-be-its-hackers-328864.html.

135 Michael Birnbaum, 'Russian subma-rines are prowling around vital undersea cables. It's making NATO nervous', Washington Post, 22 December 2017, https://www.washingtonpost.com/

world/europe/russian-submarines-are-prowling-around-vital-undersea-cables-its'-making-nato-nervous/2017/12/22/d4c1f3da-e5d0-11e7-927a-e72eac1e73b6_story.html; Brian Weeden, 'Dancing in the dark redux: Recent Russian rendezvous and proximity operations in space', *Space Review*, 5 October 2015, http://www.thespacereview.

com/article/2839/1; Ali Watkins, 'Russia Escalates Spy Games after Years of U.S. Neglect', Politico, 1 June 2017, https://www.politico.com/story/2017/06/01/russia-spies-espionage-trump-239003.

[136] Liam Tung, 'FBI to all router users: Reboot now to neuter Russia's VPNFilter malware', ZDNet, 29 May 2018, https://www.zdnet.

com/article/fbi-to-all-router-users-reboot-now-to-neuter-russias-vpnfilter-malware/.

[137] Gerasimov, 'Vektory razvitiya voyennoy strategii'; Sergey Shoygu, 'Effektivnaya armiya: Voyuyet, stroit, uchit, lechit i ekonomit byudzhetnyye sredstva', *Voyenno-promyshlennyy kur'er*, 19 March 2019, https://www.vpk-news.ru/articles/49080.

Strategic forces

Nuclear weapons have been at the core of Soviet and Russian security concerns since their creation. Moscow's approach to its nuclear arsenal was and continues to be shaped by external and internal forces. In the case of the former, these include first and foremost Washington's nuclear plans and procurement, as well as the United States' development of conventionally armed prompt-global-strike systems and, secondarily, the behaviour of other nuclear powers. Internal forces include the to-and-fro between war-fighting and deterrence doctrine, and inter-service and defence-industrial rivalries.

The largest element of Moscow's nuclear triad remains its land-based systems, with the navy's ballistic-missile force the second leg of the capability. Russia's nuclear air arm was traditionally the poor relative in the Soviet era but is now less so. The nation's approach to its nuclear arsenal has been shaped by geography. With no year-round maritime access and falling within the crucial intercontinental range, land-basing took precedence once ballistic-missile technology was sufficiently mature. The use of silos was first favoured to improve missile survivability, but mobility is now preferred.

Soviet plans to upgrade its nuclear systems were in train in the latter part of the 1980s, only to be derailed by the dissolution of the Soviet Union in 1991 and the ensuing economic turmoil. Older systems were withdrawn from service, while replacement projects struggled with inadequate funding or were cancelled. Of the ballistic-missile projects anticipated by the US intelligence community in the late 1980s, some were cancelled while others were delayed. The navy's D-19 *Bark* submarine-launched ballistic-missile programme was abandoned in favour of what was to become the *Bulava* (SS-N-32), but with a far later entry into service than envisioned. For example, two air-launched cruise-missile projects – the Kh-80 (AS-X-19 *Koala*) variant of the NPO Mashinostroyenia *Meteorit*, and the Raduga Kh-90 (AS-X-21) – were cancelled. Two 3M25 naval variants of the *Meteorit* were also abandoned, while development of a hypersonic glide vehicle (HGV) was shelved for more than a decade.

Cutting investment, however, did not reflect reduced interest in strategic systems. There was a consensus that Russia should remain a nuclear power; as Moscow's conventional military atrophied during the

Key takeaways

NUCLEAR FORCES KEY
Nuclear forces continue to underpin Russia's strategic doctrine.

LAND REMAINS LARGEST IN TRIAD
Land-based systems will remain the largest component of the triad.

ONGOING BUT SLOWED RECAPITALISATION
The re-equipment programme is continuing, but with delays.

TACTICAL-INVENTORY UNCERTAINTY
The role of the substantial tactical inventory remains opaque.

NOVEL SYSTEMS' ROLE
Novel-systems are being developed to counter missile defence and provide a potential arms-control bargaining chip.

NUCLEAR RESPONSE
June 2020 nuclear-posture paper makes explicit threat of a nuclear response to a non-nuclear attack, if it risks Russian nuclear capabilities.

1990s, its nuclear forces grew in relative importance. The Soviet Union's 1982 public proclamations of a no-first-use approach to nuclear weapons was disposed of in 1993, and this policy change was made even clearer with a public announcement in June 2020.[1] Even so, Russia's strategic forces did not receive all the funding they needed during the 1990s to sustain and modernise, but they did considerably better financially than the conventional elements of the armed services.

Retaining a large nuclear arsenal also provided Moscow with a reminder to the rest of the world that it had once held superpower status. In the nuclear realm, Moscow remains a world leader: Russia and the US still retain by far the two largest holdings of nuclear weapons. By contrast, in economic terms, while the US has the world's largest GDP, Russia is ranked 11th in the International Monetary Fund's 2019 figures – putting it behind Italy, Brazil and Canada.[2]

Modernisation tempo

Having had to eke out its spending in the 1990s, Russia's nuclear forces benefited from the increases in defence expenditure in recent State Armament Programmes (SAP), particularly SAP 2020. Such was the investment that by late 2018 Defence Minister Sergei Shoigu declared that 82% of Russia's strategic nuclear forces' inventory was 'modern equipment', although the definition of modern was not provided.[3]

While there was debate in the 1990s as to whether Russia needed to sustain a nuclear triad of land, sea and air-delivery platforms, Moscow continues to support all three: the land-based Strategic Rocket Forces (*Raketnye voyska strategicheskogo naznacheniya*, RVSN) operating silo-based and road-mobile intercontinental ballistic missiles (ICBMs), the Russian Navy's ballistic-missile submarines and the Aerospace Forces' (VKS) cruise-missile-equipped long-range bombers. In 2019, *Krasnaya Zvezda*, the Russian defence ministry's in-house newspaper, suggested that 70% of the ICBM force was modern, with the equivalent figures 82% for the Navy and 91% for the Aerospace Forces.[4] By the end of 2019, the declared number for the Strategic Rocket Forces is at least 76%.[5] As with Shoigu's declaration, there was no attempt to define 'modern' and so such claims should be treated with circumspection. They do, however, give a sense of how the defence ministry views, or wishes its public audience to view, the renewal of its nuclear arsenal. If the figures are taken at face value, they also reflect a modernisation programme nearing completion.

The Strategic Rocket Forces' percentage of declared modern equipment roughly corresponds to the fraction of RS-24 *Yars* (SS-27 mod. 2) and RS-12M2 *Topol*-M (SS-27 mod. 1) ICBMs now in the RVSN inventory, with the RS-24 the mainstay among its ICBMs. The RS-24 was introduced in 2010, to begin replacing the RS-12M (SS-25 *Sickle*), although manufacturing issues meant the initial build-up was slow. As of mid-2020, this process was almost complete. The RS-24, however, is also intended to replace the RS-12M2. Meanwhile the service lives of the RS-18 (SS-19 *Stiletto*) and RS-20 (SS-18 *Satan*) have been extended repeatedly, as a result of delays to their successor, the RS-28 *Sarmat* (SS-X-29) liquid-fuelled ICBM. Originally intended to be replaced in the middle of the last decade, the RS-20 is now likely to be withdrawn in the next couple of years, while a small number of RS-18 missiles are likely to be retained for now.[6] The intent is to field only the RS-24, RS-28 and *Avangard* from the middle of this decade.[7]

In the case of the navy, the modern-equipment percentage can be explained if it represents the *Bulava*, the R-29RMU *Sineva* and the R-29RMU2.1 *Layner* missile systems. Similarly, it is unclear

RS-24 *YARS*
The missile system central to Moscow's strategic deterrent, during Victory Day parade rehearsals, May 2019. CREDIT: Mikhail Metzel/ TASS/Getty Images

in terms of strategic aviation what the percentage is based upon. It could reflect the number of Kh-102 (AS-23B *Kodiak*) nuclear-armed cruise missiles now in the inventory; if correct, this would suggest few of the ageing Kh-55SM (AS-15B *Kent*) now remain in service since their introduction in 1986–87.

Land-basing

Russia's Strategic Rocket Forces are divided into mobile and 'fixed' groups, and as the names suggest these cover the vehicle-mounted and silo-based missiles respectively. These are together organised in three Rocket Armies comprised of 12 missile divisions.

Eight of the 12 missile divisions are equipped with road-mobile transporter-erector-launcher (TEL) vehicles carrying solid-fuel ICBMs.[8] Within these divisions are 15 road-mobile regiments equipped with the RS-24 *Yars* (SS-27 mod. 2), forming the backbone of the land-based mobile forces. Each regiment is assessed to have nine TELs. Two additional regiments are outfitted with the RS-12M2 *Topol*-M (SS-27 mod. 1) while three more regiments retain the earlier RS-12M *Topol* (SS-25 *Sickle*). A further possible member of the *Yars* family is occasionally mentioned in the Russian media, the *Yars*-M, although its status is uncertain.[9] Continuing to field three differing road-mobile ICBMs raises inter-operability issues since the communications and battle-management systems likely differ between the three.

Given the importance and mission of the Strategic Rocket Forces, combat readiness is the priority. Units that are on duty patrol regularly with regiments deployed either from one division, or more often with regiments drawn from different divisions. In the case of the latter, units are deployed over a vast land area, with the intention of maximising their survivability in the event of war and in the face of a first strike by an enemy. The combat drills include concealment, counter-sabotage, demining and the engineering preparation of launch sites. The defence ministry has in recent years

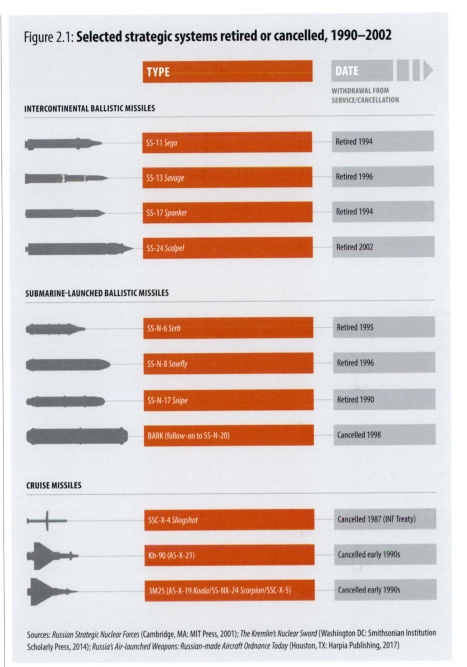

Figure 2.1: Selected strategic systems retired or cancelled, 1990–2002

TYPE	DATE
	WITHDRAWAL FROM SERVICE/CANCELLATION

INTERCONTINENTAL BALLISTIC MISSILES

SS-11 *Sego*	Retired 1994
SS-13 *Savage*	Retired 1996
SS-17 *Spanker*	Retired 1994
SS-24 *Scalpel*	Retired 2002

SUBMARINE-LAUNCHED BALLISTIC MISSILES

SS-N-6 *Serb*	Retired 1995
SS-N-8 *Sawfly*	Retired 1996
SS-N-17 *Snipe*	Retired 1990
BARK (follow-on to SS-N-20)	Cancelled 1998

CRUISE MISSILES

SSC-X-4 *Slingshot*	Cancelled 1987 (INF Treaty)
Kh-90 (AS-X-21)	Cancelled early 1990s
3M25 (AS-X-19 *Koala*/SS-NX-24 *Scorpion*/SSC-X-5)	Cancelled early 1990s

Sources: *Russian Strategic Nuclear Forces* (Cambridge, MA: MIT Press, 2001); *The Kremlin's Nuclear Sword* (Washington DC: Smithsonian Institution Scholarly Press, 2014); *Russia's Air-launched Weapons: Russian-made Aircraft Ordnance Today* (Houston, TX: Harpia Publishing, 2017)

also been investing more in escort protection including the *Typhoon*-M surveillance vehicle and the *Peresvet* laser system. The *Typhoon*-M is intended to provide support against possible ground threats such as special forces, while the *Peresvet* appears intended as a counter-space system to blind observation satellites. Further additions to ICBM convoys include the *Listva* counter-mine vehicle and the MIOM engineering-support vehicle.

As of late 2019, three regiments of RS-18 (SS-19 *Stiletto*) and eight regiments of RS-20 (SS-18 *Satan*) – both types silo-based – were in the inventory. These

legacy systems have had their service lives extended as the development of intended replacements slipped. Although most will be withdrawn in the next couple of years, some RS-18s are being retained as the launch system for the *Avangard* hypersonic glide vehicle system (SS-19 mod. 4). RS-20s are still deployed at Dombarovsky, in Orenburg oblast, while RS-18s are sited at Tatishchevo, in Saratov oblast. All silo-based RS-12M2 *Topol*-M are thought to be located at Tatishchevo. A missile division in Kozelsk in Kaluga oblast is being slowly re-equipped with RS-24 *Yars* (SS-27 mod 2). A first regiment reportedly began service with *Yars* in 2015, but work continues on re-arming the rest of the division. There are indications this may have been the result of the need to improve the security and survivability of the silo site.[10] Although most will be withdrawn in the next couple of years, a small number of RS-18 (SS-19 mod. 4) missiles will be retained to provide the initial launch capability for the *Avangard* hypersonic boost glide vehicle until development of the RS-28 *Sarmat* ICBM is complete. The Russian Ministry of Defence is now aiming to introduce the first *Sarmat* missiles into the inventory in 2021.[11]

Sea-basing

The maritime leg of the triad is also a mix of recently introduced and legacy systems. Nuclear-powered ballistic submarines (SSBNs) are divided between the Northern and Pacific fleets. The Northern Fleet has its headquarters in Severomorsk, with the SSBNs based at Gadzhiyevo, with the Pacific Fleet headquartered at Vladivostok, and the SSBNs located at Vilyuchinsk on the Kamchatka peninsula. Of the navy's 11 SSBNs, plus a single Project 941 *Akula* (*Typhoon*) in reserve, eight are with the Northern Fleet and three with the Pacific Fleet.

Two of the navy's much delayed Project 955 *Borey*-class (*Dolgorukiy*) SSBNs have been allocated to the Pacific Fleet to supplement the last remaining Project 667BDR *Kalmar* (*Delta* III). The *Delta* III carries 16 of the liquid-fuel R-29RKU-02 *Stantsia*-02, an upgraded variant of the SS-N-18 *Stingray*, while the *Borey*s each carry 16 of the new 3M30 *Bulava* (SS-N-32) solid-fuel missiles. The Northern Fleet operates one *Borey* and one improved Project 955A *Borey*-A, alongside six Project 667BDRM *Delfin* (*Delta*-IV) submarines. Each of the *Delfins* can carry 16 R-29RM-series (SS-N-23) liquid-fuel submarine-launched ballistic missiles (SLBMs). These are a mix of the R-29RMU *Sineva* and the R-29RMU2.1 *Layner*. One hundred and eight SLBMs were delivered between 2012 and 2018, and ten *Bulava* SLBMs were due to be delivered in 2019.[12] There is no official public data on warhead numbers and types, however there may be some 'universal' options, including for the *Bulava* and *Yars* 'families' of solid-fuel ballistic missiles.

The first Project 955A *Borey*-A class SSBN, the *Knyaz Vladimir*, completed most of the required trials during 2019 (including test-firing a *Bulava*) and was handed over on 12 June 2020.[13] Along with the *Knyaz Vladimir*, four more *Borey*-A hulls have been laid down.[14] The acquisition of two more *Borey*-A submarines, to bring the fleet size to ten, has also been discussed.

Air-delivered

The Aerospace Forces' heavy-bomber force consists mainly of the Tu-95MS *Bear* H, with up to 60 of the type still in the inventory, supplemented by a small number of the Tu-160 *Blackjack* aircraft. Engels and Ukrainka are the two main bases from which these types are operated. The Kh-55 (AS-15 *Kent*) has since 1983 provided the service with a nuclear-armed cruise missile. The basic Kh-55 (AS-15A *Kent*) is assessed to have been withdrawn, while many of the Kh-55SM (AS-15B) have been converted to the Kh-555 (AS-22 *Kluge*), with the nuclear package replaced with a conventional explosive warhead and with improved terminal guidance. Initial requirements work for a successor to the Kh-55 got under way in the late 1980s with the *Raketa*-2000, and the Kh-102 (AS-23B *Kodiak*) entering production around 2010. The Tu-95MS and the Tu-160 fleets are being upgraded to allow the carriage of the Kh-102 and its conventional variant the Kh-101. The *Bear* and *Blackjack* are the subject of phased modernisation projects, with the first phase involving a navigation upgrade to provide the required in-flight navigation updates for the Kh-101/102. For instance, in 2018, one Tu-160 and four Tu-95MS aircraft were modernised, with a further four Tu-95MSs modified in 2019.

BULAVA SUBMARINE-LAUNCHED BALLISTIC MISSILE
After a troubled development, now the Russian Navy's primary strategic missile. CREDIT: Ministry of Defence of the Russian Federation/TASS/Getty Images

Nuclear decision-making

The power to authorise the use of nuclear weapons rests with the Russian armed forces supreme commander, President Vladimir Putin, with the National Defence Management Centre providing central command and control.[15] This presidential role is made clear in 'The Fundamentals of the State Nuclear Deterrence Policy', which was released in June 2020.[16] The Strategic Rocket Forces' main command site is at Vlasikha near Moscow, however there are several hardened command-and-control bunkers in the Urals, including in Yamantau and Kosvinsky Kamen.[17]

Multiple redundant channels are provided to sustain communications in the event of an attack. These include multi-frequency ground-based radio, satellite communications, airborne command posts, communications aircraft and ballistic-missile-based rebroadcast.[18] Once issued, orders would be sent to hardened, silo-based and mobile command posts at the army, division, regiment and launcher levels. Naval command and force groups would also receive orders, as would SSBNs and long-range bombers. While there is the potential for greater automation in the overall command-and-control system, at present personnel are involved in all levels of decision-making. The missile-based rebroadcast,

the *Perimetr* system, is viewed as a backup channel, should all else fail.

Nuclear doctrine

The latest version of the Military Doctrine of the Russian Federation, published in 2014, identifies two prerequisites for

Map 2.1: **Selected strategic forces locations, 2020**

YOSHKAR-OLA
TEYKOVO
YURYA
VYPOLZOVO
GADZHIYEVO
KOZELSK
MOSCOW
ENGELS
TATISHCHEVO
VILYUCHINSK
DOMBAROVSKY
UKRAINKA
NIZHNY TAGIL
BARNAUL
IRKUTSK
UZHUR
NOVOSIBIRSK

⊕ AIR FORCE BASE
▬ STRATEGIC ROCKET FORCES MISSILE DIVISIONS
⊑ NORTHERN AND PACIFIC FLEETS' SSBN BASES

Sources: IISS; US Defense Intelligence Agency

the use of nuclear weapons: a nuclear or other weapon-of-mass-destruction (WMD) attack on Russia or its allies, or a conventional attack posing an existential risk.[19] How Moscow would calculate such a threat, however, remains unclear. Some details were made public in June

***AVANGARD* HYPERSONIC BOOST GLIDE SYSTEM**
President Vladimir Putin overseeing a test launch, December 2018.
CREDIT: Mikhail Klimentyev/TASS/Getty Images

2020, with the first public release of 'The Fundamentals of the State Nuclear Deterrence Policy'. A previous version of the document had been approved in 2010, but was confidential.[20] The posture paper follows the logic previously outlined in the 2014 military doctrine but goes further in discussing the conditions of nuclear use and the military dangers addressed through nuclear deterrence. The policy paper makes explicit the view that a conventional attack of any kind against civilian or military infrastructure that would undermine a nuclear retaliatory capability would risk eliciting a nuclear response.

It is worth keeping in mind that what has been made public is a strategic-planning document, not a war-fighting manual. There has also been at least passing mention of Russia's nuclear policy in a number of other official documents on doctrine, including 'The Basic Principles of State Naval Policy' (2017) and 'The Military Doctrine of the Union State of Russia and Belarus' (2001).[21] A revised version of the latter was approved in 2018 but has not yet formally entered force nor been made public.[22] Furthermore, 'The Basic Principles of State Naval Policy' includes statements that support a readiness to use nuclear weapons as a deterrent in an escalating confrontation, along with the ability to inflict damage on an adversary using 'non-strategic' nuclear weapons. The extent to which some naval thinking on nuclear weapons is driven by the ambition to conspicuously provide blue-water capability remains an open question, but this is certainly less likely where conventional capabilities are concerned.

The extension of the 'nuclear umbrella' to 'allies' is explicit in the joint Russia–Belarus doctrine. This permits Russia to use nuclear weapons should Belarus be the target of a WMD attack, or if a conventional attack proves an existential threat to Minsk.[23] The willingness to approve nuclear-weapons release under certain conditions when faced only by a conventional attack, along with articles in Russian military-scientific journals and the wider media, may have contributed to debate in the Western specialist and policymaking communities over whether Moscow has an 'escalate to de-escalate' doctrine. Such concerns were voiced in the 2018 US Nuclear Posture Review.[24] Moscow's retention of a large number of 'tactical' nuclear warheads, the breadth of systems these can be fitted to, and the lack of transparency as to how these fit into nuclear doctrine all also contribute to such concerns in the US and Europe.

The concept of 'strategic stability' is an important influence in Russia's nuclear doctrine. The initially agreed approach to the notion was established between Moscow and Washington at the end of superpower confrontation.[25] Both assented that neither would have first strike as a goal, with the emphasis rather on survivability and a second-strike capacity. As such, multiple independently targetable re-entry vehicle (MIRV) warheads married to silo-based ICBMs were viewed as particularly destabilising. Although Moscow retains an emphasis on survivability, it also sees a role for silo-based systems.

In 2019, Vladimir Leontiev, the deputy director of the Ministry of Foreign Affairs' non-proliferation department, argued that heavy silo-based ICBMs were a stabilising factor. However, he also reinforced the goal of 'strategic stability' based on the capacity to hold an adversary at threat and the inevitability of retaliation.[26] Leontiev argued that these two factors provided this desired stability.

Russia's non-strategic nuclear weapons

That Moscow retains a considerable number of nuclear warheads allocated for non-strategic roles appears beyond debate, but otherwise there is little certainty in the public domain as to the size and nature of the arsenal. In discussing this area, even the language is fogged by lack of definition: what is a tactical nuclear weapon, and how do tactical, theatre and sub-strategic differ?

Most estimates for Moscow's warhead inventory lie between 1,000 and 2,000, but it is often not clear whether such figures cover stockpiles allocated to weapons that are operationally available, or also warheads held in reserve.[27] Numerous assessed dual-capable systems are fielded by the army, the Aerospace Forces (VKS) and the navy, but again the command chain for their release to front-line units or regarding their use is unclear. These controls are likely to be restrictive.[28] Washington alleges that Moscow's non-strategic stockpile will grow during the 2020s, though it has provided no evidence to support the assertion.[29] Russia, however, is introducing several new weapons that could be dual-capable: either requiring additional warheads, or a reallocation of some existing stock if the design is compatible.

While official Russian statements on non-strategic systems are uncommon, they are not unknown. In January 2020, a defence ministry press item noted that a 9K720 *Iskander*-M (SS-26 *Stone*) unit had trained in the delivery of 'special ammunition'.[30] In this context, 'special' normally refers to a nuclear package. Some Russian defence commentators suggested this was the first official recognition that the 9K720 had a nuclear-warhead option.

The *Iskander* family also includes the 9M728 (SSC-7 *Southpaw*) and 9M729 (SSC-8 *Screwdriver*) ground-launched cruise missiles.[31] While the 9M728 has a range of around 500 kilometres, the 9M729 – the source of US and NATO assertions of the Intermediate-range Nuclear Forces (INF) Treaty breach – may have a range of up to 2,500 km.[32] Alongside the 9M723 *Iskander* ballistic missile, the 9M728 and 9M729 are also viewed by many as dual-capable, though Russia has not confirmed or refuted this.[33] It maintains that the 9M729 did not break the INF range threshold.[34] At the same time, however, Minister of Defence Sergei Shoigu was advocating the rapid development of a ground-based version of the 3M14 *Kalibr* (SS-N-30A *Sagaris*) naval land-attack cruise missile to provide a greater-range missile.[35] The 3M14 is likely the basis for the 9M729 ground-launched cruise missile.

A nuclear-only submarine-launched cruise missile, the 3M10 *Granat* (SS-N-21 *Sampson*), entered service with the Soviet Navy in 1984.[36] With a range of over 2,500 km, it was considered a strategic and a theatre nuclear weapon. The 3M10 was developed by Novator, which is the design bureau also responsible for the 3M14.[37] Several Soviet-era shorter-range anti-ship and coastal-defence missiles are also dual-capable.

In the air-launched arena, several tactical weapons – besides a stock of free-fall nuclear bombs – currently in the inventory may be dual-capable. The Kh-59M (AS-18 *Kazoo*) has a nuclear-payload option besides high-explosive and submunition warheads.[38] The Kh-59M has a range of 115 km.[39] A further development, known as the Kh-59MK2, appears similar in class to the United States' JASSM or European *Storm Shadow*/SCALP EG. This would have the potential to be dual-capable, should this enter the VKS inventory. The VKS is also assessed to have, or to have had, a nuclear-armed air-to-air missile associated with the MiG-31 *Foxhound*. The R-33S (AA-9B *Amos*) is a variant of the long-range R-33 modified to carry a nuclear warhead.[40] It is possible – if not probable – that the follow-on to the R-33, the R-37M (AA-13A *Axehead*), may also have a nuclear-armed variant.

The A-135 *Amur* anti-ballistic-missile system around Moscow also uses a nuclear warhead on the 53T6 (ABM-4A *Gazelle*) missile.[41] A long-in-development upgrade for the A-135, known as the A-235, is ongoing. The 53T6's nuclear warhead reportedly will be replaced with either a hit-to-kill or conventional warhead payload.[42] The relationship between the A-235 and the *Nudol* anti-satellite programme is unclear. Long-range surface-to-air missile (SAM) systems such as the Soviet S-200 (SA-5 *Gammon*) and S-300 (SA-10 *Grumble*) did include nuclear-warhead options, for example the 5V55S missile for the S-300.[43] It is possible that the nuclear-warhead option continued with later variants of the S-300 family and the S-400, although there has been no official confirmation of this from the Russian defence ministry.

In response to then-president George H.W. Bush's September 1991 Presidential Nuclear Initiatives, Moscow agreed to cut its holding of tactical nuclear weapons.[44] This included the removal of nuclear warheads from SAMs, with the devices to be held in 'central storage'. The Russian response also included eliminating nuclear-artillery rounds; the Soviet Union had developed and deployed 155mm and 203mm nuclear shells. Work ceased on nuclear-artillery-shell design and development in 1998. However, there is still occasional reference to a nuclear-artillery capability, the most recent an April 2020 RIA Novosti article on the 2S7M *Malka* 203mm self-propelled gun.[45] The article mentioned that the gun's munitions could include nuclear rounds.

RUSSIAN NAVY HITS WEAPONS DUMPS IN SYRIA
Russia used a conventionally armed variant of the 3M14 (SS-N-30A *Sagaris*) during its intervention in Syria, with submarines and surface vessels used as launch platforms. A nuclear-armed variant of the missile is also a distinct possibility. CREDIT: Russian Defence Ministry Press Office/TASS/Getty Images

Launch authority and policy

When to launch is contentious among Russia's nuclear academics and military commentators and may well reflect similar debate within the state's nuclear hierarchy. The traditional understanding is that the Strategic Nuclear Forces would launch on warning following the detection of an attack by space- and ground-based systems, but before any of the incoming missiles detonated. However, recent research into Soviet-era doctrine suggests that waiting for an initial detonation was at least countenanced as a means of avoiding a retaliatory strike based on erroneous information. Nevertheless, 'The Fundamentals of the State Nuclear Deterrence Policy' cites 'reliable' information for incoming ballistic missiles (without specifying either range or payload type) targeted on Russian territory as one of the conditions for possible nuclear use.[46]

The structure of nuclear forces in the late Soviet era appeared designed to survive an initial attack and retain enough capacity to inflict an unacceptably high level of damage in a counterstrike.[47] Russian nuclear doctrine, according to Putin, 'does not provide for a pre-emptive strike', and that launch authorisation would be forthcoming 'only when we know for certain' that an attack is under way. He suggested that this would be based on Moscow's early-warning infrastructure. As such, this would appear to be a classic 'launch-on-warning'.[48] Furthermore, Russia continues to be concerned about an attack using advanced conventional weapons, the targets of which could include strategic deterrent systems as well as detection and command, control, communications, computers, intelligence, surveillance and reconnaissance (C4ISR) infrastructure. The behaviour of silo-based units during exercises offers a possible window into Russian thinking. Coverage of an exercise in the *Krasnaya Zvezda* newspaper suggested a scenario in which the unit had to react to a conventional attack on Russia. Drills included concealing the silos during simulated air attack, moving mobile command posts to safety and – only after complete evaluation of the scope of the enemy attack – making a decision on retaliatory strike.[49] If the conventional attack was deemed to be an existential threat to the state, then a nuclear response would be an option.

The US withdrawal from the Intermediate-range Nuclear Forces (INF) Treaty, the result of the United States' conviction that Moscow's 9M729 (SSC-8 *Screwdriver*) dual-capable ground-launched cruise missile was in material breach of the binding agreement, and the potential implications of this withdrawal raise questions for Russian nuclear doctrine. A former head of the Strategic Rocket Forces suggested that if the US deployed intermediate- and short-range ballistic and ground-launched cruise missiles in Europe, then Moscow could respond by shifting to a pre-emptive doctrine.[50] Putin has also indicated that deployment options for dual-capable hypersonic missiles include sea-basing that would place them within reach of the continental US.[51]

The Intermediate-range Nuclear Forces Treaty

Signed between the United States and the Soviet Union on 8 December 1987, and entering into force on 1 June 1988, the INF Treaty eliminated for the first time a whole class of nuclear-delivery systems.[52] It ended 31 years later with the US withdrawal on 2 August 2019; the collapse was due to allegations of a sustained 'material breach' of the treaty.[53]

The INF Treaty prohibited the US or the Soviet Union from fielding ground-launched missiles with a range between 500 and 5,500 kilometres, irrespective of whether the systems were intended to be conventional or nuclear-armed, or dual-capable.[54] This resulted in the US removing the *Pershing* 1A, 1B and *Pershing* II ballistic missiles and the BGM-109G *Gryphon* ground-launched cruise missile from its inventory. The Soviet Union withdrew the R-12 (SS-4 *Sandal*), R-14 (SS-5 *Skean*), *Temp-S* (SS-12 *Scaleboard*), *Pioneer* (SS-20 *Saber*) and OTR-23 *Oka* (SS-23 *Spider*) ballistic missiles and the SSC-X-4 *Slingshot* ground-launched cruise missile. Yet it was a ground-launched

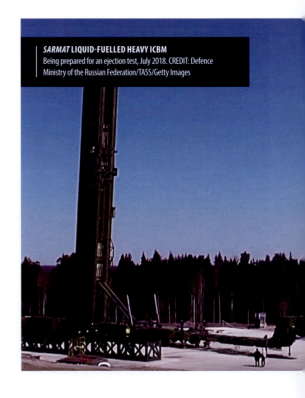

SARMAT LIQUID-FUELLED HEAVY ICBM
Being prepared for an ejection test, July 2018. CREDIT: Defence Ministry of the Russian Federation/TASS/Getty Images

cruise-missile development that led to the treaty's eventual collapse.

In 2014, the US publicly alleged that Russia had violated the treaty in relation to the prohibition regarding ground-launched cruise missiles.[55] It had first raised the issue with Moscow in 2013. The missile in question was later identified as the 9M729 (SSC-8 *Screwdriver*). By the end of 2018, the US and its NATO allies had determined that Russia had begun to deploy the 9M729.[56] The US associated the 9M729 with the Novator missile-design bureau. The latter has a history of developing cruise missiles, including the 3M10 (SS-N-21 *Sampson*) on which the SSC-X-4 was based. The 9M729 is likely a development of the 3M14 (SS-N-30A *Sagaris*) naval land-attack cruise missile now widely fielded in the Russian fleet. The 3M14 is estimated to have a range of up to 2,500 km, and a land-based variant would have a similar range performance. Russia has deployed at least three brigades that are equipped, at least in part, with the 9M729.

As of mid-2020, Russia has maintained that the 9M729 was INF-compliant, with actually less range than the 9M728 (SSC-7 *Southpaw*).[57] However, a 2,000–2,500 km-class dual-capable ground-launched cruise missile would put almost all of Europe within range from the west of Russia, and it would have utility from a military perspective.

Map 2.2: **Notional maximum engagement of a 2,000–2,500 km-range ground-launched cruise missile fired from western Russia**

- – – 2,000 KM RANGE
- – – 2,500 KM RANGE

Source: IISS

Recapitalising the strategic arsenal

Two external factors influencing Russian doctrine are government and military perceptions of the United States' long-range precision conventional-weapons developments, and Washington's missile defence. Improving survivability and possessing a greater capacity to defeat missile defences are pillars of Moscow's strategic-weapons modernisation – its response to how it views US developments. The continuing shift from silo-based to mobile ICBMs and the introduction, if belatedly, of the *Borey*-class SSBN armed with the *Bulava* SLBM are in part intended to improve the survivability of Moscow's deterrent. Improving the survivability of silo-based systems has occasionally also been raised with the

use of what is called 'active protection', including the use of smoke screens, though there has been little public mention of this for some time.

The perceived need to be able to overcome US actual or projected missile defences is the argument most often made for upgrades to existing systems, and for the planned introduction of novel weapons such as the *Avangard* boost-glide system, *Burevestnik* (SSC-X-9 *Skyfall*) nuclear-powered ground-launched cruise missile and *Poseidon* (*Kanyon*) nuclear-powered uninhabited underwater vehicle (UUV). (Of note, the *Burevestnik* and *Kanyon* systems fall outside the New Strategic Arms Reduction Treaty (New START) strategic arms-control agreement.) For ballistic missiles, Moscow has also increasingly adopted shortened boost phases, along

with depressed trajectories to make detection and tracking more difficult.

The economic travails of the 1990s and the impact on defence spending meant that legacy missiles have had to be kept in service far longer than initially planned, as successor projects were delayed or shelved. The service lives of the RS-20 (SS-18 *Satan*) and RS-18 (SS-19 *Stiletto*) have been repeatedly extended. Both were introduced into the Soviet Union's ICBM inventory in the 1980s. A particular problem in recent years has been the support of the RS-20. This missile was from the Ukrainian Yuzhnoye Design Office. Russia's annexation of Crimea in 2014, and its continuing military support for Ukrainian separatists, brought any lingering prospect of support to a halt. Moscow's latest SAP, SAP 2027, reportedly includes re-equipping 20 silo-based regiments with the *Sarmat* (SS-X-29) by the end of the period covered.[58] This would finally replace all RS-20 and RS-18 missiles and likely also the silo-based RS-12M2 *Topol*-M (SS-27 mod. 1). The last of the RS-18s to be replaced will be those retained as the launch system for *Avangard* until they are replaced with the *Sarmat*. As well as the obvious draw on finances, maintaining ageing systems also ties up part of the industrial community and the human resources that could otherwise be involved in the development and support of successor missile systems.

Russia regularly tests its strategic systems, for assurance, to examine upgrade performance and for demonstra-tion purposes. Notable recent examples include a Tu-160 launching a full-war load of the Kh-101/102 cruise missile at a single target set in the Pemboy training range in November 2018.[59] The extent to which this test was intended to examine the reliability of multiple missiles in a salvo firing has not been made public. The firing test may also have been geared to examine modifications introduced to the missile in the light of the Syrian combat experience. While Russia's use of land-attack cruise missiles in the civil war in Syria was generally successful, some early firings of the conventionally armed Kh-101 did not reach the intended targets. A similar if not quite so extensive firing was carried out from the *Borey*-class SSBN *Yuri Dolgorukiy*, which launched four *Bulava* missiles at targets on the Kura training range in Kamchatka, in May 2018. This was the first time the *Bulava* had been salvo-fired.[60]

Command-and-control systems have also been upgraded alongside the delivery mechanisms. The Il-80 *Maxdome* airborne command post – based on the Il-86 wide-body airliner – has been the subject of a number of upgrades, as has the Il-82 radio-relay aircraft with which it is associated. Design work on a successor to the Il-80, using the Il-96 airframe, started in 2015. The Il-22M11 *Sokol* radio-relay aircraft and the Tu-142MR *Bear* J have likely also been the subject of systems upgrades.[61]

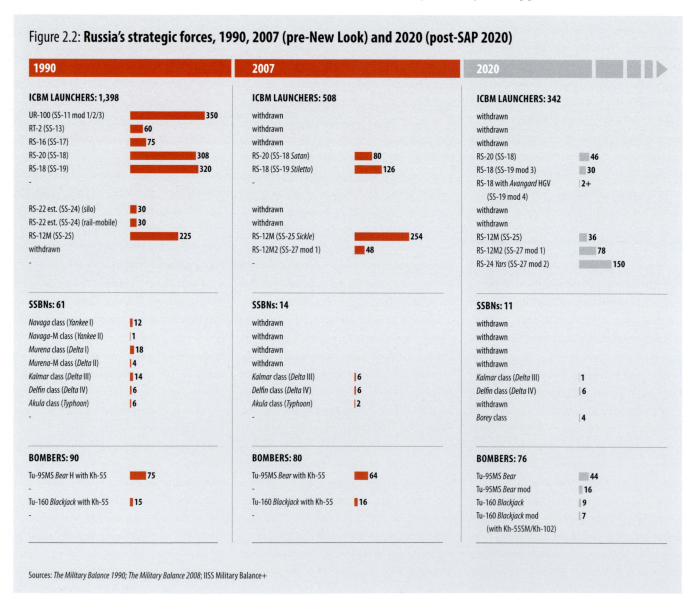

Figure 2.2: **Russia's strategic forces, 1990, 2007 (pre-New Look) and 2020 (post-SAP 2020)**

1990		2007		2020	
ICBM LAUNCHERS: 1,398		**ICBM LAUNCHERS: 508**		**ICBM LAUNCHERS: 342**	
UR-100 (SS-11 mod 1/2/3)	350	withdrawn		withdrawn	
RT-2 (SS-13)	60	withdrawn		withdrawn	
RS-16 (SS-17)	75	withdrawn		withdrawn	
RS-20 (SS-18)	308	RS-20 (SS-18 *Satan*)	80	RS-20 (SS-18)	46
RS-18 (SS-19)	320	RS-18 (SS-19 *Stiletto*)	126	RS-18 (SS-19 mod 3)	30
-		-		RS-18 with *Avangard* HGV (SS-19 mod 4)	2+
RS-22 est. (SS-24) (silo)	30	withdrawn		withdrawn	
RS-22 est. (SS-24) (rail-mobile)	30	withdrawn		withdrawn	
RS-12M (SS-25)	225	RS-12M (SS-25 *Sickle*)	254	RS-12M (SS-25)	36
withdrawn		RS-12M2 (SS-27 mod 1)	48	RS-12M2 (SS-27 mod 1)	78
-		-		RS-24 *Yars* (SS-27 mod 2)	150
SSBNs: 61		**SSBNs: 14**		**SSBNs: 11**	
Navaga class (*Yankee* I)	12	withdrawn		withdrawn	
Navaga-M class (*Yankee* II)	1	withdrawn		withdrawn	
Murena class (*Delta* I)	18	withdrawn		withdrawn	
Murena-M class (*Delta* II)	4	withdrawn		withdrawn	
Kalmar class (*Delta* III)	14	*Kalmar* class (*Delta* III)	6	*Kalmar* class (*Delta* III)	1
Delfin class (*Delta* IV)	6	*Delfin* class (*Delta* IV)	6	*Delfin* class (*Delta* IV)	6
Akula class (*Typhoon*)	6	*Akula* class (*Typhoon*)	2	withdrawn	
-		-		*Borey* class	4
BOMBERS: 90		**BOMBERS: 80**		**BOMBERS: 76**	
Tu-95MS *Bear* H with Kh-55	75	Tu-95MS *Bear* with Kh-55	64	Tu-95MS *Bear*	44
-		-		Tu-95MS *Bear* mod	16
Tu-160 *Blackjack* with Kh-55	15	Tu-160 *Blackjack* with Kh-55	16	Tu-160 *Blackjack*	9
-		-		Tu-160 *Blackjack* mod (with Kh-55SM/Kh-102)	7

Sources: *The Military Balance 1990*; *The Military Balance 2008*; IISS Military Balance+

Burevestnik (SSC-X-9 *Skyfall*)

On 8 August 2019, an explosion near the Nynoksa naval missile test range in northern Russia resulted in a radiation spike and the deaths of five specialists from Rosatom, the state-owned atomic-energy corporation, while other personnel were injured. Moscow has not yet identified the system involved, but a candidate is the *Burevestnik* (SSC-X-9 *Skyfall*) nuclear-powered cruise missile.[62]

The explosion did not occur during a firing but perhaps when a recovery attempt was under way after the missile went through a prolonged period of submersion due to an earlier failed test launch.[63] The missile may have been submerged for well over 12 months prior to the attempted recovery. Following the event, imagery showing a badly damaged barge with a recovery crane on the shoreline at Nynoksa appeared on social media.

While the defence ministry has released some test footage of the ground-launched missile, and of partly covered test items in a final assembly building, no technical information on the weapon has been released.[64] The missile configuration, however, suggests a subsonic weapon, with the wing design reminiscent of the Kh-101/Kh-102 (AS-23A/B *Kodiak*) family of long-range cruise missiles designed by Raduga. A Rosatom subsidiary, the All-Russian Scientific Research Institute of Experimental Physics, has been associated with the project.[65] Given that the nuclear-reactor element of the project is by far the most demanding, the project may be led by its provider, rather than the air-vehicle designer.

The *Burevestnik* was one of several developments revealed by President Vladimir Putin in his speech to the Federal Assembly on 1 March 2018; these projects were couched in terms of Moscow's response to Washington's 2002 withdrawal from the Anti-Ballistic Missile Treaty and the United States' perceived wider aims.[66] Putin saw Washington attempting to create 'a global missile defence system … for countering strategic arms that follow ballistic trajectories. These weapons form the backbone of our nuclear deterrent forces.'[67]

The benefit of a cruise missile using a nuclear-powered engine as the sustainer motor is very long endurance. Assuming the propulsion unit can be made to work, the limiting factor on flight time may be other mechanical elements of the air vehicle, for example those that require lubrication.

Testing of the *Burevestnik* was under way no later than 2017. Some of the early tests likely were to ensure that the large booster motor used to launch the missile from the ground operated and separated correctly. The missile may also use additional conventional booster motors to allow the nuclear reactor to begin to provide adequate thrust. The transition to and the sustainment of nuclear propulsion is a considerable engineering challenge, and there have been US reports of numerous failures.

The US has also considered nuclear propulsion for cruise-missile applications. In the 1960s, the US Air Force funded Project Pluto, an attempt to design and develop a nuclear ramjet-powered cruise missile. It was abandoned as impractical in 1964, following a seven-year effort.

Today's and tomorrow's inventory

Russia deploys four different ICBMs, if one counts the RS-12M2 and RS-24 as the same family, with the RS-12M, RS-18, and RS-20 as separate types.[68] Moscow has not disclosed the number of the legacy RS-18 and RS-20 liquid-fuel heavy ICBMs that still remain in the inventory, though a notable decrease in the number of deployed warheads declared under the New START in late 2017 may have reflected a number of these types being finally retired. The SS-19 mod. 3 has up to six MIRVs per missile, while the SS-18 mod. 5 has ten. Despite mobile systems offering greater survivability, Moscow continues to invest in multi-warhead silo-based ICBMs. As previously noted, Ministry of Foreign Affairs officials contend that such weapons are not destabilising, or at least no more so than heavy bombers, since both are arguably as vulnerable to a first strike. In the case of the heavy bomber the argument is made that the deployment of aircraft could be viewed as escalatory by an adversary, even if this was not the intention.

By the end of the current SAP, the aim is that all the RS-18s and RS-20s will have been retired, as will the road-mobile RS-12M *Topol* (SS-25 *Sickle*). RS-12M regiments are being re-equipped with the RS-24 *Yars* (SS-27 mod. 2). By the end of 2019, four regiments continued to field the RS-12M. Given that the missiles were deployed between 1985 and 1992, their replacement is pressing; even having had a service-life extension, they are near life-expired.[69]

As of the end of 2019, the Strategic Rocket Forces have re-equipped 15 mobile and two silo-based regiments with *Yars*, with up to an additional 12 regiments to be added over the course of SAP 2027 (2018–27).[70] Alongside re-equipping mobile units with the missiles and TELs, the rearmament also includes new support and patrol vehicles. The pace of re-equipping units, however, can be variable. The 54th Guards Missile Division (Teykovo), despite often being considered 'rearmed', retains a mix of RS-12M2 *Topol*-M and RS-24 *Yars*.

Similarly, the pace of deployment of the silo-based RS-24 with the 28th division at Kozelsk appeared slow. This may in part be the result of the need for construction work at the site including improving the command posts. There have also been suggestions that a point-defence system was being tested at the Kozelsk site, and this may also have contributed to the sluggish speed of re-equipping.

The defence ministry has not made public exactly how many RS-24 missiles have been produced, but 109 missiles, a mix of mobile and silo-based, were delivered from 2012 to 2018.[71] The aim for 2019 was to deliver 21 *Yars*; the defence ministry stated that three more regiments were to be converted to the type by the end of that year.[72] The head of the Strategic

Rocket Forces, Colonel-General Sergei Karakayev, said in November 2019 that more that 150 *Yars* missiles had been delivered.[73] The goal for 2020 is the delivery of 22 missiles. Whether this number is indicative of a near-maximum annual production for the Votkinsk Machine Building Plant responsible for making the RS-24 is uncertain. Two further variants of the *Yars* are occasionally mentioned, with one at least deployed. The *Yars*-M may be associated with the RS-26 *Rubezh* development programme, while what has been labelled the *Yars*-S has been deployed with the 14th, 35th and 39th missile divisions in Yoshkar-Ola, Barnaul and Novosibirsk in addition to the basic *Yars*.[74] The *Yars*-S may differ from *Yars* in warhead yield, and there has been speculation that a post-boost vehicle has also been developed as a counter to missile defences.[75]

Something old, something new

The Reagan-era Strategic Defense Initiative spurred Moscow's interest in hypersonic boost-glide systems as one counter to anti-missile developments, with NPO Mashinostroyenia working on the *Albatros* project in the late 1980s. Shelved in the early 1990s, the work fed into what was to become known as Project 4202.[76] Flight testing resumed in 2001 or 2004 using a modified RS-18, though this missile may not necessarily have been the intended operational launch system.[77] The RS-18 was ageing by the early 2000s; it is a 1970s design that entered the Soviet inventory from the beginning of the 1980s. A development contract for a successor to the RS-18, the *Sarmat*, was placed in 2011, but the programme has suffered delay.[78] The RS-18 service life has already been stretched to 36 years; the last missiles delivered were in 1984, and a further extension is now under way to stretch this beyond 2020 to support the initial *Avangard* deployment.[79] A regiment from the 13th Missile Division in Dombarovsky was the first to begin fielding *Avangard* (SS-19 mod. 4) at the end of 2019. The *Avangard* is almost certainly a nuclear-only system, not least of all because it is being deployed as part of the Strategic Rocket Forces. Moscow has also deemed conventionally armed ICBMs as being destabilising, as is evident in its opposition to Washington's Prompt Global Strike initiative.

As aforementioned, the longer-term hypersonic-glide-vehicle launch system, the *Sarmat*, has suffered from a number of development and manufacturing delays. Test-launch infrastructure has been built at Plesetsk, and work carried out at Uzhur, where the missile will be deployed.[80] Ejection tests of the cold-launch mechanism were carried out in 2017 and 2018, with flight tests then expected to follow in 2019. As of April 2020, however, a full flight test had yet to be carried out. Unconfirmed reports suggested five flight tests would be carried out prior to the missile entering the inventory, now planned for 2021.[81] The 62nd Missile Division, based at Uzhur, will deploy the missile, eventually replacing its four regiments of RS-20.[82]

The association of *Sarmat* with *Avangard* had been the source of speculation for some years, but informal confirmation emerged in late 2018 when a Russian television programme showed an animation depicting the separation of three hypersonic glide vehicles from a *Sarmat*-like booster.[83] Russia maintains that *Avangard* and *Sarmat* can be dealt with as part of the New START. To this end, it showed *Avangard* to US inspectors in November 2019. Russian Foreign Minister Sergei Lavrov said these systems 'are covered by the treaty', and that Moscow would propose these are included as and when New START is extended.[84] As of August 2020, Washington had yet to decide on extending the treaty, due to expire in February 2021.

Along with NPO Mashinostroyenia, *Avangard* rival missile designer the Moscow Institute of Thermal Technology may be working on a hypersonic-glide body associated with the name *Anchar*-RV.[85] The institute is also the designer of the *Yars* missile, which had led to speculation there may be a relationship between the two.

AVANGARD HYPERSONIC BOOST GLIDE SYSTEM
En route to a test launch, July 2018. CREDIT: Defence Ministry of the Russian Federation/TASS/PA Images

Nuclear propulsion

The two most surprising developments that President Putin touted in his 1 March 2018 address were what are now referred to as *Burevestnik*, a nuclear-powered very long-endurance cruise missile, and the *Poseidon* nuclear-powered long-endurance UUV.[86] The *Burevestnik* (SSC-X-9 *Skyfall*) project has likely been under way for the better part of two decades, although many of the flight tests so far have resulted in failure. While both are intended to be nuclear-armed, *Poseidon* (*Kanyon*) may have a secondary conventional role. Large UUVs can carry surveillance- and intelligence-gathering payloads and could also be used for minelaying.

The diesel–electric-powered *Sarov* test submarine was used for *Poseidon* trials, but it is planned to be deployed before the end of 2020 on the Project 09852 *Belgorod* submarine launched in spring 2019.[87] The *Belgorod* is reportedly able to carry up to six *Poseidon* UUVs.

Air and naval recapitalisation

Following a long and troubled development, the *Bulava* submarine-launched ballistic missile continues in production at Votkinsk, while the Krasnoyarsk Machine-Building Plant has been involved with the R-29RMU *Sineva* and R-29RMU2.1 *Layner* SLBM projects. The R-29RM *Shtil* (SS-N-23 *Skiff*) entered service in 1986 and production ceased by the late 1990s.[88] However, in 1999 an improved version entered production, the R-29RMU *Sineva*, with this missile beginning to be fielded on the *Delfin*-class SSBNs beginning in 2007.[89] A further upgrade, the R-29RMU2.1 *Layner*, was introduced from the beginning of 2014.[90] The *Layner* appears to be a warhead and penetration-aids improvement package for the *Sineva*.

The extension of the R-29 family is due to the delays in the navy's SLBM replacement plans. Work on a new SLBM was under way in the early 1990s to provide the primary armament for the Project 955 *Borey*-class submarines. This was led by the Makeyev Design Bureau with the *Bark* programme. Four failed flight tests led to *Bark* being cancelled in 1997 and the Moscow Institute of Thermal Technology being given the contract to develop a missile for the Project 955s.[91] The *Borey–Bulava* combination will eventually replace the *Delfin* and *Sineva–Layner*, with the latter two being withdrawn by around the end of this decade.

The problems with *Bulava* prompted speculation that the programme would follow a similar trajectory to *Bark* and be cancelled. The possibility of a *Bulava-2* or even a new liquid-fuel missile have been suggested, but there has been no official confirmation of any such project.[92]

The inaugural Project 955A hull *Knyaz Vladimir* was expected to be delivered to the navy in 2018, then 2019, but this only occurred in June 2020. Three *Borey*- and one *Borey*-A-class SSBNs are already in service, with four *Borey*-As in build. The *Borey*-A is meant to have an improved acoustic signature, while other upgrades include a better sensor suite. Two further developments of the *Borey* have occasionally been mentioned in the Russian press, the *Borey*-B and the *Borey*-K. The latter is a proposed design that would fit the submarine with land-attack cruise missiles.

Work is also under way on the *Laika* next-generation submarine research-and-development project as a part of SAP 2027. The design is intended to be modular, with one ambition being the ability to fulfil both nuclear-powered attack submarines and SSBN requirements.[93] As of June 2020, this aim has yet to be met.

The air leg of Moscow's nuclear triad has always been the smallest of the three. As of 2020, it continues to be based on a nearly 70-year-old design (the prototype Tu-95 *Bear* was first flown in 1952), along with a handful of the Tu-160 *Blackjack* (first flown in 1981). The Soviet intent had been to have a 100-strong Tu-160 fleet that, when combined with the T-60S medium-bomber project, would have likely formed the core of the Air Force's nuclear delivery aircraft from the turn of this century. Instead the T-60S was cancelled and production of the Tu-160 halted at the end of 1992, only just

TU-95MS *BEAR* H
Though the Tu-95 prototype first flew in the early 1950s, the Tu-95MS *Bear* H remains the Russian Air Force's most numerous long-range bomber.
CREDIT: Tatyana Belyakova/TASS/Getty Images

over one-third of the way through planned production. The type entered service in 1987 with the 184th Bomber Regiment in Prylyuky, Ukraine. The dissolution of the Soviet Union in 1991 left all the operational aircraft in newly independent Ukraine; of these, eight Tu-160s were handed back to Russia, and a further ten were scrapped.[94] Moscow was left with 16 Tu-160s from which to form a squadron within the 121st Heavy Bomber Aviation Regiment based at Engels. The operational strength of the squadron is considerably less than 16 aircraft as the small fleet is in the process of a staged upgrade. Up to May 2020, only seven Tu-160s could be seen regularly on publicly available satellite imagery of Engels. At least a further four airframes were at Kazan, including two aircraft recently upgraded to the Tu-160 mod. 1 standard. Including these, so far seven aircraft have been modified. The modifications allow the Tu-160 to carry the Kh-101/102 (AS-23A/B *Kodiak*) nuclear-armed cruise missile. As well as upgrading existing airframes, Moscow has also re-started production of the Tu-160. The first of ten Tu-160M aircraft ordered in 2018 is now in assembly at Kazan and serial deliveries to the Aerospace Forces are to begin in 2023.[95]

The venerable Tu-95MS is also being upgraded, with at least a quarter of the up to 60-strong fleet having undergone a modest modification programme to allow the carriage of the Kh-101/102.[96] Similarly, the life of the Tu-22M *Backfire* C is being extended, with the modified aircraft known as the Tu-22M3M. Absent an air-to-air refuelling capability, the Tu-22M was not included in New START. An air-to-air refuelling capability now appears to be part of the upgrade.

Russia is also working on a design to meet the Aerospace Forces' PAK-DA (*Perspektivnyy aviatsionnyy kompleks dalney aviatsii*), Future Aviation Complex Long-Range Aviation requirement, though the pace of the project has slowed. The design is assumed to be a subsonic low-observable aircraft. The extent to which Russia retains the design and manufacturing capacity to produce two strategic bombers in parallel is an open question. There have been suggestions that if additional new-build Tu-160s were to be bought then the number of aircraft required to meet the PAK-DA requirement would be cut. It was announced that there were plans to order additional Tu-160s in May 2019.[97]

While the Kh-102 has replaced the Kh-55SM as the Aerospace Forces' primary air-launched nuclear-armed cruise missile, further developments also continue. There has been occasional reference to a project known as Kh-BD – BD is the Russian abbreviation for 'long range', which is associated with air-launched cruise-missile development. This could be an extended-range variant of the Kh-102, similar to the Kh-55SM that increased the range of the baseline Kh-55. Along with subsonic-cruise-missile development, the VKS is also looking to introduce one or more hypersonic-cruise-missile designs into the strategic-bomber inventory. The abbreviation GZUR (*giperzvukovaya upravlyayemaya raketahypersonic*, or guided missile) is associated with a 1,500 km-range Mach 6-class weapon.

MOLODETS RAIL-MOBILE ICBM
Russia was developing a follow-on known as *Barguzin*, but the project has been shelved. CREDIT: Andrew Too Boon Tan/Getty Images

Holding pattern

Two strategic projects, at least, were shelved as a result of deliberations on SAP 2027. The RS-26 *Rubezh* road-mobile ICBM and the *Barguzin* rail-based system were both at least paused, with reports suggesting there was inadequate funding to support all the strategic projects.[98] The RS-26 was initially cause for Washington's charges that Russia was violating the INF Treaty given that its range skirts the 5,500 km upper threshold of the now-defunct treaty. Instead the focus of US accusations became the 9M729 (SSC-8 *Screwdriver*) mobile ground-launched cruise-missile system. *Barguzin* meanwhile risks following a similar course to the RT-12UTTh *Molodets* (SS-24 *Scalpel* mod. 1) rail-based ICBM, which after a short service life was withdrawn in 2005. (The missile was a Ukrainian design.)

Revisiting the *Rubezh* – quite possibly a variant of the RS-24 *Yars*, which had completed research and development and was notionally expected to be deployed in 2017 – is still an option.[99] It may be viewed as a countermove should Washington deploy intermediate-range ballistic systems. Of particular concern to Russia is that militarily significant Russian territory including the Kamchatka and Chukotka peninsulas would fall within easy reach if the US were to deploy intermediate-range ballistic-missile systems in the western part of the continental US.

The *Barguzin* rail-mobile ICBM may also be related to *Yars* or to *Bulava*. The intent was to provide the Strategic Rocket Forces with a third launch system to complement silo-based and road-mobile systems. Ejection tests were carried out in 2016. Rail-basing, however, appears to have lost out to other systems that were deemed more attractive.

New START stops?

Washington's ambiguity on whether it will extend the New START strategic arms-control treaty has been increasingly matched by Moscow's public claims that it wants the treaty sustained, if perhaps with new provisions. New START will expire 5 February 2021 unless Russia and the US agree an extension of between 12 and 60 months. Showing *Avangard* to US inspectors in November 2019 may have been intended to signal to Washington that Moscow remained in compliance.[100] During his 19 December 2019 press conference, Putin said he was 'ready … to extend the existing New START as is'.[101] Moscow has also stated it is willing to include *Avangard* and *Sarmat* under New START, on the basis that Washington agrees to its extension.[102] *Burevestnik* and *Poseidon* fall outside the treaty definitions, which is of benefit to Moscow and to the detriment of the treaty goals.

As of the end of August 2020 obstacles remain, not least of all owing to the lack of clarity from the US over any willingness to compromise in order to extend the treaty. US Defense Secretary Mark Esper has suggested he wants to see it cover theatre nuclear weapons, while President Donald Trump wants future strategic-arms agreements to include China. Esper's aim will likely meet implacable opposition in Moscow, while drawing China into any deal in such a short period would seem wildly optimistic. China has dismissed any involvement in trilateral nuclear-arms control.

Figure 2.3: **The Soviet Union and Russia: strategic arms controls**

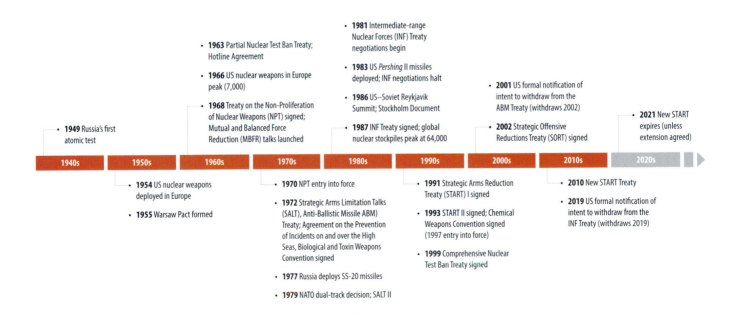

Source: *The Military Balance 2019*

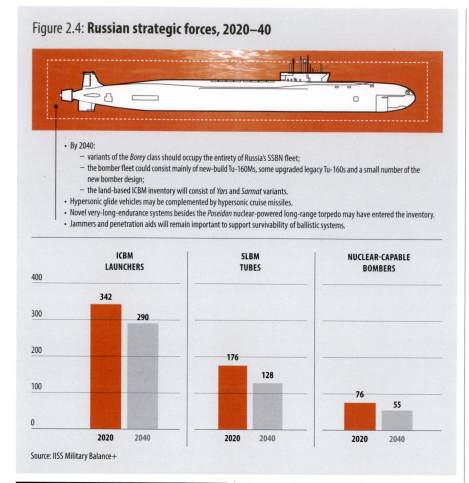

Figure 2.4: **Russian strategic forces, 2020–40**

- By 2040:
  - variants of the *Borey* class should occupy the entirety of Russia's SSBN fleet;
  - the bomber fleet could consist mainly of new-build Tu-160Ms, some upgraded legacy Tu-160s and a small number of the new bomber design;
  - the land-based ICBM inventory will consist of *Yars* and *Sarmat* variants.
- Hypersonic glide vehicles may be complemented by hypersonic cruise missiles.
- Novel very-long-endurance systems besides the *Poseidon* nuclear-powered long-range torpedo may have entered the inventory.
- Jammers and penetration aids will remain important to support survivability of ballistic systems.

	ICBM LAUNCHERS		SLBM TUBES		NUCLEAR-CAPABLE BOMBERS	
	342	290	176	128	76	55
	2020	2040	2020	2040	2020	2040

Source: IISS Military Balance+

Conclusion

That Russia will continue to be a significant nuclear power for the foreseeable future is a near certainty. Less so is whether Moscow will remain a nuclear-armed state framed within a bilateral or multilateral arms-control architecture, and the extent to which the novel weapons it is now developing will feature in its inventory.

The Strategic Rocket Forces will remain first among the three nuclear legs of the triad, with missile survivability a priority.

The navy's SSBNs will also continue to provide a core component of nuclear deterrence. The future shape and role of the air element of the deterrent force remains harder to discern. Should the Aerospace Forces continue to support new-build production of the Tu-160 and the development and manufacture of a design to meet its PAK-DA requirement, it is conceivable that it could have two bombers in production and at the same time only one multi-role tactical fighter, the Su-57 *Felon*. There is the question as to whether the defence budget and the defence-

aerospace industrial base can support two long-range-bomber programmes – a doubt only strengthened by the impact of the COVID-19 pandemic on the Russian economy. The ability, however, to hold at threat European targets with dual-capable, cruise-missile-equipped bomber aircraft does confer a degree of flexibility arguably absent from both the Strategic Rocket Forces and the SSBN fleet. This, along with the prestige of the deterrence mission, suggests that the Aerospace Forces will remain committed to sustaining a place in Russia's strategic forces.

For the navy, the *Borey* and *Borey*-A submarines will provide its element of the strategic deterrent for the next two decades and beyond. Less certain is whether the *Bulava* will remain these vessels' armament throughout the course of their service lives. Such has been the difficult development of this SLBM that there have been more than occasional suggestions that a possible successor missile design is being considered.

Meanwhile, the Strategic Rocket Forces should by the latter part of the 2020s field only the RS-24, *Sarmat* and *Avangard*, with most regiments equipped with mobile TELs. The RS-26 *Rubezh* could also re-emerge as an addition to the RVSN inventory and appears more likely than renewed investment in the *Barguzin* rail-mobile system. How the Strategic Rocket Forces might integrate some of the novel systems now in development – such as *Poseidon* (*Kanyon*), *Burevestnik* and hypersonic cruise missiles – remains to be seen, as does how these could be accommodated within Moscow's thinking on deterrence.

Notes

1 Nikolai Sokov, 'Modernization of Strategic Nuclear Weapons in Russia: The Emerging New Posture', Monterey Institute for International Studies, May 1998, p. 3, http://www.armscontrol.ru/start/publications/ns9812.htm.

2 'The Top 20 Economies in the World', Investopedia, 18 March 2020, https://www.investopedia.com/insights/worlds-top-economies/#countries-by-gdp.

3 'Defence Minister of the Russian Federation addresses extended session of Defence

Ministry Board Session', 18 December 2018, p. 2, http://mil.ru/files/files/Doklad%20Ministra%28en%29.pdf.

4 Marina Shcherbakova, 'Vooruzhennye Sily RF. Razvitie s 2012 po 2018 god', *Krasnaya Zvezda*, 9 January 2019, http://redstar.ru/

vooruzhyonnye-sily-rf-razvitie-s-2012-po-2018-god.

5 President of Russia, 'Defence Ministry Board meeting', 24 December 2019, http://en.kremlin.ru/events/president/news/62401.

6 Interfax-AVN, 'Russia to develop new ballistic missile by end of 2016 – commander', BBC Monitoring, 16 December 2009, https://monitoring.bbc.co.uk/product/m18ksac8.

7 S.V. Karakaev, 'Raketnyye voyska strategicheskogo naznacheniya sovremennoy rossii', *Military Thought*, 3 December 2019, http://vm.ric.mil.ru/Stati/item/229465.

8 Hans M. Kristensen and Matt Korda, 'Russian nuclear forces, 2019', *Bulletin of Atomic Scientists*, vol. 75, no. 2, March 2019, https://www.tandfonline.com/doi/full/10.1080/00963402.2019.1580891; authors' own estimations.

9 'Raketnyy polk na Altaye perevooruzhili na novyye kompleksy "Yars-S"', RIA Novosti, 27 December 2019, https://ria.ru/20191227/1562950140.html; Ivan Safronov, 'Putin ob' yavil nazvaniye novoy rakety sredney dal'nosti', *Vedomosti*, 24 December 2019, https://www.vedomosti.ru/politics/articles/2019/12/24/819588-novoi-raketi.

10 'First regiment of Kozelsk missile division rearmed with Yars missiles – source', TASS, 29 November 2018, http://tass.com/defense/1033480.

11 'Pervyye seriynye rakety "Sarmat" postupyat na vooruzheniye v 2021 godu', TASS, 3 February 2020, https://tass.ru/armiya-i-opk/7669389.

12 'Armiya Rossii Kardinalno Obnovlena', *Krasnaya Zvezda*, 13 March 2019, http://redstar.ru/armiya-rossii-kardinalno-obnovlena; Ministry of Defence of the Russian Federation, 'Tezisy doklada zamestitelya Ministra oborony Rossiyskoy Federatsii Alekseya Krivoruchko na Edinom dne priyemki voyennoy produktsii 12 aprelya 2019 goda', 12 April 2019, https://function.mil.ru/news_page/person/more.htm?id=12225535@egNews.

13 'Istochnik: pervyy modernizirovannyy "Borey" "Knyaz' Vladimir" mogut peredat' VMF v kontse maya', TASS, 6 May 2020, https://tass.ru/armiya-i-opk/840887; Ministry of Defence of the Russian Federation, 'The "Knyaz Vladimir" ballistic missile submarine went to the White sea starting its first base-to-base passage being part of the submarine force of the Northern Fleet', 29 June 2020, https://eng.mil.ru/en/news_page/country/more.htm?id=12299600@egNews.

14 President of the Russian Federation, 'Meeting with senior Defence Ministry officials and defence industry executives', 3 December 2019, http://en.kremlin.ru/events/president/news/62228.

15 Jeffrey G. Lewis and Bruno Tertrais, 'The Finger on the Button: The Authority to use Nuclear Weapons in Nuclear-Armed States', CNS Occasional Paper no. 5, James Martin Center for Nonproliferation Studies, February 2019, pp. 10–12, https://www.nonproliferation.org/wp-content/uploads/2019/02/Finger-on-the-Nuclear-Button.pdf.

16 President of the Russian Federation, 'Ob Osnovakh gosudarstvennoy politiki Rossiyskoy Federatsii v oblasti yadernogo sderzhivaniya', 2 June 2020, http://publication.pravo.gov.ru/Document/Text/0001202006020040.

17 Tatyana Lyashko, 'Sekretnyy Bunker: kak vyglyadit iznutri Tsentral'nyy Komandnyy Punkt RVSN', Zvezda TV channel, 16 December 2018, https://tvzvezda.ru/news/forces/content/201812160901-68x6.htm.

18 Nikolai Spasskiy, *Russia's Arms and Technologies. The XXI Century Encyclopedia. Volume 1 – Strategic Nuclear Forces* (Moscow: Oruzhie i Tekhnologi, 2000), pp. 106–15.

19 'Voyennaya Doktrina Rossiyskoy Federatsii', *Rossiyskaya Gazeta*, 30 December 2014, https://rg.ru/2014/12/30/doktrina-dok.html.

20 'Medvedev utverdil voyennuyu doktrinu i osnovy gosudarstvennoy politiki v oblasti yadernogo sderzhivaniya do 2020 goda', Interfax, 5 February 2010, https://www.interfax-russia.ru/main/medvedev-utverdil-voennuyu-doktrinu-i-osnovy-gospolitiki-v-oblasti-yadernogo-sderzhivaniya-do-2020-goda.

21 President of the Russian Federation, 'Ob utverzhdenii Osnov gosudarstvennoy politiki Rossiyskoy Federatsii v oblasti voyenno-morskoy deyatel'nosti na period do 2030 goda', 20 July 2017, http://ivo.garant.ru/#/document/71725734/paragraph/1:1; Highest State Council of the Union State, 'O Voyennoy doktrine Soyuznogo gosudarstva', 26 December 2001, http://docs.cntd.ru/document/456089527.

22 President of the Russian Feederation, 'O Voyennoy doktrine Soyuznogo gosudarstva', 19 December 2018, http://docs.cntd.ru/document/551976250.

23 President of the Russian Federation, 'Ob utverzhdenii Osnov gosudarstvennoy politiki Rossiyskoy Federatsii v oblasti voyenno-morskoy deyatel'nosti na period do 2030 goda', 20 July 2017, http://ivo.garant.ru/#/document/71725734/paragraph/1:4.

24 US Department of Defense, 'Nuclear Posture Review', February 2018, p. 30, https://media.defense.gov/2018/Feb/02/2001872886/-1/-1/1/2018-NUCLEAR-POSTURE-REVIEW-FINAL-REPORT.PDF.

25 Office of the White House press secretary, 'Soviet–United States Joint Statement on Future Negotiations on Nuclear and Space Arms and Further Enhancing Strategic Stability', George Bush Presidential Library and Museum, 1 June 1990, https://bush41library.tamu.edu/archives/public-papers/1938.

26 'Article by Deputy Director of the Department for Nonproliferation and Arms Control of the Ministry of Foreign Affairs of Russia Vladimir L. Leontiev "Message received. Attempt at distance communication with the U.S. State Department" published in the magazine "Independent Military Review" April 12, 2019', Ministry of Foreign Affairs of the Russian Federation, 12 April 2019, http://www.mid.ru/en/web/guest/foreign_policy/international_safety/regprla/-/asset_publisher/YCxLFJnKuD1W/content/id/3613093.

27 Igor Sutyagin, 'Atomic Accounting', Royal United Services Institute, Occasional Paper, November 2012, p. 2, https://rusi.org/sites/default/files/201211_op_atomic_accounting.pdf; US Defense Intelligence Agency, 'Russia Military Power', 2017, p. 31, https://www.dia.mil/Portals/27/Documents/News/Military%20Power%20Publications/Russia%20Military%20Power%20Report%202017.pdf?ver=2017-06-28-144235-937.

28 US Defense Intelligence Agency, 'Russia Military Power'.

29 US Senate Foreign Relations Committee, 'Countering Russian Intimidation and Aggression and Building a Better Security Environment, testimony by Christopher A Ford', 3 December 2019, p. 2, https://www.foreign.senate.gov/imo/media/doc/120319_Ford_Testimony.pdf.

30 Ministry of Defence of the Russian Federation, 'In Buryatia, military personnel of the BBO missile compound worked out the issues of delivering special ammunition to a conditional area', 22 January 2020, https://function.mil.ru/news_page/country/more.htm?id=12271891.

31 Ministry of Defence of the Russian Federation, 'Russian Defence Ministry briefs military attaches with presentation of 9M729 missile of *Iskander-M* complex', 23 January 2019, https://eng.mil.ru/en/news_page/country/more.htm?id=12213705@egNews.

32 US Office of the Director of National Intelligence, 'Director of National Intelligence Daniel Coats on Russia's Intermediate-range Nuclear Forces (INF) Treaty Violation', 30 November 2018, https://www.dni.gov/index.php/newsroom/speeches-interviews/speeches-interviews-2018/item/1923-director-of-national-intelligence-daniel-coats-on-russia-s-inf-treaty-violation.

33 *Ibid.*

34 Ministry of Defence of the Russian Federation, 'Russian Defence Ministry briefs military attaches with presentation of 9M729 missile of *Iskander-M* complex'.

35 RIA Novosti, 'Russia to "develop new missiles by 2020" after INF suspension', BBC Monitoring, 5 February 2019, https://monitoring.bbc.co.uk/product/c2oolifm.

36 'STRATEGICHESKIY PROKHODNYY KOMPLEKS 3K10 "GRANAT"', Bastion-Karpenko, http://bastion-karpenko.ru/complex-3k10-granat.

37 *Ibid.*

38 Piotr Butowski, *Russia's Air-launched Weapons* (Houston, TX: Harpia Publishing, 2017), p. 37.

39 *Ibid.*

40 *Ibid.*, p .54

41 'Modernizatsiya rossiyskoy PRO zatronet znamenituyu sistemu A-135', VPK, 10 December 2014, https://vpk.name/news/122861_modernizaciya_rossiiskoi_pro_zatronet_znamenituyu_sistemu_a-135.html.

42 *Ibid.*

43 'C-300', Encyclopaedia Russia, 19 May 2014, https://weapons-russia.ru/article/s-300.

44 Susan J. Koch, 'The Presidential Nuclear Initiatives of 1991–92', Center for the Study of Weapons of Mass Destruction, National Defense University, NDU Press, September 2012, p. 14, https://inss.ndu.edu/Portals/68/Documents/casestudies/CSWMD_CaseStudy-5.pdf.

45 RIA Novosti, 'Russian army gets modernised Malka nuclear capable gun', BBC Monitoring, 16 April 2020, https://monitoring.bbc.co.uk/product/c201ma9i.

46 President of the Russian Federation, 'Ob Osnovakh gosudarstvennoy politiki Rossiyskoy Federatsii v oblasti yadernogo sderzhivaniya'.

47 'Does Russia have a launch-on-warning posture? The Soviet Union didn't', Russian strategic nuclear forces, 29 April 2019, http://russianforces.org/blog/2019/04/does_russia_have_a_launch-on-w.shtml.

48 President of the Russian Federation, 'Meeting of the Valdai International Discussion Club', 18 October 2018, http://en.kremlin.ru/events/president/news/58848.

49 Roma Biryulin, 'S Zadachami i Vvodnymi Raketchiki Spravilis', *Krasnaya Zvezda*, 1 October 2018, http://redstar.ru/s-zadachami-i-vvodnymi-raketchiki-spravilis.

50 Oleg Odnokolenko, 'General-polkovnik Viktor Yesin: "Esli amerikantsy vse-taki nachnut razvorachivat' svoi rakety v Evrope, nam nichego ne ostanetsya, kak otkazat'sya ot doktriny otvetno-vstrechnogo udara i pereyti k doktrine uprezhdayushchego udara"', *Zvezda Weekly*, 8 November 2018, https://zvezdaweekly.ru/news/t/2018117102-oiaAI.html.

51 President of the Russian Federation, 'Meeting with representatives of Russian news agencies and print media', 20 February 2019, http://en.kremlin.ru/events/president/transcripts/comminity_meetings/59865.

52 US Department of Defense, 'Inactive Strategic Treaties: Intermediate-Range Nuclear Forces (INF) Treaty: INF Treaty: Executive Summary', https://www.acq.osd.mil/tc/inf/INFexecsum.htm.

53 US Department of State, 'U.S. Withdrawal from the INF Treaty on August 2, 2019', 2 August 2019, https://www.state.gov/u-s-withdrawal-from-the-inf-treaty-on-august-2-2019.

54 US Department of Defense, 'Inactive Strategic Treaties: Intermediate-Range Nuclear Forces (INF) Treaty: INF Treaty: Executive Summary'.

55 US Department of State, 'Adherence to and Compliance with Arms Control, Nonproliferation, and Disarmament Agreements and Commitments', 31 July 2014, https://2009-2017.state.gov/t/avc/rls/rpt/2014/230047.htm.

56 Jim Garamone, 'NATO Agrees: Russia in Material Breach of INF Treaty', US Department of Defense, 5 December 2018, https://www.defense.gov/Explore/News/Article/Article/1705843/nato-agrees-russia-in-material-breach-of-inf-treaty.

57 Ministry of Defence of the Russian Federation, 'Russian Defence Ministry briefs military attaches with presentation of 9M729 missile of *Iskander-M* complex'.

58 RIA Novosti, 'Highlights of Russia's arms procurement programme for 2018–2027', BBC Monitoring, 27 December 2019, https://monitoring.bbc.co.uk/product/c201cj5a.

59 RIA Novosti, 'Russia says bomber dropped 12 cruise missiles in November drill', BBC Monitoring, 18 December 2018, https://monitoring.bbc.co.uk/product/c2oohub1.

60 'Defence Minister of the Russian Federation addresses extended session of Defence Ministry Board Session'.

61 Ministry of Defence of the Russian Federation, 'V Nizhnem Novgorode zavershaetsya razrabotka modernizirovannykh vozdushnykh punktov upravleniya', 30 May 2019, https://function.mil.ru/news_page/country/more.htm?id=12234123@egNews.

62 Interfax, 'Kremlin hits back at Trump remarks on missile blast', BBC Monitoring, 13 August 2019, https://monitoring.bbc.co.uk/product/c2010g06.

63 Thomas Nilsen, 'Norway's intelligence chief fears more accidents with Russia's reactor-powered weapons systems', *Barents Observer*, 11 February 2020, https://thebarentsobserver.com/en/security/2020/02/

norways-intelligence-chief-fears-more-accidents-russias-reactor-powered-weapons.

64 Ministry of Defence of the Russian Federation (@mod_Russia), 'Cruise missile with Burevestnik nuclear unit', Twitter, 19 July 2018, https://twitter.com/mod_russia/status/1019911273914478592?lang=en.

65 Matthew Bodner, 'Russian nuclear body says deadly blast was caused by nuclear power project, not powerful new missile', *Telegraph*, 12 August 2019, https://www.telegraph.co.uk/news/2019/08/12/russian-nuclear-body-says-deadly-blast-caused-nuclear-power.

66 President of the Russian Federation, 'Presidential Address to the Federal Assembly', 1 March 2018, http://en.kremlin.ru/events/president/news/56957.

67 *Ibid*.

68 Dmitry Andreev and Igor Zotov, 'Yarsy pridut na zamenu', *Krasnaya Zvezda*, 12 November 2017, http://archive.redstar.ru/index.php/component/k2/item/35045-yarsy-pridut-na-zamenu.

69 'Strategic Rocket Forces', Russian strategic nuclear forces, 20 January 2020, http://www.russianforces.org/missiles.

70 IISS, *The Military Balance 2020* (Abingdon: Routledge for the IISS, 2020), p. 194.

71 'Armiya Rossii Kardinalno Obnovlena', *Krasnaya Zvezda*.

72 Ministry of Defence of the Russian Federation, 'Tezisy doklada zamestitelya Ministra oborony Rossiyskoy Federatsii Alekseya Krivoruchko na Edinom dne priyemki voyennoy produktsii 12 aprelya 2019 goda'.

73 'RVSN poluchayut okolo 20 strategicheskikh kompleksov "Yars" v god – komanduyushchiy', Interfax-AVN, 29 November 2019, https://www.militarynews.ru/story.asp?rid=1&nid=522672&lang=RU.

74 'Istochnik: raketnyy kompleks "Yars-M" budet vveden v ekspluatatsiyu v Rossiyskoy Federatsii v 2017 godu', RIA Novosti, 10 May 2016, https://ria.ru/20160510/1430561300.html; 'RVSN v IV kvartale 2017 goda poluchili 21 raketu strategicheskuyu raketu "Yars" – Minoborony (rasshirennaya versiya)', Interfax-AVN, 31 January 2018, https://www.militarynews.ru/story.asp?rid=1&nid=472511&lang=RU.

75 Ankit Panda, 'Revealed: Russia's New Experimental ICBM Warheads', *Diplomat*, 4 October 2017, https://thediplomat.com/2017/10/revealed-russias-new-experimental-icbm-warheads.

76 'Summary of Project 4202 developments', Russian strategic nuclear forces, 25 April 2016, http://russianforces.org/blog/2015/06/summary_of_the_project_4202_de.shtml.

77 *Ibid*.

78 *Rossiskaya Gazeta*, 'Russia reveals new nuclear missile', BBC Monitoring, 28 October 2016, https://monitoring.bbc.co.uk/product/c1d8z117.

79 'Russia extends service life for SS-19 Stiletto ICBMs to over 36 years', TASS, 28 May 2019, http://tass.com/defense/1060382.

80 Ivan Safronov, 'Kontroliruetsya vsya kooperatsiya – ot zakazchika do poslednego gvozdya', *Kommersant*, 17 December 2018, https://www.kommersant.ru/doc/3833614.

81 *Vedomosti*, 'Russia to start RS-28 *Sarmat* missile tests in 2020 – paper', BBC Monitoring, 30 October 2019, https://monitoring.bbc.co.uk/product/c201730g.

82 'Official reveals which army's division will be one of the first to get Sarmat ICBMs', TASS, 17 December 2018, http://tass.com/defense/1036338.

83 'U RF Poyavilsya novyy vid vooruzheniya', Russia 24, 26 December 2018, https://youtu.be/wGXFIkHhNy8.

84 Interfax, 'Russia ready to include new weapons in key arms deal', BBC Monitoring, 22 December 2019, https://monitoring.bbc.co.uk/product/c201bwyx.

85 'V Rossii sozdadut letatel'nyy giperzvukovoy apparat Anchar-RV', RIA Novosti, 3 March 2020, https://ria.ru/20180822/1527027179.html.

86 'Putin's Remarkable Historic March 1 Speech in Moscow', Russia Insider, 1 March 2018, https://russia-insider.com/en/putins-remarkable-historic-march-1-speech-moscow-video-excerpts-full-transcript/ri22667.

87 'Russia floats out first nuclear sub that will carry Poseidon strategic underwater drones', TASS, 23 April 2019, http://tass.com/defense/1055188.

88 'Strategic fleet', Russian strategic nuclear forces, 4 January 2020, http://www.russianforces.org/navy.

89 *Ibid*.

90 Interfax-AVN Military News Agency, 'Russian Navy takes into service *Layner* ICBM', BBC Monitoring, 2 April 2014, https://monitoring.bbc.co.uk/product/m1bs1qbx.

91 'Status of Russia's SLBM programs', Russian strategic nuclear forces, 7 January 2005, http://russianforces.org/blog/2005/01/status_of_russias_slbm_program.shtml.

92 Alexandra Georgievich and Ivan Safronov, 'U trillionov est' dva sojuznika – armija i flot', *Kommersant*, 18 December 2017, https://www.kommersant.ru/doc/3500710.

93 'Research into Russia's fifth generation subs well in progress – Navy's commander', TASS, 18 March 2020, http://tass.com/defense/1131767.

94 'Ukraine dismantles last strategic Tu-160 bomber, Tu-22M bomber', *Kyiv Post*, 2 February 2001, https://www.kyivpost.com/article/content/ukraine-politics/ukraine-dismantles-last-strategic-tu-160-bomber-tu-7277.html?cn-reloaded=1.

95 Interfax-AVN Military News Agency, 'Russian minister outlines new military aviation projects', BBC Monitoring, 29 August 2019, https://monitoring.bbc.co.uk/product/c2011suy; 'Minoborony RF poluchit pervuyu novuyu konstruktsiyu Tu-160M v 2021 godu', https://www.interfax.ru/russia/685426.

96 IISS, *The Military Balance 2020*, p. 195.

97 President of the Russian Federation, 'Conversation with employees of Gorbunov Kazan Aviation Plant', 13 May 2019, http://en.kremlin.ru/events/president/news/60506.

98 'Avangard hypersonic missiles replace *Rubezh* ICBMs in Russia's armament plan through 2027', TASS, 22 March 2018, http://tass.com/defense/995628.

99 'Istochnik: raketnyy kompleks "Yars-M" budet vveden v ekspluatatsiyu v Rossiyskoy Federatsii v 2017 godu', RIA Novosti.

100 Interfax, 'Russia ready to include new weapons in key arms deal'.

101 President of Russia, 'Vladimir Putin's Annual Press Conference', 19 December 2019, http://en.kremlin.ru/events/president/transcripts/statements/62366.

102 Interfax, 'Russia ready to include new weapons in key arms deal'.

Ground Forces

Russia's Ground Forces (*Sukhoputnye voyska*, SV) have undergone far-reaching modernisation and restructuring since the end of the Soviet Union. The years immediately following the Soviet collapse were a time of crisis for the army. Funding dwindled, as it did for the other services, with Ground Forces modernisation programmes and soldiers' pay and conditions all suffering. The sheer size of the army that Russia inherited from the Soviet Union compounded matters. Formations from the Soviet army had returned from long-established bases in Eastern Europe, while others had been transferred to the new (former Soviet) republics, though a number remained stationed along Russia's long land borders and, occasionally, in other territories (including disputed territories).

In 1994, the Ground Forces' order of battle still included 17 tank divisions and 57 motor-rifle divisions, with around 780,000 personnel (including personnel from five airborne divisions). Of these personnel, it was estimated that about 450,000 were conscripts.[1] There was also, in the period before the reforms began, a 'disproportionately large' number of officers and warrant officers, with many of these posts intended to support the expansion of the force under mobilisation.[2] In 2020, the Ground Forces' combat order of battle comprised two tank and six motor-rifle divisions, two tank, 22 motor-rifle, 16 artillery, 12 missile and 15 air-defence brigades, as well as a single 'machine-gun artillery' division in the Kuril Islands.[3] There are continuities with the Soviet-era forces – such as in military culture, the persistence of conscript service, equipment and even (once more) in force structure – but increasingly there are significant breaks with the past. The bulk of today's Ground Forces reflect the planning laid down in defence minister Anatoly Serdyukov's 'New Look' reorganisation from 2008 onwards, with significant modifications after Serdyukov's successor Sergei Shoigu took over in 2012; one example is the re-establishment of tank and motor-rifle divisions after 2013.

Importantly, the mass-mobilisation model that had characterised Soviet and Russian military formations up to the late 1990s, and also influenced judgements of military readiness, has been abandoned. Russia has since developed military units held at a higher state of readiness and staffed by contract-based military personnel (*kontraktniki*). Under

Key takeaways

A FORCE RESHAPED

The New Look reshaped Russia's Ground Forces and ended the mass-mobilisation model. Full professionalisation has not been achieved, and long-term recruitment targets have not been met, but a 'critical mass' of contract-service personnel has been recruited and retained.

TEST AND ADJUST

Russia has shown a willingness to adjust and even upend structural changes. Divisions were reintroduced, intended to better command and equip formations in large-scale conflict. Battalion tactical groups remain a way of generating contract-staffed formations.

ARMOUR UPGRADES

The new *Armata* platforms will enter service later and in fewer numbers than originally envisaged. Focus instead shifted to modernising and upgrading existing systems.

ARTILLERY AND LONG-RANGE STRIKE

Established systems are being modernised alongside the development of new artillery platforms, indicating that massed fires as well as precision strike still occupies a key place in SV thinking.

MISSILE CAPABILITY

Significant investments have been made in modernising battlefield rocket and missile capabilities, with improvements made to range as well as targeting.

HIGHER READINESS AND GREATER MOBILITY

The Airborne Forces escaped reorganisation under the New Look, but the force faces decisions on its future including the balance, or choices, between airborne, air-mobile or ground-manoeuvre roles. The creation of a Special Operations Command has given Russia additional rapid-reaction options.

T-72B3 MAIN BATTLE TANK
From the 2nd Guards Motor-rifle Division, manoeuvring during an exercise at the Alabino range, July 2020. CREDIT: Sergei Bobylev/TASS/Getty Images

Figure 3.1: **Russian Army, Airborne and Coastal forces: order of battle, 2007 and 2020**

2007

LENINGRAD AND MOSCOW MILITARY DISTRICTS

SF bde/regt	3
tk div	2
MR div	2
MR bde	4
AB div	3
arty/MRL bde/regt	8
SSM bde	3
SAM bde	3

NORTH CAUCASUS MILITARY DISTRICT

SF bde	2
MR div	3
MR bde	5
AB div	1
arty/MRL bde/regt	4
SSM bde	1
SAM bde/regt	3

VOLGA–URAL, SIBERIAN AND FAR EASTERN MILITARY DISTRICTS

SF bde	5
tk div	1
MR div	11
MR bde	1
MGA div	5
AB bde	3
arty/MRL bde/regt	16
SSM bde	5
SAM bde	7

AB	airborne	recce	reconnaissance
arty	artillery	regt	regiment
bde	brigade	SF	special forces
div	division	SAM	surface-to-air missile
MGA	machine-gun artillery	SSM	surface-to-surface missile
MR	motor-rifle	tk	tank
MRL	multiple-rocket launcher		

2020

NORTHERN AND WESTERN JOINT STRATEGIC COMMANDS

SF bde	3
recce bde	1
tk div	1
tk bde/regt	2
MR div	3
MR bde/regt	7
AB div	3
arty/MRL bde	6
SSM bde	4
SAM bde	5

SOUTHERN JOINT STRATEGIC COMMAND

SF bde/regt	4
recce bde	2
MR div	2
MR bde	5
coastal bde	1
AB div	1
AB bde	1
arty/MRL bde/regt	4
SSM bde	3
SAM bde/regt	4

CENTRAL AND EASTERN JOINT STRATEGIC COMMANDS

SF bde	3
tk div	1
tk bde	1
MR div	1
MR bde	14
MGA div	1
AB bde	3
arty/MRL bde/regt	8
SSM bde	6
SAM bde	8

Sources: *The Military Balance 2008*; IISS Military Balance+

the old mass-mobilisation system, units would in a time of crisis be brought up to wartime strength by an influx of reservists and equipment from specialised storage bases; in peacetime many units were understrength or only staffed as cadre formations, and lacking much of the equipment they would need to go to war.[4] The number of combat-ready formations was far below the total in the order of battle: before the 2008 reforms, only 17% of army units were 'stand-by combat ready units'.[5]

Thirty years after the end of the Soviet Union, Russia is finally moving towards generating military forces of the type that were envisaged by theoreticians such as Nikolai Ogarkov as far back as the early 1980s: a military establishment with a streamlined command structure and more mobile and better trained forces, held at a high state of readiness and able to more rapidly bring to bear strike capabilities. In some ways this owes much to a confluence of factors including the wars in Chechnya and in Georgia, and Russia's relatively poor, though improving, military performance in these campaigns; the appointment of officials tasked with reforming the armed forces; high-level political support; and, after the mid-2000s, an improvement in defence funding that enabled some of the reform aspirations and meant that new and upgraded equipment was able to start flowing into the Ground Forces.

Nevertheless, the process has not been uniformly smooth. Initial reform attempts intended to truncate the Soviet-era command-and-control structure (which was originally designed to support the mass-mobilisation process) were sub-optimal and were adjusted to today's structure (of Military Regions and Joint Strategic Commands) after 2010. The reforms introduced after 2008 – which reshaped the Ground Forces' structure with the transition from divisions and regiments to brigades – were also subsequently adjusted, as were similarly far-reaching structural changes to the Air Force. Moreover, while plans have persisted to increase contractor numbers, and numbers are creeping up towards the long-stated goal of 425,000 contractors, conscription continues. With the term of service only one-year long (having been reduced from 24 to 18 and then 12 months between 2007 and 2008), this undoubtedly has an effect on military capability, particularly when these conscripts only serve for a few months after basic training before departing. (This problem is likely more acute in Ground Forces units where the limited complexity of equipment – in comparison to the Air Force or navy – might lead such personnel to predominate.) It has, perhaps, spurred initiatives designed to attract and retain contractors and ensure that these troops fill the posts in high-readiness formations, as well as important structural change, not least in finally realising the (also well established) concept of battalion tactical groups (BTGs). Meanwhile, assessments of the combat power of Russia's brigades and BTGs combined with a changing appreciation of possible future conflicts to prompt a further adaptation after 2013, with the return of divisional formations.

Structural change in post-Soviet Russia

The collapse of the Soviet Union led to a number of initiatives to restructure the Ground Forces. Within the context of a severely diminished economy, Russia inherited large numbers of military formations and weapons that the authorities had to distribute, store and maintain, also having to house units returning from former bases in newly independent states; one outcome was that this helped impel the process of reducing the armed forces' establishment strength.

Plans early in the 1990s to reform the armed forces under defence minister Pavel Grachev were focused – principally because of funding problems – on the long-discussed mobile-force concept rather than any significant reform of the mobilisation-deployment model. The mobile force

aimed to generate motor-rifle brigades held at high readiness. These formations were intended to be independent of mobilisation-deployment requirements, being fully staffed according to their wartime table of organisation and equipment (TOE). Three independent mobile-force brigades were activated that were, bar some combat-service-support components, intended to be self-sustaining formations. (The full mobile-force concept was intended to also include naval infantry, airborne and military-aviation units, but economic and political factors combined to mean that only these three motor-rifle brigades were established out of the mobile-force model.)[6]

The lack of full-strength high-readiness forces, and problems deriving from the mass-mobilisation-focused command structure, were felt during the First Chechen War (1994–96). Failure to issue a mobilisation order meant that units like the 131st Motor-rifle Brigade had to deploy with their peacetime TOE, rather than being brought to full strength by the mobilisation of reservists. This led to ad hoc means to bring units to strength, bringing in reinforcements at short notice from other formations, and even assigning trade specialists to infantry roles. After the end of the First Chechen War, then-defence minister Igor Rodionov began the task of keeping some army units at full strength.

The 'combat-ready formations' initiative, which continued under Rodionov's successor Igor Sergeyev, was intended to result in some divisions having at least one regiment fully staffed and equipped to its wartime TOE, though it remained difficult to establish units that were consistently fully staffed. The persistence of the mass-mobilisation model and issues around conscription (such as evasion and poor health) were among those factors hindering the wider establishment of combat-ready formations.

The Second Chechen War (1999–2000) provided the first test of the combat-ready initiative. For Russia, experience in the war led to an improvement in the cohesion of units deployed and in the combat

effectiveness of these forces. Relatively well-equipped and well-trained units were deployed, and this did not depend on politicians deciding to issue a mobilisation order. However, only the 74th Motor-rifle Brigade and the 205th Motor-rifle Brigade deployed at full strength; the armed forces decided to deploy only modular BTGs from other combat-ready formations, rather than units in their entirety.

Understood to have been developed by General Anatoly Kvashnin, BTGs allowed the armed forces to limit the numbers deployed on operations by only deploying the combat-ready components of larger units. They typically comprised either a motor-rifle or tank battalion augmented by an artillery battalion, a tank (or motor-rifle) company, an anti-aircraft and an anti-tank battery, and other combat-support elements. The parent brigades and divisions of these BTGs were used as personnel-replenishment feeders. In addition to the Ground Forces, BTGs were also formed out of the Airborne Forces' (*Vozdushno-desantnye voyska*, VDV) divisions and brigades and the Naval Infantry. (The war also saw initiatives designed to reduce the numbers of conscripts deployed to combat.)[7]

Through all these various attempts at reform, however, Russia had not fully tackled the problem that the mass-mobilisation model and conscription posed for the generation of combat-ready forces. Reducing numbers of conscripts and increasing the number of *kontraktniki* was one way that the defence ministry thought it could improve. While attempts at attracting contractors had been made in the 1990s, it was only with the 2003 initiative on the 'Transition of permanent readiness units to professional service' that real progress began. Trials began with a regiment of the 76th Airborne (now Air Assault) Division (Pskov), which continued until 2005 when the programme was expanded. Only a few years later, however, this initiative was deemed to have effectively failed; as Makarov noted in early 2010, not enough contractors were being recruited.[8]

After the August 2008 war with Georgia, a number of factors coalesced to finally give the necessary impetus to a throughgoing reform process. During the war, Russia's forces performed better than before, but still not as well as expected by the Kremlin. Meanwhile, defence funding started to rise as Russia's economy improved. The effects were particularly far-reaching for the Ground Forces, as was made clear after defence minister Anatoly Serdyukov, in post since 2007, unveiled his New Look reforms in October 2008.

The New Look – the transition to brigades

As well as a number of significant organisational changes relating to overall command and control, the most eye-catching aspects of Serdyukov's reforms for the Ground Forces related to the disbanding of cadre units and a transition to a combat-ready army, and the extensive structural reforms to the army. Divisions and regiments were to transform into brigades. It was felt that these changes would finally end the mass-mobilisation model, reduce the size of the army and lead to a force that was permanently combat-ready. The land forces' organisational reform into brigade structures was designed to produce forces geared towards addressing comparatively small wars and expeditionary operations. This approach was shaped by Russia's experience in Georgia and also informed by the initiatives of the preceding decade. Brigades would be more mobile and independent, with more organic combat support and combat-service support, without recourse to assets held at the divisional level.

The reorganisation led to some problems, not least with the decision that brigades were by 2015 to be reorganised according to 'light', 'medium' and 'heavy' formations. The plan was that heavy brigades would be composed of units with main battle tanks (MBTs) and infantry fighting vehicles (IFVs); medium brigades of units with IFVs and armoured personnel carriers (APCs); and light brigades of units with APCs and other light armoured vehicles.[9] Importantly, these units were to be capable 'of conducting independent action and providing [their] own organic support'.[10] Tests of this concept began in 2010, but by 2015 it had been discontinued; by that time, views about the utility of wholesale 'brigadisation' had also changed, and divisions were making a return.

The return of divisions

The requirement to re-establish division-level formations appears to pre-date the seizure of Crimea in early 2014 and the conflict in Ukraine's Donbas region, even if these episodes sharpened thinking on the subject. The first two conversions were the 4th Tank Division and 2nd Motor-rifle Division, recreated on the basis of the 4th Tank Brigade and the 5th Motor-rifle Brigade in May 2013.[11] The illustrious history of these

KURGANETS-25 INFANTRY FIGHTING VEHICLES
At the Alabino range during rehearsals for the Victory Day parade, April 2017. CREDIT: Valery Sharifulin/TASS/Getty Images

divisions, based in the western environs of Moscow, may have played a part in the re-establishment decision; there is, possibly, additional symbolism in that they had been among the first units to transform to brigades. Nonetheless, this change in structure also suggests that the army had begun to reconsider the operational utility of the slimmed-down Operational Strategic Command–army operational command–brigade command structure created under the New Look, seeing a renewed role for an intermediate level of command between armies and brigades in large-scale operations against peer or near-peer opponents and one that could better command incoming formations. Another imperative seemed to be the re-establishment of formations that could more easily provide divisional-level combat support and combat-service support assets that would be useful in high-intensity combat.[12]

In 2016, a second wave of divisional activations began, two years after Moscow's decision to intervene militarily in Ukraine and subsequent rising tension with Western states. Four motor-rifle brigades drawn from the Central, Southern and Western military districts were disbanded and their personnel and equipment used to form the initial elements of three new motor-rifle divisions along Russia's borders with Belarus and Ukraine. In addition, one tank brigade and one more motor-rifle brigade in the Central Military District were converted to form the basis of a new tank division on the Kazakh border and the 42nd Motor-rifle Division, which had been disbanded in 2009, was reformed from three motor-rifle brigades based in Chechnya. At the end of 2018, two more motor-rifle brigades were used to create a further formation, the 127th Motor-rifle Division, on Russia's border with China.

It would seem that the intention is for these new divisions to have a 'square' establishment similar to that seen in the Soviet era, with four manoeuvre regiments (three motor-rifle regiments and

Figure 3.2: **Specimen Battalion Tactical Group (BTG) order of battle**

Source: IISS

one tank regiment in a motor-rifle division, and three tank regiments and one motor-rifle regiment in a tank division) along with supporting artillery and air-defence regiments. In practice, however, this remains more of an aspiration: the first two divisions were formed with only two manoeuvre regiments each and have now both added a third but show no signs yet of further expansion. Most of the new divisions were likewise formed with only one or two manoeuvre regiments and have had to slowly generate extra regiments as personnel and equipment has become available. As of early 2020, the 90th Tank Division at Cherbarkul and the 150th Motor-rifle Division near Rostov appear to have formed four manoeuvre regiments each, but the 3rd, 42nd and 144th motor-rifle divisions all have three and the recently formed 127th Motor-rifle Division only two.

Of the three possible limiting factors in creating and expanding these new formations – infrastructure, equipment and personnel – the last appears to be the most problematic. The growth in the number of Ground Forces formations after 2014 – not just in terms of new divisions but also in additional fire-support, combat-support and combat-service-support brigades and regiments – has generally outstripped the growth in contract personnel. This has led to questions over whether the staffing of these new formations is only being made possible by accepting that existing formations elsewhere will be understrength and concerns about a return to pre-Serdyukov problems of endemic personnel shortages and 'ghost' or 'paper' formations.

The Battalion Tactical Group (BTG)

Under the New Look, with the reorganised Ground Forces – and conscripts only serving for a single year from 2008 – the generation of effective combat power became almost entirely dependent on the number of available contract personnel. With recruitment of such personnel remaining stubbornly low in the late 2000s and early 2010s, it was soon apparent that the vast majority of New Look brigades would not be able to deploy and operate with their paper establishment – they simply would not have sufficient numbers of contract personnel.

Therefore, in September 2012, it was reported that due to shortages in equipment and contract personnel in combat brigades, battalion tactical groups would be formed in each military district.[13] At the time, battalions were staffed by a mix of conscript and contract personnel, but the BTGs would be generated by concentrating the contract manpower of each brigade into a single reinforced battalion, with the aim that this was 100% staffed by contractors.

The battalion tactical group concept is not, in itself, a new idea. Originally intended as a way of generating self-sufficient battalion battlegroups capable of independent operations, the BTG was seen as a particularly useful tactical unit for the 'local wars' that the Ground Forces expected to fight in the 1990s and 2000s. A BTG usually comprised between 700 and 900 personnel, being typically formed of a motor-rifle or tank battalion reinforced with infantry or armour as appropriate, as well as artillery, air-defence, electronic-warfare and other combat-support and combat-service-support assets from its parent brigade or regiment; they would be structured according to the task required.

Alongside the total number of contract personnel employed in the armed forces, the total number of available battalion tactical groups has, in official speeches, become a key metric of Ground Forces modernisation. In 2014, the BTG concept was used to generate combat power for operations in Ukraine and, by September 2016, Chief of the General Staff (CGS) Valery Gerasimov declared that the ambition now was for each manoeuvre brigade or regiment to be able to generate two BTGs each.[14] To facilitate this, formations were dividing their combat battalions between two fully contract-manned units and one fully staffed by conscripts, with the former used as the basis of the BTGs.

Because both tank and motor-rifle brigades and regiments have four manoeuvre battalions as standard, not three, the implication of this plan is that the fourth may be used to reinforce the other three with the necessary infantry (for tank formations) or tanks (for motor-rifle formations). This would suggest that these fourth battalions, as well as relevant artillery and other combat-support units, may remain a contract/conscript mix, perhaps with individual companies assigned as contract or conscript.

The BTG conundrum

At the time of Gerasimov's 2016 statement, the combined Ground Forces and the Airborne Forces were only able to muster 66 BTGs from a total of 56 brigades and regiments, though there were ambitions to expand this total to 125 by 2018.[15] Official pronouncements suggest that this duly came to pass, with 126 BTGs being declared formed by September 2018 and 136 by March 2019.[16] However, this rapid doubling of BTG numbers – in 30 months – came at a time when the total number of contract personnel appeared to have stalled. It is possible that this simply reflects the time taken in inte-grating new personnel and equipment before generating an operational battle-group and that the BTG number will now, in turn, come to a standstill. Alternatively, it is possible that many BTGs are currently understrength, once more raising concerns about possible 'ghost' formations.

There remains a debate around whether BTGs are only intended for use in limited 'local wars' or whether they are also intended to serve in large-scale inter-state conflicts, though the former was certainly a key factor in their formation. There is also disagreement over the extent to which their use indicates continuing struggles to deploy operational brigades and regiments or because they offer tactical value per se.[17]

It is possible that, in both cases, the issue is not so much one of 'either/or' as it is a matter of degree. Most official statements about the role of BTGs have emphasised their utility as independent tactical units in local wars, a role the New Look brigades were originally supposed to fill. However, the combined-arms units that have been generated appear equally useful as sub-components of larger formations, whether or not they are still explicitly called BTGs. It seems hard to presume that Russia would not seek to organise its combat forces in brigades/regiments/divisions for larger operations as opposed to simply expecting BTGs to operate as the primary tactical organisa-tion – but that is not the same thing as saying that they would not be used at all.

Similarly, it is possible that while the shift from a brigade-centric to a battalion-centric force-generation concept may have been forced on the army and VDV – indeed, the shortage in contract personnel makes it difficult to see how this would not have been the case – the BTGs them-selves still had their own tactical merits for Russia's operational requirements.

Company Tactical Groups

In recent years, the armed forces have increasingly exercised formation compo-nents as company tactical groups as well as the more well-known battalion tactical group. Perhaps based on recent operational experience, exercises of these formations are designed – according to an interview with Major-General Rustam Muradov – to train companies and supporting formations such that 'the company cannot and should not act alone'.[18] According to Muradov, the company commander should be in a posi-tion to be able to conduct reconnaissance and call in artillery, among other tasks. It is possible that this initiative is intended to drive unit cohesion as well greater freedom of action, and potentially (bearing in mind the developments that have taken place in command-and-control capacities) more devolved command responsibility among company-level officers.

Ground Forces' equipment developments

In common with the other armed services, the Ground Forces have been slated to receive significant amounts of new and upgraded equipment under recent State Armament Programmes (*Gosudarstvennaya programma vooruzheniya*, SAPs). However, the SV has fallen behind the others in terms of new deliveries. Indeed, the overall proportion of 'modern' equipment in the Ground Forces' tank, APC and IFV inventory was just under 30% by 2020, though this figure was heavily influenced by the large number of legacy APCs and IFVs in service. For tanks, the 'modern' figure was just under 70%. Nonetheless, the overall percentage was well short of the aspiration in the early years of SAP 2020 that the Ground Forces' equipment inventory would – like other services – comprise 70% 'modern' weaponry by 2020.[19] Thousands of armoured vehicles were to be procured, as well as new artillery systems, trucks and other vehicles. A priority was placed on new command-and-control systems for the land forces, as well as new soldier systems, such as *Ratnik*. However, financial and developmental problems have led to delay in key areas and – permeated with the lessons of combat operations – have led to a drive to modernise existing platforms as well as procure new equipment. At the same time, the current SAP – for the 2018–27 period – will have an additional effect on the Ground Forces in that it is believed to prioritise aerospace and maritime projects. Within this latest SAP, it is estimated that the Aerospace Forces' (VKS) projects comprise 35%, the navy 30%, the Ground Forces 17%, the Strategic Rocket Forces 10% and the Airborne Forces 8%.[20] It is unclear whether this, and the still lagging 'modernised' total for the SV, will lead either to renewed effort to flow in new equipment or to a more public explanation of what, in this context, 'modern' actually means.

Armoured fighting vehicles

In 2015, several new armoured vehicle designs appeared at the 9 May Victory Day parade. A new main battle tank, the T-14, and a new heavy IFV, the T-15, rolled through central Moscow – both based on the *Armata* universal combat platform. Also at the parade was the new *Koalitsiya*-SV self-propelled gun, the *Kurganets*-25 IFV and the *Bumerang* wheeled APC.

When they first emerged, these vehicles attracted considerable attention in the West as well as in Russia. They seemed to herald a new era for Russian armoured capability, with the design's emphasis on crew protection seemingly based on lessons of recent wars (including urban combat in Chechnya) and potentially anticipating future conflict scenarios.[21] Notable apparent improvements appeared to armour, sensors, munitions and self-defence capability.[22] The T-14 MBT removed the crew from the turret altogether, with the crew compartment located in the hull. Although Rostec had announced at the end of 2019 that the T-14 would soon be delivered, this likely meant delivered to the state-test regime and it remained unclear when, or indeed whether, the 2nd Motor-rifle Division would receive the vehicles that it had, in 2018, been reported it would receive.[23]

Early in the period of SAP 2020, it was envisaged that some 2,300 modern main battle tanks would be acquired. This number alone would have been sufficient to enable a reasonably wholesale replacement of existing front-line MBTs, and it soon became clear that a mix of modernised and new vehicles (including T-14s) would be counted towards the target.[24] Moreover, even though Moscow may have hoped initially to procure large numbers of T-14s, funding and production problems led to a reassessment of the procurement ambitions.[25]

In July 2018, Deputy Prime Minister (and, until 2018, deputy defence minister) Yuri Borisov articulated these recalibrated ambitions and said that Russia was not planning a 'massive transition to next generation armored vehicles'. Cost was one factor given by Borisov, though he also said that 'the current armoured equipment is being upgraded and performing excellently'.[26] This was perhaps an indication of the way that thinking was moving within the defence ministry's senior leadership, with this likely also informed by these vehicles' emerging development schedule. At the Army-2017 exhibition, Borisov said that over 100 *Armata* vehicles were being procured under an earlier contract, and it emerged at the Army-2018 exhibition that Uralvagonzavod was contracted to deliver 132 T-14 and T-15 armoured vehicles based on the *Armata* chassis.[27]

The direction of travel was indeed apparent in 2017. In that year, SV commander-in-chief Colonel-General Oleg Salyukov said that 'fundamentally new' platforms like *Armata*, *Kurganets*-25 and *Bumerang* were in 'the final stage of development'. High-readiness units, meanwhile, were being re-equipped with 'modern' BMP-3 and BTR-82A vehicles and, from 2018, they were to receive the 'upgraded BMP-2 with the *Berezhok* fighting compartment'. Meanwhile, 'the basis of the tank fleet is made up of modern vehicles. They are being upgraded to the level of T-72B3, T-90M and T-80BVM tanks.'[28]

T-14 MAIN BATTLE TANKS
In Moscow during rehearsals for the Victory Day parade, May 2015.
CREDIT: Kirill Kudryavtsev/AFP/Getty Images

Figure 3.3: Russia's T-14 main battle tank

The T-14 is Russia's latest main battle tank (MBT) project; it is the principal variant of the new *Armata* platform. Publicly revealed in 2015, the type is still undergoing testing, and it is likely that serial production versions will not reach the ground forces for some years to come. Upon service entry, the T-14 will be the first MBT to feature an uncrewed main turret and one of the few to incorporate a hard-kill active protection system. Its size – more comparable to Western counterparts than its predecessors – may also signify a greater emphasis on protection and firepower over mobility.

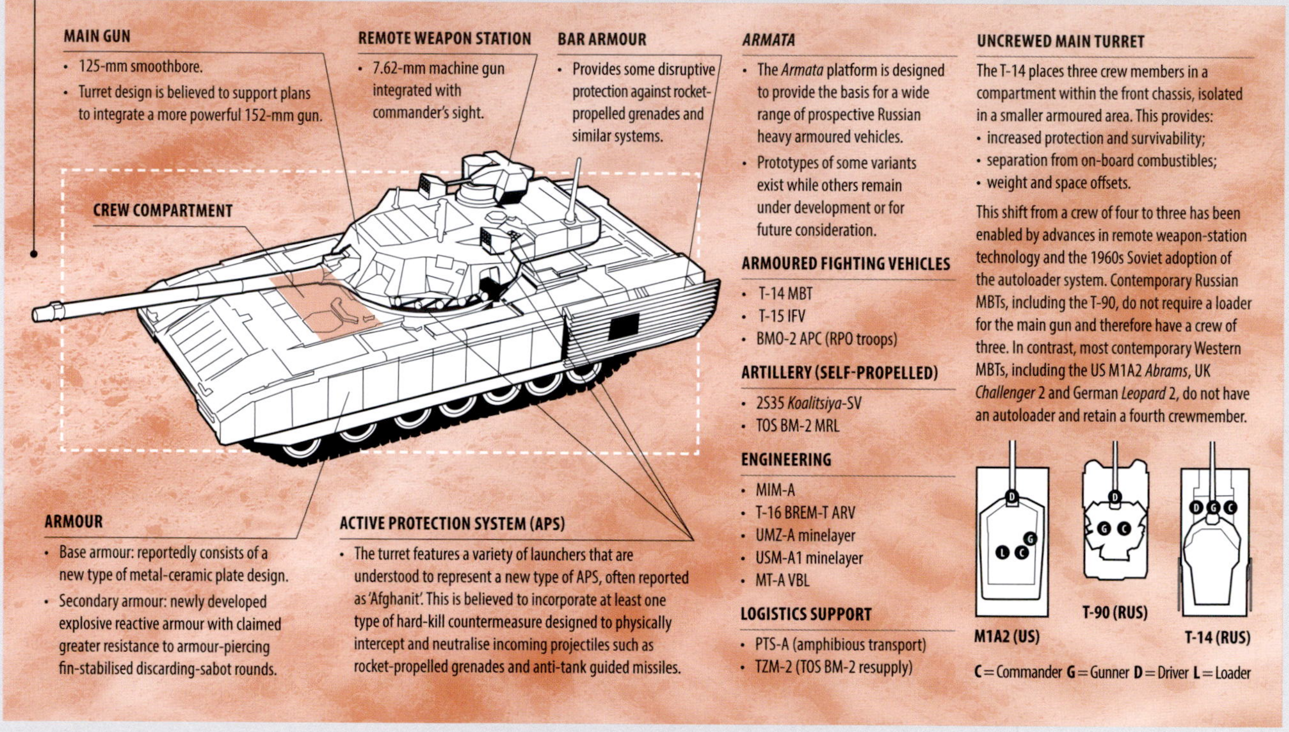

MAIN GUN
- 125-mm smoothbore.
- Turret design is believed to support plans to integrate a more powerful 152-mm gun.

REMOTE WEAPON STATION
- 7.62-mm machine gun integrated with commander's sight.

BAR ARMOUR
- Provides some disruptive protection against rocket-propelled grenades and similar systems.

CREW COMPARTMENT

ARMATA
- The *Armata* platform is designed to provide the basis for a wide range of prospective Russian heavy armoured vehicles.
- Prototypes of some variants exist while others remain under development or for future consideration.

ARMOURED FIGHTING VEHICLES
- T-14 MBT
- T-15 IFV
- BMO-2 APC (RPO troops)

ARTILLERY (SELF-PROPELLED)
- 2S35 *Koalitsiya*-SV
- TOS BM-2 MRL

ENGINEERING
- MIM-A
- T-16 BREM-T ARV
- UMZ-A minelayer
- USM-A1 minelayer
- MT-A VBL

LOGISTICS SUPPORT
- PTS-A (amphibious transport)
- TZM-2 (TOS BM-2 resupply)

UNCREWED MAIN TURRET

The T-14 places three crew members in a compartment within the front chassis, isolated in a smaller armoured area. This provides:
- increased protection and survivability;
- separation from on-board combustibles;
- weight and space offsets.

This shift from a crew of four to three has been enabled by advances in remote weapon-station technology and the 1960s Soviet adoption of the autoloader system. Contemporary Russian MBTs, including the T-90, do not require a loader for the main gun and therefore have a crew of three. In contrast, most contemporary Western MBTs, including the US M1A2 *Abrams*, UK *Challenger* 2 and German *Leopard* 2, do not have an autoloader and retain a fourth crewmember.

ARMOUR
- Base armour: reportedly consists of a new type of metal-ceramic plate design.
- Secondary armour: newly developed explosive reactive armour with claimed greater resistance to armour-piercing fin-stabilised discarding-sabot rounds.

ACTIVE PROTECTION SYSTEM (APS)
- The turret features a variety of launchers that are understood to represent a new type of APS, often reported as 'Afghanit'. This is believed to incorporate at least one type of hard-kill countermeasure designed to physically intercept and neutralise incoming projectiles such as rocket-propelled grenades and anti-tank guided missiles.

M1A2 (US) — L C G
T-90 (RUS) — G C
T-14 (RUS) — D G C

C = Commander G = Gunner D = Driver L = Loader

Source: *The Military Balance 2018*

Indeed, variants of the T-72 currently constitute by far the most numerous main battle tank in Russian service. The T-72 was originally conceived in the 1970s as a cheaper and less complex alternative to the T-64 and, incorporating many of the advances seen in the T-64, was designed to be easier to manufacture. The tank has had a series of upgrades in order to improve its serviceability, protection and offensive capability. The T-72B variant was the basis for Russia's most recent operational MBT design, the T-90. The T-80, meanwhile, derives from the T-64 design.

As it is unlikely in the near term that production of T-90 variants or the new T-14 *Armata* MBT will be able to or are intended to replace the range of T-72 variants in service, in upgraded forms T-72s will likely remain at the centre of Russia's armoured forces for the foreseeable future. T-72 variants are also flowing into VDV units as well as the SV, as the Airborne Forces look to build heavier armoured units. The T-72B3 obr. 2011 variant was produced between 2012 and 2016 and a new-standard T-72B3 first appeared in 2016 (obr. 2016), entering service in 2017; over the decade these vehicles have seen improved protection and fire-control systems (neither version is understood to have active protection, instead employing *Kontakt*-5 and *Relikt* reactive-armour packages).[29] So while there may still be an aspiration to transition, in time, to a new generation of vehicles, the timescale for this has been modified significantly and in the medium term the tank fleet will comprise a mix of upgraded-legacy designs and modest numbers of wholly new designs.

Moreover, as in the West, in Russia the understanding of potential future operating environments may also be changing, and so too may the resulting design requirements and operational concepts. The renewed appreciation of the potential for high-intensity ground combat and the need for adequate vehicle numbers to equip existing and new units will, when combined with the cost and development timelines for the new platforms, likely occasion yet more upgrades. Indeed, while the Ground Forces are now focused on the modernisation of systems such as T-72, BMP and its multiple-rocket launchers (MRLs), a Russian analyst has also posited 'intermediate' improvements including to BMP-3s, T-90Ms and improved artillery systems, perhaps by doing so bridging the gap until the next generation of vehicles (possibly including more uninhabited and robotic systems) finally emerges.[30] This seems the trajectory to be followed under SAP 2027: one of parallel development. Indeed, in late 2018 the defence ministry decided to modernise T-80s that would otherwise have been decommissioned, while announcements in 2020 indicated that further T-90As were to be upgraded to T-90M standard (there are reportedly also some new builds); the aim is now said to be that the armed forces will have 900 'truly modern' tanks by 2027.[31]

Moreover, the numbers so far ordered for *Armata*, and remaining uncertainty over the offensive and defensive systems that will emerge on the production (as opposed to trial) T-14 tank, also raise questions about how this vehicle and its associated *Armata* platforms are planned to be employed in combat. It is unclear, for instance, whether the vehicles are intended to be concentrated in certain units or distributed more widely, or used in combination with other assets, or whether they might be employed for certain tasks or in specific roles (such as an armoured spearhead). There has been discussion about whether they might also change the way Russian armour and infantry interacted on the battlefield, increasing protection and mobility for embarked infantry as well as supporting firepower – at least, this is how Uralvagonzavod officials seemed to envisage employing these new-type platforms when speaking in 2016.[32] At the same time, the *Armata* platform's derivatives might offer a 'more streamlined means' of production and maintenance.[33]

Although the T-15 heavy IFV has seen a similarly slow development process, it is an example of how the defence industry may be looking to use this generation of vehicles to drive industrial efficiencies in future. The T-15, *Kurganets*-25 and *Bumerang* are understood by US analysts to accept similar turrets, possibly the *Epoch* or *Bumerang*-BM, of which different weapons fits have been seen.[34] It is possible, therefore, that they would use similar systems and manufacturing processes, which might lead to more efficient production. The new 'combat modules' are another recent development and have been retrofitted to existing vehicles. In 2018, deliveries began of upgraded

BMP-2s with the *Berezhok* combat module (BMP-2M) to units in the Central Military District. *Berezhok* has four ready-loaded *Kornet* anti-tank guided missiles (ATGMs) flanking a 30-mm cannon.[35] The turret on the T-15, meanwhile, reportedly has been changed from the earlier 30-mm gun and *Kornet*-equipped system to the AU-220M, equipped with a 57-mm gun (manufactured by the Burevestnik Research Bureau) and the *Ataka* ATGM.[36] It is unclear whether this is a temporary or permanent change. Meanwhile, the defence ministry said in May 2020 that upgraded BMP-3s with the *Epoch* combat

module as well as more *Berezhok*-equipped BMP-2s would be fielded.[37] These developments, when taken together, seem to reflect a desire to also deliver more close-combat fire support.

This certainly seems to have been one of the factors that prompted the (still troubled) development of the latest BMPT vehicle, the *Terminator*.[38] Designed with the intention of supporting infantry and armour, this vehicle has also undergone capability upgrades. Originally mounting a 30-mm cannon with a grenade launcher and *Kornet* ATGM, this was improved to carry a twin 30-mm auto-cannon and

Figure 3.4: Russian Army, Airborne and Coastal forces: selected artillery and missile inventories, 2007 and 2020

2007		2020	
SELF-PROPELLED GUN/HOWITZERS: 6,123		**SELF-PROPELLED GUN/HOWITZERS: 2,055**	
2S1	2,875	2S1	245
2S3	1,618	2S3	850
2S5	950	2S5	100
2S19	550	2S19/2S19M	500
-		2S19M2/2S33	300
2S7	130	2S7M	60
TOWED GUN/HOWITZERS: 12,770		**TOWED GUN/HOWITZERS: 420**	
D-30	4,645	D-30	170
M-46	650		
2A65	750	2A65	200
2A36	1,100	2A36	50
D-20	1,075	-	
M-1943	700	-	
ML20	100		
MULTIPLE-ROCKET LAUNCHERS: 4,072		**MULTIPLE-ROCKET LAUNCHERS: 924**	
BM-21	2,500	BM-21/*Tornado*-G	586
BM-16	50	-	
9P138	516	-	
9P140	900	9P140	218
9A52	106	9A52	100
		Tornado-S	20
GUN/MORTARS AND MORTARS: 3,483		**GUN/MORTARS AND MORTARS: 1,236**	
2S9/2B16	883	2S9	250
2S23	50	2S23	42
-		2S9-SM	30
-		2S34	50
-		2B16	124
2S12	920	2S12	700
2S4	430	2S4	40
PM-38	900	-	
M-160	300	-	
SHORT-RANGE MISSILE LAUNCHERS: 174		**SHORT-RANGE MISSILE LAUNCHERS: 160**	
9K79-1	162	-	
9K720	12	9K720	160
		MEDIUM-RANGE MISSILE LAUNCHERS: 16	
		with 9M729	16+

Sources: *The Military Balance 2008*; IISS Military Balance+

Ataka ATGMs. Although this platform was deployed to Syria – likely for operational tests, as with other Russian equipment – a production contract has yet to be issued. Syria has also been used as a test bed for other Ground Forces equipment, including the *Typhoon* protected vehicle, and a range of lightly armoured vehicles including the *Tigr*. Indeed the Ground Forces, and designers, have taken a range of lessons from the conflict in Syria. Regarding the *Terminator*, for instance, there have been reports that another variant might be based on the *Armata* chassis to improve protection, with the guns possibly upgraded to 57 mm to improve penetration.[39] Involvement in military action in Ukraine and Syria also led to lessons for other elements of the Ground Forces.

Air defence

The air-defence element of Russia's Ground Forces (*Protivo vozdushnaya oborona sukhoputnye voyska*, PVO SV) fared less well in SAP 2020 compared to its Aerospace Forces equivalent, if better than other elements of the Ground Forces when it came to procurement. Strategic air defence of the homeland, rather than tactical air defence of manoeuvre forces, was the primary focus of the 2020 SAP regarding surface-to-air missile (SAM) systems. Large-scale acquisition of the S-400 (SA-21 *Growler*) appeared to be the ground-based air-defence priority, with the target of 56 battalion sets, most for the Aerospace Forces, nearly met by mid-2020.[40]

The PVO SV as of mid-2020 had 15 SAM brigades, primarily for medium- and long-range air defence, while army manoeuvre brigades also include point and short-range systems at the battalion and regimental levels.[41] As with the Aerospace Forces air defence, the army also adopts a layered in-depth approach, with system-engagement ranges providing overlapping capabilities.

Army air-defence units continued for the most part to be equipped with the same systems as in 2010, even if some of the SAMs were upgraded versions. Notable among these were the introduction from 2014 of the 9K333 *Verba* (SA-29) shoulder-launched point-defence missile, upgraded variants of the 9K330 *Tor* (SA-15 *Gauntlet*) short-range system from 2017, the *Buk*-M3 (SA-27) medium-range SAM system that began to be introduced from 2016, and the S-300V4 (SA-23) long-range air- and missile-defence system from 2014.[42]

Eleven of the 15 brigades are equipped with variants of the medium-range *Buk* family, mainly the 9K317 *Buk*-M2 (SA-17 *Grizzly*) and 9K317M *Buk*-M3 (SA-27). The remaining four brigades are equipped with either the S-300V (SA-12A/B *Gladiator/Giant*) or S-300V4 (SA-23) long-range system.

The army may also be trying to rationalise its ground-based air-defence inventory, supported by the 2027 SAP. A project known as '*Standart*' was launched in 2018 aimed at supporting the modernisation of the army's air defences.[43] A further aim would seem to be the closer integration of the air-defence systems deployed.[44]

The *Buk*-M3 will continue to replace the *Buk*-M2 at the brigade level, with the latter no longer being procured.[45] Three brigades have now been re-equipped with the *Buk*-M3, while at least five have the *Buk*-M2, and a further three are still outfitted with the 9K37 *Buk*-M1-2 (SA11B *Gadfly*). The *Buk*-M1-2 units will almost certainly be re-equipped with the *Buk*-M3 in the next couple of years. The *Buk*-M3 uses a more capable missile than previous variants of the *Buk*. The 9M317M missile is also containerised, with the mid-body wing of the previous *Buk*-associated missiles absent. The two remaining legacy

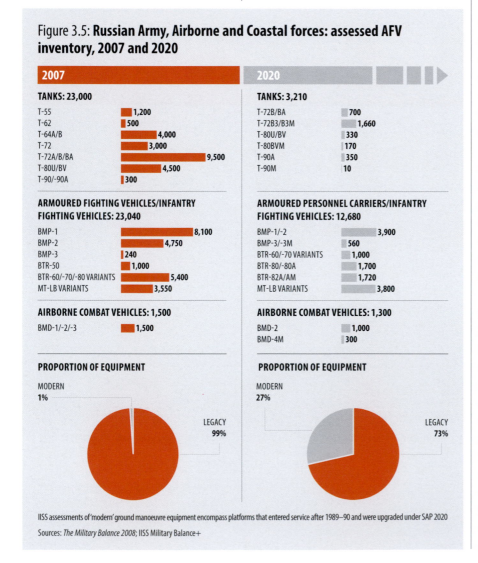

Figure 3.5: **Russian Army, Airborne and Coastal forces: assessed AFV inventory, 2007 and 2020**

2007

TANKS: 23,000

T-55	1,200
T-62	500
T-64A/B	4,000
T-72	3,000
T-72A/B/BA	9,500
T-80U/BV	4,500
T-90/-90A	300

ARMOURED FIGHTING VEHICLES/INFANTRY FIGHTING VEHICLES: 23,040

BMP-1	8,100
BMP-2	4,750
BMP-3	240
BTR-50	1,000
BTR-60/-70/-80 VARIANTS	5,400
MT-LB VARIANTS	3,550

AIRBORNE COMBAT VEHICLES: 1,500

BMD-1/-2/-3	1,500

PROPORTION OF EQUIPMENT

MODERN 1%

LEGACY 99%

2020

TANKS: 3,210

T-72B/BA	700
T-72B3/B3M	1,660
T-80U/BV	330
T-80BVM	170
T-90A	350
T-90M	10

ARMOURED PERSONNEL CARRIERS/INFANTRY FIGHTING VEHICLES: 12,680

BMP-1/-2	3,900
BMP-3/-3M	560
BTR-60/-70 VARIANTS	1,000
BTR-80/-80A	1,700
BTR-82A/AM	1,720
MT-LB VARIANTS	3,800

AIRBORNE COMBAT VEHICLES: 1,300

BMD-2	1,000
BMD-4M	300

PROPORTION OF EQUIPMENT

MODERN 27%

LEGACY 73%

IISS assessments of 'modern' ground manoeuvre equipment encompass platforms that entered service after 1989–90 and were upgraded under SAP 2020

Sources: *The Military Balance 2008*; IISS Military Balance+

S-300V brigades will likely receive the S-300V4 over a similar period.

Tor-M2 deliveries will also continue as part of SAP 2027.[46] Like the Buk-M3, the latest version of the Tor family to enter SV PVO service has a new missile, and like the Buk-M3 it offers improved performance and a greater missile load per launch vehicle. So far at least six battalion sets of the Tor-M2 have been delivered.[47] The Tor-M2 will likely continue to be used to replace earlier versions of the system, as well as the 9K33 Osa-AKM (SA-8B Gecko). Alongside the 9K33, other ageing systems that the PVO SV is also looking to replace are the Strela-10 (SA-13 Gopher) and the ZSU-23-4 Shilka. The former may be succeeded by the Sosna (SA-X-25). This short-range air-defence system completed state tests in 2017, but as of mid-2020 it was uncertain whether a production order had yet been placed. The intended ZSU-23-4 replacement is the 2S38 Derivatsiya 57-mm self-propelled anti-air gun. This system will begin state acceptance trials in 2021.

The 2S38 may also be a part replacement for the 2K22 Tunguska (SA-19 Grison), which entered production in the mid-1970s. The Pantsir-S (SA-22 Greyhound) was intended as the successor to the 2K22, however the SV rejected the system in 2012

on the basis that it did not meet its requirement. A combination of the Tor-M2, Sosna and the 2S38 may instead be the route it pursues.

Along with considering reducing the number of types of tactical air-defence systems in the SV inventory, the Standart research as described will also focus on closer integration and at least improved interoperability between the various command-and-control systems now in use.

Artillery modernisation

Artillery has long held a central place in the Ground Forces' concepts of operations and inventories. Their importance is reflected in their position within the TOE of a tank or motor-rifle brigade. As has been noted, a Russian motor-rifle brigade will frequently 'have two self-propelled artillery battalions, a rocket artillery battalion and an anti-tank battalion (with primarily direct-fire systems) before it is augmented with additional artillery support from its parent unit'.[48]

Similar to the tank fleet, Russia's artillery modernisation under SAP 2020 was publicly focused on new-generation equipment. The Koalitsiya-SV 152-mm self-propelled gun first appeared in the 2015 Victory Day parade and is slated to replace the ageing 2S19 Msta system. However,

the first batch of eight Koalitsiya-SV howitzers, based on the T-90 chassis, were only delivered for state tests to the Central Military District in May 2020. (These tests are planned to be completed in 2022.)[49] Therefore, Russia is pursuing a dual strategy in artillery modernisation too: developing the Koalitsiya while modernising existing equipment. Indeed, the Uraltransmash CEO said in a 2019 interview that the modernisation plans for the 2S19 Msta and also the 2S3 Akatsiya were related to the Koalitsiya being 'a machine of the future'.[50]

Tactical considerations have led Russia to also focus on modernising older heavy artillery systems, such as the ageing 2S7 Pion, which is being modernised as the 2S7M Malka, as well as the 2S4 Tulpan 240-mm self-propelled mortar.[51] Lessons from Syria and Ukraine, notably in relation to engagements against fortified positions and the requirement for heavier firepower, have likely informed such choices, as have financial factors: using such systems may also be more cost-effective than employing missile systems.[52] The 2S7M was being tested at the end of 2019, after import substitution reportedly allowed the production of a Russian-origin gearbox, in place of the Ukrainian-origin equipment in the earlier generation of vehicles.[53]

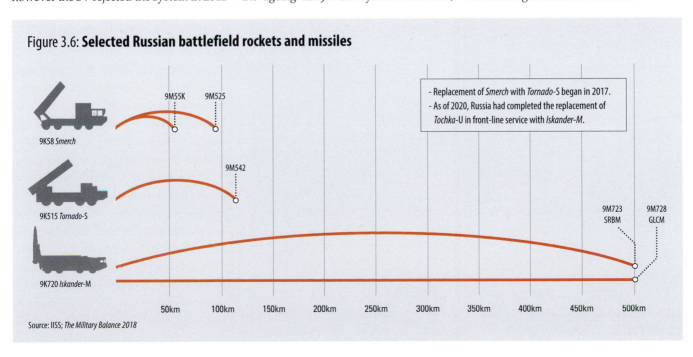

Figure 3.6: Selected Russian battlefield rockets and missiles

- Replacement of Smerch with Tornado-S began in 2017.
- As of 2020, Russia had completed the replacement of Tochka-U in front-line service with Iskander-M.

9K58 Smerch — 9M55K, 9M525

9K515 Tornado-S — 9M542

9K720 Iskander-M — 9M723 SRBM, 9M728 GLCM

50km 100km 150km 200km 250km 300km 350km 400km 450km 500km

Source: IISS; The Military Balance 2018

Map 3.1: Russia's *Iskander* missile units, 2020

448TH MISSILE BRIGADE
Kursk
Contract: Aug 2017
Delivered: Nov 2019

152ND MISSILE BRIGADE (NAVY)
Kaliningrad
Contract: Aug 2011
Delivered: Nov 2017

26TH MISSILE BRIGADE
Luga
Contract: 2010
Delivered: Mid-2011

112TH MISSILE BRIGADE
Shuya
Contract: Aug 2011
Delivered: Jul 2014

1ST MISSILE BRIGADE
Krasnodar
Contract: Aug 2011
Delivered: Nov 2013

WESTERN MILITARY DISTRICT

NORTHERN FLEET

SOUTHERN MILITARY DISTRICT

CENTRAL MILITARY DISTRICT

EASTERN MILITARY DISTRICT

12TH MISSILE BRIGADE
Mozdok
Contract: Aug 2011
Delivered: Nov 2015

92ND MISSILE BRIGADE
Totskoye Vtorye
Contract: Aug 2011
Delivered: Nov 2014

107TH MISSILE BRIGADE
Birobidzhan
Contract: Aug 2011
Delivered: Jul 2013

N.K.
Znamensk
Contract: Aug 2017
Delivered: Apr 2019

119TH MISSILE BRIGADE
Elanskiy
Contract: Aug 2011
Delivered: Nov 2016

103RD MISSILE BRIGADE
Ulan-Ude
Contract: Aug 2011
Delivered: Jul 2015

3RD MISSILE BRIGADE
Gorny
Contract: Aug 2011
Delivered: Jun 2017

20TH MISSILE BRIGADE
Ussuriysk
Contract: Aug 2011
Delivered: Jun 2016

Source: IISS Military Balance+

9K720 *ISKANDER*-M (SS-26 *STONE*) LAUNCHER
Firing a 9M723 missile at the Sary-Shagan training ground in Kazakhstan during the *Tsentr* 2019 military exercise, September 2019.
CREDIT: Russian Defence Ministry/TASS/Getty Images

Rocket and missile artillery

Russia's missile and rocket-artillery units have been a notable area of progress for the Ground Forces under SAP 2020, particularly the completion of the rearmament of its missile brigades. All ten units that operated the 120 kilometre-range 9K79-1 *Tochka*-U (SS-21 *Scarab*) have now been re-equipped with the 9K720 *Iskander*-M (SS-26 *Stone*) which has a range of over 500 km, while three additional *Iskander* brigades were formed in the Southern and Eastern military districts.[54] This total of 13 *Iskander* brigades includes the brigade located in Kaliningrad under the Coastal Defence forces.

Iskander is notable not only in giving a significant range increase over the previous *Tochka* missiles, but also because the system is dual-capable and is also equipped with two different types of missile: the 9M723 solid-fuelled missile that is understood to be capable of following an aeroballistic trajectory in order to complicate the task for missile defences; and the 9M728 cruise missile. Some doubt has been cast on the reported 500-km ranges of both.[55] Meanwhile, the US and its NATO allies also contend that the Russian 9M729 (SSC-8 *Screwdriver*) ground-launched cruise missile has a range of over 500 km (it was the system at the heart of US allegations that Russia breached the 1987 Intermediate-range Nuclear Forces Treaty). As of 2019, three of the battalions were co-located with *Iskander* brigades: Elansky (119th), Mozdok (12th) and Shuya (112th).[56] The launch vehicle for this system and its degree of commonality with the 9P78 *Iskander* transporter-erector-launcher remains unclear; the vehicle for the 9M729 missile may or may not be longer, but its overall visual similarity complicates identification. Rocket artillery has also been modernised, with the *Tornado*-S MRL constituting a modernisation of the existing *Smerch* system with guidance improvements, and the modernisation and recent combat deployment (to Syria) of the TOS-1 thermobaric MRL system.

So, it is possible that Russia is pursuing complementary strands to its artillery modernisation. As in other Ground Forces modernisation plans, these reflect the lessons of recent wars and a still evolving appreciation of how conflict might unfold in future. Artillery modernisation is focused on the development of more precise weapons, but also of weapons capable of massed artillery strikes, increasing the range of missions that artillery can perform, as well as increasing firepower in divisions and brigades, enabling artillery to better support manoeuvre formations.[57] Perhaps to this end, Russian military leaders have in recent years made strides towards improving the ability to find targets, engage them rapidly and then conduct rapid battle-damage assessment, so allowing for fire adjustment if required: to better find, fix and strike.[58] The Ground Forces are looking to improve this capability by further integrating uninhabited systems into the targeting process, both for conventional artillery and missile units and introducing other equipment to improve reconnaissance, target acquisition and fire control.[59]

Combat support and combat-service support

The Ground Forces' equipment has seen improvements in other areas, including in electronic warfare, with systems like the *Krasukha*-4, and in command and control, with the *Strelets* system beginning to be rolled out. Since the conflicts in Georgia and Chechnya, Russia has made efforts to revitalise its electronic-warfare capability.[60] The mission to seize Crimea in 2014 was supported by the RB-314V *Leer*-3 system equipped with uninhabited aerial vehicles (UAVs) and the *Lorandit* communications-intelligence (COMINT) system. Russia deployed to Syria the 1RL257 *Krasukha*-4 jammer, the L-175V/VE *Container/Khibiny* and *Leer*-3 systems.[61] There have also been reports of the deployment of the RB-301B *Borisoglebsk*-2 electronic-warfare COMINT system and the *Repellent*-1 counter-UAV system.[62]

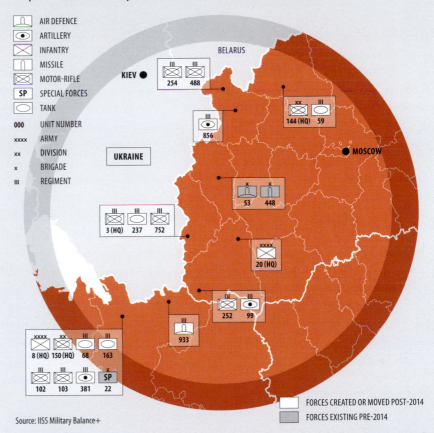

Map 3.2: **Russian Army units near Ukraine's border, 2020**

Source: IISS Military Balance+

KOALITSIYA-SV SELF-PROPELLED GUN
In Moscow during the Victory Day parade, May 2015.
CREDIT: Host photo agency/RIA Novosti/Getty Images

Command-and-control improvements for ground troops include the *Strelets* handheld system, which can reportedly integrate with the Aerospace Forces' *Metronom* system and the VDV's *Andromeda*-D, though it's unclear how far these are distributed throughout formations rather than prioritised for high-readiness formations.[63] Other equipment developments have included a seeming revitalisation of bridging capability. This exists at brigade level, with tank and motor-rifle brigades retaining a bridging company, but in late 2019 a US analyst reported (with reference to Russian media sources) that this capability was being reintroduced at the operational (army) level.[64] Meanwhile, the re-establishment of organic repair units continues, carrying on the process of unpicking the New Look initiative of outsourcing this function.[65]

The roles of Russia's Ground Forces

There has been speculation that 2020 will bring the release of a new Russian military doctrine.[66] While this can be anticipated by analysts, study of past documents cast some light on the intended roles for Russia's land forces. The end of the Cold War and the collapse of the Soviet Union led to a change in orientation. This meant far less emphasis on planning for a large-scale war requiring mass mobilisation, while the near-simultaneous outbreak of conflicts in Russia's former republics, and assessments that these smaller conflicts might dominate military requirements, drove a reassessment of priorities and structures.

The reforms after 2008 'were intended to streamline command and control, in order to give the Russian military a command structure more capable of responding to regional and low-intensity threats' while also providing greater overall utility through improved equipment and the end of the mass-mobilisation model.[67] The Kosovo conflict in 1999 is said to have marked a watershed, indicating that

Russia's conventional forces needed to be ready for 'high-technology warfare' rather than necessarily be postured in case of 'local or regional wars in the south'.[68] Recent iterations of Russia's military doctrine have been studied for references to how Moscow views the international political environment as well as NATO, and also any changes in Russia's views of nuclear and non-nuclear deterrence.[69] Principal external military dangers in 2014 included NATO's capability generation and bringing its 'military infrastructure' closer to Russia's borders, though in that year NATO was still viewed, as it was in 2010, as a 'military danger' rather than a 'military threat'.[70] NATO expansion and technical developments, such as in missile defence and prompt global strike, were noted as key challenges. There are references to increased international tensions, but there is still a focus on regional security risks as well as 'a tendency towards shifting the military risks and military threats to the information space and the [Russian Federation's] internal sphere'.[71] Though there is doubtless a greater appreciation of the possibility of high-intensity conflict with Western states, another major factor prompting Russia's military organisation and guiding its basing remains the possibility of conflict in territories of the former Soviet Union. Indeed, an interesting development, which would gain attention one year later, was that the 2014 doctrine also indicated that the armed forces could be deployed outside Russia; the doctrine used the term *operativno*, 'a Russian term which is notoriously easy to mistranslate but which invariably implies a degree of speed and urgency'.[72]

For the land forces, these regional and local challenges of the 1990s – and the problems that Russia's military establishment had in fielding forces able to efficiently tackle them – helped spur restructuring initiatives in order to produce more responsive and mobile formations.

After stuttering attempts at generating higher-readiness forces in the 1990s, more recent initiatives, such as the gener-

ation of composite force structures in the form of battalion tactical groups, have increased Russia's ability to field more usable units more quickly. Moreover, since 2013 and the beginning of the return to divisional-level formations, these units are connected to the more substantial fire- and logistics-support capabilities that would help improve their utility in a major confrontation.

At the same time, the introduction of new equipment has honed existing areas of competence, such as in artillery, by introducing new capabilities like UAVs alongside new missile and rocket-artillery pieces and also by improving the capacity of Russia's artillery personnel to quickly find, fix and strike targets. This qualitative improvement has been helped by more professionalisation with an increasing proportion of contractors and initiatives to create more effective non-commissioned-officer structures, in improved equipment and better training, as well as in combat experience: for instance, Russia has been careful in rotating through Syria a significant number of higher-ranking military commanders and has used the conflict as a test bed for some equipment.

Indications of how Russia's Ground Forces may be employed can be derived from the remarks of key leaders, insights from recent and current operations, and the structural and equipment choices that Russia has taken. For instance, the move away from a mass-mobilisation structure and the generation of higher-readiness, fully staffed components indicates an intent to generate troops that could be more quickly and more cohesively deployed than under the previous mass-mobilisation model, and so better able to tackle challenges that might arise on Russia's periphery.[73] That said, with land borders at Russia's scale, garrisoned forces also provide deterrent value, establish 'presence' and also constitute a potentially coercive tool (as in the units that have been established near the Ukrainian border after 2014 and in a manner similar to the concentration of forces that takes place when units are deployed for military exercises).

The desire to generate higher-readiness and deployable formations has also led to what could be seen as complementary developments between the Ground Forces and the VDV. In the VDV, the shift once more towards generating combat units outfitted with heavier equipment perhaps reflects the reality that some of its formations will – as in the recent past – be deployed as ground-manoeuvre formations, and that their air-portable armour lacks punch and protection. Nonetheless, they are continuing to improve their air portability with parachute and air-mobile (heliborne) air assault. But the Ground Forces may also be moving in the latter direction. Russian defence ministry press releases since late 2018 have reported on developments of air-mobile groups within motor-rifle battalions of the Southern Military District. In January 2020

it was reported that an exercise that month was due to include elements of the 49th Combined Arms Army in an air-mobile role (Russian analysts indicated subsequently that this would likely be the 205th Motor-rifle Brigade at Budyonnovsk).[74] Regardless, it is only one among a series of exercises held in the Southern Military District and indicates a desire to improve the air portability of some Ground Forces units.

In recent years, Russian officials have also discussed the integration of advanced military technologies, improvements to the reconnaissance and command-and-control capacities of land forces, changing military threats to the country and the deployment overseas of Russia's troops on operations; the last is within the context of what has been termed by CGS Gerasimov a 'strategy of limited action'.[75] Although there may be attention on strategies including those that require the integration of all arms of state power (i.e., including non-military as well

as military tools), the generation of military forces – and land forces – trained and equipped for conventional ground combat still occupies a key place in Russian military thinking. Indeed, the modernisation of armour and artillery – and parallel drives to improve the strike range of these systems – together with the moves to improve command and control, organisation and deployability, all point to the continued importance to the Ground Forces of the ability to conduct rapid deep-strike operations. Although it may be true that Russia today possesses within its Ground Forces a better trained and equipped combat core, and this may be capable of more effectively addressing its leaders' military objectives than in the 1990s and 2000s, it is also important to remember that the Ground Forces comprise only one component of Russia's high-readiness formations: intervention capability also rests in its naval infantry and Spetsnaz units, and in the Airborne Forces.

MI-8AMTSH HELICOPTERS
Preparing to land during the *Vostok* 2018 exercise, September 2018.
CREDIT: Vadim Savitsk/TASS/Getty Images

Russia's Airborne Forces

Traditionally considered a key element of the high command's strategic reserve, Russia's Airborne Forces (VDV) today provide the core of Russia's rapid-reaction force.[76] It comprises four divisions (two parachute and two air assault) and five independent brigades, combat support and combat-service support (a brigade and a battalion) and a command element. It began its 90-year history as part of the Soviet Air Force, then the army, before gaining separate status and it continues as an independent branch of the armed forces, under the control of the chief of the General Staff. The aim is that the VDV can respond to a range of threats in Russia or abroad within 24 hours.[77]

The VDV was under threat in the initial drafts of the 2008 New Look, and the force's independence and size were at risk. The proposals included cutting combat strength by half, with two of the existing four divisions to be disbanded. However, the VDV ended up being the formation least affected by the New Look and reform plans were never fully implemented; in common with the Strategic Rocket Forces, it retained its divisional and regimental structures.[78] During the Cold War, its mission set included deep-strike and interdiction operations and, today, combat tasks allocated to the VDV include air assault and insertion into enemy territory, as well as providing a blocking force, if required, in response to an enemy breakthrough.[79]

The New Look reform proposals stemmed from practical concerns – because there was a shortage of military transport aircraft – as well as a view that there was little conceptual clarity about the purpose of the VDV. Indeed, reform and development of the VDV in the post-Soviet period was carried out without a clearly defined official concept. It is arguable that this uncertainty persists, even though there are today two official documents (from 2014 and 2018) intended to guide the VDV's future direction.[80] For instance, as of 2020 the VDV's force development seems to be concurrently focused in three directions: on traditional airborne – parachute – operations; on the development of heavier ground motor-rifle-style units supported (once more) by additional armour; and on experimentation around the development of heliborne air-assault formations.

The force is slated to expand further in size. The 237th Air Assault Regiment (Pskov) was formed in December 2018, within the 76th Air Assault Division also at Pskov. This meant that the 76th now had three manoeuvre regiments; divisions previously only had two. Meanwhile, analysts also report that the 7th and 76th divisions are being expanded with tank battalions.[81] There is a plan to add a fifth division by 2025 – a further air-assault unit – so that there will then be two airborne and three air-assault divisions, as well as an artillery-brigade-sized unit.[82] This additional division will be created by converting the 31st Air Assault Brigade into the 104th Air Assault Division. There are also less-developed plans to include aviation, anti-aircraft and missile-defence units in the VDV.[83]

Personnel

The VDV's personnel strength reduced from 64,000 at the end of the Soviet Union to 48,000 by 1997 and between 30,000 and 35,000 by 2012.[84] The decision, in 2013, to include the army's three air-assault brigades helped boost numbers to 45,000, and this remains the VDV's total strength as of mid-2020.[85] During 2014 there was some discussion, as part of the reform process, as to whether to try to nearly double the size of the force by 2020, and while this was not pursued at the time it now seems to have been effectively readopted with the plan to include additional regiments, plus a division, by 2025.[86]

A further 2020 target related to increasing the percentage of professional soldiers within the overall establishment strength. Set at 80%, this aim has almost been met. The VDV was among the first to see units convert to a professional structure. The 98th Airborne Division, the 7th Air Assault Division and the 45th Special Operations Brigade have seen increasing numbers of *kontraktniki*, though they still contained conscripts, and selected battalions were fully manned by contract personnel in order to facilitate BTG generation.

The original plan had been to make all units fully professional by 2008, but this proved unachievable, with the possible exception of the 31st Air Assault Brigade. During 2007 some units were 90% professional, but the aim to transfer

PARATROOPERS FROM THE AIRBORNE FORCES
Jumping from an Ilyushin Il-76MD heavy transport aircraft during an exercise at the Zhitovo training area, July 2020. CREDIT: Alexander Ryumin/TASS/Getty Images

the VDV to contract service suffered from insufficient funding.[87] As a result, by mid-2010, the share of contract-service personnel had fallen to 31%.[88] Renewed funding from 2012 again allowed the service to prioritise the move to contract soldiers, and a target of 80% was set for 2020: enough to field 22 contract-staffed battalion tactical groups.[89] By 2015 there was parity between contractor and conscript numbers, and by 2018 the percentage of contract soldiers had risen to 70%, with more than 30,000 out of 45,000 VDV personnel being contractors.[90]

Re-equipment and expansion

The VDV's 2014 and 2018 planning documents broadly aligned with the State Armament Programme. The first had been developed alongside what was to have been the 2016–25 SAP, before this was delayed and succeeded with SAP 2027, which paralleled the 2018 VDV plan.[91] The re-equipment programme was in part intended to support the VDV's status as a rapid-reaction force, though heavier ground-combat equipment was also on the list.

The airborne and air-assault role indicates a requirement for equipment to be air-portable by the Air Force's fixed- and rotary-wing transport aircraft. The armoured-vehicle inventory, widely used in both Chechen wars, was intended to be recapitalised as part of SAP 2015, though these ambitions failed because of procurement-planning issues, as well as problems with budgets and equipment costs.[92]

The problems of the 2015 plan were taken into account with SAP 2020, and VDV acquisition plans were increased. In keeping with the wider equipment-percentage targets for 'modern' equipment set by the ministry, the VDV was supposed to have a 63% 'modern' inventory by 2020.[93] While no definition of 'modern' has been provided, the broad extent of the intended equipment recapitalisation can be gleaned by recalling that the ministry was reporting only a 20% 'modern' inventory in 2011.[94] Equipment deliveries up to 2020 have included T-72B3 main battle tanks and BTR-82AM infantry fighting vehicles for the conventional combat and armoured-reconnaissance role, and BMD-4Ms and BTR-MDMs, in order to update the VDV's airborne combat-vehicle fleets (and a contract for BMD-2Ms in lieu of a full BMD-4M fleet). There are also plans to acquire the upgraded *Sprut*-SDM1 as an air-portable fire-support vehicle, following the curtailment of the original *Sprut*-SD programme. Other equipment developments are understood to be aimed at enhancing mobility and command and control, combined with improved capacity to operate at extended range.[95]

Future roles?

An inevitable consequence of some of the VDV's specific equipment requirements, particularly related to air-portable vehicles, is that there is as a consequence limited commonality with the Ground Forces. There also remains a question as to the future utility of parachute assaults.[96] Since 2017, drills have again been carried out at the regimental level and above, combining parachute-dropped and air-landed units. Training exercises have also included two or three airborne formations being used in conjunction with other branches of the armed forces.[97] In July 2018, the 137th Airborne Regiment of the 106th Airborne Division held regimental-level tactical exercises in Ryazan oblast which included the air movement of a parachute regiment (some 1,200 personnel), and supporting vehicles and equipment, using 66 Il-76MD *Candid* transport aircraft. The drill was the largest in the last two decades.[98] Trials were also carried out during the *Vostok* 2018 military exercises of a 'new type' of mobile unit, intended for deployment by helicopter rather than fixed-wing aircraft.[99] The *Tsentr* 2019 military exercises saw further developments, with a regimental-level airdrop conducted by the 217th regiment of the 98th Airborne Division, and an air-assault operation involving the 31st Air Assault Brigade.[100] In remarks after the exercise, Minister of Defence Shoigu said that it was the first time since *Zapad* 1981 that an airborne regiment and more than 200 pieces of equipment were landed; referring to the Air Assault Brigade's participation in an air-landing exercise, he said it was part of a continuing experiment.[101]

The VDV already provides Moscow with a capable mobile high-readiness force; its air-assault formations are already based close to areas of current or potential concern: the Baltic states, Crimea and Central Asia. Moreover, its equipment inventory has benefited from a decade of sustained investment. But this experimentation in heliborne air assault and continued airdrop exercises is taking place at the same time as the VDV is also introducing more heavy armour suitable for conventional ground combat. Moreover, the VDV's vertical-assault capability remains constrained by the comparative lack of suitable heavy military transport aircraft and transport helicopters. Airlift constraints mean that the VDV's existing armoured vehicles are inferior to those of the Ground Forces, while at the same time the heavier armoured procurements under way will further stress the VDV's mobility capabilities. Indeed, how much emphasis there will be in future on the Airborne Forces' parachute role remains an open question.

Special forces

The capability of Russia's special forces (*sily spetsial'nogo naznacheniya*, Spetsnaz) has been demonstrated recently in Crimea from 2014 and in Syria from 2015. However, while Russia has long had special forces, the authorities have in recent years increased investments in and significantly reorganised this capability, notably after the beginning of the New Look reforms.

Then-defence minister Anatoly Serdyukov and General Nikolai Makarov, the chief of the General Staff, backed a plan put forward by what in effect was a working group to set up a special-operations force as part of the New Look. The special forces envisaged by Serdyukov and Makarov were to be substantially different to the special forces created during the Soviet era. Moves to implement the working group's findings began in 2009; however, in common with other aspects of the New Look, they have been developed further by Shoigu and Gerasimov. In 2013, Gerasimov announced that new Special Operations Forces (*Sily Spetsial'nikh Operatsiy*, SOF) had been created. Mobile and held at high readiness, this capability was intended to be used, Gerasimov reportedly said, 'not only in the country, but also beyond its borders'.[102]

Spetsnaz and the SOF

Established in the 1950s, by the end of the Soviet Union in 1991 there were 14 Spetsnaz brigades, and this fell to seven by 2008. Prior to the New Look, the Spetsnaz were subordinated to the 8th Directorate in the Main Intelligence Directorate (*Glavnoe razvedyvatel'noe upravlenie*, GRU) of the General Staff and to military district commands.[103]

It would be wrong to directly equate the Spetsnaz with Western special forces, particularly units tasked with unconventional tactics.[104] Spetsnaz units were mostly intended for deep reconnaissance in enemy territory along with ambushing enemy forces and carrying out raids against enemy sites such as weapons depots.[105] The use of Spetsnaz during Russia's war in Afghanistan reflected this, although their role was to be expanded in the first and second Chechen wars. In addition to 'traditional' roles, units were tasked with targeted checks in settlements and with the use of ad hoc roadblocks. The expansion of the role saw units also used for tactical reconnaissance and carrying out general security and policing tasks. Training for more specialist Spetsnaz roles had to be neglected.

It was partly because of the experience in Chechnya that some within the defence ministry began to push to set up a smaller, more 'elite' force, including GRU Colonel Vladimir Kvachkov.[106] Kvachkov advocated using the Spetsnaz as the basis for new special-operations forces, with Spetsnaz brigades to be reassigned from the GRU to a new command. These units were to be far more selective in terms of personnel, with more demanding training.

Interest culminated in a working group coordinated in 2009–10 by Igor Medoyev, defence minister Serdyukov's special-forces aide, while the work was led by General Vladimir Maistrenko, the deputy chief of staff of the North Caucasus Military District (who had held Medoyev's position in 2009).[107]

At the same time, existing Spetsnaz units were being reduced in size as part of the New Look, and responsibility for them was transferred from the GRU to the Intelligence Directorate of the Ground Forces headquarters. By moving Spetsnaz to the Ground Forces, their focus shifted towards the intelligence requirements of military districts.

The formation of the Special Operations Forces

These reforms were instituted under CGS Makarov, who had repeatedly pointed out shortcomings with the existing Spetsnaz, including understrength units, lack of training for the types of wars most likely to occur and an obsolete organisational structure. Makarov also criticised the number of conscripts allocated to Spetsnaz units.[108] Efforts were made to bring the brigades to full strength, but the reforms effectively turned the Ground Forces' Spetsnaz into battlefield-surveillance brigades. Makarov was looking to establish a command-level structure to manage the SOF. However, the plan to establish Special Operations Forces did not keep pace with the reform of the Spetsnaz, and the creation of the 346th Special Forces Brigade and the 'elite' 25th Special Forces Regiment is understood to owe much to this delay. These units were established in 2011–12 for operations in the north Caucasus, ostensibly to provide security for the 2014 Winter Olympics.

The arrival of Sergei Shoigu and Valery Gerasimov as defence minister and CGS heralded a change in direction and the eight brigades and one regiment were reassigned to the 8th Directorate of the Main Directorate of the General Staff (unofficially still called the GRU). Indeed, the overall aim of establishing the SOF was to create a mobile high-readiness force, trained and equipped to carry out 'special tasks' in peace and war and, as such, it constituted an attempt to create a force distinct from the existing Spetsnaz. The unit chosen as the core of the SOF was military unit 92154, which had been formed in 1999, with Makarov's support, and located in Senezh, near Solnechnogorsk. The personnel were nearly all officers or warrant officers. Ten years later, a Special Operations Forces Directorate (Unit 99450) was set up in Senezh, under the armed forces high command. This directo-

rate was converted into the Special Operations Forces Command, as announced by Gerasimov in 2013.[109] A second SOF unit, 01355, was formed in April 2010 in Kubinka, Moscow region, while a further unit, 43292, was established in November 2014, again in Senezh. This unit was a focus for training. In 2014, following the annexation of Crimea, an additional SOF centre, known as Unit 00317, was set up in Sevastopol.[110]

While in post, Makarov had suggested up to nine SOF brigades would be established. One analyst estimates that there may be around 1,500 personnel at Senezh, with perhaps a total of around 3,000 personnel in the SOF.[111] There has been considerable investment in the SOF; from 2012–14 the equivalent of US$120 million was spent on construction work in Senezh to support unit development. Reflecting its status, the SOF Command is a direct customer for weapons and equipment, placing it on a par with other major branches of the armed forces.

Operational employment

While SOF units were used to provide security for the 2014 Winter Olympics, the force came to greater prominence with the seizure of Crimea in March 2014. SOF units acted as one of the main forces in the military mission. As well as the SOF, personnel from the GRU special-forces unit, the VDV's 31st Air Assault Brigade and the 810th Naval Infantry Brigade were also involved in operations.[112]

The SOF involvement was even more substantial in Russia's 2015 intervention in the Syrian civil war. SOF personnel have been involved in some way in most of the ground combat activity resulting from Moscow's intervention. Units were used to engage insurgent groups, attack key enemy sites and act as forward air controllers. They also took part in combat search-and-rescue missions and acted as protection units for visiting Russian delegations.[113] SOF personnel were involved in the capture of Palmyra and Aleppo. Combat experience in Syria is being used to help shape the development of the SOF, with the majority of personnel gaining at least one operational tour. For the defence ministry, it may also have underscored the value of this relatively small-scale elite cadre within the Russian armed forces.

Conclusion

Russia's Ground Forces have undergone significant change since the end of the Soviet Union. There are fewer formations and personnel, and equipment inventories have been transformed. Russia's Ground Forces are today a more capable force, with elements held at a higher state of readiness and possessing recent combat experience. The same holds true for other formations, with the Airborne Forces and reorganised special forces seen as a key component of Russia's high-readiness capability.

Although the lessons of Russia's military performance in the wars in Chechnya and Georgia heavily informed the decision to embark on the far-reaching New Look military-reform programme outlined in October 2008, some Russian military leaders had previously advocated more professional and higher-readiness forces, and a shift away from the mass-mobilisation concept that had held a central place in Soviet military thinking.

The decision to transition to a brigade structure was designed to generate formations capable of more-independent self-sustaining missions of the sort that were anticipated on Russia's periphery, but lessons arising from experimentation with brigades, and from increased tensions with the West and with Ukraine (and the fighting there), contributed to Moscow's decision to reintroduce divisions.

For Russia's land forces, as well as its other military services, the military reforms have been tested and adjusted as required. Increased numbers of exercises have been used to improve readiness while personnel, and some equipment, have also been tested operationally, in Syria as well as in Ukraine.

The Ground Forces' inventory has changed significantly since the Soviet era, in number as well as capability, but some of the equipment aspirations outlined in the early years of SAP 2020 have been subject to delay and cancellation. Because of this, the inventory of the Ground Forces in the immediate future will consist of some wholly new equipment types but not in the number originally envisaged, as well as a large number of platforms with a 1980s or 1990s design heritage that have been heavily modernised. Moreover, with uncertain economic prospects potentially imperilling future budget allocations, another key issue for the Ground Forces, as well as the Airborne Forces, will be to maintain focus on their equipment-modernisation requirements amid competing demands from the other services.

Notes

1   IISS, *The Military Balance 1995–96* (Abingdon: Routledge for the IISS, 1996), p. 113.

2   Mikhail Barabanov, Konstantin Makienko and Ruslan Pukhov (eds), 'Military Reform: Towards the New Look of the Russian Army', Valdai Discussion Club Analytical Report, July 2012, p. 7, https://valdaiclub.com/files/11447.

3   Totals for SV only and exclude Coastal and Airborne forces. In 2020, other formations relevant to ground-manoeuvre capability included four VDV divisions and four VDV brigades; units in three Coastal Forces Army Corps (Northern Fleet, Kaliningrad, Crimea); elements of the naval infantry; and brigade-sized units stationed outside Russia, such as the 201st Military Base in Dushanbe, Tajikistan.

4   See Chapter 1, 'Personnel and the mass mobilization legacy', and the interesting discussion of the reserve system in Christopher Donnelly, *Red Banner: The Soviet Military System in Peace and War* (Coulsdon: Jane's Information Group, 1988), p. 157.

5   Barabanov, Makienko and Pukhov, 'Military Reform: Towards the New Look of the Russian Army', p. 7.

6   Aleksey Gayday, 'Reform of the Russian Army', in Mikhail Barabanov (ed.), *Russia's New Army* (Moscow: Centre for Analysis of Strategies and Technologies, 2011), p. 12, http://www.cast.ru/files/book/NewArmy_sm.pdf; A.S. Iskrenko, 'Development of post-War domestic views on the role and place of types and branches of the armed forces in solving the problems of the military security of the state history and modernity', *Bulletin of the Academy of Military Sciences*, no. 2, 2005, pp. 15–21, http://militaryarticle.ru/vestnik-akademii-voennykh-nauk/2005-vavn/10564-razvitie-poslevoennyh-otechest-vennyh-vzgljadov-na.

7   Gayday, 'Reform of the Russian Army', p. 15; Colin Robinson, 'The Russian Ground Forces Today: A Structural Status Examination', *Journal of Slavic Military Studies*, vol. 18, no. 2, 2005, p. 192.

8   Gayday, 'Reform of the Russian Army', p. 17; Dmitry Gorenburg, 'Sharp Cuts in Contract Soldiers Coming', *Russian Defence Policy* blog, 2 June 2010, https://russiandef-policy.com/2010/06/02.

9   IISS, *The Military Balance 2012* (Abingdon: Routledge for the IISS, 2012), p. 187.

10   Lester Grau and Charles Bartles, 'Factors Influencing Russian Force Modernisation', Changing Character of War Centre, University of Oxford, September 2018, p. 2, http://www.ccw.ox.ac.uk/blog/2018/9/19/factors-influencing-russian-force-moderniza-tion-by-dr-lester-grau-and-charles-k-bartles.

11   Russian Ministry of Defence, 'Vossozdany gvardeyskaya Tamanskaya ordena Oktyabr'skoy Revolyutsii Krasnoznamennaya ordena Suvorova motostrelkovaya i Kantemirovskaya ordena Lenina Krasnoznamennaya tankovaya divizii', 4 May 2013, https://function.mil.ru/news_page/country/more.htm?id=11735703@egNews.

12   Michael Kofman suggests that the experience of deploying BTGs to Ukraine 'exposed two problems for Russia's Western MD'. The first was the lack of permanently

based units with sustainment capacities to support a long-term deployment and the second was the 'absence of a larger formation that could take in battalions from other military districts and command them in the field, i.e. no divisional structure'. See Michael Kofman, 'Russia's New Divisions in the West', Russian Military Analysis, 7 May 2016, https://russianmilitaryanalysis. wordpress.com/2016/05/07/russias-new-divisions-in-the-west.

13 'Genshtab sozdast na baze brigad postoy-annoy gotovnosti usilennyye batal'ony', Interfax, 19 September 2012, https://www. interfax.ru/russia/266406.

14 Dmitry Gorenburg, 'Contractees in BTGs', Russian Defence Policy blog, 17 September 2016, https://russiandefpolicy.com/tag/btg.

15 'Chislo batal'onnykh takticheskikh gruppirovok v rossiyskoy armii pochti udvoitsya', TASS, 14 September 2016, https://tass.ru/armiya-i-opk/3620165; 'Kolichestvo batal'onnykh grupp, sostoyashchikh iz kontraktnikov, v rossi-yskoy armii cherez dva goda dostignet 125 – nachal'nik Genshtaba VS RF', Interfax-ABH, 14 September 2016, https://www.militarynews.ru/story. asp?rid=1&nid=425709&lang=RU.

16 'Tezisy vystupleniya nachal'nika General'nogo shtaba Vooruzhennykh Sil Rossiyskoy Federatsii na brifinge, posvy-ashchennom podgotovke manevrov voysk (sil) «Vostok-2018»', Ministry of Defence of the Russian Federation, https://struc-ture.mil.ru/mission/practice/all/more. htm?id=12194449@egNews; 'Chislo kontrak-tnikov v rossiyskoy armii udvoilos' za shest' let', RIA Novosti, 11 March 2016, https://ria. ru/20190311/1551688468.html.

17 It is possible, for instance, that as well as offering an offensive capability, BTGs may offer a defensive capability in large-scale combat operations.

18 'Teoriya bez praktiki mertva', Krasnaya Zvezda, 14 August 2019, http://redstar.ru/ teoriya-bez-praktiki-mertva/?attempt=1; 'V Yuzhnom voyennom okruge provedeny dvustoronniye ucheniya s uchastiyem boleye 130 rotnykh takticheskikh grupp', Ministry of Defence of the Russian

Federation, 9 November 2018, https:// function.mil.ru/news_page/country/more. htm?id=12195026@egNews; 'Rotnyye takticheskiye gruppy rossiyskoy voyennoy bazy YUVO v Abkhazii provedut dvusto-ronniye ucheniya', TV Zvezda, 29 August 2018, https://tvzvezda.ru/news/forces/ content/201808291650-mil-ru-uh95l.html.

19 IISS assessments of 'modern' ground-forces equipment includes platforms that entered service after 1989–90 and upgraded under SAP 2020. So, for the Ground Forces' manoeuvre forces this includes T-72B3/ B3M, T-80U/BV, T-80BVM, T-90/T-90A, T-90M, BMP-3/-3M and BTR-82A/-82AM. The Russian defence ministry's figures for the proportion of 'modern' Ground Forces equipment are higher, though it remains difficult to reconcile the stated percentages against assessed inventories because the Russian defence ministry has not precisely defined what constitutes 'modern' equipment in this context (even if its definition too can be taken to encom-pass new-build and upgraded combat platforms and weapons purchased or modernised in the post-Soviet period). See, for instance, 'Vo vseoruzhii: rossiys-kaya armiya prodolzhayet obnovleniye', Rostec, 23 March 2020, https://rostec.ru/ news/vo-vseoruzhii-rossiyskaya-armiya-prodolzhaet-obnovlenie.

20 Viktor Murakhovsky, Facebook post, 27 April 2020, https://www.facebook.com/ photo.php?fbid=3689242037816261.

21 Franz-Stefan Gady, 'Revealed: Russia's Deadly New Tank Force', Diplomat, 24 April 2015, https://thediplomat.com/2015/04/ revealed-russias-deadly-new-tank-force; 'Russia's new Armata tank gets new genera-tion reactive armour', TASS, 16 June 2015, https://tass.com/russia/801081; 'Russia unveils new Armata tank for WW2 victory parade', BBC, 5 May 2015, https://www.bbc. co.uk/news/world-europe-32478937.

22 That said, Russian analyst Alexey Nikolsky has reported an industry source as saying that issues remain with vehicle protec-tion as well as with the procurement of 'cheap, high-precision ammunition'. See Alexey Nikolsky, 'Sukhoputnyye

voyska dobilis' bol'shikh uspekhov, no yest' i nedostatki', Vedomosti, 11 March 2019, https://www.vedomosti.ru/politics/ articles/2019/03/11/796128-suhoputnie-voiska-nedostatkami.

23 '"Rostekh" nazval srok postu-pleniya v VS pervoy partii tankov "Armata"', Izvestia, 19 November 2019, https://iz.ru/944839/2019-11-19/ rostekh-nazval-srok-postupleniia-v-vs-pervoi-partii-tankov-armata; Nikolay Surkov, Alexey Ramm and Evgeny Andreev, 'Tamanskaya "diviziya budu-shchego"', Izvestia, 22 February 2018, https://iz.ru/708875/nikolai-surkov-aleksei-ramm-evgenii-andreev/ tamanskaia-diviziia-budushchego.

24 Dmitry Gorenburg, 'Tanks in GPV-2027', Russian Defense Policy, 20 February 2020, https://russiandefpolicy.com/tag/gpv.

25 Alexander Khramchikhin, 'Prezhdevremennyy otkaz ot broni', Nezavisimaya Gazeta, 20 February 2020, https://nvo.ng.ru/arma-ment/2020-02-20/1_1082_tanks.html.

26 'Current armored vehicles in excellent condition, no need to switch to next genera-tion – Borisov', Interfax, 30 July 2018.

27 The contract for 132 is understood to have been signed in 2015 and deliveries were first planned to take place from the end of 2018. 'Russian Defense Ministry to get 100 Armata tanks', TASS, 24 August 2017, https://tass.com/defense/961838; 'Russian Armed Forces start getting Armata tanks – Deputy PM Borisov', Interfax, 21 August 2018; 'Uralvagonzavod signed six state contracts at the Army 2018 forum', Interfax, 23 August 2018; Ilya Kramnik, 'Prodolzheniye serii: chto zakupyat v ramkakh gosprogrammy', Izvestia, 14 January 2019, https://iz.ru/833462/ ilia-kramnik/prodolzhenie-serii-chto-zaku-piat-v-ramkakh-gosprogrammy.

28 Oleg Salyukov, 'Sukhoputnyye voyska vykhodyat na novyy uroven', Izvestia, 1 October 2017, https://iz.ru/651606/ oleg-saliukov/sukhoputnye-voiska-vykhodiat-na-novyi-uroven.

29 'Kakim stal tank T-72 posle modernizatsii', VPK, 31 October 2017, https://www.vpk-

news.ru/news/39657.

30 Kramnik, 'Prodolzheniye serii: chto zakupyat v ramkakh gosprogrammy'.

31 Mathieu Boulegue and Richard Connolly, 'Russia's New State Armament Programme: Implications for the Russian Armed Forces and Military Capabilities to 2027', Chatham House, May 2018, https://www.chathamhouse.org/sites/default/files/publications/research/2018-05-10-russia-state-armament-programme-connolly-boulegue-final.pdf; Dmitry Gorenburg said (regarding the T-80BVM) that 'the ground troops often prefer its gas turbine over diesel for extreme cold in the Arctic and Eastern MD'; see Gorenburg, 'Tanks in GPV-2027'; Ivan Safronov, 'Minoborony opredelilos' s planami razvitiya tankovykh voysk', *Vedomosti*, 13 February 2020, https://www.vedomosti.ru/politics/articles/2020/02/13/823042-minoboroni-opredelilos; 'Plany postavok tankov v Vooruzhennyye Sily Rossii', BMPD, 17 February 2020, https://bmpd.livejournal.com/3935520.html.

32 'Ideologiya boevoy sistemy budushchego', VPK, 22 July 2016, https://vpk.name/news/159847_ideologiya_boevoi_sistemyi_budushego.html?new#new. Reports of new weapons, such extended range ammunition, would also seem to indicate that it was intended to engage targets from distance. See Alexei Ramm and Alexei Kozachenko, '"Armata" stanet superubiytsey tankov', *Izvestia*, 7 September 2018, https://iz.ru/783243/aleksei-ramm-aleksei-kozachenko/armata-stanet-superubiitcei-tankov.

33 'Russian Military Power: Building a Military to Support Great Power Aspirations', US Defense Intelligence Agency, 2017, https://www.dia.mil/Portals/27/Documents/News/Military%20Power%20Publications/Russia%20Military%20Power%20Report%202017.pdf.

34 Lester Grau and Charles Bartles, 'The Russian Way of War: Force Structure, Tactics, and Modernisation of the Russian Ground Forces', Foreign Military Studies Office, 2016, p. 221, https://www.armyu-

press.army.mil/Portals/7/Hot%20Spots/Documents/Russia/2017-07-The-Russian-Way-of-War-Grau-Bartles.pdf.

35 'Berezhok', KBP Instrument Design Bureau, http://www.kbptula.ru/ru/razrabotki-kbp/kompleksy-vooruzheniya-legkobronirovannoj-tekhniki/berezhok.

36 'BMP na platforme "Armata" poluchila novyye orudiya i rakety', *Izvestia*, 18 August 2018, https://iz.ru/779288/2018-08-18/bmp-na-platforme-armata-poluchila-novye-orudiia-i-rakety; 'Russian defense firm at final stage of developing new combat module', TASS, 5 February 2020, https://tass.com/defense/1116721; 'Poyavilos' video ispytaniy noveyshego boyevogo modulya AU-220M', *Izvestia*, 5 February 2020, https://iz.ru/972499/2020-02-05/poiavilos-video-ispytanii-noveishego-boevogo-modulia-au-220m.

37 Russian Ministry of Defence, 'Sovremennyye boyevyye mashiny postupyat v Sukhoputnyye voyska do kontsa 2020 goda', 24 May 2020, https://function.mil.ru/news_page/country/more.htm?id=12293986@egNews.

38 BMPTs are not a new concept. See 'Istoriya poyavleniya BMPT', *Military Review*, 23 April 2013, https://topwar.ru/27164-istoriya-poyavleniya-bmpt.html; Vladimir Tuchkov, '"Terminator-3": groza natovskikh soldat i borodatykh insurgentov', VPK, 1 July 2020, https://www.vpk-news.ru/articles/57581.

39 Tuchkov, '"Terminator-3": groza natovskikh soldat i borodatykh insurgentov'.

40 See, for example, IISS, *The Military Balance 2020* (Abingdon: Routledge for the IISS, 2020), p. 201.

41 *Ibid.*, p. 195.

42 Interfax-AVN, 'Russian military news agency reports on deliveries to the army, navy', BBC Monitoring, 15 October 2014, https://monitoring.bbc.co.uk/product/m1c54b4c; *Rossiskaya Gazeta*, 'Russian forces get first new Tor-M2 SAM regiment', BBC Monitoring, 15 April 2017, https://monitoring.bbc.co.uk/product/c1dg8zqk; *Izvestia*, 'East Russia brigades gets Buk-M3 surface-to-air missile systems', BBC

Monitoring, 14 June 2017, https://monitoring.bbc.co.uk/product/c1dinb7t; 'Firing drills featuring hypersonic S-300V4 missile system to be held in Russia's south', TASS, 3 April 2015, https://tass.com/russia/787069.

43 *Izvestia*, 'Russia begins ground troops air defence standardisation programme', BBC Monitoring, 10 July 2018, https://monitoring.bbc.co.uk/product/c1dpfv63.

44 *Ibid.*

45 *Izvestia*, 'Russian air defence unit on Caucasus border to get latest Buk-M3 system', BBC Monitoring, 22 July 2020, https://monitoring.bbc.co.uk/product/c201wrxz.

46 'Russian defense ministry to sign long term contract for modernized Tor-family systems', TASS, 21 December 2018, https://tass.com/search?searchStr=Tor-M2%202027&sort=date.

47 Samuel Cranny-Evans, 'Russia receives final contracted Tor-M2 air defence system', *Jane's Defence Weekly*, 22 October 2019, https://customer.janes.com/Janes/Display/FG_2420387-JDW.

48 Scott Boston and Dara Massicot, 'The Russian Way of Warfare: a primer', RAND Corporation, 2017, p. 10, https://www.rand.org/content/dam/rand/pubs/perspectives/PE200/PE231/RAND_PE231.pdf.

49 IISS, Military Balance+ database.

50 'V Rossii prokhodyat ispytaniya odnoy iz moshchneyshikh pushek v mire', RIA Novosti, 17 December 2019, https://ria.ru/20191217/1562466756.html. See also the interview with Dmitry Semizorov, CEO of Uraltransmash, at 'Dmitriy Semizorov: artustanovka "Koalitsiya-SV" obgonyayet vremya', RIA Novosti, 17 December 2019, https://ria.ru/20191217/1562434256.html.

51 'Odnu iz samykh moshchnykh pushek ispytyvayut v Rossii v uluchshennom variante', *Izvestia*, 17 December 2019, https://iz.ru/955104/2019-12-17/odnu-iz-samykh-moshchnykh-pushek-ispytyvaiut-v-rossii-v-uluchshennom-variante; Alexey Leonkov, 'Vystrelil i skrylsya: zachem nuzhny novyye samokhodki "Lotos" i "Drok"', *Rossiyskaya Gazeta*, 22 July 2019, https://rg.ru/2019/07/22/

vystrelil-i-skrylsia-zachem-nuzhny-novye-samohodki-lotos-i-drok.html.

52 For information on Russian artillery modernisation, see Anton Lavrov, 'Russia's Military Reforms from Georgia to Syria', Center for Strategic and International Studies, November 2018, p. 12, https://csis-website-prod. s3.amazonaws.com/s3fs-public/ publication/181106_RussiaSyria_WEB_ v2.pdf?sM_hVtQoqs4_TTU9rSTS_sDJJvcB. IPg; Michael Peck, 'The Big Guns are Here: Russia is Bringing Back Its Cold War "God of War" Heavy Artillery', *National Interest*, 20 September 2018, https://nationalinterest.org/blog/buzz/ big-guns-are-here-russia-bringing-back-its-cold-war-god-war-heavy-artillery-31607; Charles Bartles, 'Russian Heavy Artillery: Leaving Depots and Returning to Service', *OE Watch*, vol. 8, no. 9, September 2018, https://community.apan.org/wg/tradoc-g2/ fmso/p/oe-watch-issues; 'Odnu iz samykh moshchnykh pushek ispytyvayut v Rossii v uluchshennom variante', *Izvestia*, 17 December 2019.

53 'Dmitriy Semizorov: artustanovka "Koalitsiya-SV" obgonyayet vremya', RIA Novosti.

54 Roger McDermott, 'Russia's Iskander Missile System and the Collapse of the INF Treaty', Eurasia Monitor, Jamestown Foundation, 22 January 2020, https://jamestown.org/program/ russias-iskander-missile-system-and-the-collapse-of-the-inf-treaty; 'V Yuzhnom voyennom okruge sformirovana novaya raketnaya brigada', BMPD blog, 19 March 2019, https://bmpd.livejournal. com/3574400.html.

55 Although doubt has been cast on this by some analysts: see Dmitry Stefanovich, Twitter, https://twitter.com/KomissarWhipla/ status/1216123867191808000.

56 Douglas Barrie, 'Ground-launched cruise missiles, Europe and the end of the INF Treaty?', IISS Military Balance Blog, 15 February 2019, https://www.iiss.org/ blogs/military-balance/2019/02/inf-treaty-ground-launched-cruise-missiles; Alexey Ramm and Bogdan Stepavoy, 'Raketnoye

ob' yedineniye: brigadam "Iskanderov" uvelichili ognevuyu moshch', *Izvestia*, 16 December 2019, https://iz.ru/952462/ aleksei-ramm-bogdan-stepovoi/ raketnoe-obedinenie-brigadam-iskanderov-uvelichili-ognevuiu-moshch.

57 Grau and Bartles, 'The Russian Way of War: Force Structure, Tactics, and Modernisation of the Russian Ground Forces', p. 260; Connolly and Bouleague, 'Russia's New State Armament Programme: Implications for the Russian Armed Forces and Military Capabilities to 2027', p. 25.

58 Lester Grau and Charles Bartles, 'The Russian Reconnaissance Fire Complex Comes of Age', Changing Character of War Centre, University of Oxford, May 2018, http://www.ccw.ox.ac.uk/blog/2018/5/30/ the-russian-reconnaissance-fire-complex-comes-of-age.

59 *Ibid.*; Roman Kresul and Alexey Ramm, 'Po sledu drona: "Iskandery" poluchat "glaza i ushi"', *Izvestia*, 21 August 2019, https:// iz.ru/912228/roman-kretcul-aleksei-ramm/ po-sledu-drona-iskandery-poluchat-glaza-i-ushi; Bogdan Stepovoy and Anton Lavrov, '"Penitsillin" idot v razvedku: artilleriyu navedut na tsel' elektronnyye kompleksy', *Izvestia*, 6 May 2020, https://iz.ru/1007743/ bogdan-stepovoi-anton-lavrov/ penitcillin-idet-v-razvedku-artilleriiu-navedut-na-tcel-elektronnye-kompleksy; Anton Lavrov, in 'Russia's Military Reforms from Georgia to Syria', Center for Strategic and International Studies, 2018, p. 8, writes that the ground forces have tested in Syria a prototype UAV with a laser designator for guided artillery shells. In 'The Russian Way of War', Lester Grau and Charles Bartles have an extended discussion of Russia's artillery modernisation (pp. 260–5).

60 See 'Radioelektronnaya bor'ba: na strazhe efira', Rostec, 15 April 2020, https://rostec. ru/news/pomekhi-v-efire-o-radioelek-tronnoy-borbe.

61 IISS, *The Military Balance 2020*, p. 14.

62 *Ibid.*, p. 15.

63 Grau and Bartles, 'The Russian Reconnaissance Fire Complex Comes of Age', p. 14.

64 Ray Finch, 'Strengthening Russian Army

Ground Mobility', *OE Watch*, vol. 9, no. 9, September 2019, p. 3, https://community. apan.org/wg/tradoc-g2/fmso/p/oe-watch-issues.

65 Alexander Kolpakov and Ivan Abakumov, 'Rossiyskaya armiya gotovitsya forsirovat' reki Yevropy', *Vzglyad*, 30 July 2019, https:// vz.ru/society/2019/7/30/989911.html; 'Pontonno-mostovyye polki i remontnyye batal'ony vernutsya v vooruzhennyye sily Rossii', *Kommersant*, 29 July 2019, https:// www.kommersant.ru/doc/4046269.

66 Not last because the 2014 Military Doctrine indicates, in paragraph four, that it takes into account a number of other documents 'up to 2020'. See 'The Military Doctrine of the Russian Federation', 25 December 2014, https://rusemb.org.uk/press/2029.

67 Grau and Bartles, 'Factors Influencing Russian Force Modernisation', p. 2.

68 Alexei G. Arbatov, 'The Transformation of Russian Military Doctrine: Lessons Learned from Kosovo and Chechnya', The Marshall Center Papers, no. 2, July 2000, https://www.marshallcenter.org/ en/publications/marshall-center-papers/ transformation-russian-military-doctrine-lessons-learned-kosovo-and-chechnya/ transformation-russian-military.

69 'Voyennaya doktrina Rossiyskoy Federatsii', Security Council of the Russian Federation, 2014, http://www.scrf. gov.ru/security/military/document129; Margarete Klein, 'Russia's New Military Doctrine: NATO, the United States and the "Colour Revolutions"', SWP Comments, February 2015, https://www.swp-berlin. org/fileadmin/contents/products/ comments/2015C09_kle.pdf; 'The Military Doctrine of the Russian Federation', 25 December 2014, https://rusemb.org.uk/ press/2029; Dara Massicot, 'Anticipating a New Russian Military Doctrine in 2020: What it Might Contain and Why it Matters', War on the Rocks, 9 September 2019, https://warontherocks.com/2019/09/ anticipating-a-new-russian-military-doctrine-in-2020-what-it-might-contain-and-why-it-matters; and Stephen Main discusses the 2000 doctrine in this CSRC pamphlet: S.J. Main, 'Russia's Military

Doctrine', Conflict Studies Research Centre, Occasional Brief 77, April 2000, https://www.files.ethz.ch/isn/96824/00_Apr.pdf.

70 'Voyennaya doktrina Rossiyskoy Federatsii', Security Council of the Russian Federation.

71 Ibid.

72 Keir Giles, 'The Military Doctrine of the Russian Federation 2010', Research Review, NATO Defense College Research Division, February 2010, p. 7, http://www.ndc.nato.int/news/news.php?icode=126; 'Voyennaya doktrina Rossiyskoy Federatsii', Security Council of the Russian Federation.

73 There is an element of continuity here, of course, with Soviet-era discussions on rapid mobility in war, given – for instance – the limitations of the mobilisation system. Peter Vigor's book Soviet Blitzkrieg Theory (London: Macmillan Press, 1983) contains useful material relating to Soviet-era discussions of mobility and surprise in war. Meanwhile, in 2019, CGS Gerasimov indicated that Russia's strategy of 'active defence' still included military (as well as non-military) means acting on the basis of surprise, decisiveness and continuity of strategy action. See Dave Johnson, 'General Gerasimov on the Vectors of the Development of Military Strategy', Russian Studies Series 4/19, NATO Defence College, http://www.ndc.nato.int/research/research.php?icode=585.

74 'Aeromobil'naya gruppa soyedineniya YUVO v Dagestane otrabotala posadku v vertolet i vysadku', Ministry of Defence of the Russian Federation, 27 December 2019, http://contract.mil.ru/sel_contract/news/more.htm?id=12209835@egNews&_print=true. This referred to an exercise including the motor-rifle unit of the 58th Army (Vladikavkaz) that was, according to Russian analysts, the 136th Separate Motor-rifle Brigade (Buynaksk). See the blog of Moscow-based think tank CAST ('Aeromobil'nyye gruppy v sostave motostrelkovykh batal'onov', BMPD, 24 January 2020, https://bmpd.livejournal.com/3913090.html).

75 See Valery Gerasimov, 'Vectors of the development of military strategy', Krasnaya Zvezda, 4 March 2019, http://redstar.ru/

vektory-razvitiya-voennoj-strategii/; Johnson, 'General Gerasimov on the Vectors of the Development of Military Strategy'; Massicot, 'Anticipating a New Russian Military Doctrine in 2020: What it might contain and why it matters'. Also see Aleksandr V. Rogovoy and Keir Giles, 'A Russian View on Landpower', Letort Papers, Strategic Studies Institute, US Army War College, April 2015, https://publications.armywarcollege.edu/pubs/2329.pdf.

76 'Vystupleniye nachal'nika General'nogo shtaba Vooruzhennykh Sil Rossiyskoy Federatsii – pervogo zamestitelya Ministra oborony Rossiyskoy Federatsii generala armii Valeriya Gerasimova na otkrytom zasedanii Kollegii Minoborony Rossii 7 noyabrya 2017 g', Ministry of Defence of the Russian Federation, 7 November 2017, https://function.mil.ru/news_page/world/more.htm?id=12149743%40egNews.

77 Ministry of Defence of the Russian Federation, 'Vozdushno-desantnyye voyska segodnya', https://www.mil.ru/files/files/85vdv/vdvtoday.html.

78 Alexey Nikolsky, 'Minoborony sobirayetsya udvoit' chislennost' Vozdushno-desantnykh voysk', Vedomosti, 6 August 2014, https://www.vedomosti.ru/politics/articles/2014/08/07/udvoenie-vdv.

79 V.I. Shaykin, 'Istoriya sozdaniya i puti razvitiya vozdushno-desantnykh voysk: ot rozhdeniya do pochtennogo vozrasta', Ryazan Higher Aircraft Command School, 2013, p. 206, http://www.rvvdku-vi.ru/assets/files/knigi/elita_2.pdf.

80 See, for example, Michael Kofman, 'Rethinking the Structure and Role of Russia's Airborne Forces', Russia Military Analysis: A Blog on the Russian Military, 30 January 2019, https://russianmilitaryanalysis.wordpress.com/2019/01/30/rethinking-the-structure-and-role-of-russias-airborne-forces; 'Prinyata novaya kontseptsiya razvitiya VDV', VPK, 1 September 2014, https://vpk-news.ru/news/21638; Alexsey Zakvasin, '"My vozrodim diviziyu": kak izmenyatsya Vozdushno-desantnyye voyska Rossii k 2030 godu', Russia Today, 7 May 2018, https://russian.rt.com/russia/article/510528-vdv-

plan-razvitiya-shamanov.

81 Kofman, 'Rethinking the Structure and Role of Russia's Airborne Forces'.

82 Zakvasin, '"My vozrodim diviziyu": kak izmenyatsya Vozdushno-desantnyye voyska Rossii k 2030 godu'; 'V VDV sformiruyut pyatuyu diviziyu: Obshchaya chislennost' desantnikov budet uvelichena', TASS, 22 February 2019, https://tass.ru/armiya-i-opk/6146423.

83 Ministry of Defence of the Russian Federation, 'Armeyskaya aviatsiya, podrazdeleniya protivovozdushnoy i protivoraketnoy oborony voydut v formirovaniya VDV', 16 November 2018, https://structure.mil.ru/structure/forces/airborne/news/more.htm?id=12204365@egNews.

84 Vadim Selemenev, 'O prichinakh rasformirovaniya 105-y gvardeyskoy vozdushno-desantnoy Venskoy Krasnoznamennoy divizii', Desantura, 2 November 2010, https://desantura.ru/articles/25705/?PAGEN_2=2; 'Den' Vozdushno-desantnykh voysk v Rossii', RIA Novosti, 2 August 2012, https://ria.ru/20120802/713733392.html; IISS, The Military Balance 2012 (Abingdon: Routledge for the IISS, 2012), p. 192.

85 Yuri Gavrilov, 'Parashyut na tanke: Na baze VDV sozdadut "bystryye" voyska', Rossiyskaya Gazeta, 1 June 2015, https://rg.ru/2015/05/30/armiya-site.html; Igor Zotov, 'Mobil'nyy obereg derzhavy', Krasnaya Zvezda, 2 August 2017, http://archive.redstar.ru/index.php/newspaper/item/33982-mobilnyj-obereg-derzhavy; Alexander Pinchuk, 'Pered krylatoy gvardiyey otkryvayutsya novyye gorizonty', Krasnaya Zvezda, 1 August 2018, http://redstar.ru/pered-krylatoj-gvardiej-otkryvayutsya-novye-gorizonty; Alexander Tikhonov, 'Desant narashchivayet mobil'nost' i moshch'', Krasnaya Zvezda, 22 February 2019, http://redstar.ru/desant-narashhivaet-mobilnost-i-moshh.

86 'VDV Rossii v 2014 godu popolnilis' brigadoy spetsnaza i tremya batal'onami razvedki', TASS, 1 January 2015, https://tass.ru/armiya-i-opk/1682653.

87 Shaykin, 'Istoriya sozdaniya i puti razvitiya vozdushno-desantnykh voysk: ot rozh-

deniya do pochtennogo vozrasta', p. 199; Konstantin Rashchepkin, 'Net sily, sposobnoy nas uderzhat: Segodnya – Den' Vozdushno-desantnykh voysk', *Krasnaya Zvezda*, 2 August 2003, http://old.redstar. ru/2003/08/02_08/1_01.html; Konstantin Rashchepkin, 'VDV – Voyska Dlya Voyny', *Krasnaya Zvezda*, 2 August 2005, http:// old.redstar.ru/2005/08/02_08/3_01.html; Konstantin Rashchepkin and Viktor Pyatkov, 'Gordimsya sluzhboy V VDV', *Krasnaya Zvezda*, 2 August 2006, http://old. redstar.ru/2006/08/02_08/1_01.html.

88   'Vladimir Shamanov: VDV Rossii gotovy k resheniyu boyevykh zadach', RIA Novosti, 2 August 2010, https://ria. ru/20100802/260908344.html.

89   Olga Kirillova, 'Desantnikov perevedut na kontraktnuyu osnovu v uskorennom rezhime', *Kommersant*, 31 July 2013, https://www.kommersant.ru/doc/2245188; Alexander Tikhonov, '"Golubyye berety" Rossii: 2 avgusta desantniki so svoyst-vennym im razmakhom otmetili Den' VDV', *Krasnaya Zvezda*, 3 August 2016, http:// archive.redstar.ru/index.php/newspaper/ item/29874.

90   Gavrilov, 'Parashyut na tanke: Na baze VDV sozdadut "bystryye" voyska'; Ministry of Defence of the Russian Federation, 'Komanduyushchiy VDV prinyal uchastiye v rasshirennom zasedanii Kollegii Minoborony Rossii', 18 December 2018, https://function.mil.ru/news_page/world/ more.htm?id=12208660@egNews.

91   'Perspektivy "krylatoy pekhoty" Vozdushno-desantnyye voyska poluchat BMD-4M, BTR "Rakushka", modern-izirovannyy "Sprut" i upravlyayemyye parashyuty', VPK, 6 August 2013, https:// vpk-news.ru/articles/16986; Zakvasin, '"My vozrodim diviziyu": kak izmenyatsya Vozdushno-desantnyye voyska Rossii k 2030 godu'.

92   'Minoborony RF planiruyet zakupit' 69 kompleksov "Topol'-M" do 2015 goda', RIA Novosti, 13 July 2006, https://ria.ru/20060713/51302181.html; 'Gosudarstvennyye programmy vooruz-heniya Rossii. Dos'ye', TASS, 26 February 2018, https://tass.ru/info/4987920.

93   Alexsey Krivoruchko, 'Put' v novoye desya-tiletiye', *Radioelectronic Technologies*, no. 1, 2020, p. 6, http://www.promweekly.ru/ archive/kret/KRET_1-2020.pdf.

94   'V soyedineniya i voinskiye chasti VDV postupayet novoye vooruzheniye i voyen-naya tekhnika', Ministry of Defence of the Russian Federation, 2 February 2011, https://function.mil.ru/news_page/ country/more.htm?id=10831822@egNews. Interestingly, Dmitry Gorenburg's blog, on 29 March 2020 and reporting on Defence Minister Shoigu's 'government hour', indicated that 'modern' equipment accounted for only 16% of the total, with serviceable equipment accounting for 47%. Moreover, the housing crisis arising from the cuts in officer numbers was also worse than admitted at the time. See 'The Rest of Government Hour', Russian Defense Policy, 29 March 2020, https:// russiandefpolicy.com/2020/03/29/the-rest-of-government-hour.

95   Tikhonov, 'Desant narashchivayet mobil'nost' i moshch''.

96   Anton Lavrov, 'Voyska tumannogo naznacheniya', *Kommersant*, 8 February 2010, p. 58, https://www.kommersant.ru/ doc/1475967.

97   'Nikolay Ignatov: VDV po komande budut v lyuboy tochke Arktiki v nuzhnoye vremya', RIA Novosti, 13 July 2017, https:// ria.ru/20170713/1498419173.html; Alexander Tikhonov, 'Krylataya gvardiya vykhodit na poligony', *Krasnaya Zvezda*, 28 May 2018, http://redstar.ru/krylataya-gvardiya-vyhodit-na-poligony.

98   Pinchuk, 'Pered krylatoy gvardiyey otkryvayutsya novyye gorizonty'; Victor Khudoleev, 'Krylataya gvardiya v boyu ne drognet', *Krasnaya Zvezda*, 14 November 2018, http://redstar.ru/krylataya-gvardiya-v-boyu-ne-drognet.

99   Khudoleev, 'Krylataya gvardiya v boyu ne drognet'; Tikhonov, 'Desant narashchivayet mobil'nost' i moshch''.

100 See Charles Bartles, 'Airborne Operations in the Tsentr-2019 Exercise', *OE Watch*, November 2019, p. 11, https://community. apan.org/wg/tradoc-g2/fmso/m/oe-watch-articles-singular-format/333626.

101 Ministry of Defence of the Russian Federation, 'Ministr oborony Rossii podvel itogi ucheniya "Tsentr-2019"', 15 November 2019, https://function. mil.ru/news_page/country/more. htm?id=12262127@egNews.

102 Mikhail Ivanov, '"Vezhlivyye lyudi" otmechayut godovshchinu', *Gazeta*, 27 February 2017, https://www.gazeta.ru/ army/2017/02/27/10547549.shtml.

103 There were (and are) other special forces, such as the KGB's 'Alfa' and 'Vympel' units (now subordinate to the Federal Security Service), while today's Foreign Intelligence Service (SVR) has its own 'Zaslon' unit.

104 It was only after reforms launched in 2013 by CGS Gerasimov and GRU Colonel-General Igor Sergun that unconventional warfare 'became part of the spetsnaz forces' toolkit'. See Alexey Ramm, 'Russian Military Special Forces', in Ruslan Pukhov and Christopher Marsh (eds), *Elite Warriors: Special Operations Forces from Around the World* (Moscow: EastView Press, 2017), p. 3.

105 Their introduction in the 1950s was, some analysts contend, prompted by Western states' introduction of long-range battle-field missiles. See, for example, Bartles and Grau, *The Russian Way of War: Force Structure, Tactics, and Modernisation of the Russian Ground Forces*, p. 279; Mark Galeotti, 'Spetsnaz: Operational Intelligence, Political Warfare, and Battlefield Role', George C. Marshall European Center for Security Studies, February 2020, https://www.marshallcenter. org/en/publications/security-insights/ spetsnaz-operational-intelligence-political-warfare-and-battlefield-role-0; Roger McDermott, 'Putin's Secret Force Multiplier: Special Operations Forces, International Centre for Defence and Security – Estonia', 15 May 2016, https:// icds.ee/putins-secret-force-multiplier-special-operations-forces.

106 Kvachkov was to gain wider public atten-tion when he was arrested in 2005 after allegedly planning to murder former deputy prime minister Anatoly Chubais. He was jailed in 2013 for creating a terrorist group, though this conviction was annulled in 2019.

107 Alexey Nikolsky, 'Russian Special Forces: Eight Years and Three Wars', in Ruslan Pukhov and Christopher Marsh (eds), *Elite Warriors: Special Operations Forces from Around the World* (Moscow: EastView Press, 2017), p. 24.

108 See Grau and Bartles, 'The Russian Way of War: Force Structure, Tactics, and Modernisation of the Russian Ground Forces', p. 281.

109 Grau and Bartles, *ibid.*, p. 282, suggest that this command has no Western equivalent and 'that it appears more of a branch proponent than an actual functional command'.

110 Nikolsky, 'Russian Special Forces: Eight Years and Three Wars', p. 23.

111 *Ibid.*, pp. 24–6. Nikolsky estimates up to 2,500, citing available media reporting as well as documents relating to the construction of facilities at Senezh.

112 *Ibid.*, p. 28.

113 Alexey Mikhailov, 'Za "chernyy yashchik"', VPK, 14 December 2015, https://vpk-news.ru/articles/28495.

Naval forces

There is a well-established and broad consensus in defence-analytical circles about the general character and trajectory of the Russian Navy's (*Voyenno-morskoy flot*) development in recent times and into the near future. It is what some observers have described as a 'dual fleet'.[1] These are, first, submarines and small or medium-sized multi-purpose surface combatants for deterrence and defence-in-depth of Russia's home territories and near waters; and, secondly, submarines and larger, mainly legacy Soviet-era, surface combatants to project influence and at least the image of power, if not the full reality of it, close to home but also, and more importantly, in a 'blue-water' role in international seas.

However, there is less consensus on the extent to which this approach has been successful in delivering on Moscow's declared naval ambitions and in producing a full coherent set of capabilities that amount to or promise a real revival of Russian naval fortunes in the longer term. In part, this is due to different interpretations of those ambitions, set against the background of a long historical debate over the appropriate and actual role of the navy in Russia's (and, for much of the twentieth century, the Soviet Union's) overall defence strategy and posture.

Has it been essentially a supporting element of a land-dominant military, or does it and should it possess a strategic value of its own that bestows as well as reflects great-power status or ambition? Such questions also depend on what geostrategic context is considered, including scenarios of enduring competition and confrontation short of actual military action as well as full-scale armed conflict. Many of the capabilities in the current Russian naval inventory, including those more recently developed and brought into service, are particularly well suited to the former, but perhaps less so to the latter.

This divergence of views is also partly due to the considerable focus there has been on the often significant challenges faced by and delays in Russia's naval rearmament programme and what that presages for the future in terms of constraining Russia's naval potential. There is little doubt that there has been considerable reinforcement and modernisation of Russia's naval capabilities, particularly since the so-called 'locust years' in the immediate aftermath of the end of the Cold War, but the degree to which these capabilities are sustainable and amount

Key takeaways

LONG-RANGE LAND-ATTACK CAPABILITY
The advent of precision-guided conventionally armed long-range land-attack capabilities in significant numbers has increased the utility of Russian naval forces.

HYPERSONIC CRUISE MISSILES
Of further significance will be the advent of very high-speed cruise missiles in the fleet.

PRECISION STRIKE IN PERSPECTIVE
The transformation of the Russian naval forces' capabilities in long-range precision strike need to be assessed alongside those of other nations, particularly the United States.

AMBITIONS UNFULFILLED
While significant capability improvements are beginning to be delivered, Russia will still struggle to fulfil its naval ambitions.

SUBMARINE-FLEET PRIMACY
Despite delays, sustaining and modernising the submarine fleet remains at the heart of Russia's future naval-capability potential.

POWER-PROJECTION UNCERTAINTY
Growing numbers of modern blue-water surface platforms may not fully compensate for dwindling legacy assets. Future power-projection capabilities rest on the uncertain prospects for Russia's aircraft-carrier programme and new large amphibious ships, and possible increasing use of submarines in this role.

STRATEGIC PRIORITY AREAS
The Black Sea and the Mediterranean have become strategic priority areas in naval terms.

to a full revival of Russian naval power is open to debate.

In terms of the utility of naval forces in the context of Russia's overall national strategy and the navy's contribution to strategic deterrence, one game-changer that has come to the fore in the last decade is the advent of a modern long-range precision-guided land-attack cruise missile (LACM) capability – essentially the *Kalibr* family of weapons – aboard the navy's surface ships and, perhaps more importantly, on its submarines. This capability (often known as the '*Kalibr*-isation of the fleet') debuted operationally in sea-launched strikes against targets in Syria in October and December 2015.[2] The implications of this development feature

prominently in Russia's current naval doctrine and policy pronouncements. However, for Moscow, what actual military and strategic effect the capability can deliver, particularly in the long term, and how exactly it fits into Russia's overall strategy, is more problematic.

Russia's actions in Ukraine and annexation of Crimea, followed by its intervention in Syria, meant that the naval aspects of its military-modernisation programme were to some extent overshadowed as the rest of the world – particularly the West – came to terms with an assertively revanchist Russia. Naval forces appeared to play only a minor supporting role in these events. There were, nevertheless, significant underlying maritime drivers behind

Moscow's actions in Crimea, which have resulted in an important rebalancing of naval power and influence in the Black Sea (and the elevation of the Black Sea Fleet's significance), the eastern Mediterranean and beyond – for so long a neglected theatre in terms of Russia's naval activity and prioritisation. The revival of Moscow's naval presence in the Mediterranean is likely to bolster, but will also benefit from, Russia's military footprint in Syria – not least the port of Tartus.

The subsequent assertiveness of Russia's naval activity in more general terms, on the back of its recent capability reinvestment, has also prompted a refocus on the place of the navy in Moscow's designs, more than making up for any

Figure 4.1: **Russian Navy: '*Kalibr*-isation' of the fleet**

RUSSIAN VESSELS IN SERVICE ARMED WITH 3M14T/K *KALIBR*-NK/PL (SS-N-30A)

PROJECT NUMBER	RUSSIAN DESIGNATION	NATO DESIGNATION	TYPE	QUANTITY	FLEET(S)	ENTERED SERVICE
885	*Yasen*	*Severodvinsk*	SSGN	1	Northern	2015
06363	*Varshavyanka*	Improved *Kilo*	SSK	7	Black Sea; Pacific	2014–19
677	*Lada*	*Petersburg*	SSK	1	Northern	2010
22350	n.k.	*Gorshkov*	FFGHM	2	Northern	2018–20
11356	n.k.	*Grigorovich*	FFGHM	3	Black Sea	2016–17
11661K	n.k.	*Gepard* II	FSGM	1	Caspian	2012
21631	*Buyan-M*	*Sviyazhsk*	FSGM	8	Caspian; Baltic; Black Sea	2014–19
22800	*Karakurt*	*Uragan*	FSG	2	Baltic	2018–19
TOTAL				**25**		

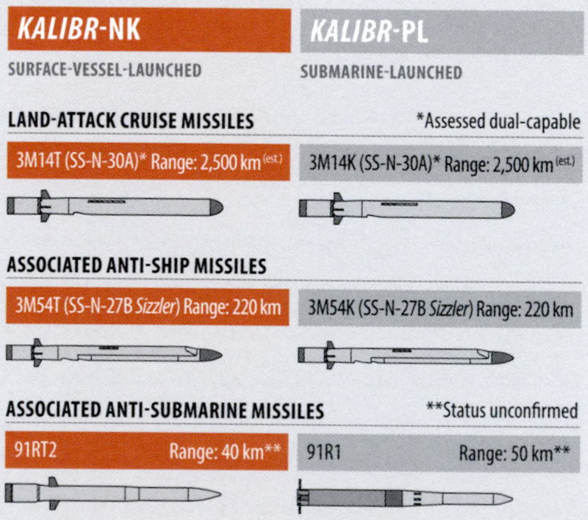

KALIBR-NK
SURFACE-VESSEL-LAUNCHED

KALIBR-PL
SUBMARINE-LAUNCHED

LAND-ATTACK CRUISE MISSILES   *Assessed dual-capable

| 3M14T (SS-N-30A)* Range: 2,500 km (est.) | 3M14K (SS-N-30A)* Range: 2,500 km (est.) |

ASSOCIATED ANTI-SHIP MISSILES

| 3M54T (SS-N-27B *Sizzler*) Range: 220 km | 3M54K (SS-N-27B *Sizzler*) Range: 220 km |

ASSOCIATED ANTI-SUBMARINE MISSILES   **Status unconfirmed

| 91RT2   Range: 40 km** | 91R1   Range: 50 km** |

NEW-BUILD RUSSIAN VESSELS UNDER CONTRACT THAT WILL BE ARMED WITH 3M14T/K *KALIBR*-NK/PL (SS-N-30A)

PROJECT NUMBER	RUSSIAN DESIGNATION	NATO DESIGNATION	TYPE	TOTAL QUANTITY ORDERED	QUANTITY REMAINING TO DELIVER	FLEET(S)	ORIGINALLY PLANNED TO ENTER SERVICE	ACHIEVED/ CURRENT PLANNED DELIVERY DATES	NOTES
08851	*Yasen-M*	n.k.	SSGN	8	8	Northern; Pacific	2013–18 (first six)	2020–26	
06363	*Varshavyanka*	Improved *Kilo*	SSK	6	5	Pacific	2019–21	2019–22	Second batch
677	*Lada*	*Petersburg*	SSK	5	4	Northern	2001 (first of class); 2009–10 (second and third boats)	2010; 2020–21 (second and third); 2026–27 (fourth and fifth)	Fourth and fifth boats ordered 2019
22350	n.k.	*Gorshkov*	FFGHM	8	6	Northern	2014–18	2019–25	
23550	*Ivan Papanin*	n.k.	PSOH	2	2	Northern	2019–20	2021–22	Models of class have shown it can be fitted with containerised *Kalibr*
20386	*Derzkiy*	Improved *Steregushchiy* II	FFGHM	2	2	Northern	2017–18	2020–21	
21631	*Buyan-M*	*Sviyazhsk*	FSGM	12	4	Black Sea	2013–23	2014–23	
22800	*Karakurt*	*Uragan*	FSG	18	16	All minus Caspian	2018–26	2018–26	
TOTAL				**61**	**47**				

Source: IISS Military Balance+

Note: missiles not drawn to scale

previous lack of attention to the maritime domain. Moreover, President Vladimir Putin's Russia has demonstrated that it is not shy about exploiting the utility of naval power, at the very least as a coercive diplomatic and deterrent tool.

Whether, how much and where Moscow is prepared to invest in that tool in the future is an open question. However, there are new capabilities on the horizon, not least in the realms of hypersonic and uninhabited or remote systems, which could result in a further step change in Russia's naval capabilities. The ability to fully exploit these technological prospects will remain constrained by the country's naval defence-industrial and technological base and infrastructure shortcomings.

Doctrinal context

There has been a long tradition in Russia of aspiring to and periodically pursuing great-power blue-water naval capabilities but regularly reverting to a more limited naval posture centred closer to home and subordinated to the requirements of primarily a great land power. This oscillation was reflected to a large extent in the early decades of the Soviet Union. However, the aftermath of the Second World War and the years of the Cold War saw the remarkable emergence of the Soviet Navy as a vast maritime force of global reach, mainly under the stewardship of its long-serving commander-in-chief Admiral Sergei Gorshkov, who occupied the post from 1956 to 1985.

There were multiple factors behind this rise, but among the more significant was the change brought about by the advent of long-range strategic nuclear weapons and the role played by nuclear-powered ballistic-missile submarines (SSBNs). As well as arguing that these and other technological changes (including the threats posed by the United States' aircraft-carrier formations and SSBNs) elevated the navy to a primary rank among the Soviet armed forces, Gorshkov became the cham-

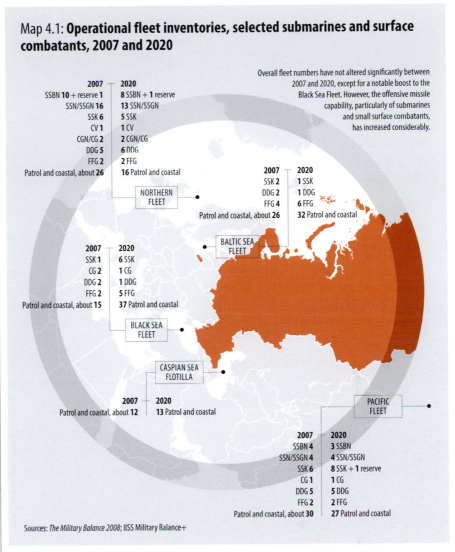

Map 4.1: **Operational fleet inventories, selected submarines and surface combatants, 2007 and 2020**

Overall fleet numbers have not altered significantly between 2007 and 2020, except for a notable boost to the Black Sea Fleet. However, the offensive missile capability, particularly of submarines and small surface combatants, has increased considerably.

NORTHERN FLEET

2007	2020
SSBN 10 + reserve 1	8 SSBN + 1 reserve
SSN/SSGN 16	13 SSN/SSGN
SSK 6	5 SSK
CV 1	1 CV
CGN/CG 2	2 CGN/CG
DDG 5	6 DDG
FFG 2	2 FFG
Patrol and coastal, about 26	16 Patrol and coastal

BALTIC SEA FLEET

2007	2020
SSK 2	1 SSK
DDG 2	1 DDG
FFG 4	6 FFG
Patrol and coastal, about 26	32 Patrol and coastal

BLACK SEA FLEET

2007	2020
SSK 1	6 SSK
CG 2	1 CG
DDG 2	1 DDG
FFG 2	5 FFG
Patrol and coastal, about 15	37 Patrol and coastal

CASPIAN SEA FLOTILLA

2007	2020
Patrol and coastal, about 12	13 Patrol and coastal

PACIFIC FLEET

2007	2020
SSBN 4	3 SSBN
SSN/SSGN 4	4 SSN/SSGN
SSK 6	8 SSK + 1 reserve
CG 1	1 CG
DDG 5	5 DDG
FFG 2	2 FFG
Patrol and coastal, about 30	27 Patrol and coastal

Sources: *The Military Balance 2008*; IISS Military Balance+

pion and chief architect of an oceanic role for the navy. It is possible to contend that this role was postulated in the context of an essentially defensive military strategy, and it is notable that it was also under Gorshkov that the 'bastion' concept of protecting the navy's strategic submarines (using heavily defended bodies of water) became a central doctrinal tenet.[3]

However, Gorshkov bequeathed to Russia an incomplete force structure, with the final pieces of the jigsaw – specifically full-size aircraft carriers – only just beginning to be put in place when the Soviet Union collapsed, with only one such vessel ever entering service. There then followed a dramatic hollowing out of the fleet, with the nadir of its fortunes perhaps symbolised by the devastating loss of the *Antey*-class (*Oscar* II) submarine *Kursk* on 12 August 2000. In 2001,

Russian SSBNs conducted just one patrol, in 2002 none.[4]

That was just a few months after Putin became president, but despite the *Kursk* setback, he displayed an ostentatious early interest in the potential of the navy to parade Russia's continuing great-power status on the world stage, even if this may have been primarily a façade at that point.[5] Like Russia's other armed forces, substantive naval modernisation and enhancement efforts came after 2008, following the lessons of the war with Georgia and in the context of an improved economy.

A number of official Russian defence and naval strategy documents, including a new maritime doctrine in 2001, have emerged since Putin's ascendance. Early on, they were already painting a broad picture of Russia's increasing interest in the maritime domain, both strategically

Figure 4.2: **Russia's naval shipbuilding programme – selected construction times**

Shipbuilding delays have had a significant impact on Russia's naval modernisation. Construction times for prototypes of the last nuclear-powered submarine designs were particularly extended. There have been recent improvements. However, deliveries of certain surface-ship designs have continued to be plagued by problems, including the supply of propulsion systems in part as a result of the Ukraine crisis. In comparison, series construction of conventionally powered submarines of the *Varshavyanka*-class (Improved *Kilo*) design appears to have proceeded relatively smoothly.

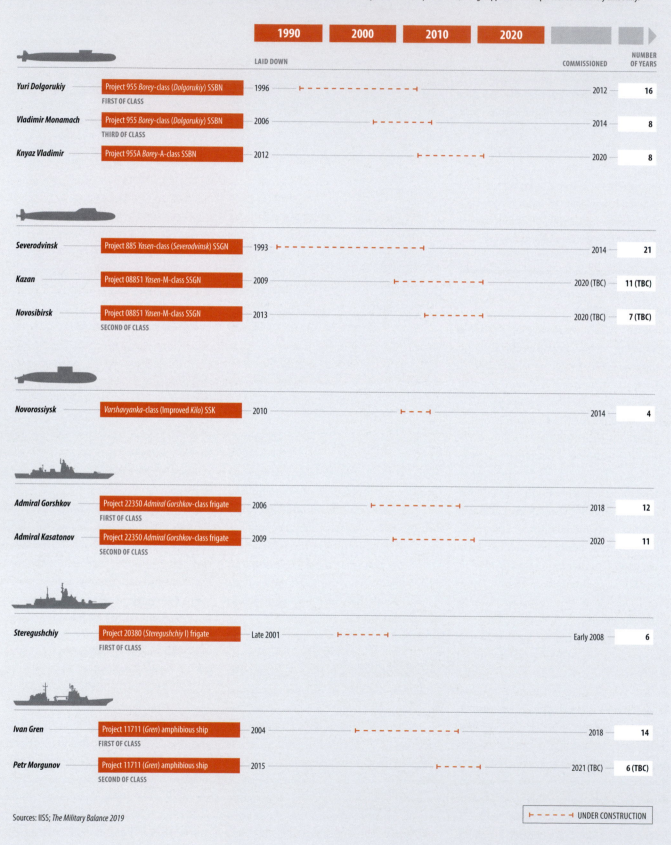

		LAID DOWN					COMMISSIONED	NUMBER OF YEARS
Yuri Dolgorukiy	Project 955 *Borey*-class (*Dolgorukiy*) SSBN — FIRST OF CLASS	1996					2012	16
Vladimir Monamach	Project 955 *Borey*-class (*Dolgorukiy*) SSBN — THIRD OF CLASS	2006					2014	8
Knyaz Vladimir	Project 955A *Borey*-A-class SSBN	2012					2020	8
Severodvinsk	Project 885 *Yasen*-class (*Severodvinsk*) SSGN	1993					2014	21
Kazan	Project 08851 *Yasen*-M-class SSGN	2009					2020 (TBC)	11 (TBC)
Novosibirsk	Project 08851 *Yasen*-M-class SSGN — SECOND OF CLASS	2013					2020 (TBC)	7 (TBC)
Novorossiysk	*Varshavyanka*-class (Improved *Kilo*) SSK	2010					2014	4
Admiral Gorshkov	Project 22350 *Admiral Gorshkov*-class frigate — FIRST OF CLASS	2006					2018	12
Admiral Kasatonov	Project 22350 *Admiral Gorshkov*-class frigate — SECOND OF CLASS	2009					2020	11
Steregushchiy	Project 20380 (*Steregushchiy* I) frigate — FIRST OF CLASS	Late 2001					Early 2008	6
Ivan Gren	Project 11711 (*Gren*) amphibious ship — FIRST OF CLASS	2004					2018	14
Petr Morgunov	Project 11711 (*Gren*) amphibious ship — SECOND OF CLASS	2015					2021 (TBC)	6 (TBC)

Timeline scale: 1990 | 2000 | 2010 | 2020

⊢-----⊣ UNDER CONSTRUCTION

Sources: IISS; *The Military Balance 2019*

and economically, and renewed assertions that Russia needs a strong navy to remain a great power. Precisely what the threats facing Russia are deemed to be has evolved in response to geostrategic developments and defence-technological changes. Russia's naval strategy and policy proclamations have also lately received increasingly weighty and high-profile political endorsement.

That has certainly been true of the most important current documents. These include the latest version of the Maritime Doctrine of the Russian Federation, published in July 2015, which was announced by Putin himself, and the Fundamentals of the State Policy of the Russian Federation in the Field of Naval Operations for the Period until 2030, which was signed by Putin on 20 July 2017.[6]

Maritime doctrine, 2015

The new maritime doctrine asserts a broad ambition to safeguard national interests on the world's oceans and reinforce Russia's standing among the leading maritime powers. Moscow's priority geographical areas are also extensive, including the Atlantic, Pacific and Indian oceans, the Arctic and Antarctic, and the Caspian Sea, although it is evident that these regions are not given equal attention.

The Atlantic is clearly a major area of focus, with the maritime doctrine citing as a key factor NATO encroachment into Russia's sphere. The same is true of the Arctic, where the doctrine indicates that Russia aspires to ensure free transit access to the Atlantic and Pacific, protect economic resources and enable the commercial exploitation of the Northern Sea Route. Moscow's ambition to create an effective and permanent naval presence in the Mediterranean is highlighted, while the growing significance of the Pacific is also emphasised, including the development of friendly relations with China and other regional states. In contrast, the Indian Ocean receives rather cursory attention.

This doctrine is also a broad and to some extent ritualistic affirmation of Russia's maritime stakes and credentials across the sweep of activities, from the military to the commercial, industrial, environmental and scientific – similar to the documents that preceded it. However, it is the 2017 policy document that in many ways offers greater substance on Russia's naval ambitions and which has attracted more pointed attention and commentary.

Naval operations policy document, 2017

Much critical attention has focused on Russia's seemingly illusory declared ambition to remain the world's second-most-powerful navy and the policy's exposition of blue-water power-projection aspirations.[7] Such critiques may have some validity. However, other observers have suggested that, while both this and the maritime doctrine may express broad global ambitions, their centres of gravity lay elsewhere in a more pragmatic and achievable set of policy goals, mainly closer to home.[8]

It should be recognised that the 2017 policy document reflects a period when there had been significant progress in the modernisation of Russia's naval forces. Moreover, the capabilities vested in its submarine force, including the SSBNs, would be sufficient to preserve the Russian Navy's position as the second-ranked global naval force in terms of overall firepower, at least for the rest of the decade, although not in broader terms of general naval capability and potential.

The document asserts that Russia retains the status of a great maritime power, able to support its national interests in any of the world's oceans. It also asserts that the oceans will grow in importance, not least with the expansion of offshore economic activity on the continental shelf, as general competition between states intensifies.[9]

The military threats the document highlights are the build-up of 'strategic high-precision sea-based non-nuclear weapons systems' and sea-based ballistic-missile defence (BMD) close to Russia's shores – points that perhaps explain the high-profile but very low-level 'buzzing' of the BMD- and cruise-missile-equipped destroyer USS *Donald Cook* by two Russian Su-24 *Fencer* attack aircraft in the Baltic Sea in April 2016 (and similar incidents earlier in the Black Sea involving the same ship).[10] Particular attention is paid to the issue of what the policy document describes as the United States' 'global strike' systems, which include a major naval component.[11]

The essence of the document from a military-technical point of view is that the

TULA (DELTA IV) AND YURI DOLGORUKIY (PROJECT 955 BOREY)
Examples of ballistic-missile submarines that have been key to the rise in the navy's strategic significance from Soviet times to now.
CREDIT: Alexander Galperin/Sputnik

PROJECT 11356 (*GRIGOROVICH*) FRIGATE
Firing a 3M14T *Kalibr* cruise missile at a target in Syria from the Mediterranean Sea, June 2017. CREDIT: Russian Defense Ministry Press Service/ TASS/Getty Images

advent of new capabilities, specifically high-precision nuclear and non-nuclear weapon systems, endows the navy with a new role, or 'qualitatively new objective', within the overall Russian defence strategy – namely the ability to destroy an opponent's military and economic potential by striking vital facilities from the sea.[12] It has been suggested that this is a 'fleet on shore' capability that even Gorshkov's navy in the Cold War did not possess to the same degree.[13] The policy document also contends that the navy is one of the most effective instruments of strategic

(nuclear and non-nuclear) and conventional deterrence, including as a counter to US global-strike capabilities.[14]

Other key elements set out in the policy include: the assertion that, during a period of military escalation, the readiness to use non-strategic (i.e., tactical) nuclear capabilities is an effective deterrent; the importance of 'inter-theatre manoeuvre' and 'under-ice navigation'; the improvement in the operational capability of the Black Sea Fleet; and securing a permanent presence in the Mediterranean and other strategically important areas. The

document contends that the armed forces' modernisation and technical-development priorities should include naval strategic nuclear forces, conventional naval task groups for non-nuclear strategic deterrence and the formation of battlegroups in remote areas. Other objectives include establishing 'qualitatively new conventional forces'. There is also a clear, if brief, reference to the ambition to produce a new aircraft carrier.[15]

This policy document argues that only the presence of a strong navy will secure Russia's position in a multipolar world in the twenty-first century, and that Russia 'must possess balanced fleets in all strategic areas' by 2030.[16] However, this could be taken as either grandiose rhetoric or as a manifesto to justify the navy's position in internal defence-policy and budgetary arguments.

The reality is that Russia is not in a position to produce or operate what would traditionally be considered a balanced fleet on a scale to justify second-rank global status. Whether or not that is really the intention, or just a rhetorical flourish on top of the real core missions of the fleet, can be debated. These missions are essentially contributing to the national defence and deterrence posture; fielding and protecting a sea-based strategic nuclear force; defending Russia's maritime approaches; conducting naval diplomacy in the broad oceans; and in particular to exert influence in situations short of full armed conflict with a peer or near-peer competitor.

The naval capabilities that have been delivered in recent years and that will enter service in this decade should not be underestimated.[17] Indeed, the backbone of Russia's capabilities are clearly strategic nuclear forces and, up to 2025, long-range precision cruise missiles. Beyond 2025, hypersonic and autonomous systems will likely increasingly feature. Even so, recent experience suggests that, even if focusing on the more pragmatic elements of its naval policy ambitions, Russia will still struggle to fulfil its plans in full measure.

Figure 4.3: **Fundamentals of the State Policy of the Russian Federation in the Field of Naval Operations for the Period Until 2030**

KEY HIGHLIGHTS

- The Russian Federation still maintains the status of a great maritime power, possessing maritime potential that supports the implementation and defence of its national interests in any area of the World Ocean.

- The Navy is one of the most effective instruments of strategic (nuclear and nonnuclear) deterrence, including preventing 'global strike'.

- With the development of high-precision weapons, the Navy faces a qualitatively new objective: destruction of enemy military and economic potential by striking its vital facilities from the sea.

- The Russian Federation will not allow significant superiority of naval forces of other states over its Navy and will strive to secure its position as the second most combat capable Navy in the world.

- The primary objectives in the modernisation and development of the Navy are: a) establish a balanced Navy structure; b) maintain the combat potential of the naval strategic nuclear forces at a high level; c) establish a qualitatively new conventional naval force.

- The primary armament of the undersea, surface and coastal forces of the Navy through 2025 will be long-range high-precision cruise missiles.

- After 2025, hypersonic missiles and various unmanned autonomous systems, including unmanned underwater vehicles, will be supplied to equip the undersea, surface, and coastal forces of the Navy.

- There are plans for a naval aircraft carrier.

- By 2030 the Russian Federation must possess powerful balanced fleets in all strategic areas consisting of ships intended to carry out missions in near and far sea zones and ocean areas.

Source: Russia Maritime Studies Institute, US Naval War College

Naval forces and the Syria campaign

The Russian Navy has made two particularly high-profile interventions in the Syria campaign, one more successful than the other. However, its most significant contributions have come in other ways, including the supply of materiel.

On 7 October 2015 came the operational debut of a Russian sea-based land-attack cruise missile (LACM) capability, when 26 3M14T Kalibr-NK LACMs were launched from four minor warships in the Caspian Sea.[18] Another strike with 18 weapons from the same platforms followed on 20 November.[19] On 8 December, the submarine-launched variant of the same weapon was fired operationally for the first time by the Project 06363 Varshavyanka-class (Improved Kilo) submarine Rostov-on-Don, which launched four missiles from the eastern Mediterranean Sea.[20] There have been further sporadic missile strikes using a variety of platforms, and the Russian Navy says it has launched more than 100 such missiles.[21]

These strikes sent a significant geopolitical message to the outside world and highlighted a major element of Russia's modernised naval capability. They also underscored its potential. However, their actual operational effect may have been relatively modest. They were a reminder that Russia still has a small (but growing) number of Kalibr-equipped platforms, each with a modest (normally eight-cell) magazine capacity. For comparison, in two separate strikes against targets in Syria in April 2017 and April 2018, the US Navy launched respectively 59 and 66 Tomahawk LACMs (and nearly 300 during the missile's operational debut in 1991 in the 42-day Operation Desert Storm).[22]

The other high-profile intervention in the Syria campaign in 2016–17 was the deployment of the aircraft carrier Admiral Kuznetsov with accompanying warships, including the nuclear-powered heavy cruiser Pyotr Velikiy. The carrier had undertaken Mediterranean deployments in 2011–12 and in 2014. The timing of the later deployment leant it greater significance, helping Moscow exert diplomatic influence and signal Russia's revived great-power status. Russia's naval leadership may also have meant the deployment to reinforce its case for a continued and potentially modernised carrier capability.[23]

If the latter intention was indeed the case, the mission – the carrier's first operational deployment – may have been counterproductive. After initial international concern over the deployment, there was much comment about the carrier's poor condition. The ship deployed with nine Su-33 Flanker D and four MiG-29KR Fulcrum aircraft and a mix of Ka-27, Ka-29 and Ka-52K helicopters.[24] It operated off Syria from 8 November 2016 until early January 2017. A MiG-29 was lost in an accident on 13 November and an Su-33 on 5 December, both apparently the result of failures with the ship's arrestor gear. After that, the fixed-wing air group chiefly operated from Hmeimim air base in Syria.[25]

The lack of operational effectiveness, the loss of two aircraft in accidents and the transfer of most of the air group ashore have been well documented. However, if the deployment's core mission had been diplomatic impact, it may still have been at least a qualified success.

Of greater significance, though, in terms of Russian Navy support for the Syria campaign has been the so-called 'Syrian Express' supply operation delivering materiel and personnel from the Black Sea ports of Novorossiysk and Sevastopol to the Syrian port of Tartus. This has been sustained utilising amphibious ships of the Ropucha and Alligator classes from the Black Sea Fleet and former merchant vessels bought up as naval auxiliaries.[26]

The other key element of Moscow's involvement in Syria has been the re-establishment

TAPIR-CLASS (ALLIGATOR) LANDING SHIP ORSK
Transiting the Dardanelles en route to the Mediterranean, April 2018.
CREDIT: Engin Oren/Anadolu Agency/Getty Images

and strengthening of a persistent Russian naval presence in the Mediterranean. This is mainly centred on Black Sea Fleet units, but with ships from other fleets regularly being assigned as reinforcements. In August 2018, the navy assembled its most significant Mediterranean flotilla up to that point, in part as a show of force. It consisted of at least ten surface ships and two submarines, many of them equipped with *Kalibr* missiles. The flotilla included the *Atlant*-class (*Slava*) cruiser *Marshal Ustinov*, the navy's three *Admiral Grigorovich*-class frigates, the *Burevestnik*-class (*Krivak* II) frigate *Pytlivyy*, three *Buyan*-M (*Sviyashsk*) corvettes and two Project 06363 *Varshavyanka*-class (Improved *Kilo*) submarines.[27]

As well as providing a direct covering and supporting force for the Syria mission, this ongoing presence is clearly meant as a deterrent to US and NATO activity and has become a complicating factor in US-led and NATO operational planning in and around the eastern Mediterranean, including to support missions in Syria. The Russian Navy has continued to maintain a heightened presence in the area, including with some of its most modern platforms.

Connected to this is the other key pillar of Russia's involvement in Syria, the port of Tartus. Russia established its naval presence there under an agreement with Syria in 1971. The berths at the port have been of considerable value, although other support facilities have always been limited.[28] The Syria crisis changed that, and in January 2017 Damascus and Moscow signed a 49-year agreement for Moscow to lease and expand the Tartus facility. This decision was no doubt made with a view to improving support to Russia's Mediterranean naval presence. In December 2019 Moscow announced that it would invest 34.95 billion roubles (US$500 million) in developing Tartus.[29]

In 2015 Russia had signed an agreement with Cyprus to allow its warships access to port facilities there.[30] Although Russian vessels also call at other such ports in the Mediterranean, the further development of Tartus will be significant not just regionally but as a facility to support Russia's global naval deployments and therefore the country's broader power-projection ambitions.

ADMIRAL KUZNETSOV
The aircraft carrier whose deployment to support the Syria operation attracted much attention, in the Mediterranean Sea, November 2016.
CREDIT: Andrei Luzik/TASS/Getty Images

In organisational terms, the Russian Navy is divided into four main fleets – Northern, Pacific, Baltic and Black Sea – and the Caspian Sea Flotilla. However, the geostrategic backdrop – not least Moscow's perceptions of NATO as a threat, the resurgence of the perceived need to protect Russia's SSBN force in a revived 'bastion' concept, and the growing significance of the Arctic and a desire to protect the Northern Sea Route – have tended to reinforce the traditional primacy of the Northern Fleet.[31] The extent to which the Northern Fleet was meant as a vehicle in any actual conflict to launch a concerted battle with NATO over sea lines of communication in the North Atlantic was long debated during the Cold War. The same is now true of the revived Northern Fleet, as its capability to deter NATO forces continues to develop.[32]

The Pacific Fleet, which had been neglected over a long period and has tended to receive the least attention in recent times, has experienced a partial revival. Its strategic nuclear forces have been renewed as part of Russia's overall deterrent strategy. Meanwhile, it has received reinforcement, albeit limited, to aid in its ability to act as a reminder that Russia is a Pacific player and to forge influence and relations in the region, especially with China.[33]

The Baltic Fleet has received an injection of new capabilities as part of a general strengthening of Russia's posture in that region, while the international attention that the mass clear-out of top commanders in 2016 also received underscored the current sensitivities and geopolitical pressures in that region.[34] Nevertheless, it is perhaps the Black Sea Fleet – for so long a backwater formation – that has been the winner in terms of reinforcement. Made possible by the annexation of Crimea, the dramatic improvement in Russia's military/strategic position in the Black Sea has been founded principally in reinforced land-based systems. However, a greatly strengthened and still improving Black Sea Fleet has been a springboard to a bolstered Russian presence in and around the eastern Mediterranean and beyond.[35]

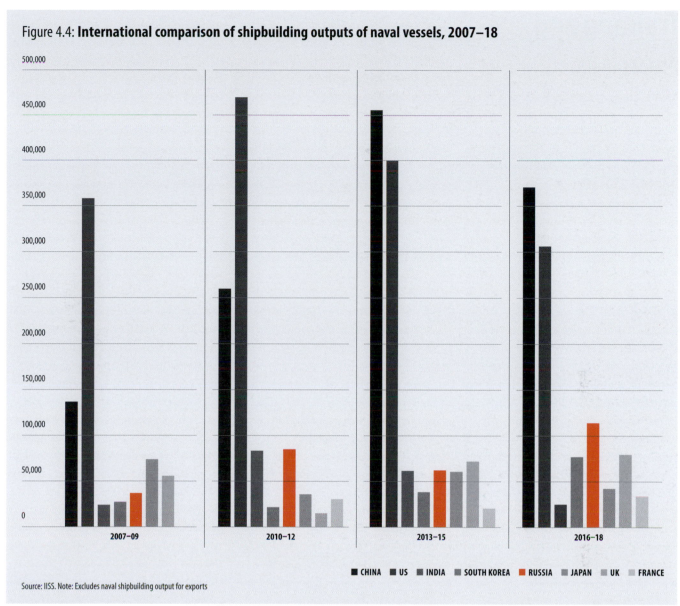

Figure 4.4: **International comparison of shipbuilding outputs of naval vessels, 2007–18**

2007–09   2010–12   2013–15   2016–18

■ CHINA ■ US ■ INDIA ■ SOUTH KOREA ■ RUSSIA ■ JAPAN ■ UK ■ FRANCE

Source: IISS. Note: Excludes naval shipbuilding output for exports

Naval rearmament plan

The major signal of a potential change in the navy's fortunes came with the introduction of the State Armament Programme (SAP) 2020, approved in December 2010 and covering the period 2011–20. It allocated 4.4 trillion roubles (US$150 billion) or 23.4% of the total funding – the largest share, excluding strategic nuclear forces – to naval rearmament.[36] The creation of a new naval force centred around newly built strategic and tactical submarines and modern and modified surface ships armed with long-range precision weapons was already an intention.[37]

The SAP aimed to produce by 2020 eight of the new Project 955 *Borey*-class (*Dolgorukiy*) SSBNs, eight multi-purpose nuclear-powered submarines, eight diesel-electric submarines and at least 50 new surface combatants, including 15 frigates. Also part of the plan were up to four French *Mistral*-class large amphibious-assault ships (LHDs).

In terms of planned upgrades to legacy Soviet-era platforms, highlights included the intended restoration and modernisation of possibly all four Project 1144 *Orlan*-class (*Kirov* I) nuclear-powered battle cruisers.[38] Only one of these cruisers was still in service at that time, with the other three supposedly 'in reserve' (although the prospects for the lead ship, *Admiral Ushakov*, were always in doubt due to its poor material state).[39]

However, the seeds of disappointment were present almost from the outset, due to the weakness of Russia's naval defence-industrial base and key supply chains, as well as the incomplete development of some new naval systems. This was compounded from 2014 by the fallout from the Ukraine crisis and Russia's annexation of Crimea, which had a disproportionate impact on the shipbuilding sector. The export to Russia of gas turbines from Ukraine and diesel generators from Germany for the main propulsion systems of a range of the navy's surface combatants stopped.[40] The subsequent downturn in the Russian economy, in part as a direct result of economic sanctions over Ukraine, further hit the navy's procurement plan.

Training and exercises

The move to a more professional force is one of the most important qualitative improvements in Russia's naval capabilities. Following the instigation of the military reforms process in 2008, pay, conditions and benefits for naval personnel also improved considerably.[41]

This increased investment in personnel, particularly from 2010 when the SAP was agreed, was accompanied by a significant rise in navy activity, including exercises, compared to previous levels (albeit from very low levels in some cases). As NATO commanders were publicly noting increased Russian submarine activity from about 2014–15, then-commander-in-chief of the Russian Navy Admiral Viktor Chirkov in June 2015 pointed to not only an increase of 30% in time under way by submarines and surface ships compared to 2013, but also a 20% rise in the number of naval exercises.[42]

The focus in terms of increased activity and exercises has been the Black Sea and Mediterranean areas, in line with Russia's increased strategic attention there. In 2016, in the aftermath of the annexation of Crimea, the Russian Navy launched ambitious amphibious manoeuvres in the Black Sea, at a time when it was also engaged in exercises with China's People's Liberation Army Navy (PLAN) in the South China Sea.[43]

A significant element of recent exercises has been the development of 'inter-fleet interoperability' – to be able to swing units from one theatre to another as required. Mixed fleet deployments to the Mediterranean provide invaluable training opportunities and thereby increase operational capability, enabling the rapid integration of different fleets in support of operations.

Further large-scale exercises have continued to develop since 2016. In August and September 2017, a large flotilla based on Russia's Northern Fleet undertook 'combat readiness' manoeuvres in parallel with the integrated *Zapad* 2017 exercises, which also involved Belarus, in and around the Baltic region.[44] A year later, the *Ocean Shield* series of naval manoeuvres was instigated, focusing first on the Mediterranean and Black seas. *Ocean Shield* 2019, which concentrated on the northern waters of the Baltic, Barents and Norwegian seas and the North Atlantic, was significantly larger than the previous year's exercise.

These exercises included significant elements aimed at developing the navy's ability to operate integrated with, in particular, the Aerospace Forces and in contested environments.[45] While *Ocean Shield* 2019 kicked off in the Baltic Sea, Russian ships also operated significantly forward into the Norwegian Sea.

Most major and minor exercises and general training appear to be undertaken in the context of developing the navy's abilities to operate as part of a joint and integrated layered defence concept designed to protect the Russian homeland. Nevertheless, there has also been conspicuous training activity both to further Moscow's message that it remains a great power and to revitalise and sustain the navy's ability to operate at range. Particularly notable in this respect has been Russia's burgeoning joint-exercise programme with China. While such exercises have been under way since the mid-2000s, they have taken on increased momentum since the events of 2012. Initially centred on Chinese home waters, in May 2015 a Russo-Chinese joint exercise was held in the Mediterranean and in July 2017 for the first time in the Baltic Sea.[46]

Also of note were joint manoeuvres between the Chinese, Iranian and Russian navies in the northern Arabian Sea in late 2019, in the wake of the renewed tensions in the region, including over international freedom of navigation. Just prior, in November 2019, the Russian missile cruiser *Marshal Ustinov*, the flagship of the Northern Fleet, conducted a first joint exercise with the Chinese and South African navies in the South Atlantic, off the Cape of Good Hope.[47]

However, perhaps the clearest signal of the navy's intention to sustain its ability to deploy globally was the deployment carried out by Russia's newest blue-water surface combatant in service with the fleet, *Admiral Gorshkov*, at the head of a small Northern Fleet flotilla. The flotilla visited the Mediterranean and the Indian Ocean, then China before returning via the eastern Pacific, the Panama Canal and Cuba.[48] However, this global deployment also underscored the navy's limited capacity to undertake such missions compared to the Chinese and US navies.

PROJECT 22350 FRIGATE *ADMIRAL GORSHKOV*
Arriving in Havana, Cuba as part of a circumnavigation cruise to demonstrate Russia's global deployment capability, June 2019.
CREDIT: Adalberto Roque/AFP/Getty Images

One of the most striking shortfalls in achieving SAP 2020's goals involves the Project 885/08851 *Yasen-/Yasen*-M nuclear-powered guided-missile submarines (SSGNs). The original plan called for eight boats to be in service by 2020. At most, only three will have been delivered to the navy by that deadline. Another notable shortfall was in the delivery of the Project 22350 (*Gorshkov*) frigates, caused by the challenges of developing and integrating new systems and the effects of the Ukrainian gas-turbine cut-off.[49]

Significantly, SAP 2020 may prove to be the high-water mark in terms of funding allocations for naval rearmament. The Coastal Missile and Artillery Forces have also benefited from the acquisition of the 3K60 *Bal* (SSC-6 *Sennight*) and 3K55 *Bastion* (SSC-5 *Stooge*) anti-ship missile systems as part of SAP 2020. The period of geostrategic upheaval and economic uncertainty following the Ukraine crisis saw the successor SAP delayed considerably. SAP 2027 was eventually approved in December 2017.

What has been reported on SAP 2027 suggests that the navy is likely to receive a reduced share of funding. One estimate has indicated that it might be only about 60% of the previous funding level, out of an overall allocation for defence procurement that was about on par with the previous programme, at least in nominal terms.[50]

This scenario suggests that it will continue to be difficult for the navy to pursue aspirations for new platform classes that were raised as prospects, such as a new destroyer class, but not progressed in any meaningful sense in the previous SAP. This will result in a basic core of Russia's strategic nuclear and conventional naval deterrence and warfighting capability centred on submarines and relatively small surface combatants, equipped with precision long-range-strike capabilities, and a blue-water force still mainly of Soviet-era legacy platforms.[51] SAP 2027 appears to reflect greater official acknowledgement of Russia's current economic realities and the limitations of what the country's still impaired shipbuilding industry can deliver.[52]

The 2027 programme can be characterised as a consolidation agenda that is more pragmatic than its predecessor, particularly as far as naval armaments are concerned.[53] Naval procurement is a long-term undertaking, both in terms of platform construction and maintaining vessels during their service lives. It would seem to be particularly so in the case of Russia.

SAP 2020 bequeathed a legacy of new ship construction that should see a significant enhancement of the navy's overall firepower, albeit behind schedule. However, precisely what the shape and overall size of the fleet will be in the future

remains uncertain. It will depend not only on the fate of new programmes but also on the prospects for sustaining the Soviet-legacy blue-water fleet on which the navy will still rely for a large proportion of its operational tonnage and global reach.

Sub-surface naval power

In 1989, as the Cold War was drawing to a close, the inventory of the Soviet Navy stood at 349 submarines, including 69 strategic submarines, and 151 principal surface combatants, including four *Kiev*- or modified *Kiev*-class hybrid aircraft carriers, 37 cruisers and 52 destroyers. Within a few years, much of this fleet was tied up and rotting or being scrapped. By 2007, on the eve of the start of Russia's military reform and modernisation push, those numbers were some 49 submarines (14 of which were SSBNs) and around 28 principal surface combatants, including the aircraft carrier *Admiral Kuznetsov*, five cruisers and 16 destroyers. By 2020, the active fleet was made up of 48 submarines, 11 of them SSBNs, and 33 principal surface combatants. The key difference is that among the fleet's current flotilla of minor warships are six platforms equipped to carry 3M14T *Kalibr*-NK (SS-N-30A *Sagaris*) dual-capable LACMs.[54]

It has been said that the Russian Navy, like the Soviet Navy before it, 'looks best

PROJECT 20380 (*STEREGUSHCHIY* I)
The name ship of the class, which has evolved into one of the most successful modern Russian surface-warship designs. CREDIT: Igor Zarembo/Sputnik

underwater'.[55] Indeed, modernising and sustaining the submarine fleet remains at the heart of the navy's future and the SSBN force is the service's highest priority. One outcome of this focus was proclaimed in June 2015 by then-commander-in-chief Admiral Chirkov, when he announced that 'combat duty deployments' of strategic submarines were up almost 50% compared to two years previously, and time under way by submarines overall and surface ships was up 30%.[56]

Admittedly, this increase is likely to have been from a low base, but it came during a period when US and NATO naval commanders were warning of levels of Russian submarine activity not seen since the Cold War.[57] Most strikingly, the then commander of the US Navy's 6th Fleet co-authored an article that spoke of a 'Fourth Battle of the Atlantic':

> Once again, an effective, skilled, and technologically advanced Russian submarine force is challenging us. Russian submarines are prowling the Atlantic, testing our defenses, confronting our command of the seas, and preparing the complex underwater battlespace to give them an edge in any future conflict.[58]

This statement was clearly meant to grab attention and encourage discussion, but it may have been counterproductive in terms of its messaging, appearing to exaggerate a threat for effect. Nevertheless, it reflected a real change in the geopolitical backdrop, the readiness of Russia's submarine forces and unease in NATO over the level of its own preparedness.

By 2010, as SAP 2020 was being finalised, in terms of SSBNs the Russian Navy had at its disposal one *Akula*-class (*Typhoon*), six *Delfin* (*Delta* IV), five *Kalmar* (*Delta* III) and the first of the new Project 955 *Borey* class (*Dolgorukiy*), *Yuri Dolgorukiy*, which was still undergoing sea trials and therefore had limited operational capability.[59] Except for the *Yuri Dolgorukiy*, all the other

boats had been commissioned between 1977 and 1990 and were between 20 and 33 years old in operational terms.

Flagship submarine programme

It is a reflection of the sometimes parlous state of even Russia's flagship submarine-building programme that the first *Borey*, which was laid down in November 1996, reportedly incorporates the bow and stern sections of an Project 09711 *Schuka*-B-class (*Akula* II) nuclear-powered attack submarine (SSN), while the second of class reportedly includes the sections of two different abandoned Project 971 *Schuka*-B-class (*Akula* I) SSNs. The first *Borey* took 16 years to complete, from start of construction to commissioning in December 2012.[60] However, a significant factor in this delay was a succession of difficulties in developing the planned principal weapon for the class, first the failed *Bark* missile programme and ultimately the *Bulava* (SS-N-32) submarine-launched ballistic missile.[61] *Bulava* was not declared operational until 2018, when the *Yuri Dolgorukiy* (which serves with the Northern Fleet) carried out a successful salvo firing of four missiles.[62]

The second boat of the class, *Alexander Nevsky*, was laid down on 19 March 2004 and commissioned nearly ten years later, transferring to the Pacific Fleet after a 42-day 'inter-theatre' transit (30 of them submerged) using the Northern Sea Route, during which the vessel supposedly remained undetected until its arrival.[63] The third *Borey*, *Vladimir Monomakh*, took just over eight years from being laid down to commissioning, and also serves with the Pacific Fleet. In both cases, the boats' transfers to the Pacific Fleet were delayed due to technical difficulties. The *Borey* class purportedly has significant enhancements over previous Russian SSBNs in terms of stealth and speed (reportedly up to 29 knots, although not on operational patrol).[64]

In 2012, keel laying began on the first of an enhanced Project 955A *Borey*-A design, *Knyaz Vladimir*, with a modified, more streamlined hull and fin configu-

ration, improved acoustic performance and manoeuvrability, and an improved weapons-control system. Four further *Borey*-A boats have been laid down and orders for a further two were expected in the near future.[65] It was originally planned to hand over *Knyaz Vladimir* to the fleet in 2017, but after a number of delays this was pushed back to June 2020.[66] The second improved boat, *Knyaz Oleg*, could be delivered before the end of 2020.[67] If these goals are achieved, it would mean a reduction in construction and delivery time of an SSBN class to under seven years.

The current construction and commissioning schedule for the *Borey* class is far from the original aspiration to have eight *Borey* submarines in service by 2020. Nevertheless, the remaining boats could be delivered between 2022 and 2025. It has also been reported that an order for two additional *Borey*-A submarines is planned; these could be ready for service before the end of the decade.[68] This could allow the progressive retirement of the remaining six *Delta* IV submarines and one *Delta* III submarine that are currently between 30 and 42 years old. Even if some of these legacy boats are retained beyond the end of this decade, a possible ten *Borey*/*Borey*-A submarines in the Russian fleet by the beginning of the 2030s would constitute a significant capability and a relatively homogeneous class of SSBNs that would be considerably newer than the US Navy's 14 ageing *Ohio*-class SSBNs. The *Ohio*s are currently scheduled to serve for about 42 years each and to start retiring in 2027 before the first of the replacement *Columbia*-class SSBNs is ready for service in 2031.[69] Indeed, by the end of that decade, Russia's SSBN force is likely to be proportionally the most modernised major arm of the naval service. There is also continuing speculation about a further update to the SSBN design called *Borey*-B and possibly an SSGN variant dubbed *Borey*-K.[70]

Despite the delays, Russia's SSBN development represents a considerable achievement, not least given that it is centred on the Sevmash shipyard at

Severodvinsk on the White Sea, Russia's sole provider of nuclear-powered submarines and the largest shipyard in the country, with just under 30,000 employees.[71] A key concern for Moscow over the coming period will be balancing the navy's production requirements with maintaining a stable and steady flow of work to sustain this critical element of Russia's naval defence-industrial base.

Yasen class

Even more than the *Borey* class, the Russian submarine programme that has captured the most attention, particularly in NATO states – at least perhaps until the debut of the heavily modified *Oscar* II submarine *Belgorod* and its *Poseidon* nuclear-armed large uninhabited underwater vehicle (UUV) – has been the Project 885/08851 *Yasen/Yasen*-M SSGNs. This was underscored by the reaction of senior US Navy officers to the arrival of the prototype vessel, *Severodvinsk*.[72] However, inevitably, the prioritisation of new SSBNs appears to have had an impact on these other major submarine programmes.

Given the lethality, firepower and stealthiness they could represent in a naval warfare context (as opposed to a strategic nuclear exchange involving SSBNs), these SSGNs are in some ways the new capital ships of the Russian Navy. Even so, the reaction to the *Yasen* class in Western states may be somewhat surprising given that the SSGN's design origins date back to the 1980s and *Severodvinsk* was first laid down in 1993. Nevertheless, the class represents a significant step forward in terms of acoustic signature and systems, and it has a considerable weapons suite consisting of eight four-cell SM-346 vertical launch tubes for 3M14K (SS-N-30A *Sagaris*) *Kalibr*-PL dual-capable LACMs and 3M54K (SS-N-27B *Sizzler*), 3M54K1 (SS-N-27) and 3M55 (SS-N-26 *Strobile*) *Onyx* anti-ship missiles.[73]

The *Yasen*-Ms incorporate several improvements and modifications compared to the prototype boat. They are some ten metres shorter and have a modi-

PROJECT 08851 *YASEN*-M CRUISE-MISSILE SUBMARINE *KAZAN*
The launch of the first improved version of this significant new class of nuclear-powered submarine, March 2017. CREDIT: Sergey Mamontov/Sputnik

fied bow design apparently incorporating a new sonar array.[74] They may also have eight instead of ten torpedo tubes.[75]

The *Severodvinsk* has remained the sole operational *Yasen* for seven years. The first *Yasen*-M has experienced an extended construction and trials period lasting ten years. Its entry into service, now expected sometime in 2020, has been delayed on several occasions.

Five more *Yasen*-Ms have been in various stages of construction and fitting out at Sevmash, and all could reasonably be expected to be in service by 2024–25. An order for a further two was placed in 2019; these vessels were both laid down in July 2020 and could also enter service before the end of the decade.[76] A force of up to nine *Yasen/Yasen*-Ms would be formidable but unlikely to completely fulfil Russia's SSGN/SSN requirements.

Legacy nuclear-powered submarines

Older boats are likely still to be required in service. However, the overhaul and modernisation of these vessels have been impacted even more than the new submarine construction plans. Chief among these plans has been the ambition to modernise the remaining eight *Antey* (*Oscar* II) submarines, and in particular to replace their 24 3M45 *Granit* (SS-N-19) anti-ship missiles with up to 72 *Kalibr*-PL missiles.[77] Reports over the years have variously spoken of all eight, six or four of the boats being converted. Such modification would turn these vessels from (albeit formidable) anti-ship threats into multi-purpose platforms. However, the indications are that possibly only two of these vessels may be undergoing such a transformation, and that the prospects for any other submarines in this class receiving the upgrade in the near future, if at all, may be limited.[78] If this is the case, it would considerably affect the navy's overall arsenal of seagoing *Kalibr* capability.

The rest of the nuclear-powered submarine fleet presents a very mixed and uncertain picture. The notional backbone of the SSN force has been 11 Project 971/971U/09711 *Schuka*-B (*Akula* I/II) commissioned between 1988 and 2001, and there has been a long-term plan to upgrade them to operate *Kalibr*.[79] However, a significant number have been essentially non-operational for several years awaiting overhaul and modernisation. One boat, *Vepr*, has emerged from refit and in early 2020 was on sea trials, and another, *Tigr*, is set to go through modernisation and emerge in 2023, apparently equipped to operate *Kalibr*.[80]

The navy also operates two Project 945A *Kondor* (*Sierra* II) SSNs from the 1990s, which have reportedly been active recently, and a single Project 945 *Barracuda* (*Sierra* I), which is reportedly kept in reserve. There are also three more elderly Project 971 Schuka (*Victor* III) in the fleet.[81] The state of the attack-submarine fleet of SSGNs and SSNs suggests that the need for a long-mooted 'fifth-generation' attack submarine is high. There has been much speculation but little concrete information about a design concept known as *Khaski* (or *Husky*), and more recently the *Laika* design displayed in model form in 2019, which may be the basis of the new attack-submarine class.[82] This class is aimed at being more affordable and less complex than the *Yasen*-M, and is possibly of a modular design, but still with considerable offensive capability, such as the ability to accommodate *Kalibr* and the *Tsirkon* hypersonic missile.

Conventional submarines

The one other area of success in the Russian submarine force has been the expanding role of conventionally powered boats (albeit not quite as originally intended by the navy). Six improved, *Kalibr*-equipped Project 06363 *Varshavyanka* (Improved *Kilo*) submarines have been delivered to the Black Sea Fleet, and a similar number of this design are destined for the Pacific Fleet. The first of these Pacific-bound boats was handed over to the navy in November 2019, the second has been on trials and is expected to join the fleet in 2020, two more are under construction at St Petersburg and the final two are expected to be laid down soon for delivery in the middle of the decade.[83]

There has been less success in Russia's efforts to develop an air-independent-propulsion (AIP) system for its conventional submarines, which was expected to be fitted to the Project 677 *Lada* class (*Petersburg*). However, an AIP system has not been brought into service and the *Lada* has not proved to be a successful design.[84] This has led the navy to persevere with its *Varshavyanka* design, which has paid dividends in terms of this class of submarine's high-profile role in the Black Sea Fleet of late, and particularly as *Kalibr*-shooters in the Syria conflict.

The prospective employment of an AIP plant on a Russian submarine still appears undecided.[85] In the meantime, the *Lada* programme continues fitfully: the lead submarine, *Sankt Peterburg*, apparently continues on sea trials some ten years after first being commissioned, while two more improved versions are now close to completion after long delays and an order for a further two was placed in June 2019.[86]

Special-mission submarines

The other potentially significant capability enhancement in the sub-surface domain will be Russia's special-mission submarines, particularly those associated with the deployment of the new *Poseidon* nuclear-armed UUV, which has excited more speculation than any other recent Russian naval weapons system. Very significant resources have clearly been devoted to this programme and its associated capabilities. The plan was for the first 'mother ship' submarine to host *Poseidon*, a heavily modified *Oscar* II boat, *Belgorod*, to begin trials in 2020, which are set to last two to three years. *Belgorod* is also able to operate other UUVs.[87] Another *Poseidon*-capable submarine, *Khabarovsk*, this time thought to be a heavily modified *Borey* design, was also scheduled for launch during 2020.[88]

It has been reported that Russia will eventually deploy 32 *Poseidon*s aboard four submarines split between the Northern and Pacific fleets.[89] The development of *Poseidon* may have much to do with Moscow's concerns about US BMD system developments, but its precise capabilities and therefore concept of operations remain obscure.

Another prominent recent addition to the specialist fleet has been the 'mother ship' submarine *Podmoskovye*, a stretched *Delta* IV submarine that hosts the deep-submersible AS-12 *Losharik*, the latter – and

PROJECT 06363 *VARSHAVYANKA*-CLASS (IMPROVED *KILO*) CONVENTIONALLY POWERED SUBMARINE *ROSTOV-ON-DON*
Which became, in 2015, the first Russian submarine to launch an operational land-attack cruise-missile strike. CREDIT: Vasiliy Batanov/Sputnik

possibly also the mother ship – is thought to have been involved in a fire in the Barents Sea in July 2019 that killed 14 naval officers, raising questions about their operational status, at least for a period.[90]

These specialist vessels are operated by an organisation called the Main Directorate of Deep-Sea Research (or GUGI), which is not part of the mainstream navy and reports directly to the defence ministry. GUGI also operates oceangoing research ships such as the *Yantar* class and has special-forces divers and elite submariners.

Russia's strategic sub-surface capabilities have been enhanced by the arrival of the Project 22010 *Yantar*-class hydrographic survey ships. The first was completed in 2015 and has been engaged in a number of high-profile missions since, and a second ship, *Almaz*, is nearing completion.[91]

Together, these submarines and other vessels add up to a considerable specialist capability that places Russia in the leading rank of states developing and exploring the underwater battlespace.

Progress on the surface

In some ways, developments in the surface navy mirror those of the sub-surface fleet: significant challenges and delays in the production of new vessels, but a considerable transformation of capability now under way. At the same time, these programmes have fared considerably better than the modernisation of legacy platforms. However, the evolution of the surface fleet, and particularly the introduction of new types of vessels that have become more consequential for Russia's overall defence and naval strategies, has perhaps been more startling than has been the case in the underwater domain.

Part of the public impact of the *Kalibr* strikes on Syrian targets in October 2015 was not just that Russia had debuted a sea-launched LACM capability on operations. It was also that it had done so from very modest surface platforms quite unlike those from which the US Navy had been

PROJECT 21631 *BUYAN*-M (*SVIYAZHSK*) CORVETTE *SERPUKHOV*
One of a growing number of small modern Russian surface combatants with a powerful offensive missile armament. CREDIT: Alexander Galperin/Sputnik

regularly carrying out cruise-missile strikes for nearly two and a half decades – 950-tonne *Buyan*-M (*Sviyazhsk*) corvettes and the 1,960-tonne *Dagestan* (*Gepard* II).[92]

Small craft

From the 1960s, the Soviet Navy had a strong tradition of endowing its small near-waters patrol craft and corvettes with a powerful anti-ship cruise-missile capability, as exemplified by the *Moskit*- (*Osa*), *Molnya*- (*Tarantul*) and *Ovod*-I-class (*Nanuchka*) vessels. Some of these craft have continued to play an important and under-acknowledged part in the Russian Navy's near-waters inventory and will continue to do so for a few more years. In a sense, the navy's latest capability builds on this tradition and mindset. However, *Kalibr*'s land-attack element and the range potential of at least 1,500 kilometres are transformational.

The navy now has at least eight *Buyan*-Ms (*Sviyazhsk*) in service – each with an eight-cell 3S14 UKSK universal

vertical launch system (VLS) for 3M14T *Kalibr*-NK LACMs – with several more under construction. These ships are being joined by the more capable *Karakurt*-class (*Uragan*) boats, which have the same eight-cell VLS installation, the first of which commissioned in December 2018.[93] It is reported that at least 18 *Karakurt*s are planned, although delivery continues to be held up by problems with the supply of Russian-made diesel engines.[94] Nevertheless, there are set to be at least 30 vessels of these two classes in the fleet.

Frigates

The prototype of the successful 2,200-tonne multipurpose Project 20380 (*Steregushchiy* I) frigate commissioned in 2008. Nine subsequent improved ships of this class are either under construction or in service. Perhaps more significantly, an outgrowth of these designs has been two Project 20385 *Gremyashchiy*-class frigates, the first of which is in trials, which add an eight-cell 3S14 UKSK universal

PROJECT 22350 (*GORSHKOV*) FRIGATE *ADMIRAL GORSHKOV*
The first of a new breed of blue-water surface combatant that is likely to play a big part in Russia's future naval line-up. CREDIT: Peter Kovalev/ TASS/Getty Images

VLS to their equipment, enabling the use of *Kalibr*.[95] However, any plans for further ships were complicated because of engine-supply problems and the need to substitute Russian diesels for the German units that were blocked due to sanctions.[96] The design has been further developed into the 3,400-tonne Project 20386 *Derzkiy* class (Improved *Steregushchiy* II), which is also expected to be *Kalibr*-capable, and of which three are apparently planned.[97]

Replacing legacy platforms

As a result of the lack of investment in both shipbuilding programmes and infrastructure development in the 1990s and early 2000s, when policy changes and renewed funding opened the way to the possibility of reviving its fleet of larger blue-water-capable ships, the Russian Navy had limited options. The navy only had a core

of outwardly impressive-looking legacy blue-water platforms used for naval diplomacy and prestige deployments. The design that emerged to recapitalise the navy's blue-water capability and begin to replace some of the older legacy platforms was what has become the 5,400-tonne Project 22350 *Admiral Gorshkov*-class frigates. This design was aimed at being multipurpose, in contrast to the previous generation of specialist platforms.

However, the *Gorshkov* class has been subjected to a particularly tortuous production process that has resulted in the project becoming the poster child for Russia's naval-modernisation struggles.[98] This was caused by Russia's endemic shipbuilding shortfalls and, as the navy had fallen behind in terms of manufacturing equipment for larger oceangoing platforms, the need to concurrently develop and incorporate new

systems. In addition, the Ukrainian gas-turbine-supply cut-off and the requirement to develop and switch to a Russian supply chain has been a compounding problem. Related complications included the development of a new area air-defence system, the 3K96-2 *Poliment-Redut* (SA-N-28), and its integration into the rest of the *Gorshkov*'s systems.[99] The basic ship design also includes two eight-cell 3S14 UKSK VLSs for *Kalibr*-NK.

The name ship of the class, *Admiral Gorshkov*, finally commissioned in July 2018, 12 years after having been laid down. This marked the end of a near-two-decade hiatus in the commissioning of a fully fledged blue-water vessel into the Russian Navy.[100] However, production has fallen far short of the original hope of six ships commissioned by 2020. The ultimate ambition is to have 15–20 *Gorshkov*-class ships in the fleet.

As a stopgap because of delays in the *Gorshkov* programme, the navy embarked in 2010 on a plan to build six relatively modest 4,000-tonne Project 11356 *Admiral Grigorovich*-class frigates, based on the *Talwar*-class frigates built for the Indian Navy (and all ultimately derived from the *Krivak* series of frigates). This promised a well-balanced, well-armed (with an eight-cell 3S14 UKSK VLS for *Kalibr*) class of six medium-sized frigates, but it too has been beset by the problem of gas-turbine supply. Three vessels have been completed, and the first two have maintained Russia's naval presence in the Mediterranean Sea. Another two are being completed for India, which will itself build a further two of the class for its own navy.[101]

The number of modern blue-water-capable surface combatants in Russia's navy therefore remains low but should steadily grow during this decade with further deliveries of *Gorshkov*-class ships. The second ship in the class, *Admiral Kasatonov*, finally commissioned in July 2020. The first four ships have been or will be completed to the original design. The next four will be to a modified design, with 24 instead of 16 UKSK VLS launch cells.[102] It is also reported that subsequent vessels will be completed

Figure 4.5: **Principal surface combatants: generational change**

During the Soviet era, the navy developed its principal surface combatants into specialist roles. The *Sovremenny* class was developed in the 1970s as a surface-warfare platform and was complemented by the near-contemporary Project 1155 *Fregat*-class (*Udaloy*), which had a greater focus on anti-submarine warfare. The new *Admiral Gorshkov* class stems from a different design philosophy aiming for a more multi-purpose platform, enabled by new weapons systems and the adoption of vertical-launch-system technology. Although the first genuinely blue-water surface combatants to emerge since the Cold War, the *Admiral Gorshkov* class is significantly more compact than the last-generation Soviet principal surface combatants. However, some growth is anticipated in later class variants in order to incorporate greater firepower.

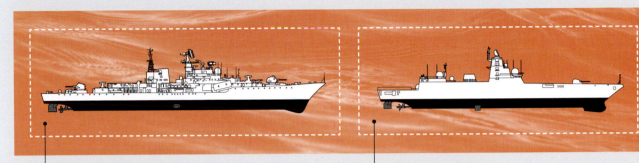

PROJECT 956 *SARYCH* (*SOVREMENNY* I)

- Full-load displacement: 8,000 tonnes

- Length overall: 156 metres

- First entered service: 1980

- Armament:
  - **2** quad launchers with 2M80 *Moskit* (SS-N-22 *Sunburn*) anti-ship missile
  - **2** twin 3S90 launchers with 9M317 *Yezh* (SA-N-7B) surface-to-air missile
  - **2** twin DTA-53-956 533mm torpedo tubes with 53-65K heavy-weight torpedo/SET-65K heavy-weight torpedo
  - **2** RBU 1000 *Smerch* 3 anti-submarine mortar
  - **4** AK630 close-in weapons system
  - **2** twin AK130 130-mm guns
  - Capacity: **1** Ka-27 *Helix* anti-submarine-warfare helicopter

PROJECT 22350 (*GORSHKOV*)

- Full-load displacement: 5,400 tonnes

- Length overall: 135 metres

- First entered service: 2018

- Armament:
  - **2** 8-cell 3S14 UKSK vertical launch system with 3M14T *Kalibr*-NK (SS-N-30A) dual-capable land-attack cruise missile/3M54T (SS-N-27 *Sizzler*) anti-ship missile/3M54T1 (SS-N-27) anti-ship missile/3M55 *Oniks* (SS-N-26 *Strobile*) anti-ship missile/91RT2 anti-submarine missile
  - **4** 8-cell 3S97 vertical launch system with 3K96-2 (SA-N-28) surface-to-air missile
  - **2** quad 324mm torpedo tubes with MTT lightweight torpedo
  - **2** 3M89 *Palash* close-in weapons system (CADS-N-2)
  - **1** A-129M *Armat* 130-mm gun
  - Capacity: **1** Ka-27 *Helix* anti-submarine-warfare helicopter

Source: *The Military Balance 2020*

---

to an enlarged, potentially 8,000-tonne design with 48 UKSK cells.[103]

Design work on these vessels – informally dubbed 'Super *Gorshkovs*' – has been under way since about 2013, although the plan for such ships was first publicly announced by then-commander-in-chief Admiral Chirkov in December 2014.[104] The ships appear to have been an on–off project ever since. If they are to proceed now, they are unlikely to appear in the fleet until the late 2020s or early 2030s.

The fate of the Super *Gorshkov* project is inextricably linked with Moscow's level of ambition to revive the navy's blue-water capabilities more broadly and therefore to proceed with other often-mooted major warship projects. Foremost among these are Russia's intentions in terms of its aircraft-carrier capability.[105]

Aircraft carriers

Russia, and the Soviet Union before it, has had a changeable attitude towards aircraft carriers. Soviet leader Nikita Khrushchev was famously dismissive of their value and vulnerability. However, he appointed Gorshkov to head the navy, who did as much as anyone to advance the case of large aviation-capable platforms. The admiral did this through the acquisition of a series of hybrid platforms leading to the construction of the 59,000-tonne *Admiral Kuznetsov* (or *Riga* as it was initially) with an estimated capacity of up to 39 fixed-wing aircraft and helicopters. A second ship was only completed in 2012 as part of China's People's Liberation Army Navy and a larger nuclear-powered vessel did not get beyond the early construction stage before the dissolution of the Soviet Union

saw the project cancelled and the unfinished ship scrapped.

Officially designated a heavy aircraft-carrying cruiser, *Kuznetsov* as built did not qualify as a pure aircraft carrier in the Western and particularly US sense, given the amount of installed weaponry (including 3M45 *Granit* (SS-N-19 *Shipwreck*) anti-ship missiles), which curtailed the ship's aviation capacity. However, for most observers, the distinction is over-precise.

The ship's subsequent service, in strictly operational terms, has been unspectacular and dogged by a reputation for unreliability. Yet the amount of speculation there has been over the years about the ship's prospects and plans for a potential successor or successors is a testament to the power of the aircraft carrier as a symbol of maritime great-power status, even or perhaps especially in Russia.

Naval aviation

Much of the discussion about the possibilities for Russia's naval aviation capability focuses on the prospects for the aircraft carrier *Admiral Kuznetsov* and its air group. However, the centre of gravity of Russia's maritime air-power aviation lies elsewhere, not least in its land-based air elements and in components not operated by the navy.

In 2016–17, *Admiral Kuznetsov* deployed on the Syria operation with a modest mixed air group that included a total of 13 fixed-wing aircraft, nine Su-33 *Flanker* Ds (air-superiority fighters with a limited air-to-ground capability) and four modern and multi-role MiG-29KR *Fulcrum*s. The air wing also included Ka-27 anti-submarine warfare (ASW) and Ka-31 airborne early-warning (AEW) helicopters, while the Ka-52K attack helicopter made its operational debut aboard the carrier.

The navy's Su-33 (17 aircraft) and MiG-29KR/KUBR (22 aircraft) inventories severely limit its operational air-power potential, even without issues of aircrew availability and carrier operational qualification, which have been significant problems.[106] If Russia is to possess an adequate naval aviation capability, much will depend not only on the fate of the carrier itself, but also on what level of investment there will be in new aircraft and particularly pilot numbers and training.

During the Soviet era, the navy operated regiments of long-range missile-armed bombers, culminating in the Tu-22M3 *Backfire* C medium supersonic bomber equipped with the Kh-22 (AS-4 *Kitchen*) anti-ship missile. All the older Tu-22s have been retired and the remaining 60 newer Tu-22s were transferred to the Long-Range Aviation component of the Aerospace Forces in 2011. However, they retained the anti-ship role. Thirty of the airframes are due to be modernised to Tu-22M3M standard, able to launch the Kh-32 (AS-4A mod) anti-ship missile.[107] The first modernised aircraft was delivered in 2018.[108]

Also in the maritime-strike role, naval aviation operates the Su-24M *Fencer* and increasing numbers of replacement Su-30SM *Flanker* H aircraft with each of its main fleets.[109] These latter are capable of carrying the Kh-31 (AS-17B *Krypton*) anti-ship missile.

In terms of long-range maritime patrol, naval aviation is undertaking upgrades to the Tu-142 *Bear*-F and Il-38 *May* aircraft. However, this is an area of relative weakness, particularly in the context of ASW. The inventory of these aircraft is estimated at 44, made up of 12 Tu-142MK/MZ *Bear* F, ten Tu-142MR *Bear* J, 15 Il-38 and seven upgraded Il-38N *May* aircraft.[110]

This is also the case in terms of the navy's shipborne ASW capability, in the shape of the venerable Ka-27 *Helix* helicopter. However, an updated 'digitised' version, the Ka-27M, is reported to be entering service during 2020, with the first units going to the Baltic Sea Fleet.[111]

In the absence in refit of the *Kuznetsov*, Ka-31 AEW helicopters have been deployed with the Black Sea Fleet, including aboard at least one surface combatant at sea.[112] This may be a way of deploying these aircraft in a dispersed way in order to enhance Russia's AEW capabilities among the different fleets when the carrier is not available.

The troubled progress of *Admiral Kuznetsov*'s latest refit suggests that the ship will not be available to return to the fleet before 2022 at the earliest. Even then, and despite the refit, its readiness and serviceability – and indeed its long-term prospects, notwithstanding the continuing prestige value of operating a carrier – are likely to be open to question. A key factor may be whether the navy's proposed new large amphibious-assault ships materialise, and what power-projection capability they could potentially deliver in combination with Ka-52K attack and Ka-31 AEW helicopters.

In May 2005, then navy commander-in-chief Admiral Vladimir Kuroyedov announced a plan to build at least two new aircraft carriers (one for the Northern Fleet, one for the Pacific Fleet), with construction starting in 2010 for service to begin from 2016–17.[113] Furthermore, the intention for construction to begin in 2010 was reinforced in 2008 by then-president Dmitry Medvedev.[114] In 2009, the navy was discussing developing five to six aircraft-carrier groups by 2050–60.[115]

Such ambitions appeared to fly in the face of the realities: whether there were the facilities to undertake such a programme, given the loss of the Ukrainian shipyards that had previously built such ships, and the fact that there appeared to be no funding in the then-current SAP to start such a project.[116] Nevertheless, the ambition for a new aircraft carrier was explicitly stated in the 2017 navy policy document.

The subsequent economic downturn in Russia, and the poor showing of *Kuznetsov* on its deployment to the eastern Mediterranean, may have encouraged the sceptics, including then-first deputy prime minister Dmitry Rogozin.[117] However, the navy is working to keep the aircraft-carrier idea alive, and in recent years competing future concepts have emerged. In 2015, the Project 23000 *Shtorm* design of 90,000–100,000 tonnes, rivalling US carriers in size, was revealed.[118] Another new heavy aircraft-carrier design, the 80,000–90,000 tonne Project 11430 *Lamantin*, was displayed at the St Petersburg International Naval Show in July 2019, along with a design for a smaller 44,000-tonne vessel.[119] The different designs have claimed onboard aircraft capacities ranging from 46 to 90 aircraft.

Funding reportedly exists in SAP 2027 for research and development on a new aircraft carrier, and a recent report suggests a possible order for a new carrier in 2025.[120] In January President Putin was observed viewing a display on Russia's future aircraft-carrier plans.

Russia's own long-range precision-weapons developments mean it has been among the countries to pose questions about the future utility and survivability of aircraft carriers in a full great-power military confrontation. As these weapons designs evolve, such questions will surely weigh in the deliberations over carriers in Moscow. Russia seems likely to be reluctant to give up on its aircraft-carrier ambitions, not least because of carrier-procurement plans under way elsewhere in the world but also because carriers continue to show their value in a range of disparate contingencies. Nevertheless, the prospect of a new Russian carrier capability emerging before the 2030s seems unlikely.

The prospects for *Kuznetsov* will be influenced by and have a bearing on these deliberations. The ship is currently in a refit that has been notable for a number of accidents and delays. The scope of the refit was also drastically cut to save costs and is being limited chiefly to repairs of the main machinery, including new boilers, with plans to upgrade electronics and other systems scrapped.[121] The carrier is unlikely to emerge before 2021. However, if some of the ship's reliability issues have been addressed, it is possible it could play a useful role well into the 2030s.

Cruisers and destroyers

An important element in the prospects for the navy's future carrier capability is the need to invest not just in the ship (and its air group) but also the supporting features. For Russia, this is tied up with replacing its ageing fleet of large cruisers and destroyers. Most of these are currently equipped with legacy weapons systems that would likely not perform well in a modern, contested maritime environment.

The focus in recent years has been the now almost-mythical Project 23560 *Lider*-class destroyer, a design concept that has evolved into an extraordinary 17,000–19,000-tonne nuclear-powered vessel of cruiser proportions.[122] However, scepticism about the need for and practicalities of such a design, including Russia's ability to build and afford it, suggest that it is unlikely to turn into a realistic proposition.[123] *Lider* design work appeared to have stopped in 2020. Although the same apparently also occurred on the Project 22350M Super *Gorshkov*, that programme is more mature (and less ambitious) and more likely to come to fruition, especially as the navy will need such a vessel in the long run to replace its older ships.[124]

Unfortunately for the navy, aspirations for instead modernising many of the fleet's large legacy platforms have yielded negligible results amid rising doubts about the cost-effectiveness of this approach. The highest hopes, and biggest disappointment, up to now

have centred on the modernisation of the *Orlan*-class (*Kirov* I) heavy nuclear-powered cruiser *Admiral Nakhimov*. The ship has been awaiting refurbishment since the late 1990s. Talk of a refit in the mid-2000s appeared to come to nothing. After reports of further modernisation progress, work appears only to have begun in earnest in 2015, initially with a plan to finish in 2018.[125] The current stated completion date is 2021 but is more likely to be 2022 at the earliest.[126] However, this modernisation is expected to yield a ship able to carry up to 80 *Kalibr* – or ultimately even hypersonic *Tsirkon* – missiles.

Meanwhile, the planned refit of the only *Kirov*-class ship to remain operational, *Pyotr Velikiy*, looks set to proceed in the near future. However, there still may be questions over this modernisation, which could – like that of the *Kuznetsov* – be curtailed on cost grounds, and when the ship may return to service afterwards. However, the navy would surely want to keep such a prestigious warship in service.

Second only in size to the *Kirov*s are the three *Atlant*-class (*Slava*) cruisers, which have seen significant service in terms of maintaining a deployed high-profile Russian naval presence, not least in the Mediterranean. Of these, *Marshal Ustinov* emerged from an overhaul and modest modernisation in 2016.[127] *Moskva*, the oldest of the three, is also emerging from a refit that could keep it in service until the end of the 2020s, by which time the ship (and more pointedly its weapons systems) will be 47 years old. The prospect of the significant modernisation of any of these ships appears slender, even if they continue to fulfil a prestige role for the navy.

Russia's remaining oceangoing surface fleet is made up of the *Sarych*- (*Sovremenny* I) and *Fregat*-class (*Udaloy* I) ships. Seventeen *Sovremenny* destroyers were originally built but only three remain in service and their futures appear limited, while the *Udaloy* I has in many ways been the workhorse of the oceangoing fleet.[128] At the same time, ambitions to modernise

the eight remaining *Udaloy* I (including one modified *Udaloy* II) have been significantly delayed from the last decade to the present one.[129] At best, fewer than the full number may be modified, although those that are should be transformed from being 'large anti-submarine ships' into multi-purpose vessels, including the fitting of the 3S14 UKSK VLS, and be re-rated from destroyers to frigates.

Marshal Shaposhnikov, whose five-year refit has finally been completed, is believed to be the first of the *Udaloy*-I class to undergo this transformation. If the modernisation programme goes ahead, it could yield a significant supplement of multi purpose blue-water platforms, albeit ageing ones. However, the programme is likely to be a protracted one, which may raise doubts as to whether it will ever be entirely fulfilled.[130]

Amphibious vessels

Despite the navy's efforts, the least modernised arm of the Russian surface fleet has been its amphibious ships. The mainstays of the amphibious flotilla have been the large *Ropucha*- and *Ropucha* II-class landing ships built between the 1970s and early 1990s. In the early 2000s, a new class of Project 11711 (*Gren*) large landing ships was planned. However, the first ship, *Ivan Gren*, commissioned only in June 2018 after 14 years under construction. The sea trials and commissioning of a second ship, *Pyotr Morgunov*, have been delayed by technical difficulties.[131]

This design is likely now to be limited to just two vessels. Instead, two ships of an improved design were laid down in April 2019, although there are already reported delays over the design modifications.[132] Potentially of greater significance, in July 2020 Russia laid down two 'Universal Landing Ships' or LHDs of approximately 25,000 tonnes.[133] This revives the navy's ambition that was originally to have been met by the now-aborted deal with France for at least two *Mistral*-class LHDs. (The *Mistral* deal was stopped because of the Ukraine crisis and the two completed ships were eventually sold to Egypt.)

Supposedly, these Universal Landing Ships could be ready in 2026 and 2027. However, such reports and forecasts should be treated with caution. Nonetheless, the construction of at least two modern LHDs, which would be by far the largest warships built for the Russian Navy since the Cold War, could provide an earlier and more cost-effective boost to Russia's naval power-projection capability than, for example, focusing entirely on a new aircraft-carrier programme. Particularly if paired with the new Ka-52K attack helicopter and the Ka-32 anti-submarine helicopter, the LHDs would be impressive, flexible platforms.

Such additions could herald a shift in the potential role of Russia's Naval Infantry. The new amphibious ships certainly go hand in hand with some modernisation of the equipment and upgrading of units of the Naval Infantry, notably those with a focus on Arctic operations, like the 61st Naval Infantry Brigade attached to the Northern Fleet. The Naval Infantry does not compare either in scale or role with the US Marine Corps. However, it represents a relatively elite force now totalling five brigades and a regiment.

Reportedly, Naval Infantry units have been engaged in Ukraine and Syria. However, in their traditional role they have been focused more on relatively short-range coastal defence and manoeuvre missions. The bolstering of their own capabilities, and the advent of more capable amphibious ships, could see a shift to a more expeditionary role.

Another structural weakness that has held back Russia's blue-water and power-projection capabilities, both in Soviet times and now, has been the relative lack of afloat support. The Russian practice has generally been to replenish fuel while under way using a bow/stern method, which is far less efficient than the abeam method favoured in major Western navies. However, the handing over in January 2020 of the abeam-

replenishment-equipped *Akademik Pashin*, the first of the Project 23130 replenishment tankers and the first such vessel to be delivered since the Cold War, suggests a significant evolution in replenishment capability.[134] Five more Project 23130 vessels are planned.[135] However, the design is a modest 9,000 tonnes full-load displacement, and this hardly compares, for example, with the large investment China has been putting in to developing its afloat-support capability in pursuit of its own blue-water naval ambitions.

Counting the *Kalibrs*, counting on *Tsirkon*

Beyond its sea-based strategic nuclear forces, so much of the potential strategic effect that the Russian Navy will be able to yield appears to be based around the *Kalibr*-isation of the fleet, that investment in long-range precision strike that has been at the heart of Russian policy planning for at least a decade. However, for all the impact that has had and attention it has received, what it means in capability terms is not clear-cut.

The number of *Kalibr*-capable vessels in service with the fleet has fallen far short of initial expectations. For example, it can be estimated that as of the end of 2019 the Russian Navy had in service around 20 vessels (submarines and small and medium surface combatants) with the capacity to launch with either VLS cells or torpedo tubes some 180 *Kalibr* missiles of different variants.[136] Although that is not the totality of the navy's precision offensive-strike capabilities, particularly in terms of anti-ship systems, it is still a relatively modest overall capability.

The navy is undoubtedly on the cusp of a significant transformation as many of its delayed shipbuilding programmes begin to bear fruit. Even given the experience of shortfalls, it would be reasonable to calculate that by the end of this decade the navy will be able to field in service the launch capacity for 1,550 *Kalibr* or

equivalent weapons, using VLS cells or torpedo tubes, from more than 80 vessels, including submarines and small, medium and large surface ships, many of them powerful new platforms.

To put this in context, the US Navy at the end of 2019 boasted some 10,276 VLS cells aboard submarines and surface ships capable of firing *Tomahawk* land-attack cruise missiles (TLAMs).[137] That may be only a notional figure, since most of the Mk 41 and Mk 57 VLSs on the US surface ships would be given over to Standard SM-2, -3 and -6 air-defence and BMD missiles. Nevertheless, even if only a quarter of the surface-ship cells were given over to housing TLAMs, that would leave a total potential of 3,445 TLAMs across the fleet, as well as room for 6,831 Standard Missiles to defend against incoming missile salvoes.

However, there is another potential game-changer on the horizon in the shape of hypersonic weapons. The first test-launch of Russia's *Tsirkon* hypersonic missile from a ship took place in February 2020 from the frigate *Admiral Gorshkov* in the Barents Sea, and the missile reportedly flew in excess of 500 km.[138] An accelerated programme of further tests is said to be planned. Submarine trials are expected by 2024–25, aboard a *Yasen*-M.[139] The clear intention is to deploy the missile widely among submarines and ships currently equipped or being built to operate *Kalibr*. The addition of hypersonic weapons in numbers would represent a significant challenge to any potential adversary.

Enduring weaknesses
Despite this, there are enduring weaknesses in the fleet's make-up, including in anti-submarine-warfare (ASW) capability – potentially a critical area, given the navy's priority missions of defending Russia's maritime approaches and protecting the country's at-sea strategic nuclear forces. These weaknesses will be addressed somewhat with the arrival of new platforms such as submarines and additional

Figure 4.6: **Russia's 'Kalibr corvette' revolution**

The introduction of new corvette designs with a heavy offensive missile capability, including land-attack cruise missiles, has been a particular feature of the country's naval modernisation programme, in some ways shifting the balance of the fleet's capabilities.

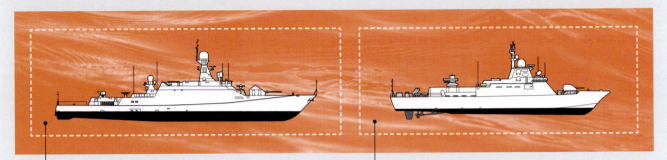

PROJECT 21631 *BUYAN*-M (*SVYAZHSK*)

- Approximate full-load displacement: 950 tonnes

- Length overall: 74 metres

- Armament:
  - **1** 8-cell 3S14 UKSK vertical launch system
    - 3M14T *Kalibr*-NK (SS-N-30A *Sagaris*) land-attack cruise missile
    - 3M54T (SS-N-27B *Sizzler*) long-range anti-ship missile
    - 3M54T1 (SS-N-27) long-range anti-ship missile
    - 3M55 *Oniks* (SS-N-26 *Strobile*) long-range anti-ship missile
  - **2** x sextuple 3M47 *Gibka* ship-guided missile launch system
    - *Igla*-1M (SA-N-10 *Grouse*) point-defence surface-to-air missile
  - **1** AK630M-2 close-in weapons system
  - **1** 100-mm A-190-01 naval gun

PROJECT 22800 *KARAKURT* (*URAGAN*)

- Approximate full-load displacement: 800 tonnes

- Length overall: 67 metres

- Armament:
  - **1** x 8-cell 3S14 UKSK vertical launch system
    - 3M54T (SS-N-27B *Sizzler*) long-range anti-ship missile
    - 3M54T1 (SS-N-27) long-range anti-ship missile
    - 3M55 *Oniks* (SS-N-26 *Strobile*) long-range anti-ship missile
    - 3M14T *Kalibr*-NK (SS-N-30A) land-attack cruise missile
  - **2** AK630M close-in weapons system (later ships equipped with *Pantsir*-M SAM)
  - **1** 76-mm AK-176MA naval gun

Source: *The Military Balance 2020*

Gorshkovs and *Steregushchiys* and developments of those designs. But the reported development of an anti-submarine variant of the *Karakurt* class (*Uragan*) may be acknowledgement that more needs to be done in this area.[140] Another uncertainty is the extent to which Russia continues to pursue non-acoustic approaches to ASW, such as wave tracking, and the degree to which advances in data processing, for example, could enhance the effectiveness of such approaches.[141]

While much attention has been focused on the fact that Russia's new generation of small surface combatants punch above their weight in terms of offensive firepower, concern has also been expressed domestically about their vulnerability in a peer or near-peer engagement, due in particular to a lack of air-defence capability. Hence, it is planned that later vessels in the *Karakurt* class will be armed with the *Pantsir*-M air-defence system.[142]

Beyond these endeavours, a key element of the effectiveness of the fleet, as it is being constituted for near-waters operations, is the integration of naval elements with other elements, including missile batteries and land-based air defence. Efforts continue to develop these capabilities.[143]

Whatever the specific limitations of the Russian Navy's developing inventory in terms of full-spectrum capabilities and the ability to generate balanced fleets for blue-water operations as referenced in the latest policy declaration, there is no doubt that these new capabilities will pose challenges for potential adversaries. Even a single *Yasen*-M submarine in the North Atlantic or a handful of smaller combatants in waters around the peripheries of Russian territories, armed with *Kalibr* or more significantly *Tsirkon*, would pose problems and exert pressure or influence in both periods of tension short of armed conflict and during an actual armed confrontation.

Conclusion

Both in strategic terms and in the detail of capability and equipment, there has been a considerable gap between some of Russia's declarations of naval ambition and the reality of what has been delivered. However, that is not to deny that considerable capability improvements have been achieved. In that sense, Russia's naval ambitions should perhaps not be taken literally, but they should be taken seriously.

For all the alarm expressed in NATO states and elsewhere about a Russian naval resurgence in the last decade, the results palpably failed to live up to Russia's own modernisation goals. But, because of programmes set in motion, the coming decade could produce significantly more in terms of actual capability transformation, albeit within certain limits. Yet this will depend on continued funding.

The limits of achievable modernisation may not produce a truly global navy, but they could produce a naval force that is well adapted to the reality of what Russia most likely is – an assertive major regional power with a desire for some global reach. The Russian Navy may be in poor shape relative to the highest levels of official ambition and that of the Soviet Navy during the Cold War, but it may be well adapted to the actual needs and approach of the state. The investments being made in terms of weapons systems are certainly in line with those of an assertive foreign policy.

Putin has shown himself to be enamoured of the potential of naval power as an instrument of policy. Whatever the navy's long-term trajectory, he may ultimately be interested in it more as a diplomatic lever for deterrence and display than as a robust war-fighting instrument. Nevertheless, that type of navy still requires a significant level of investment if it is to have enduring effect.

Beyond the navy's overall effectiveness, a key factor in its utility recently has been Putin's willingness to use it boldly, even aggressively, as observed in Syria. However, as other navies continue to develop their own capabilities and the balance of power at sea evolves, there may be only a limited window of opportunity for the Russian Navy to adapt further, retain its strategic influence and replace those legacy capabilities on which it still relies before they become increasingly exposed and turn into liabilities.

Notes

1 Richard Connolly, 'Towards a Dual Fleet? The Maritime Doctrine of the Russian Federation and the Modernisation of Russian Naval Capabilities', NATO Defense College Russian Studies, June 2017, http://www.ndc.nato.int/news/news.php?icode=1061.

2 Lee Willett, 'Game changer: Russian sub-launched cruise missiles bring strategic effect', *Jane's International Defence Review*, 27 April 2017, https://janes.ihs.com/Janes/Display/idr19220-idr-2017.

3 For a discussion of this, see Bryan Ranft and Geoffrey Till, *The Sea in Soviet Strategy* (London: Palgrave Macmillan, 1983), pp. 71–83.

4 Milan Vego, 'The Russian Navy revitalized', *Armed Forces Journal*, 1 May 2009, http://armedforcesjournal.com/the-russian-navy-revitalized.

5 Thomas R. Fedyszyn, 'Putin's "Potemkin-Plus" Navy', *US Naval Institute Proceedings*, vol. 142, no. 5, May 2016, https://www.usni.org/magazines/proceedings/2016/may/putins-potemkin-plus-navy.

6 'Maritime Doctrine of the Russian Federation', Russia Maritime Studies Institute, US Naval War College, July 2015, https://digital-commons.usnwc.edu/cgi/viewcontent.cgi?article=1002&context=rmsi_research; 'Fundamentals of the State Policy of the Russian Federation in the Field of Naval Operations for the Period until 2030', Russia Maritime Studies Institute, US Naval War College, July 2017, https://digital-commons.usnwc.edu/rmsi_research/2.

7 Dmitry Gorenburg, 'Russia's New and Unrealistic Naval Doctrine', War on the Rocks, 26 July 2017, https://warontherocks.com/2017/07/russias-new-and-unrealistic-naval-doctrine.

8 Liv Karin Parnemo, 'Russia's Naval Development – Grand Ambitions and Tactical Pragmatism', *Journal of Slavic Military Studies*, vol. 32, no. 1, January 2019, https://www.tandfonline.com/doi/abs/10.1080/13518046.2019.1552678.

9 'Fundamentals of the State Policy of the Russian Federation in the Field of Naval Operations for the Period until 2030', pp. 3–4.

10 *Ibid.*, p. 5; Phil Stewart, 'Russia jets make "simulated attack" passes near US destroyer: US', Reuters, 13 April 2016, https://www.reuters.com/article/us-usa-russia-simulate-dattack-idUSKCN0XA1UW.

11 'Fundamentals of the State Policy of the Russian Federation in the Field of Naval Operations for the Period until 2030', p. 11.

12 *Ibid.*, p. 12.

13 Richard Connolly, 'Fundamentals of the State Policy of the Russian Federation in the Field of Naval Operations for the Period until 2030, Document Review', NATO Defence College, Russian Studies Series, January 2019, http://www.ndc.nato.int/research/research.php?icode=574.

14 'Fundamentals of the State Policy of the Russian Federation in the Field of Naval Operations for the Period until 2030', p. 11.

15 *Ibid.*, pp. 14–15.

16 *Ibid.*, p. 15.

17 Michael Kofman and Jeffrey Edmonds, 'Why the Russian Navy is a more capable adversary than it appears', *National Interest*, 22 August 2017, https://nationalinterest.org/feature/why-the-russian-navy-more-capable-adversary-it-appears-22009.

18 'Russian missiles "hit IS in Syria from Caspian Sea"', BBC News, 7 October 2015, https://www.bbc.co.uk/news/world-middle-east-34465425.

19 'Syria crisis: massive Russian air strikes on "IS targets"', BBC News, 20 November 2015, https://www.bbc.co.uk/news/world-europe-34882503.

20 Christopher P. Cavas, 'Russian Submarine Hits Targets in Syria', *Defense News*, 8 December 2015, https://www.defensenews.com/breaking-news/2015/12/08/russian-submarine-hits-targets-in-syria.

21 Interfax, 'Russian navy commander gives details about Syria operation', BBC Monitoring, 8 February 2018, https://monitoring.bbc.co.uk/product/c1d0swrp.

22 Michael R. Gordon et al., 'Dozens of US missiles hit air base in Syria', *New York Times*, 6 April 2017, https://www.nytimes.com/2017/04/06/world/middleeast/us-said-to-weigh-military-responses-to-syrian-chemical-attack.html; 'US-led strikes on Syria: what was hit?', BBC News, 16 April 2018, https://www.bbc.co.uk/news/world-middle-east-43769332; Norman

Polmar and Thomas B. Allen, 'Naval weapon of choice', *USNI Naval History*, February 2016, https://www.usni.org/magazines/naval-history-magazine/2016/february/naval-weapon-choice.

23 Neil MacFarquhar, 'Russian Carrier is bound for Syria, Flexing Muscle but Risking Malfunction', *New York Times*, 21 October 2016, https://www.nytimes.com/2016/10/22/world/europe/russia-admiral-kuznetsov-syria.html.

24 Anton Lavrov, 'The Russian air campaign in Syria: a Preliminary Analysis', CNA, June 2018, pp. 24–5, https://www.cna.org/CNA_files/PDF/COP-2018-U-017903-Final.pdf.

25 Sean O'Connor, Jeremy Binnie and Tim Ripley, 'Russian carrier jets fly from Syria, not Kuznetsov', *Jane's Defence Weekly*, 1 December 2016, https://janes.ihs.com/Janes/Display/jdw63916-jdw-2017.

26 Jonathan Saul and Maria Tsvetkova, 'Russia supplies Syria mission with old cargo ships bought from Turkey', Reuters, 15 December 2015, https://www.reuters.com/article/us-russia-syria-ships/russia-supplies-syria-mission-with-old-cargo-ships-bought-from-turkey-idUSKBN0TY2BG20151215.

27 *Izvestia*, 'Daily says Russian warships in Mediterranean meant to "stop US"', BBC Monitoring, 28 August 2018, https://monitoring.bbc.co.uk/product/c2006fe0.

28 Christopher Harmer, 'Russian Naval Base Tartus', Institute for the Study of War backgrounder, 31 July 2012, http://www.understandingwar.org/sites/default/files/Backgrounder_Russian_NavalBaseTartus.pdf.

29 Henry Foy, 'Russia to invest $500m in Syrian port of Tartus', *Financial Times*, 17 December 2019, https://www.ft.com/content/f52bdde6-20cc-11ea-b8a1-584213ee7b2b.

30 'Cyprus signs deal to allow Russian navy to use ports', BBC News, 26 February 2015, https://www.bbc.co.uk/news/world-europe-31632259.

31 Pavel K. Baev, 'Threat Assessments and Strategic Objectives in Russia's Arctic Policy', *Journal of Slavic Military Studies*, vol. 32, no. 1, January 2019, https://www.tandfonline.com/doi/full/10.1080/13518046.2019.1552662.

32 Igor Sutyagin, 'Russia's New Maritime Doctrine: Attacking NATO's Sea Lanes of Communication in the Atlantic – Sustainability, Future Capabilities and Potential Countermeasures', RUSI Defence Systems, 28 August 2015, https://rusi.org/publication/rusi-defence-systems/russia%E2%80%99s-new-maritime-doctrine-attacking-nato%E2%80%99s-sea-lanes.

33 Igor Delanoë, 'Russia's Navy in the Pacific: the Forgotten Fleet?', *US Naval Institute Proceedings*, vol. 144, no. 7, July 2018, https://www.usni.org/magazines/proceedings/2018/july/russias-navy-pacific-forgotten-fleet.

34 Ivan Nechepurenko, 'Russia fires dozens of military officers in Baltic region', *New York Times*, 30 June 2016, https://www.nytimes.com/2016/07/01/world/europe/russia-fires-dozens-of-military-officers-in-baltic-region.html.

35 Michael Petersen, 'The Naval Power Shift in the Black Sea', War on the Rocks, 9 January 2019, https://warontherocks.com/2019/01/the-naval-power-shift-in-the-black-sea.

36 IISS, *The Military Balance 2013* (Abingdon: Routledge for the IISS, 2013), pp. 202–03.

37 *Ibid*.

38 *Ibid*.

39 *Ibid*.

40 Konstantin Bogdanov and Ilya Kramnik, 'The Russian Navy in the 21st Century: the legacy and the new path', CNA Occasional Paper, October 2018, https://www.cna.org/CNA_files/PDF/IOP-2018-U-018268-Final.pdf.

41 Michael Kofman and Norman Polmar, 'New Russian Navy: Part 1 – Towards Smaller Ships and Professional Sailors', *US Naval Institute Proceedings*, vol. 42, no. 12, December 2016, https://www.usni.org/magazines/proceedings/2016/december/new-russian-navy-part-1-toward-smaller-ships-and-professional.

42 Interfax-AVN, 'Russian naval activities, submarine deployments on the rise – commander', BBC Monitoring, 17 June 2015, https://monitoring.bbc.co.uk/product/m1ci72fx.

43 Donald Thieme, 'Russian Military Activities from South China Sea to Sevastopol', USNI News, 14 September 2016, https://news.usni.org/2016/09/14/analysis-russian-military-activities-from-south-china-sea-to-sevastopol.

44 Atle Staalesen, 'Powerful Navy flotilla sets out from Kola Bay as Russia starts Zapad-2017', *Barents Observer*, 15 September 2017, https://thebarentsobserver.com/en/security/2017/09/powerful-navy-flotilla-sets-out-kola-bay-russia-starts-zapad-2017.

45 Roger McDermott, 'Russia rehearses multi-platform warfare in the Baltic Sea', Real Clear Defense, 7 August 2019, https://www.realcleardefense.com/articles/2019/08/07/russia_rehearses_multi-platform_warfare_in_the_baltic_sea_114647.html.

46 Michael Paul, 'Partnership on the High Seas', SWP Comment, no. 26, June 2019, https://www.swp-berlin.org/fileadmin/contents/products/comments/2019C26_pau.pdf.

47 Ministry of Defence of the Russian Federation, 'Missile cruiser Marshal Ustinov leaves Cape Town for exercise with frigates of South Africa and China in the South Atlantic', 28 November 2019, https://eng.mil.ru/en/news_page/country/more.htm?id=12264033@egNews&_print=true.

48 IISS, *The Military Balance 2020* (Abingdon: Routledge for the IISS, 2020), p. 176.

49 Tom Waldwyn, 'Russia's Admiral Gorshkov frigate: commissioned at last', IISS Military Balance blog, 13 August 2018, https://www.iiss.org/blogs/military-balance/2018/08/russian-navy-admiral-gorshkov-frigate.

50 Dmitry Gorenburg, 'Russia's Military Modernisation Plans 2018–2027', PONARS Eurasia, Policy Memo no. 495, November 2017, http://www.ponarseurasia.org/memo/russias-military-modernization-plans-2018-2027; Delanoë, 'Russia's Navy in the Pacific: the Forgotten Fleet?'

51 Richard Connolly and Mathieu Boulegue, 'Russia's New State Armament Programme', Chatham House Research Paper, May 2018, https://www.chathamhouse.org/sites/default/files/publications/research/2018-05-10-russia-state-armament-programme-connolly-boulegue-final.pdf.

52 Conrad Waters, *Seaforth World Naval Review 2019* (Barnsley: Seaforth Publishing, 2018).

53 Tomas Malmlöf, 'Russia's New Armament Programme – Leaner and Meaner', FOI Swedish Defence Research Agency, March 2018, https://www.foi.se/en/foi/reports/report-summary.html?reportNo=FOI%20MEMO%206365.

54 All data from IISS, *The Military Balance* (various editions).

55 Norman Polmar and Michael Kofman, 'Russian Navy: Part 3 – Impressive Beneath the Waves', *US Naval Institute Proceedings*, vol. 143, no. 2, February 2017, https://www.usni.org/magazines/proceedings/2017/february/russian-navy-part-3.

56 Interfax-AVN, 'Russian naval activities, submarine deployments on the rise – commander'.

57 Jeremy Bender, 'US Navy official: Russian submarine activities are at their highest since the Cold War', Business Insider, 19 April 2016, https://www.businessinsider.com/russias-submarine-activities-are-at-their-highest-since-the-cold-war-2016-4?r=US&IR=T.

58 James Foggo and Alarik Fritz, 'The Fourth Battle of the Atlantic', *US Naval Institute Proceedings*, vol. 142, no. 6, June 2016, https://www.usni.org/magazines/proceedings/2016/june/fourth-battle-atlantic.

59 *The Military Balance 2010* (Abingdon: Routledge for the IISS, 2010), pp. 224–25.

60 See Stephen Saunders, *Jane's Fighting Ships, 2018–2019* (Coulsdon: IHS Markit, 2018).

61 *Ibid.*

62 *Izvestia*, 'Acceptance of Russia's Bulava missile, test history revisited', BBC Monitoring, 3 July 2018, https://monitoring.bbc.co.uk/product/c1dpfvea.

63 'Secrets from Russia's "undetectable" Borey-class submarine', TASS, 7 April 2020, https://monitoring.bbc.co.uk/product/c201ljf4.

64 *Ibid.*

65 'Russia's top brass to sign deal for two more Borey-A strategic nuclear-powered subs', TASS, 21 February 2020, https://tass.com/defense/1122941.

66 TASS, 'Advanced nuclear-powered sub *Knyaz Vladimir* to be delivered to Russian navy by late June', BBC Monitoring, 13 April 2020, https://tass.com/defense/1143771.

67 Nikolai Novichkov, 'Russian Navy to receive new and overhauled submarines', *Jane's Defence Weekly*, 25 March 2020, https://janes.ihs.com/Janes/Display/FG_2735760-JDW.

68 Zvezda TV, 'Russian military TV profiles nuclear submarine', BBC Monitoring, 8 March 2020, https://monitoring.bbc.co.uk/product/c201iobl.

69 'Navy Columbia (SSBN-826) Class Ballistic Missile Submarine Program: Background and Issues for Congress', Congressional Research Service, 22 March 2020, https://fas.org/sgp/crs/weapons/R41129.pdf.

70 TASS, 'Russia may build Borey-K nuclear subs with cruise missiles – source', BBC Monitoring, 20 April 2019, https://tass.com/defense/1054714.

71 *Rossiyskaya Gazeta*, 'Russia's Sevmash ship-yard sets out submarine production plans', BBC Monitoring, 19 December 2019, https://monitoring.bbc.co.uk/product/c201bp1q.

72 Dave Majumdar, 'US Navy impressed with new Russian attack boat', USNI News, 28 October 2014, https://news.usni.org/2014/10/28/u-s-navy-impressed-new-russian-attack-boat.

73 IISS, *The Military Balance 2020*, p. 197.

74 *Izvestia*, 'Russian website describes Project 885 Yasen-M submarine upgrade', BBC Monitoring, 6 April 2020, https://monitoring.bbc.co.uk/product/c201m42l.

75 *Ibid.*

76 Tim Ripley, 'Second Yasen-M submarine launched', *Jane's Navy International*, 2 January 2020, https://janes.ihs.com/Janes/Display/FG_2639325-JNI.

77 'Russia's Project 949A Oscar II to be modified for Kalibr missile systems', Navy Recognition, 9 March 2017, https://www.navyrecognition.com/index.php/news/defence-news/2017/march-2017-navy-naval-forces-defense-industry-technology-maritime-security-global-news/4966-russia-s-project-949a-oscar-ii-submarines-to-be-modified-for-kalibr-missile-systems.html.

78 *Izvestia*, 'Production of Russia's Kalibr cruise-missile platforms at standstill', BBC Monitoring, 6 December 2018, https://monitoring.bbc.co.uk/product/c200h23i.

79 IISS, *The Military Balance 2020*, pp. 196–97.

80 *Izvestia*, 'Russia to refit Project 971 class submarine *Tigr* by 2023', BBC Monitoring, 3 February 2020, https://monitoring.bbc.co.uk/product/c201fq6t.

81 IISS, *The Military Balance 2020*, p. 197.

82 H.I. Sutton, 'Husky SSN', Covert Shores, 30 December 2019, http://www.hisutton.com/Husky_SSN.html.

83 Franz-Stefan Gady, 'First Project 636.3 Kilo-class attack sub to enter service with Russia's Pacific Fleet this month', *Diplomat*, 22 November 2019, https://thediplomat.com/2019/11/first-project-636-3-kilo-class-attack-sub-to-enter-service-with-russias-pacific-fleet-this-month.

84 Mark Episkopos, 'Meet Russia's new Lada-class submarine: the next "stealth" threat to the US Navy?', *National Interest*, 25 February 2019, https://nationalinterest.org/blog/buzz/meet-russias-new-lada-class-submarine-next-stealth-threat-us-navy-45522.

85 'Russian Navy undecided on submarine to trial air-independent engine', RIA Novosti, 16 December 2019, https://monitoring.bbc.co.uk/product/c201cli2.

86 'Analysis: St Petersburg submarine expects upgrade for new arms trials – take 1', Navy Recognition, 23 April 2020, https://www.navyrecognition.com/index.php/focus-analysis/naval-technology/8309-analysis-st-petersburg-submarine-expects-upgrade-for-new-arms-trials-take-1.html.

87 Franz-Stefan Gady, 'Russia's new nuclear torpedo-carrying sub to start sea trials in June 2020, *Diplomat*, 10 September 2019, https://thediplomat.com/2019/09/russias-new-nuclear-torpedo-carrying-sub-to-begin-sea-trials-in-june-2020.

88 *Ibid.*

89 TASS, 'Source says Russia to arm four subs with nuclear drones', BBC Monitoring, 12 January 2019, https://monitoring.bbc.co.uk/product/c200jlnz.

90 James Glanz and Thomas Nilsen, 'A Deep-diving Sub. A Deadly Fire. And Russia's Secret Undersea Agenda', *New York Times*, 20 April 2020, https://www.nytimes.com/2020/04/20/world/europe/russian-submarine-fire-losharik.html.

91 'What makes Russia's new spy ship Yantar special?', BBC News, 3 January 2018, https://www.bbc.co.uk/news/world-europe-42543712.

92 Lee Willett, 'Punching up: Russia's smaller surface fleet builds bigger impact', *Jane's International Defence Review*, 1 December 2017, https://janes.ihs.com/Janes/Display/FG_686758-IDR.

93 IISS, *The Military Balance 2020*, p. 198.

94 FlotProm, 'Russian naval diesel production still mired in problems', BBC Monitoring, 23 March 2020, https://monitoring.bbc.co.uk/product/c201kono.

95 *Jane's Fighting Ships, 2018–2019.*

96 Ria Novosti, 'German engines on Project 20385 corvettes to be replaced by Russian ones', BBC Monitoring, 12 May 2015, https://monitoring.bbc.co.uk/product/m1cfyc5p.

97 'Project 20386 corvettes fully substitute Project 11356 frigates, Russian navy official says', Mil.Today, 3 June 2019, http://mil.today/2019/Navy51.

98 Paul Schwartz, 'Admiral Gorshkov Frigate Reveals Serious Shortcomings in Russia's Naval Modernization Program', Center for Strategic and International Studies, 10 March 2016, https://www.csis.org/analysis/admiral-gorshkov-frigate-reveals-serious-shortcomings-russia%E2%80%99s-naval-modernization-program.

99 Waldwyn, 'Russia's Admiral Gorshkov frigate: commissioned at last'.

100 *Ibid.*

101 Franz-Stefan Gady, 'Russia to deliver 2 guided-missile frigates to India by 2024', *Diplomat*, 7 February 2020, https://thediplomat.com/2020/02/russia-to-deliver-2-guided-missile-frigates-to-india-by-2024.

102 TASS, 'Russian report says new frigates to carry 24 Tsirkon missiles', BBC Monitoring, 17 April 2020, https://monitoring.bbc.co.uk/product/c201mfcv.

103 Dmitry Zhavoronkov, 'Russian Navy is heading for three series of frigates of Project 22350', Flotprom, 1 May 2020, https://flot-prom.ru/2020/%D0%9E%D0%B1%D0%B E%D1%80%D0%BE%D0%BD%D0%BA% D0%B0100.

104 Alexey Ramm and Evgeny Dmitriev, 'Super Gorshkov gains a thousand tons', *Izvestia*, 5 April 2017, https://iz.ru/news/668261.

105 IISS, *The Military Balance 2020*, pp. 176, 219.

106 IISS, *The Military Balance 2020*, pp. 199–200.

107 Michael Kofman and Norman Polmar, 'Russian navy part 3: naval aviation taking flight again … slowly', USNI Proceedings, March 2017, https://www.usni.org/magazines/proceedings/2017/march/new-russian-navy-part-3-naval-aviation-taking-flight-againslowly.

108 *Izvestia*, 'Russian paper looks at prospects for naval aviation strike force', BBC Monitoring, 23 May 2019, https://monitoring.bbc.co.uk/product/c200u59g.

109 IISS, *The Military Balance 2020*, pp. 199–200.

110 *Ibid.*

111 *Izvestia*, 'Russia to deploy latest Ka-27M helicopter in Baltic to hunt NATO submarines', BBC Monitoring, 2 January 2020, https://monitoring.bbc.co.uk/product/c201dnh4.

112 Zvezda TV, 'Russia deploys naval radar-picket helicopters to Crimea', BBC Monitoring, 13 March 2020, https://monitoring.bbc.co.uk/product/c201jla7.

113 Interfax, 'Russia developing new aircraft carrier', BBC Monitoring, 15 May 2005, https://monitoring.bbc.co.uk/product/30030802.

114 Vladimir Petrov, 'Medvedev orders construction of aircraft carriers for Russian navy', *Jane's Defence Weekly*, 14 October 2008, https://janes.ihs.com/Janes/Display/jdw38048-jdw-2008.

115 Interfax-AVN, 'Russia to start building new aircraft carriers in 2012–13 – navy source', BBC Monitoring, 9 June 2009, https://monitoring.bbc.co.uk/product/m1873kbx.

116 Interfax-AVN, 'Russian navy chief comments on work to design new aircraft carrier by 2020', BBC Monitoring, 23 November 2012, https://monitoring.bbc.co.uk/product/m1au3r1z.

117 'Russian deputy premier casts doubt on new carrier', Rossiya 1 TV, 20 May 2017, https://monitoring.bbc.co.uk/product/c1dhn3jn.

118 Nikolai Novichkov, 'Russia developing Shtorm supercarrier', *Jane's Defence Weekly*, 14 May 2015, https://janes.ihs.com/Janes/Display/jdw58641-jdw-2015.

119 *Rossiyskaya Gazeta*, 'New aircraft carrier project unveiled at Russian navy show', BBC Monitoring, 10 July 2019, https://monitoring.bbc.co.uk/product/c200xz28.

120 'Russia to start development of nuclear-powered aircraft carrier in 2023 – source', TASS, 7 May 2019, https://tass.com/defense/1057234.

121 Interfax, 'Russian carrier refit funding to be halved – source', BBC Monitoring, 14 October 2017, https://monitoring.bbc.co.uk/product/c1dmpexd.

122 David Majumdar, 'Russia wants a new 18,000-ton nuclear-powered guided missile destroyer', *National Interest*, 31 July 2018, https://nationalinterest.org/blog/buzz/russia-wants-new-18000-ton-nuclear-powered-guided-missile-destroyer-27322.

123 *Ibid.*

124 'Northern Design Bureau suspended work on a promising nuclear destroyer', Interfax, 18 April 2020, https://www.interfax.ru/russia/704920.

125 *Izvestia*, 'New Russian defence industry boss surveys shipbuilding morass', BBC Monitoring, 16 May 2018, https://monitoring.bbc.co.uk/product/c1dp9nq4.

126 *Ibid.*

127 'After five years of upgrade, destroyer "Marshal Ustinov" is back in Barents Sea', *Barents Observer*, 23 May 2017, https://thebarentsobserver.com/en/security/2017/05/after-5-years-upgrade-destroyer-marshal-ustinov-back-barents-sea.

128 *Jane's Fighting Ships, 2018–2019.*

129 Karl Soper, 'Russian Udaloy destroyer modernized for land-attack mission', *Jane's Defence Weekly*, 18 June 2019, https://janes.ihs.com/Janes/Display/FG_2110350-JDW.

130 *Ibid.*

131 'Russian amphibious assault ship to resume sea trials', Shephard News, 7 May 2020, https://www.shephardmedia.com/news/naval-warfare/russian-amphibious-assault-ship-resume-sea-trials.

132 Interfax-AVN, 'Construction of Russia's Project 11711 landing ships delayed by design changes', BBC Monitoring, 27 June 2019, https://monitoring.bbc.co.uk/product/c200xgyy.

133 'Russia to spend $1.3bln to construct two helicopter carriers – source', TASS, 10 April 2020, https://tass.com/defense/1142751.

134 Tim Ripley, 'Russia to build five more auxiliary tankers', *Jane's Navy International*, 23 January 2020, https://janes.ihs.com/Janes/Display/FG_2652879-JNI.

135 *Ibid.*

136 IISS, *The Military Balance 2020*, pp. 196–99.

137 *Ibid.*

138 'Russia test-launches Tsirkon hypersonic missile from ship for first time',

TASS, 27 February 2020, https://tass.com/defense/1124339.

139 'Russia to test-fire Tsirkon missile from subs in "2024–2025"', RIA Novosti, 14 April 2020, https://monitoring.bbc.co.uk/product/c201m706.

140 *Izvestia*, 'Russia to convert Project 22800 ships for anti-submarine role', BBC Monitoring, 5 November 2019, https://monitoring.bbc.co.uk/product/c2017tho.

141 Norman Polmar and Edward C. Whitman, 'Russia poses a nonacoustic threat to US subs', *US Naval Institute Proceedings*, vol. 143, no. 10, October 2017, https://www.usni.org/magazines/proceedings/2017/october/russia-poses-nonacoustic-threat-us-subs.

142 *Izvestia*, 'Russia: project 22800 ships to get naval version of Pantsir system', BBC Monitoring, 13 April 2020, https://monitoring.bbc.co.uk/product/c201mtlb.

143 *Izvestia*, 'Russian report describes warship, air defences "guidance loop"', BBC Monitoring, 19 March 2020, https://monitoring.bbc.co.uk/product/c201ljmf.

Aerospace Forces

Soviet military aviation was a source of pride and a symbol of communist progress, celebrated in official publications like *Herald of the Air Fleet*, irrespective of the occasionally inflated propaganda of the air and air-defence forces.[1] The collapse of the Soviet Union in December 1991 ushered in over a decade of stagnation and decay for the Air Force (*Voyenno-vozdushnye sily*, VVS).[2] Morale collapsed, while multiple combat, transport and special-mission aircraft and strategic-weapons projects were shelved as the economic turmoil of the 1990s saw defence expenditure plummet.[3] For a few fortunate programmes this amounted to only a suspension. The break-up of the Soviet Union also fragmented the previously integrated defence-aerospace manufacturing and supply base.

Today, Russian air and space power has been re-established as a credible – albeit far smaller – force capable of again undertaking operations that were beyond its capacity in the 1990s and early 2000s.[4] The Air Force would in the late 1990s or early 2000s have been very hard pressed to mount an operation on the scale of its involvement in Syria, for example.

For the Air Force, the post-Soviet downward spiral reached its nadir in 1996 when it did not fund even a single new aircraft. According to former Aerospace Forces (*Vozdushno-kosmicheskie sily*, VKS) chief Colonel-General Viktor Bondarev, the service 'received practically no new equipment in the 20 years since the 1990s'.[5] Combat readiness also disintegrated by the mid-1990s as an inability to pay for aviation fuel severely cut flying hours.[6] In the immediate aftermath of the Soviet Union's end, a lack of realism amid senior Air Force ranks meant that procurement ambitions were sustained on paper even when little to no funding was available.[7] The Air Force would continue to suffer throughout the 1990s, and there would be little sign of any recovery until well into the first decade of the twenty-first century.[8]

The role of the Russian Aerospace Forces

From the outset of the Cold War, the Soviet Union viewed attack from the air as an existential threat, and today the aerospace domain is viewed in a similar vein by Russia's military leadership. The doctrine of

Key takeaways

SU-35S *FLANKER* M
The entry into service in significant numbers of the Su-35S *Flanker* M provides the Air Force with a modern multi-role fighter.

UPGRADED MISSILES
Upgraded air-to-air and air-to-surface missiles are improving the Air Force's combat capabilities.

DEVELOPMENT DELAYS
New aircraft-development programmes continue to suffer development delays. As of 2020, the Su-57 *Felon* was running nearly a decade behind the original, overly ambitious, schedule.

TU-160M *BLACKJACK*
The parallel development and manufacturing of two heavy bombers, the Tu-160M *Blackjack* and a new design to meet the PAK-DA requirement, is a challenge.

ONGOING UNDERFUNDING
Enabler types of aircraft, such as heavy transport and tankers, continue to be underfunded.

SYRIAN INTERVENTION
The Syrian intervention has provided valuable combat experience.

the Aerospace Forces flows from Russia's Military Doctrine, which sees NATO's expansion and advanced military capabilities as a threat. Russia needs to be able to 'ensure the aerospace defence of the Russian Federation's critical facilities' and to counter an 'air or space attack'.[9]

The Aerospace Forces now includes the Air Defence Forces (*Voyska protivovozdushnoy oborony*, PVO) that were until 1998 a separate air- and ground-based force. The PVO's task was to provide air defence of the Soviet Union, while the Soviet Air Force provided frontal aviation at the theatre level, and also strategic and transport aviation.

Aerospace defence remains core to VKS doctrine, with the goal being the capacity to reduce the worst of an attack, absorb the rest and then support a counter-attack while continuing to fulfil defensive needs. Active defence would also form part of the response to an attack, for example, targeting enemy bases at extended ranges with conventionally armed medium- and long-range air-launched cruise missiles.

Structural change in post-Soviet Russia

Even in the immediate aftermath of the demise of the Soviet Union, there was recognition of the need to restructure the rump of the Air Force and Air Defence Forces that Russia had inherited from the Soviet Union.[10] The scale of the challenge and the scarcity of resources, however, condemned early efforts to failure. Air Force General Piotr Deinekin, who led the service from 1992 to 1998, stressed the need for reform, with the aim of creating a service capable of meeting the defence and security demands of the coming century.[11] Although this ambition was unfulfilled during his tenure, ensuing air-force organisational changes in post-Soviet Russia have enabled the integration of the country's air and space forces with greater success.[12]

The most notable of the late 1990s reforms was the 1998 merger of the Air Defence Forces into the Air Force.[13] Subsuming the Air Defence Forces into the Air Force had been considered in the early 1990s, but was shelved because of the cost, and more pressing and basic needs such

as improving, or in some cases simply building, housing for Air Force personnel.[14]

Formed in 1949, the Air Defence Forces had since 1954 been an equal service branch to the Soviet Air Force. In 1998, the Air Force took all of the PVO's interceptor and fighter aircraft, surface-to-air missile systems and air-defence radars.[15] The ballistic-missile warning system, Moscow's missile-defence units and space-network control previously operated by the Air Defence Forces were transferred to the Strategic Rocket Forces. These missile-defence units were rebadged as the Space Forces in March 2001.[16] This force was then included in further restructuring in 2011 to form an element of the Aerospace Defence Forces and since 2015 has formed part of the Aerospace Forces.[17]

Following consolidation, the Air Force and Air Defence Forces continued to shed units and personnel, with the merged service initially retaining just over half of the previously separate arms' total units. The Air Force had 95 aviation regiments prior to absorbing its sister service, while the Air Defence Forces had 25 aviation regiments. By 1999, there were only 70 regiments; over a third were fighter units, seven were heavy-bomber regiments and one was a tanker-aircraft unit. The planned personnel strength for 1999 was to total 184,594, a reduction of just over 45,000 compared to the two formerly independent services.[18] As of mid-2020, personnel figures were estimated to be 165,000, including conscripts.

Further restructuring occurred in 2003, when at the beginning of that year Army Aviation was subordinated to the Air Force, rather than being part of the Ground Forces.[19] The former Air Defence Forces had suffered damage to its reputation in the 1980s as a result of the shoot-down in 1983 of a Korean Airlines passenger aircraft, and the penetration of Soviet air space by a German amateur pilot in a light aircraft in order to reach Moscow in 1987.[20] Likewise, the decision to transfer the army's combat and transport helicopters to the Air Force was made in the wake

SU-35S *FLANKER* M
As of 2020, the Russian Air Force's premier multi-role combat aircraft.
CREDIT: Yuri Smityuk/TASS/Getty Images

of the downing of an Mi-26 *Halo* heavy transport helicopter and the death of 127 people aboard, in Chechnya on 19 August 2002. The resulting investigation revealed numerous failings and weaknesses in the command of the Army Aviation within the Ground Forces. Colonel-General Vitaly Pavlov, the commander of army aviation, was sacked.[21]

Some years after the transfer of Army Aviation to the Air Force in 2003, in 2011 units and aircraft belonging to the Strategic Rocket Forces and the Airborne Forces were also handed over.[22] While the navy retains an organic air capability, even here some units were transferred to the Air Force. In 2011, the navy's Tupolev Tu-22M3 *Backfire* C fleet was also moved to the Air Force.[23]

In August 2015, the Air Force and the Aerospace Defence Forces (*Voyska vozdushno-kosmicheskoy oborony*, VVKO) merged to create the Aerospace Forces.[24] This brought together most of Russia's military-aviation, air-defence and space units, including the ballistic-missile-defence system intended to protect Moscow, along with up to 130 military and dual-purpose satellites.[25] One rationale for the move was to improve Russia's ability to counter the use of air and space power in any war with a peer or near-peer rival.[26]

In 2020, the only military arms operating crewed fixed- and rotary-wing aircraft are the Aerospace Forces and the navy. When the military branches of the Russian Federation's armed forces were established in May 1992, each had their own air units but most were transferred to the Air Force and then the Aerospace Forces over time. Whether command of army rotary-wing aviation ought to reside with the air or ground forces remains an open question. As of mid-2020, the units are operationally tasked by each of the military district's Joint Strategic Commands. Initial and combat training, however, is the responsibility of the Air Force. The department tasked with army-aviation combat preparation is part of the VKS headquarters.[27]

Figure 5.1: **Air Force structural change, 2007–20**

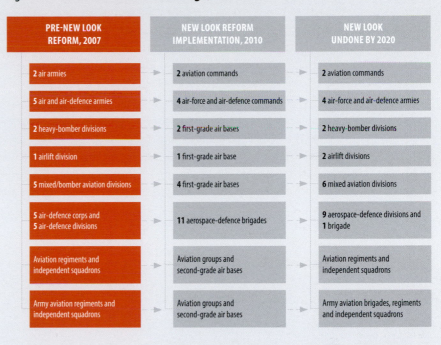

Figure 5.2: **Selected Soviet and Russian aircraft-development ambitions, 1989 and 2020**

Sources: IISS; *The Military Balance 2019*; IISS Military Balance+

Training and personnel

If you joined a Russian Air Force pilot school before 2020, the first two years of training would be earthbound, with class-based learning only. Flying training would begin in the third year of what was a five-year course. As of 2020, however, training will begin in the second year.[28] One aim of the revised training syllabus is to earlier identify candidates who will not meet the required standard, thereby saving resources in terms of trainers and trainer aircraft. Failure rates during pilot training can be significant.[29]

The VKS is suffering a shortfall in pilots and a shortage of trainer aircraft. Defence Minister Sergei Shoigu said in 2017 that the pilot numbers were understrength by around 1,300. The 2008 'New Look' (*Novy Oblik*) reform programme included an attempt to rationalise Russia's training infrastructure but resulted in unintended and unwelcome consequences, including a reduction in trainee intake.[30] Several steps were taken to offset the worst effects: aircrew tenure was lengthened and the recruitment of aircrew candidates was increased. The home of fixed-wing aviation training is the Krasnodar Higher Military Aviation College, where the revised training syllabus is being implemented.

The declining number of qualifying pilots has been exacerbated by a lack of trainer aircraft. The Aero L-39 *Albatros* is a Soviet-era jet trainer now at the very end of, if not beyond, its service life, with all the maintenance and availability challenges that this brings.[31] The L-39 prototype

Figure 5.3: **The Air Force's structure in 2007**

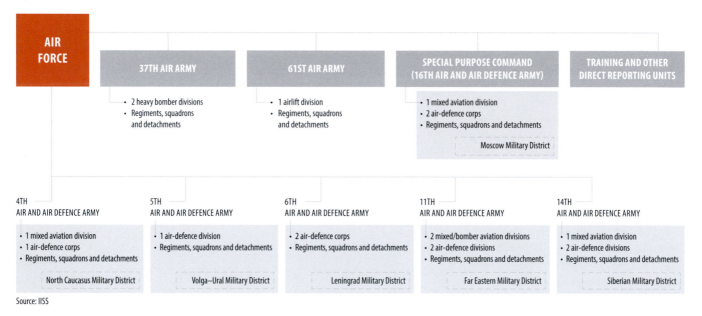

Source: IISS

Figure 5.4: **The Air Force's structure from 2010**

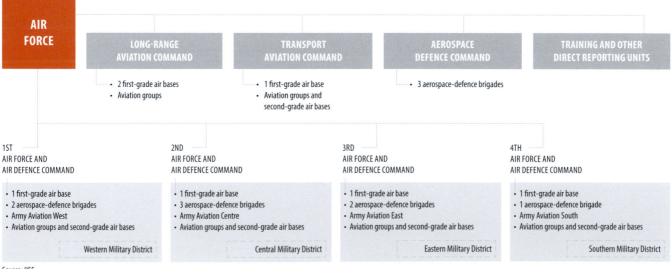

Source: IISS

was flown for the first time in 1968. The Air Force has an inventory of 150 L-39Cs, although how many of these are available given the maintenance requirements and serviceability issues is unclear. The L-39C is also increasingly ill-suited to preparing pilots for modern combat aircraft because it has analogue displays rather than a digital cockpit.

The L-39C was meant to be replaced by the Yakovlev Yak-130 *Mitten*. The Air Force's advanced-jet-trainer requirement dates to the late 1980s, with Yakovlev's Yak-UTS competing with the Mikoyan MiG-AT for the contract by the early 1990s.[32] A development of the original YAK-UTS, the Yak-130 was eventually selected over the MiG-AT design in 2002. Pilot training on the Yak-130 is carried out at the Borisoglebsk and Armavir air bases. Availability issues are also affecting the Yak-130 fleet, with a figure of 56% quoted for serviceability.[33] In the early 2000s, the Air Force intended to buy 200–300 Yak-130s, but as of 2020 had just over 100 in service. This is likely one of the reasons the L-39C has remained in service well beyond its planned out-of-service date. In addition, as of mid-2020 development work was being carried out on an avionics upgrade for the L-39 to try to address obsolescence issues.[34]

Beginning flying training a year earlier than in the previous syllabus will also allow pilots to build flight hours. One aim will be for the trainee to have greater basic competence in flying an advanced jet trainer when they transition to the combat-training element of the syllabus, and onto aircraft such as the MiG-29 *Fulcrum* or Su-27 *Flanker* in their final year, before being assigned to a combat unit.

Figure 5.5: **The development of Russia's air forces**

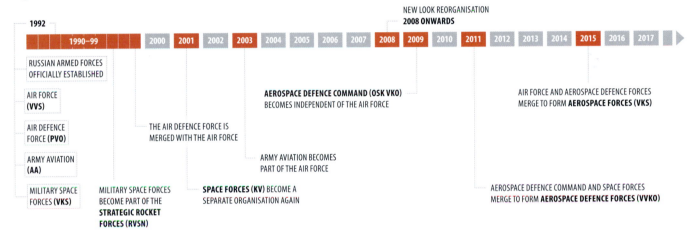

Source: IISS

Figure 5.6: **The Aerospace Forces' structure and organisation, 2020**

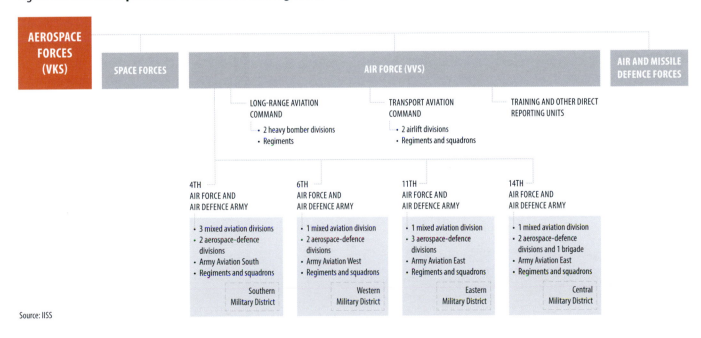

Source: IISS

The New Look and the Air Force

The most significant, and most successful, overarching post-Soviet reform of the armed services has been that dubbed the New Look.[35] This reform programme was launched by then-defence minister Anatoly Serdyukov in October 2008. Serdyukov was an economist by background. Appointed by President Vladimir Putin in February 2007, his remit from the outset may well have been to drive through such reform – not all of it was popular, particularly among the senior military.[36] The intent of the New Look was to create smaller but more immediately usable forces at a far higher state of readiness.[37] All the service arms' equipment inventories were also to be modernised, with increased and sustained defence spending to support this.[38]

In the Air Force, the Air Force and Air Defence Armies were transformed into four Air Force and Air Defence commands, each assigned to one military district. Bombers and heavy transport aircraft became the responsibility of the Long Range Aviation Command (the former 37th Air Army) and the Military Transport Aviation Command (the former 61st Air Army) respectively.[39]

The New Look also revisited an idea first mooted in the 1990s: the creation of a unit structure built around the 'air base or air station' (*aviabaza*). This replaced regiments, independent squadrons and detachments.[40] The change was more than merely rebadging, since where an air base was established, the associated air regiment or squadron (or squadrons) was merged with auxiliary units at the same site.[41] Such units would previously have been independent, with their own commands. The 'air base' approach therefore cut the number of command personnel.[42]

The reform, however, did not appear to have been planned in detail, and changes – some significant – were required during implementation.[43] At the outset of the New Look in 2008, the plan was to convert 72 regiments and a further 26 smaller units into 52 air bases.[44] During the reform's implementation in 2009, the number was cut to 33.[45] In 2010, there was more adjustment with the Air Force restructured into seven so-called first-grade air bases and eight second-grade air bases.[46] A first-grade air base was the size of a former air division and made up of several aviation groups located at numerous airfields.[47] Each group consisted normally of multiple squadrons. A second-grade air base was the size of an air regiment and located at one airfield only.[48] Five second-grade air bases were for Army Aviation and the other three were Air Force detachments in Armenia, Kyrgyzstan and Tajikistan.[49]

One aim of the New Look was to simplify the command structure by removing some of the intermediate levels, in order to increase flexibility and responsiveness. Instead it had the opposite effect, inadvertently introducing a structure that threatened to be yet more rigid. The gap in the command chain potentially made a test-and-adjust approach more difficult. In the Air Force one problem was basic geography, with some commanders attempting to manage an air base spread over more than 1,000 kilometres.[50] A particularly clear example of this was the 7000th Aviation Base, where its furthest units were stationed at Monchegorsk, 1,850 km from the air base's headquarters at Voronezh.

Given the challenges faced by defence minister Serdyukov, and the antipathy to some of the reforms among senior military, his fall was near inevitable.[51] This duly happened in 2012, amid allegations of impropriety, with the appointment of Sergei Shoigu as his successor. In post, Shoigu began to walk back some of Serdyukov's structural reforms.[52] Addressing concerns over a lack of flexibility and too rigid a command architecture, aviation groups were reconstituted as regiments while first-grade air bases became the headquarters of aviation divisions.[53]

The re-introduction of what was at face value a more traditional force structure should not, however, be taken as evidence of the overall failure of Serdyukov's reforms.[54] While the name plates for the units had reverted to language that a Soviet-era air-force officer would recognise, the internal architectural changes put in place by Serdyukov remained.[55] For example, aviation groups (second-grade bases) were once again named regiments, but the air-base structure was retained and supporting subunits did not regain independence.[56] Nonetheless, the force-structure changes introduced by the New Look were arguably the least successful element of the reform package for the Air Force, as evidenced by the rowing back on some of the more radical restructuring.

IL-76 *CANDID* HEAVY TRANSPORT AIRCRAFT
Taking off from Dyagilevo air base, March 2018. CREDIT: Alexander Ryumin/TASS/PA Images

The State Armament Programme

Russia's State Armament Programme (SAP) is a multi-volume classified set of documents setting out plans for the purchase, repair and upgrade of military equipment, and allocating and directing research and development (R&D) funding. Each SAP covers a ten-year period, with detailed expenditure plans for the first five, while the second five are only broadly described. The programme is meant to be refreshed every five years, thus overlapping with the previous SAP's second half.[57]

Throughout the 1990s and early 2000s programmes were underfunded; the planned resources and those actually made available were badly mismatched.[58] SAP 2020, covering the period from 2011 to the end of the decade, has been the most successful armament programme since the collapse of the Soviet Union. The budget for the 2020 programme was 19.4 trillion roubles (US$285 billion). This total included upward of 21% for the Air Force, intended to buy 600 new fixed-wing aircraft and more than 1,000 helicopters over the course of the decade.[59] The programme went well initially. Delivery of fixed-wing combat aircraft to the Air Force increased from 22 in 2011, to 29 in 2012, 54 in 2013, 72 in 2014 and 77 in 2015. Helicopter deliveries to the Russian armed services ran at 100–120 per year for the same period.

Two factors resulted in the initial procurement targets being missed. The decline in the barrel price of oil in 2014 hit the Russian economy, as did Western sanctions implemented in response to Moscow's annexation of Crimea.[60] In December 2018, Deputy Prime Minister Yuri Borisov said deliveries of combat aircraft consisted of 50–60 airframes annually, with the figure for helicopters at 30–40.[61] Despite the failure to meet the original target delivery rates in the second half of SAP 2020 by the end of 2019, more than 500 new aircraft and more than 700 helicopters had been delivered.[62] By comparison, the Air Force received only around a tenth of these numbers in the previous decade.[63]

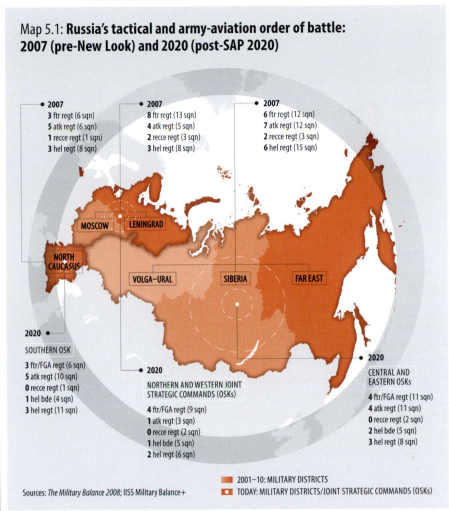

Map 5.1: **Russia's tactical and army-aviation order of battle: 2007 (pre-New Look) and 2020 (post-SAP 2020)**

2007
3 ftr regt (6 sqn)
5 atk regt (6 sqn)
1 recce regt (1 sqn)
3 hel regt (8 sqn)

2007
8 ftr regt (13 sqn)
4 atk regt (5 sqn)
2 recce regt (3 sqn)
3 hel regt (8 sqn)

2007
6 ftr regt (12 sqn)
7 atk regt (12 sqn)
2 recce regt (3 sqn)
6 hel regt (15 sqn)

MOSCOW LENINGRAD
NORTH CAUCASUS
VOLGA–URAL SIBERIA FAR EAST

2020
SOUTHERN OSK
3 ftr/FGA regt (6 sqn)
5 atk regt (10 sqn)
0 recce regt (1 sqn)
1 hel bde (4 sqn)
3 hel regt (11 sqn)

2020
NORTHERN AND WESTERN JOINT STRATEGIC COMMANDS (OSKs)
4 ftr/FGA regt (9 sqn)
1 atk regt (3 sqn)
0 recce regt (2 sqn)
1 hel bde (5 sqn)
2 hel regt (6 sqn)

2020
CENTRAL AND EASTERN OSKs
4 ftr/FGA regt (11 sqn)
4 atk regt (11 sqn)
0 recce regt (2 sqn)
2 hel bde (5 sqn)
3 hel regt (8 sqn)

2001–10: MILITARY DISTRICTS
TODAY: MILITARY DISTRICTS/JOINT STRATEGIC COMMANDS (OSKs)

Sources: *The Military Balance 2008*; IISS Military Balance+

By the end of 2019, the Air Force had taken delivery of almost 90 Su-35S *Flanker* M single-seat multi-role fighters, around 90 Su-30SM twin-seat multi-role fighters and more than 108 Su-34 *Fullback* long-range fighter/ground-attack aircraft in SAP 2020. The trainer-aircraft inventory saw a new type arrive with the delivery of 101 Yak-130 aircraft. Attack-helicopter deliveries in the same period totalled 120 Ka-52 *Alligator*s, some 70 Mi-28N/UB *Havoc*s and 60-plus Mi-35M *Hind*s, with 320 Mi-8 *Hip* medium transport helicopters also entering the inventory.

The successor State Armament Programme and strategic aviation

Such was the combined impact of the drop in oil prices and the Western sanctions that the follow-on to the SAP was delayed by almost two years.[64] What should have been SAP 2025 became instead SAP 2027 (announced in 2018) as the government attempted to deal with the impact of a more constrained economic environment. Although the allocated headline figure of 19trn roubles was the same as for SAP 2020, the two are not directly comparable: the rouble had in the interim lost half its value against the US dollar.

The recapitalisation and modernisation of its strategic forces continues to be a priority for Russia. In the air domain, this is reflected in SAP 2027 providing funding to relaunch the manufacture of an upgraded model of the Tu-160 *Blackjack*.[65] The idea of resuming Tu-160 production was first raised in public by Shoigu during a visit to the Kazan Aviation Production Association aircraft plant in April 2015.[66] The Kazan site was originally the final assembly line for the Tu-160. A decision to proceed with the development of an improved aircraft, the

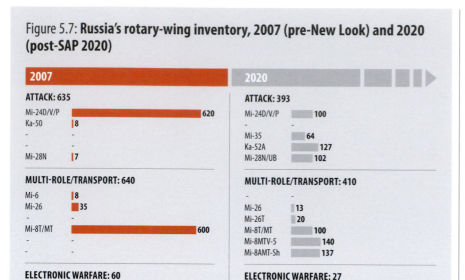

Figure 5.7: Russia's rotary-wing inventory, 2007 (pre-New Look) and 2020 (post-SAP 2020)

2007

ATTACK: 635

| Mi-24D/V/P | 620 |
Ka-50	8
Mi-28N	7

MULTI-ROLE/TRANSPORT: 640

| Mi-6 | 8 |
Mi-26	35
Mi-8T/MT	600

ELECTRONIC WARFARE: 60

Mi-8PPA	60

2020

ATTACK: 393

Mi-24D/V/P	100
Mi-35	64
Ka-52A	127
Mi-28N/UB	102

MULTI-ROLE/TRANSPORT: 410

| - | - |
Mi-26	13
Mi-26T	20
Mi-8T/MT	100
Mi-8MTV-5	140
Mi-8AMT-Sh	137

ELECTRONIC WARFARE: 27

| Mi-8PPA | 20 |
| Mi-8MTPR-1 | 7 |

Sources: *The Military Balance 2008*; IISS Military Balance+

Tu-160M, sometimes also referred to as the Tu-160M2, was likely made in 2014.

Putin then took the opportunity of a January 2018 visit to Kazan to oversee the contract signature between the defence ministry and the industry of a 160bn rouble (around US$2.2bn) order for ten Tu-160M bombers.[67] The unit cost of each aircraft is around US$249 million. The first new-build Tu-160M is due to be flown in 2021, with series production of three aircraft a year to begin from 2023.[68] While preparing to restart production, Kazan built a Tu-160, the main subcomponents of which had languished at the site since the collapse of the Soviet Union in 1991. The aircraft is known as 8-04, the fourth aircraft of the eight-production batch. It represents the 35th Tu-160 to be built, not counting ground-rig and fatigue-test airframes.

The schedule for the new-build programme appears demanding. Re-establishing manufacture of the aircraft requires an overhaul of the production tooling at the Kazan plant, and the construction of a new final assembly building is also planned. Engine manufacture for the aircraft has also restarted, after a 25-year hiatus. The Samara-based Kuznetsov received a contract in August 2014 to put into production an upgraded version of the original engine for the Tu-160, the NK-32.[69] The latest variant, the NK-32-02, is anticipated to provide a range extension of up to 13% as a result of improved fuel consumption. A small batch of the upgraded NK-32 has already been built. The Tu-160M will also use avionics and mission systems developed for the mid-life update of the small existing Tu-160 fleet.

Russia today has a fleet of 17 Tu-160s, including the latest, aircraft 8-04, with the type assigned to the 121st Heavy Bomber Aviation Regiment at Engels. Of these aircraft, seven have been upgraded to what was sometimes referred to as the Tu-160M1, or Tu-160 mod. standard.[70] This is an initial-stage upgrade with improved navigation and communication suites. This allows the aircraft to use the Kh-101/Kh-102 (AS-23A/B *Kodiak*) conventional and nuclear-armed land-attack cruise missiles. The Tu-160M standard includes a new radar, cockpit avionics, self-defence suite and additional weapons. The improved systems for the new-build Tu-160Ms will likely also be retrofitted to the existing Tu-160 aircraft where possible.

The Tu-95MS *Bear* bomber fleet is also the subject of a similar upgrade programme to the Tu-160. By mid-2020, more than 16 aircraft had undergone the initial modification to the Tu-95MS mod. standard to allow carriage of Kh-101/Kh-102 missiles.[71] By the end of the year, the Air Force should

SU-34 *FULLBACK*
Now the Russian Air Force's most capable tactical bomber, with production of an upgraded version in the pipeline. CREDIT: P. Butowski

have at least 20 Tu-95MSM mod. aircraft.[72] The full Tu-95MSM upgrade provides for new radar and data displays, an upgraded self-defence suite and improved power plant. The engine improvements will, according to Tupolev, increase the aircraft's range and payload. The first Tu-95MSM was due to be flown in 2019, but the first flight only took place in August 2020.[73]

A new bomber

Even as the Soviet Union began to collapse, the Air Force was drawing up requirements for a new strategic bomber. This late-1980s effort did not progress far, but even so there have since been sporadic efforts to outline needs for a future long-range platform. The latest, decade-long, work is to meet what is referred to as the PAK-DA (*Perspektivnyy aviatsionnyy kompleks dalney aviatsii*, Future Aviation Complex Long-Range Aviation) requirement. Initial work began in 2007 and in August 2009 Tupolev's bid was selected and the company awarded a 36-month research contract, with the project named *Poslannik* (Envoy or Courier).[74]

Tupolev prepared a preliminary design for the 'Izdeliye 80' bomber (the Tu-160 was the 'Izdeliye 70'), and this was approved in the second quarter of 2013. On 23 December 2013, the United Aircraft Corporation (UAC) was awarded a follow-on contract for the detailed design of the aircraft to meet the PAK-DA requirement, and this was given the green light in 2016.[75] By then, however, the pace of the programme had slowed; from 2015, the emphasis had shifted to restarting production of an upgraded version of the Tu-160, the Tu-160M.[76]

A prototype of the bomber could be flown by the mid-2020s. In January 2018, then-vice-prime minister Dmitry Rogozin expressed hope that the flight tests of the aircraft would start in 2023–24.[77] Minister of Trade and Industry Denis Manturov was more guarded in an August 2019 interview, saying only that work was under way within the 'established schedule', though he declined to say what this schedule was.[78]

The new bomber is most likely a subsonic all-wing design with a take-off weight of 145 tonnes and an unrefuelled range of 15,000 km (9,320 miles). If correct, this would make the design half the weight of the Tu-160 and only 20 tonnes heavier than the Tupolev Tu-22M *Backfire* C. Given the size, there is the possibility that the aircraft is a twin- rather than a four-engine design.

The Tu-22M3 is also being modernised to extend its service life and operational utility.[79] The first upgraded aircraft, dubbed the Tu-22M3M, was flown for the first time on 28 December 2018.[80] Yuri Slyusar, UAC president, said in August 2018 that the upgrade of in-service aircraft would begin

IL-76MD-90A *CANDID*
Production of this new heavy transport aircraft has been substantially delayed. CREDIT: P. Butowski

in 2021.[81] Improvements include new radar, navigation and communication suites, and a new self-defence system. The intent is to use many of the same systems that are part of the Tu-160 upgrade to provide cross-platform commonality and ease support and logistics. If the Aerospace Forces' evaluation of the Tu-22M3M prototype is positive, the upgrade could include not only operational but also stored aircraft. Several dozen Tu-22M3 aircraft remain in storage.

Although SAP 2020 has delivered upgraded bomber aircraft to the Air Force, the schedule for the PAK-DA requirement had to be reshaped to accommodate delays. The project continues to be supported in SAP 2027, but its viability – in financial and industrial-capacity terms – remains questionable.

TU-160 *BLACKJACK* **BOMBER**
Being refuelled by an Il-78 *Midas* tanker (r). CREDIT: P. Butowski

Back to the future

Russia is relaunching the production of several aircraft types from the Soviet era; it has been forced to, since intended successor designs have fallen by the wayside, or have been delayed. Moscow has resumed production of the Ilyushin Il-76 *Candid* that first flew in 1971, rather than immediately pursue a new heavy-transport design.[82] Likewise, it is to build an improved version of the Tu-160 *Blackjack*, first flown in 1981, at least delaying the PAK-DA requirement for a new bomber.[83] In civil aerospace, the government has provided funds to restart manufacture of the Ilyushin Il-114 re-

gional passenger aircraft, first flown in 1990, and the Il-96-400M wide-body passenger aircraft; the Il-96 first flew in 1988.[84] Neither was successful.

Constraints on funding post-2014 may have curtailed the pace of new programmes, but this alone does not explain such an approach. The effort to begin Il-76 production in Ulyanovsk suggests broader issues of a lack of investment in manufacturing technology and in sustaining the appropriate skills base among staff. In December 2006, the Russian government approved the launch of the Il-76MD-90A *Candid* transport's production at the Aviastar-SP factory in Ulyanovsk (in the Soviet era the aircraft was built in Tashkent,

Uzbekistan).[85] The original schedule called for the first Ulyanovsk-built aircraft to complete qualification trials by 2009. Instead, the test aircraft was flown for the first time on 22 September 2012. On 4 October 2012, the Ministry of Defence signed a contract for 39 series Il-76MD-90A aircraft to be made by 2018.[86] The first six, however, were eventually only due to be delivered in 2019, as production schedules were revised.[87] This goal was met, and as of July 2020 the eighth aircraft was in flight test. As of June 2020, there were reports the contract had been revised further, with only 13 aircraft to be covered by the old contract, and another 14 to be delivered by 2028 under a new contract.[88]

Tactical combat aircraft

Over the past decade, the VKS's tactical combat fleet has been re-equipped increasingly with new-build aircraft.

Early-model MiG-29 *Fulcrum*s and Su-27 *Flanker*s as of the end of 2019 had for the most part been replaced by Su-30SM *Flanker* H and Su-35S *Flanker* M fighters

respectively.[89] The Su-24M *Fencer* D ground-attack aircraft meanwhile is being replaced with the Su-34 *Fullback* A in the Aerospace Forces and with the Su-30SM

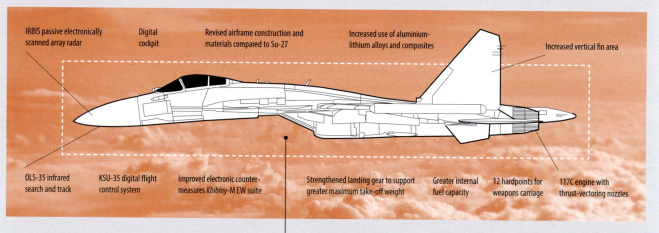

Figure 5.8: Su-35S *Flanker* M: key characteristics

IRBIS passive electronically scanned array radar

Digital cockpit

Revised airframe construction and materials compared to Su-27

Increased use of aluminium-lithium alloys and composites

Increased vertical fin area

OLS-35 infrared search and track

KSU-35 digital flight control system

Improved electronic counter-measures *Khibiny*-M EW suite

Strengthened landing gear to support greater maximum take-off weight

Greater internal fuel capacity

12 hardpoints for weapons carriage

117C engine with thrust-vectoring nozzles

The Su-27 *Flanker* family will remain the core of Russia's tactical air-combat fleet at least well into the 2030s. The Su-35S will provide the air force with its most capable multi-role fighter until the Su-57 *Felon* enters service in reasonable numbers, probably no earlier than the middle of this decade. Once the *Felon* is in service, the *Flanker* M will provide a valuable complement. The *Flanker* had perhaps an even more difficult development than the Su-57, with an airframe redesign during the early stages of the flight-test programme in the late 1970s. Since its introduction into service in 1984, the single-role *Flanker* B has evolved through various design iterations into today's multi-role *Flanker* M. Originally developed as an export product, the air force ordered a batch of 48 in 2009, and a further 50 at the end of 2015. The last of the second batch is planned to be delivered in 2020. Integration trials of the R-37M (AA-13A *Axehead*) long-range air-to-air missile were reportedly under way on the Su-35S during the first quarter of 2020.

Source: IISS; *The Military Balance 2015*

KEY CHARACTERISTICS

- Radar: IRBIS passive electronically scanned array multi-mode air-to-air and air-to-surface. Claimed detection range against a 3 m² radar cross-section target 350–400 km. Claimed 90 km detection range against a 0.01 m² RCS target

- Digital cockpit

- Engine: AL-41F (*Izdeliye* 117C) 2 x 117S turbofan engines each rated at 14,500 kg in afterburner, 8,800 kg max dry power. Thrust-vectoring nozzles

- OLS-35 infrared search and track, 90 km plus detection range (target from rear)

- 12 hardpoints:

- R-73 (AA-11A) and R-74M (AA-11B) (R-73 upgrade), maximum kinematic range 40 km

- *Alamo* family plus R-77-1 (AA-12B *Adder*) active radar-guided medium-range AAM, max range 110 km. Also the K-77M (AA-X-12C), a further development of the basic R-77

Long-range AAM

- R-37M (AA-13A *Axehead*) long-range radar-guided AAM (known as RVV-BD for export). This missile is being offered for the Su-35S. Max range is est. 280 km (200 km for RVV-BD)

- Air-to-surface includes: Kh-38 family of medium-range air-to-surface missiles, Kh-31PM (AS-17C *Krypton*) anti-radiation missile, Kh-59M family (AS-18 *Kazoo*), variety of precision-guided bombs in the navy.[90] The Air Force's reconnaissance variant of the Su-24, the Su-24MR, will be replaced by the Su-34, fitted with a range of pod-mounted reconnaissance systems.[91] In Russian Naval Aviation, the Su-24MR role is in part being met by the introduction of the *Forpost* (*Searcher* II) and *Inokhodets* (*Orion*) uninhabited aerial vehicles (UAVs).[92] The MiG-31 *Foxhound* interceptor fleet has been upgraded to the MiG-31BM *Foxhound* C standard, while much of the Su-25 *Frogfoot* close-air-support aircraft are the improved Su-25SM3 standard.[93]

Current orders for the Su-35 and Su-34 will be fulfilled in 2020. Upon completion, this will still leave up to 100 Su-24s (including about 40 Su-24MR *Fencer* E reconnaissance versions), about 70 MiG-29s (half of which are MiG-29SMTs, and not yet needing replacement) and about 80 Su-27s (12 of which are new Su-27SM3 aircraft) in the VKS inventory. Naval Aviation will

have about 30 Su-24M and ten Su-27 aircraft left to be replaced. If these types were to be renewed on a one-for-one basis, then SAP 2027 would need to include orders for a further 100 Su-34, 60–70 Su-30SM and 70–80 Su-57 *Felon*/Su-35S aircraft. This total is much smaller than in the previous programme, SAP 2020.[94] A larger order could only be based on the formation of additional operational units.

At least part of any new order would involve upgraded models of the Su-30SM and Su-34. Defence Minister Shoigu was shown the prototype of an improved variant of the Su-30SM during a visit to the Irkutsk manufacturing site in January 2019.[95] The upgrade includes the ability to use new air-to-air and air-to-surface weapons; the aircraft is fitted with the AL-41F1S turbofans used in the Su-35 fighter. Replacing the AL-31 would provide greater thrust. The situation is less clear with regard to the Su-34. An

upgrade version, the Su-34M, has been in discussion and a prototype was in development as of 2019. The upgrade covers a new central computer, improved Sh141M radar, with automatic low-level flight, the inclusion of digital-map and terrain-following navigation, and the integration of new weapons. An additional order for the Su-34 was placed at the end of 2019.[96] As of mid-2020, discussions were under way between the defence ministry and industry regarding a potential order for up to 76 Su-34M aircraft.

Felon's change of fortune

SAP 2020 included the planned acquisition of some 60 Su-57 *Felon* multi-role fighters, the first post-Soviet-era aircraft to be designed from the outset with radar-signature reduction as a key parameter.[97] This ambition went unmet, and by the end of 2019 only ten prototypes and one initial production-standard aircraft had

Figure 5.9: **Su-57 *Felon*: development and production**

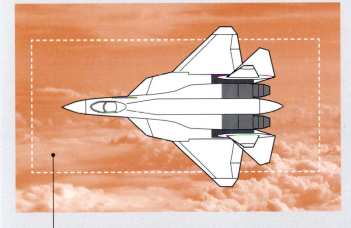

T-50 (SU-57) PROTOTYPES

SERIAL NUMBER	FACTORY NUMBER	FIRST FLIGHT	NOTES
-	T-50-0	-	Static-test airframe
-	T-50-KNU	-	Static-test airframe
051 BLUE	T-50-1	29 Jan 2010	
052 BLUE	T-50-2	3 Mar 2011	
053 BLUE	T-50-3	22 Nov 2011	
054 BLUE	T-50-4	2 Dec 2012	
055 BLUE	T-50-5	27 Oct 2013 and 16 Oct 2015	Seriously damaged by fire in 2014. Testing resumed in 2015
056 BLUE*	T-50-6	27 Apr 2016	
-	T-50-7	-	Static-test airframe
057 BLUE*	T-50-8	17 Nov 2016	
509 BLUE*	T-50-9	24 Apr 2017	
511 BLUE*	T-50-11	6 Aug 2017	

*Built to modified design with reportedly strengthened fuselage to avoid cracking issues seen in previous prototypes

The Su-57 *Felon* has had mixed fortunes since Sukhoi was selected to meet the air force's PAK-FA requirement in 2002. Overly ambitious plans to begin series production in 2010 were unachievable, and as of mid-2020 the first production aircraft had yet to be handed over to the air force. Initial plans in the 2020 State Armament Programme (SAP) to buy 60 of the type were dropped, and the SAP 2027 originally included only a small initial production batch of around 15 aircraft. The intervention of President Vladimir Putin in June 2019 saw this number increased to 76 aircraft to be delivered by the end of 2027. As of mid-2020, however, development of the long-term engine for the aircraft continued to be delayed.

TIMELINE

PLANNED

SERIES PRODUCTION PLANNED TO BEGIN	EXPECTED T-50 ISD (AS OF 2010)	EXPECTED T-50 ISD (AS OF 2017)	FIRST PRODUCTION DELIVERY DUE	AIM – 76 SU-57 3 REGIMENTS IN SERVICE
2010	2015/16	2019	2020	2027

1985	1990	1995	2000	2005	2010	2015	2020	2025	2030

ACTUAL

1986	1991	2002	2003	2010	2016	2018	2019
MIG IS SELECTED TO LEAD THE MFI FIGHTER PROJECT	DISSOLUTION OF THE SOVIET UNION	RUSSIA SELECTS SUKHOI'S T-50 PROPOSAL OVER MIG'S E-721 DESIGN	SUKHOI CONTRACTED TO DEVELOP T-50	FIRST T-50 PROTOTYPE MAKES MAIDEN FLIGHT	FIRST GROUND TESTS ON ADVANCED *IZDELIYE*-30 ENGINE	SU-57 SYRIA SHORT DETACHMENT	• SU-57 SYRIA SHORT DETACHMENT • SU-57 (T-50S-1) FIRST FLIGHT DECEMBER 2019 CRASHED 24 DECEMBER

— Target dates were not achieved

Sources: IISS; *The Military Balance 2018*

Figure 5.10: Russia's tactical aviation inventory, 2007 and 2020

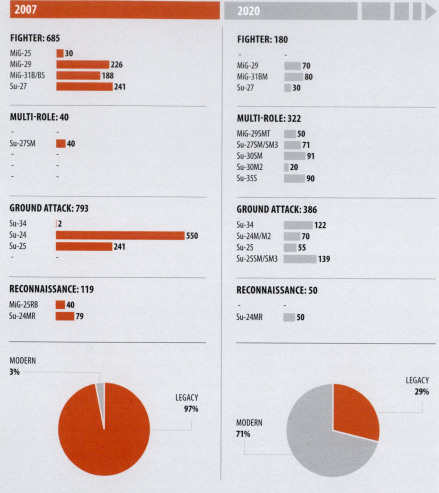

2007 **2020**

FIGHTER: 685

MiG-25	30
MiG-29	226
MiG-31B/BS	188
Su-27	241

FIGHTER: 180

-	-
MiG-29	70
MiG-31BM	80
Su-27	30

MULTI-ROLE: 40

-	-
Su-27SM	40
-	-
-	-
-	-

MULTI-ROLE: 322

MiG-29SMT	50
Su-27SM/SM3	71
Su-30SM	91
Su-30M2	20
Su-35S	90

GROUND ATTACK: 793

Su-34	2
Su-24	550
Su-25	241
-	-

GROUND ATTACK: 386

Su-34	122
Su-24M/M2	70
Su-25	55
Su-25SM/SM3	139

RECONNAISSANCE: 119

MiG-25RB	40
Su-24MR	79

RECONNAISSANCE: 50

-	-
Su-24MR	50

MODERN 3%
LEGACY 97%

LEGACY 29%
MODERN 71%

IISS assessments of 'modern' air-force equipment covers platforms that were upgraded or new-build from 1999

Sources: *The Military Balance 2008*; IISS Military Balance+

SU-57 *FELON*
Russia's latest fighter/ground-attack aircraft, which has suffered procurement delays. CREDIT: P. Butowski

been built, along with three static-test airframes. The first production aircraft crashed on 24 December 2019, before it had been delivered to the Air Force training centre at Lipetsk.[98] Furthermore, information made public on SAP 2027 indicated that only a small number of the Su-57 would be purchased during this period, perhaps as few as 15 aircraft. On 22 August 2018, Alexey Krivoruchko – the defence ministry's deputy minister for acquisition – signed a contract with UAC president Slyusar for the first production batch of two Su-57s, with delivery to the VKS due during 2020 (though not complete as of July 2020).[99]

Orders for another 13 Su-57s were later announced, with Krivoruchko suggesting that from 2023 these could be 'second-stage' aircraft fitted with a new engine.[100] Rather than the 15 or so Su-57s that SAP 2027 indicated that the Air Force would receive, the initial target was to have been ten times this number in service by the middle of the 2020s.[101] An unrealistic development schedule, technical problems and the unit cost of the aircraft combined to delay its entry into service.[102] In an interview in July 2018, Borisov put a gloss on the situation, saying: 'the Su-35 … is one of the best airplanes in the world. So there is no sense in ramping up work on the mass production of the fifth-generation aircraft.'[103] The Su-57's fortunes took a turn for the better in June 2019, however, when Putin announced that 76 Su-57s would be purchased by 2028, likely to form six squadrons of the type.[104] He also suggested that the projected acquisition cost of the Su-57 had been reduced.[105]

The order signed between Krivoruchko and Slyusar also included the purchase of six MiG-35 multi-role fighters, the latest development of the *Fulcrum*.[106] An additional 20 were to be purchased as part of SAP 2027. It is yet unknown the extent to which this is mainly an effort to support the design in the export arena, rather than any real aim on the part of the Air Force to operate the type in significant numbers.

Foxhound's further guises

Alongside an upgrade programme for the interceptor, the MiG-31 *Foxhound* has also been modified to accommodate two additional weapons: one a long-range air-to-surface weapon, the other an anti-satellite system. The MiG-31K *Foxhound* D carries the *Kinzhal* (AS-24 *Killjoy*) aero-ballistic missile.[107] The weapon, which may be designated the 9-A-7760, is an air-launched derivative of the 9M723 missile that is part of the 9K720 *Iskander*-M (SS-26 *Stone*) short-range ballistic-missile system fielded by the Russian army.[108] The dual-capable *Kinzhal* is carried on a centre-line pylon on the MiG-31K.

The MiG-31's cruise speed of Mach 2.35, and a maximum speed of Mach 2.8 at high altitude, make it particularly suited to the launch of aero-ballistic systems.[109] The combined combat range of the MiG-31K–*Kinzhal* combination is around 2,000 km. As of mid-2020, a squadron of the MiG-31K aircraft appeared to still be deployed at the 929th State Flight Test Centre at Akhtubinsk.

A further MiG-31 modification emerged in September 2018 when a MiG-31 was seen being test-flown carrying a very large weapon, again on a centre-line pylon. The project is assumed to be an anti-satellite system and appears to be a continuation of a 1980s Soviet project known as *Kontakt* (Contact) that was later shelved as the Russian economy weakened. The 'new' anti-satellite programme is also believed to be known as *Burevestnik*, with the 'Izdeliye 293' or 14A045 rocket intended to deliver a small anti-satellite payload to low-Earth orbit. The 1980s 30P6 *Kontakt* programme was based on the MiG-31D aircraft carrying the *Fakel* 79M6 missile, trials of which were carried out.[110] A further modification, the MiG-31DM, was being designed to carry the *Fakel* 95M6 missile when the programme was cancelled.[111] The 79M6 missile weighed 4,550 kilograms (10,031 lb), was launched at Mach 2.55 and an altitude of 22 km (13.67 miles), and was capable of intercepting satellites in low-Earth orbit at altitudes between 120 km and 600 km (74.5 miles to 372.8 miles).

Of the existing fleet of MiG-31s, most have already been upgraded to the MiG-31BM *Foxhound* C standard, while several dozen others are in storage and could also be upgraded or modified to provide additional *Kinzhal* or anti-satellite launch platforms. A successor design to meet the Aerospace Forces' PAK-DP (*Perspektivnyy aviatsionnyy kompleks dalnego perekhvata*, Future Aviation Complex of Long-range Interception) requirement is being considered. The MiG-31, however, will be operated well into the 2030s.[112]

Irrespective of the failed targets within SAP 2020, the Air Force's tactical-combat-aircraft inventory has improved greatly as a result of a decade-long investment in acquisition. The Su-35S provides the service with the first new-build single-seat multi-role fighter in operationally significant numbers, with the two-seat Su-30SM providing a useful complement. The Su-34 similarly arrived in credible numbers to improve markedly the service's conventional air-to-surface attack capacity.

Regenerating Russia's air-to-air arsenal

By the mid-1980s, the Soviet Air Force had a credible guided-weapons road map to complement the upgraded and new combat-aircraft types that it anticipated entering service during the 1990s and early 2000s. The air-to-air element of this was to stall for over two decades as R&D and procurement funding dropped precipitously. Only since 2015 has the Air Force finally begun to take delivery of improved air-to-air missiles (AAMs).[113]

Rather than field more capable short-, medium- and long-range AAMs

R-37M (AA-13A *AXEHEAD*)
This long-range air-to-air missile (r) could form part of the Su-35's armament, along with the R-77-1 (AA-12B *Adder*) (l). CREDIT: P. Butowski

equivalent to or better than the types fielded by the United States and European nations, the Russian Air Force had to make do with weapons designed in the 1970s. By the second decade of this century, these were verging on obsolescence, had questionable reliability, or both. The effect was to markedly reduce the force's potency in the air-to-air arena.

Of at least three types planned in the 1980s – the short-range R-30, the intended successor to the R-73 (AA-11A *Archer*); the medium-range R-77 (AA-12A *Adder*), to replace the R-27 (AA-10 *Alamo*) family; and the long-range R-37 (AA-X-13 *Axehead*), to succeed the R-33 (AA-9A/B *Amos*) – only the R-77 reached production.[114] This would be export-only for well over a decade before an improved version finally made its way into the Russian inventory. The short-range R-30 project was shelved, while the R-37 was eventually to emerge nearly two decades after it was first intended to be fielded as the R-37M.[115]

Several factors combined to reinvigorate Russia's efforts to recapitalise its AAM inventory. Worsening relations with the US and its NATO allies from the mid-2000s met an increased focus on military modernisation. This was helped by a comparatively buoyant economy and a regime willing to provide a useful increase in defence spending. With the introduction of improved-performance AAMs to complement the upgraded combat-aircraft types now in service in reasonable numbers, the Air Force poses a more credible air-to-air opponent than at any time since the collapse of the Soviet Union.

An improved variant of the R-73, the R-74M (AA-11B), entered service in 2016, three decades after work started on an R-73 upgrade.[116] The R-74M uses a new infrared seeker that offers greater detection range and a higher off-boresight angle. Meanwhile, the K-74M2 project is intended to fit the *Archer* airframe within the Su-57's smaller internal weapons bay, and perhaps with an imaging-infrared seeker.[117]

While the R-77 was exported widely as the RVV-AE, the missile did not enter service in Russia, almost certainly due to a lack of funding. Instead the Air Force looked to an improved variant of the basic missile, the R-77-1 (AA-12B), as its first active radar-guided medium-range AAM. The R-77-1 design included a number of aerodynamic refinements: the rear section was boat-tailed, and the lattice-fin mountings were recessed to make them flush with the main body.[118] These changes, when combined with a lofted trajectory, resulted in an increase in the missile's maximum engagement range to around 100 km (62 miles), compared to the basic version's 80 km (50 miles). The first test shots of the missile began in 2010, with the weapon entering the VKS inventory in 2015.

Images of the missile on an operational aircraft, an Su-35S, emerged in open sources when the Su-35S was deployed as part of the Syrian air operation. It has since been seen also on aircraft intercepted as part of NATO's Baltic Air Policing mission.

A further 'upgrade' of the R-77, the R-77M (likely the AA-X-12C), is also in development.[119] This is a more extensive project, including reportedly that the *Adder*'s lattice fin is replaced with a traditional blade fin. Solid-motor refinements, possibly including the introduction of a dual-pulse motor, will likely push the weapon's maximum engagement range to around 120 km.

The Air Force in Syria

Moscow's employment of airpower in the 1994–96 and 1999–2000 wars in Chechnya had taxed the Air Force, as did the 2008 Russo-Georgian war.[120] Neither, however, were comparable to the demands of the Syrian civil war. Russia's commitment to supporting the regime of Bashar al-Assad, if not Assad himself, required deploying and sustaining a mixed air wing at distances overseas not seen, nor practised, since the end of the Soviet Union. This was achieved by relying on an ageing air-transport fleet, similarly aged supply ships, and a range of upgraded aircraft and weapon types being debuted in combat operations.

In the Air Force's first expeditionary operation since the Soviet era, on 30 September 2015 a Russian air group deployed at Hmeimim air base, 20 kilometres (12 miles) southeast of the city of Latakia, and began combat operations in support of Syrian government forces.[121] Initially the combat air wing totalled 32 aircraft, a mix of multi-role fighters and close-air-support and attack aircraft. Combat-support helicopters later complemented fixed-wing combat types. The size of the force grew over time, with the deployment peaking at around 50 fixed-wing combat aircraft in early 2016.[122]

The most numerous aircraft deployed so far has been the Su-24M *Fencer* D, with a maximum of 14 of the type involved. The successor to the 1970s-era Su-24 design, the Su-34 *Fullback* – along with the Su-25SM *Frogfoot* – were the two next most numerous, while smaller numbers of upgraded *Flanker*s – the Su-27SM *Flanker*, Su-30SM *Flanker* H and Su-35S *Flanker* M – were also committed to the operation.[123]

False drawdown

Six months after the initial deployment, Moscow made what was to be the first of several premature withdrawal claims. President Vladimir Putin announced on 14 March 2016 the beginning of the drawdown of 'the main part of the Russian Military contingent', suggesting 'the task set for the Ministry of Defence and the Armed Forces in general is fulfilled'.[124] Shortly after Putin's statement almost one-third of the air component was pulled out, including all the Su-25s.[125]

Following the first reduction in the deployment, 12 Su-24M, four Su-34, and three or four Su-30SM and Su-35S aircraft remained at Hmeimim.[126] Irrespective of Putin's statement, however, the opposition to Assad proved more resilient than first assessed by Russia; as fighting again intensified, the air contingent was increased, though not to the same level as the peak of the original deployment. For most of the time, fixed-wing strength varied between 27 and 40 combat aircraft.[127]

By December 2016, Putin was again making a 'mission accomplished' declaration, this time during a visit to Syria. The Russian president said that Russian and Syrian armed forces had defeated the 'terrorists' and again that a drawdown of personnel should soon begin.[128] Despite Putin's rhetoric, there was little change at Hmeimim in terms of combat aircraft remaining at the base. After an increase in operations, by mid-2018 the number of deployed aircraft had finally been reduced, with around 20 aircraft remaining at the base.[129] Satellite imagery from the third and fourth quarters of 2018 showed up to eight Su-24Ms, six Su-34s and four Su-35Ss.

Support aircraft deployed included a *Beriev A-50 Mainstay* airborne early-warning (AEW) aircraft, two Ilyushin Il-20M *Coot* electronic-reconnaissance aircraft, and for a limited period a Tupolev Tu-214R electronic-reconnaissance aircraft. Transport types included the Antonov An-124 *Condor* and the Ilyushin Il-76 *Candid* to provide the air bridge between Russia and Syria.[130]

Other Russian aircraft have appeared in Syria for brief periods in order to test them in combat conditions. Several MiG-29SMT *Fulcrum* aircraft from the 929th State Flight Test Centre at Akhtubinsk were deployed in Syria between September and December 2017.[131] In February 2018, two Su-57 *Felon* fighters (aircraft numbers T-50-9 and T-50-11) were deployed there for a few days.[132] It was not until November 2018 that the defence ministry released footage showing the aircraft taking off and landing at Hmeimim. At the same time, the footage appeared to confirm earlier claims that the Su-57s were flown without Luneburg lenses to mask the aircraft's actual radar signature. The lens acts as a corner reflector, increasing the return of the aircraft when illuminated by radar. If true, and if the Air Force had not taken any other less visible measures to alter the aircraft's signature, it would have provided valuable intelligence data on the Su-57 to other interested parties in the region. In December 2019, Sergei Shoigu said the Su-57 had been deployed to Syria again but did not provide dates.[133] The MiG-31*Foxhound* interceptor was also claimed to be included among the roster of combat aircraft at Hmeimim for a brief period in November 2016.[134]

In a move arguably more symbolic than operationally significant, the Russian Navy sent its only aircraft carrier, the *Admiral Kuznetsov*, to the Syrian operation from November 2016 to January 2017. The air group on board the ship was made up of four MiG-29KR/KUBR *Fulcrum* and nine Su-33 *Flanker* D fighters, as well as Ka-52K *Hokum* attack helicopters, Ka-31 *Helix* AEW helicopters, Ka-29 *Helix* transport helicopters and Ka-27 *Helix* helicopters in the anti-submarine-warfare and search-and-rescue roles. Following problems with the carrier's aircraft-recovery system, the MiG-29 and Su-33 aircraft operated from Hmeimim. All but around 10% of the fixed-wing missions flown by the navy were from Hmeimim rather than from the aircraft carrier.[135]

Crewed aviation units were complemented by a number of uninhabited systems, most of them small. In total, the Russian military deployed around 70 uninhabited aerial vehicles (UAVs) in the Syrian civil war. Light UAVs included the *Orlan*-10, *Eleron*-3SV and *Granat*.[136] The largest to be routinely deployed was the 450 kg (1,000 lb)-class *Forpost*, a licence-built version of the Israeli *Searcher* II, while the 1,130 kg (2,500 lb)-class *Inokhodets* (*Orion*) was also tested in Syria.[137] The UAVs were used for intelligence, surveillance and reconnaissance. A tethered surveillance system was also employed: the Augur Au-17 *Bars* tethered balloon that carries an electro-optical payload.

Weapons used

While the Russian military and domestic media often stressed the use of precision weaponry, the air operation continued to rely for the most part on free-fall munitions.[138] The most widely

SU-25 *FROGFOOT* GROUND-ATTACK AIRCRAFT
At various times, one of the most numerous aircraft types deployed by Russia in Syria. CREDIT: Vadim Grishankin/Russian Defence Ministry Press and Information Office/TASS/Getty Images

used were the 250 kg (551 lb) OFAB-250-270 high-explosive fragmentation bomb and 500 kg (1,102 lb) FAB-500M-62 high-explosive bomb, both designed for personnel defeat, and the destruction of lightly armoured vehicles, infrastructure and field fortifications. Footage also showed RBK-500 cluster bombs filled with fragmentation, incendiary or anti-armour bomblets being used in Syria.[139]

Guided weapons were used most often with the Su-34 *Fullback* in the form of the KAB-500S 500 kg satellite-guided bomb.[140] This type completed state trials in 2006.[141] A number of weapons that are still in test or have recently completed development were also seen in Syria. The Zvezda-Strela (part of Russia's Tactical Missile Corp.) Kh-35U (AS-20 *Kayak*) was shown carried by an Su-34 at Hmeimim.[142] The Kh-35U is an extended-range variant of the basic Kh-35 (AS-20A *Kayak*) anti-ship missile, the latter originally designed as the 3M24 *Uran* (SS-N-25 *Switchblade*) surface-to-surface anti-ship weapon.[143] The Russian defence ministry in May 2018 also provided footage of an Su-57 releasing an air-to-surface missile, claiming it was an operational test-shot of the weapon in Syria carried out in February of that year.[144] The missile seen has previously been identified by Raduga (also a KTRV company), its manufacturer, as the Kh-59MK2.[145]

The Kh-59MK2 designation had been used initially by the manufacturer to describe a limited upgrade of the Kh-59M (AS-18 *Kazoo*), before what appeared to be a new tactical land-attack cruise missile (LACM) was shown under the same designation during the 2017 Moscow Air Show.[146] The weapon was designed to fit within the main internal bays of the Su-57. The air-to-surface stand-off weapon may be in a similar class to the European SCALP EG/*Storm Shadow* or KEPD-350 *Taurus*.

Two designs of conventionally armed long-range cruise missiles were used for the first time by the Russian Air Force during the Syrian civil war. The Kh-555 (AS-22 *Kluge*) and Kh-101 (AS-23A *Kodiak*) were carried by the Tupolev Tu-95MS mod *Bear* and Tu-160M mod *Blackjack*.[147] The Kh-555 is a conventionally armed conversion of the Kh-55 (AS-15A/B *Kent*) nuclear-armed cruise missile, and provided the Air Force with a 'shortcut' to fielding a non-nuclear long-range LACM.[148]

The Kh-101, and its nuclear variant the Kh-102 (AS-23B), have had a prolonged development. The project likely began at the end of the 1980s.[149] Originally intended to be powered by the Soyuz R128 propfan engine, this propulsion option was dropped in favour of a less ambitious approach using a turbofan from engine manufacturer Saturn. The engine pod is housed in the missile body, like the Kh-55, and is deployed only after release from a rotary launcher, or pylon.

Initial firings of the Kh-101 during the Syrian campaign were not always successful and have likely resulted in the introduction of some modifications, probably software-based.[150] The Tu-22M3 *Backfire* C carried only free-fall iron bombs for all Syrian missions.[151]

Personnel opportunities

Irrespective of contradictory and perhaps inflated figures, the Syrian commitment provided valuable combat and operational experience for the Russian Aerospace Forces. Shoigu said in August 2018: 'two thirds of flight and technical personnel had received combat practice. We have many young pilots who have 100 and more combat missions.'[152] Units were rotated frequently with the aim of achieving as large a number of personnel with combat experience as possible. However, Shoigu's comments do not match Russian defence-ministry figures released that same month. Official ministry statistics claim that combat experience was gained by '87% of tactical aviation crews, 91% of army aviation crews, 97% of transport aviation crews and 60% of strategic and long-range aviation crews'.[153] These figures are markedly higher than those given by Shoigu. According to the same ministry release, by August 2018 the Air Force had flown 39,000 combat flights, with tactical combat missions peaking at over 100 per day. Tu-95MS and Tu-160 missions totalled 66, with the Tu-22M3 reaching 369. Transport aircraft had been flown 2,785 times to support the deployment, moving over 91,000 personnel. Naval Aviation had carried out 420 combat flights, but nearly all were land-based, while UAV flights were in excess of 25,000.[154]

'Combat' losses

Aircraft losses and crew fatalities were a near inevitability in an operation of the scale of the Russia intervention in Syria. By early 2019, Russian forces had lost eight helicopters and eight fixed-wing aircraft. Of the eight helicopters (two Mi-8AMTSh *Hip*, three Mi-35M *Hind*, one Mi-24 *Hind*, one Mi-28N *Havoc* and one Ka-52 *Hokum*) six were destroyed in combat and two, the Mi-28N and the Ka-52, were lost due to flying errors.[155] An additional four Mi-24Ps were destroyed by fire on the ground at the Tiyas Miltary Airbase (also known as the T-4 air base) on 14 May 2016.[156] This was variously claimed to have been a 'terrorist' attack or caused by an accident and not as a result of combat action.[157]

Of the eight fixed-wing aircraft lost, only two were shot down. The first Russian loss in Syria was an Su-24M *Fencer* shot down on 24 November 2015 by a Turkish Air Force F-16C *Fighting Falcon*; the pilot was killed, while the navigator was rescued.[158] An Su-25SM was then shot down on 3 February 2018 by a man-portable surface-to-air missile in Idlib province, and the pilot killed.[159] Accidents during take-off resulted in the loss of an Su-24M and an Su-30SM; the crew was killed in both cases. The former loss occurred on 10 October 2017, while the latter crash happened on 3 May 2018.[160]

Accidents cost Naval Aviation two shipborne fighters from the *Admiral Kuznetsov*. On 13 November 2016, an MiG-29KR was ditched near the ship after having run out of fuel.[161] On 3 December 2016, an Su-33 crashed into the Mediterranean Sea when the arresting wire snapped on landing.[162] On both occasions the pilots survived.

The two largest death tolls were also the result of accidents, though of a different nature. Six crew and 33 passengers died when an Antonov An-26 *Coke* crashed on approach to Hmeimim on 6 March 2018.[163] Meanwhile, the Syrian Air Defense Force was to shoot down an Ilyushin Il-20M *Coot* reconnaissance aircraft on 17 September 2018, incorrectly identifying the aircraft on radar as part of an Israeli Air Force raid. All 15 personnel on board were killed.[164]

The Syrian intervention was a gamble on the part of President Putin, and for the service arms involved. It could have easily gone wrong, but instead Russian support has so far proved the turning point for Assad's regime. This was down mainly to the Russian Air Force, aided by Russian advisers on the ground. The Air Force's prestige has benefited from its success in Syria.

Long range

In the 1980s, work was under way on a further development of the MiG-31 *Foxhound*, the MiG-31M; in effect, a mid-life update to the aircraft design. At the heart of the upgrade was a replacement for the MiG-31's original long-range AAM, the R-33 (AA-9A *Amos*). The R-33 had a maximum engagement of 110 km. Work on a replacement, the K-37 (AA-X-13), was likely under way by the end of the 1970s.[165] The MiG-31M project, however, was cancelled in the economic turmoil of the 1990s, and the K-37 project fell into abeyance.[166]

Such was the importance of the long-range interceptor to the Air Force, however, that the service eventually pursued the inclusion of some of the systems intended for the new-build MiG-31M on in-service MiG-31s. The upgraded variant of the latter is known as the MiG-31BM (*Foxhound* C). Central to the modernisation programme was a further development of the K-37, the R-37M (AA-13 *Axehead*).[167] The R-37M entered Russian service in 2016 and can be used to engage targets well beyond 150 km.[168] It is also being offered for export as the RVV-BD, as part of the weapons package for the Su-35. The Su-57 could also carry the R-37M, though only externally.

The R-33 and the R-37M also likely have nuclear-armed variants.[169] A small nuclear warhead was developed for the R-33 to allow it to be used to engage groups of targets, such as cruise missiles, and the same may be the case for the R-37M. Work on another long-range AAM, known as the 'Izdeliye 810', began around 2010.[170] This missile is a further development of the R-37M and is intended for carriage in the Su-57's internal-weapons bay. This missile may have a range in excess of 250 km.

If the activity and success of the 1980s was a high point in the Soviet air-to-air weapons arena, the following decades were marked by the lows of limited investment and little procurement. It was only with the introduction of the R-77-1 that the service gained an active radar-guided medium-range AAM in 2015, almost a quarter of a century later than first planned. Russia still lacks an imaging-infrared-guided high-agility short-range AAM, where once the R-73 had been among the most capable in its class. However, successor projects are under way, albeit much later than anticipated; the introduction of the improved AAMs again marks a notable improvement in the Air Force's ability to pose a credible air-to-air threat.

Air-to-surface developments

Weapons development in the air-to-surface realm fared no better than for AAMs during the 1990s and into the early part of this century. Even the Air Force's replacement for the Raduga Kh-55 (AS-15A/B *Kent*) nuclear-armed cruise missile, the Kh-102 (AS-23B *Kodiak*), was to suffer from delayed development.[171] Arguably, however, it was in the short-to-medium-range tactical realm that the collapse in funding was felt most keenly. This was evident in the VKS's intervention in Syria where the Su-24M *Fencer* D, Su-25 and Su-34 used relatively few tactical missiles of a limited range of types. Free-fall bombs figured strongly in the weapon load-outs for missions; the Tu-22M3 *Backfire* C intermediate-range bomber, for example, dropped only unguided munitions.

The Tu-95MS mod., *Bear* H, and the Tu-160 mod, *Blackjack*, were used in Syria to employ two types of cruise missiles. The Kh-555 (AS-22 *Kluge*) was a conventionally armed variant of the Kh-55, with improved guidance, while the Kh-101 (AS-23A *Kodiak*) was the conventional version of the Kh-102.[172] The Kh-555 appears to have been an interim approach to provide the VKS with a conventionally armed land-attack cruise missile (LACM) until the delayed Kh-101 programme was eventually ready.

Like the Kh-101/102 programme, the Kh-38M project can also be tracked back

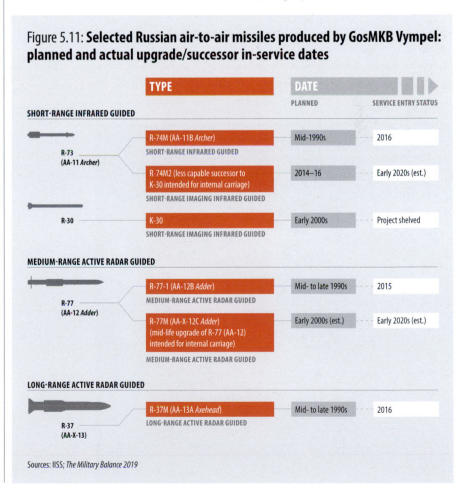

Figure 5.11: Selected Russian air-to-air missiles produced by GosMKB Vympel: planned and actual upgrade/successor in-service dates

TYPE		DATE	
		PLANNED	**SERVICE ENTRY STATUS**
SHORT-RANGE INFRARED GUIDED			
R-73 (AA-11 *Archer*)	R-74M (AA-11B *Archer*) SHORT-RANGE INFRARED GUIDED	Mid-1990s	2016
	R-74M2 (less capable successor to K-30 intended for internal carriage) SHORT-RANGE IMAGING INFRARED GUIDED	2014–16	Early 2020s (est.)
R-30	K-30 SHORT-RANGE IMAGING INFRARED GUIDED	Early 2000s	Project shelved
MEDIUM-RANGE ACTIVE RADAR GUIDED			
R-77 (AA-12 *Adder*)	R-77-1 (AA-12B *Adder*) MEDIUM-RANGE ACTIVE RADAR GUIDED	Mid- to late 1990s	2015
	R-77M (AA-X-12C *Adder*) (mid-life upgrade of R-77 (AA-12) intended for internal carriage) MEDIUM-RANGE ACTIVE RADAR GUIDED	Early 2000s (est.)	Early 2020s (est.)
LONG-RANGE ACTIVE RADAR GUIDED			
R-37 (AA-X-13)	R-37M (AA-13A *Axehead*) LONG-RANGE ACTIVE RADAR GUIDED	Mid- to late 1990s	2016

Sources: IISS; *The Military Balance 2019*

to a late-1980s requirement, though in this case to provide a successor to the Kh-25 (AS-10 *Karen*/AS-12 *Kegler*) family of short-range air-to-surface missiles, which dates back to the 1970s.[173] The Kh-38M will also provide the main successor to the Kh-29 (AS-14 *Kedge*), although the former's warhead is smaller.

Several versions of the Kh-38 are in development using semi-active laser, active radar, infrared and satellite-navigation guidance.[174] The semi-active laser-guided version, the Kh-38ML, has likely already completed state-testing and entered production. There have been contradictory claims as to whether the Kh-38ML was tested in Syria. So far, unlike the Kh-25, there has been no indication that the family will also include an anti-radiation variant. The VKS's main anti-radiation missiles are likely to be the Kh-31PM (AS-17C *Krypton*), an improved version of the Kh-31P (AS-17A), and also improved variants of the Kh-58 (AS-11 *Kilter*).

Moscow also appears to be looking to close a capability gap in its missile inventory in acquiring one or more medium-range LACMs. A missile dubbed the Kh-59MK2 was tested in Syria, which in performance terms is likely akin to the European SCALP-EG/*Storm Shadow* or the *Taurus* KEPD-350.[175] This system could also be associated with the KH-SD. However, this is a designation that has also been used with regard to a repackaged and physically smaller version of the Kh-101.[176]

The Air Force's cruise-missile inventory has been enhanced with the introduction of the Kh-101/102. Improvements similarly are in train for its tactical air-to-surface inventory, if again far later than originally planned. Syria, however, continued to show a reliance on unguided ordnance that is of increasingly limited utility in air warfare. As such, completing the development of a number of tactical guided-weapons projects and their production in substantial numbers remains of importance to the Air Force if it is to deliver fully in the air-to-surface role.

GROM, Kh-59MK2 AND Kh-58USHK (L–R)
Examples from the range of new and upgraded air-to-surface missiles being developed by Russia's Tactical Missile Corporation.
CREDIT: P. Butowski

S-400 *TRIUMF* AND *PANTSIR* ANTI-AIRCRAFT SYSTEMS IN TRAINING
The S-400 *Triumf* (SA-21 *Growler*) long-range (l) and the 96K6 *Pantsir* (SA-22 *Greyhound*) short-range (r) surface-to-air missile systems, delivered in substantial numbers as part of Russia's State Armament Programme 2020. CREDIT: Mikhail Japaridze/TASS/Getty Images

Russia's military space modernisation

Russia today maintains military and intelligence-oriented space systems that, while not at the level of the United States', are still more advanced and numerous than most other countries'.[177] The GLONASS precision-timing and -navigation constellation is fully operational, as is the new generation of EKS early-warning satellites. Moscow also maintains a fleet of capable intelligence, surveillance and reconnaissance (ISR), weather and mapping satellites to serve military needs.[178] The Russian armed forces have shown significant capacity to integrate space capabilities into military operations in Crimea, eastern Ukraine and Syria.[179] This includes using Russian space capabilities to enhance planning, targeting and coordination of their own allied forces as well as sophisticated electronic-warfare, counter-space capabilities to deny their adversaries the use of satellite communications and navigation services.

In addition, there are strong indications that Russia is developing a suite of new counter-space capabilities to undermine and deter NATO space competence in the event of a future conflict.[180] Russia has conducted multiple demonstrations of rendezvous and proximity operations on orbit, including two recent events that may have been tests of a new co-orbital anti-satellite (ASAT) called *Burevestnik*.[181] Since 2014, Russia has also conducted ten flight tests of a new direct-ascent ASAT missile system known as *Nudol*, although to date the system has not been tested against an orbital target.[182] There are also signs that Russia is upgrading its *Beriev* A-60 aircraft-based laser system, which could be used to temporarily dazzle or blind imagery satellites.[183] Finally, Russia is modernising many of its radar and telescope facilities used for space situational awareness (SSA) and partnering with other countries to expand coverage beyond its geographic boundaries.

During the Cold War, the Soviet Union was a space superpower and possessed a wide array of civil- and national-security space capabilities. Although its biggest successes came early, the Soviet Union was rightly regarded as a pioneer in many types of space activity, with its sophisticated workforce and a strong industrial base. The Cold War drove the Soviet Union and the United States to develop a spectrum of national-security space capabilities for both military and intelligence uses. Although Moscow had an early lead in powerful rockets and the rate of space launches, its satellites lagged behind the United States' in technological sophistication and performance. Nevertheless, by 1980 the Soviet Union had developed dedicated military remote-sensing satellites for ISR, particularly the detection and targeting of ships at sea; communications satellites for global and high-latitude strategic and tactical communications; missile-warning satellites for detecting launches of intercontinental ballistic missiles (ICBMs); navigation satellites for regional use by land or maritime forces; and weather and geodesy satellites to support military planning and operations. The Soviet Union also had a series of dedicated military space stations for reconnaissance and military research, and a co-orbital anti-satellite weapon system that could target satellites in low-Earth orbit.

During the 1980s, the US–Soviet military space competition accelerated. The Soviets began developing their GLONASS satellite system to provide global navigation and timing capabilities, and deploying more advanced versions of their radar-imagery and electronic-surveillance satellites for tracking and targeting ships at sea. The Reagan administration's Strategic Defense Initiative (SDI) also prompted a significant increase in Soviet counter-space and missile-defence programmes. The SDI was envisioned to involve large numbers of US space-based interceptors for destroying Soviet ICBMs as they coasted through space on the way to their targets. Although the Soviets doubted the feasibility of the SDI, the Soviet defence industry nevertheless used the concerns to propose and begin developing a wide range of ground-, air- and space-based ASAT weapon systems that could target satellites in all Earth orbits, including those that would be used for SDI. The Soviet Union also developed sophisticated ground-based radars and telescopes for detecting, tracking and targeting satellites as part of SSA, albeit with coverage limited to only the geographic area of the Soviet Union.

The break-up of the Soviet Union in 1991 and resulting economic and political challenges created delays in many of the Soviet-era military space programmes and, in some cases, resulted in programmes being completely halted, largely due to the collapse of government budgets and the absence of alternative private-sector funding. Several key ground installations, such as early-warning radars and space-launch facilities, were now located in independent countries. The next generation of Russian early-warning satellites was significantly delayed, and on-orbit failures led to coverage gaps that likely rendered the system unreliable. While the GLONASS navigation-satellite constellation was officially declared operational in 1996, older satellites began to fail faster than they could be replaced. By 2001, only nine GLONASS satellites were still operational, out of the 24 needed for full coverage, and Russian forces in the First Chechen War had to rely on the US Global Positioning System instead. Development of the new ASAT weapons systems was also placed on hold or outright cancelled.

Since the early 2000s, the Russian Federation has made reinvesting in military space capabilities a priority and is in the process of reconstituting many of the capabilities it had during the Cold War.[184] The funding for GLONASS was doubled, and new versions of the satellites started launching to replenish the constellation. Likewise, there were new commitments and funding to re-establish an early-warning satellite constellation. New programmes were started, to refresh and upgrade Russian space-based ISR capabilities. There is also evidence to suggest that Russia restarted several counter-space programmes to develop upgraded versions of Cold War-era ASAT capabilities or new capabilities that had been put on hold. In 2015, Russia reorganised its military space forces by combining space- and missile-defence units under the new Aerospace Forces.

Taken together, these activities suggest that Russia sees its space capabilities as cornerstones of its ability to defend against foreign aggression and reassert its regional dominance.

VKS surface-to-air (and space) missile development

The Soviet Union expended more effort on surface-to-air missile systems than the West, and Russia continues this tradition. Point-defence, short-, medium-, and long-range air-defence systems, ballistic-missile defence and counter-space systems all now fall within the ambit of the Aerospace Forces. All are being upgraded, if with varying results.

Generations of surface-to-air missile systems have been developed to meet actual or projected US threats, some of which failed to materialise. The United States' offensive aerospace capabilities remain the driver for Russia's air- and space-engagement capabilities. Ground-based air-defence systems did not escape the effects of the Soviet collapse. As with nearly all military research, development and manufacturing projects were often deferred, delayed or shelved. For instance, the S-350 *Vityaz* (SA-28) medium- to long-range surface-to-air missile (SAM) system and S-400 *Triumf* (SA-21 *Growler*) long-range SAM have their origins in late-1980s requirements and under original schedules would have entered service earlier than transpired.[185] An air-launched anti-satellite programme – the MiG-31D/79M6 interceptor–missile combination known as *Kontakt*, begun in the late 1970s or early 1980s – was shelved in 1991.[186]

Russia's Aerospace Defence Forces and the Air Force were merged in 2015, a move which Defence Minister Sergei Shoigu described at the time as 'the optimum way to improve the country's aerospace defences'.[187] Shoigu's comment reflects the importance given to and the fear of vulnerability that Moscow's political elite and its military ascribe to the 'aerospace sphere'.[188] Russian commentary remains replete with concern of a conventional decapitating attack; justified or not, it continues to underpin Moscow's thinking and spending on air and space defence.[189]

This was also a goal of SAP 2020, with the purchase of the S-400 and the completion of development and introduction into service of the S-500 long-range SAM as priorities.[190] Other air- and space-missile projects that benefited included the *Nudol* ground-launched anti-satellite system that is still in development, the *Samolyot*-M upgrade to the anti-ballistic-missile system around Moscow, and the S-350 *Vityaz*.[191]

Although SAP 2020 was more successful than any previous iteration, far from all targets were met, among them several air-defence-missile goals. One target that does appear to have been nearly met is the delivery of 56 battalion sets of the S-400. As of the second quarter of 2020, 48 sets had been delivered, with two more regiments due to convert during 2020. In 2012, the aim appeared to be to re-equip all the Aerospace Defence Forces' medium-to-long-range SAM regiments with the S-400 by 2020.[192] While the numerical target appears to have been hit, some of the missiles intended to form part of the S-400 suite have yet to enter service.

Re-equipping S-300 (SA-10 *Grumble*) regiments with the S-400 has taken far longer than planned, with the schedule being repeatedly revised, partly as the result of development issues, the slow build-up of manufacturing capacity and problems laid bare when the first regiment began to be re-equipped in 2007 – the 606th Regiment.[193] By 2010, only one more regimental set of the S-400 was in service, with a further five planned for that year. In turn, this had to be scaled down to two regiments by 2012.[194] The delays were reported as a reason for the dismissal of Igor Ashurbeyli – general director of the S-400 manufacturer, Almaz-Antey – in October 2011.[195] Between 2012 and 2019, the Aerospace Forces had taken delivery of 14 regimental sets of the S-400, used to replace all of the S-300PSs (SA-10B) in the Aerospace Defence Forces and many in the Air Force.[196]

The remaining Air Force S-300PS regiments – as with the 9K37 *Buk*-M1-2 (SA-11 *Gadfly*) and *Buk*-M2 (SA-17 *Grizzly*) units – are likely intended to be re-equipped with the S-350 but, like the S-400, the S-350 has also suffered from delays in development and fluctuating funding. Up to 38 battalion sets of the S-350 were reportedly to be acquired as part of SAP 2020.[197] However, as of 2020 only the first unit of the S-350 had been handed over to the missile training school at Gatchina, with a first regiment to convert in 2021.[198] As of mid-2020, a revised procurement is thought to call for the acquisition of 18 battalion sets.

The S-350 is in part a subset of the S-400 in that the primary missile for the former is the *Fakel* 9M96, which is also an element of the S-400's wider range of missiles. As fielded, the S-400 does not include all the missiles that were originally intended to form part of its arsenal, and in that sense it is more akin to the S-300PM3 upgrade proposed for the S-300PM line that it overtook. Besides not yet including either version of the 9M96, also lacking is the very long-range 40N6 missile. As of 2020, the main missiles for the S-400 are variants of the 48N6, which are also used for the S-300PM1 and PM2. The 40N6 reportedly has a maximum engagement range of 400 km, while the longest-range 48N6, the 48N6DM, has a range of 250 km. The 40N6 development has been prolonged, with the project over a decade late.[199] The short-range 9M100 also has yet to enter service, which as well as being notionally part of the S-400, may also be part of the armament for a system known as *Morfei*.[200] The status of this project remains unclear. The 9M96 and the 9M100 were likely designed first to meet a naval SAM requirement. Point defence for S-400 units is provided by the 96K6 *Pantsir* S1/S2 (SA-22 *Greyhound*) gun–missile combination, also procured in significant numbers as part of SAP 2020.

So far, the S-500 SAM has followed a similar, if less dramatic, trajectory to the S-350. Acquisition funding for the programme was part of SAP 2020, with the system meant to be in service by the middle of the 2010s. As of the beginning of 2020, the state testing of elements of the S-500 continued, with delivery yet to begin. The S-500 is meant to provide a greater engagement range than the S-400, with the capability to intercept medium-range and intercontinental-range ballistic missiles. There have been suggestions that delivery of the S-500 could begin in 2021, with other reports suggesting 2025.[201]

Tests of the *Nudol* ground-based interceptor also continued in early 2020. *Nudol* appears to be a direct-ascent anti-satellite weapon, with firings recorded from 2014.

Recapitalising the VKS's SAM arsenal did not go completely to plan in SAP 2020. It did, however, deliver more in terms of equipment and R&D progress than any previous SAP. While the S-400 remains only partially fielded in terms of its missile armament, the 40N6 as of mid-2020 appeared on the brink of being introduced into the inventory. Like its predecessor the S-300, the S-400 will almost certainly undergo numerous incremental upgrades to address shortfalls in meeting the initial ambition. The S-350 will similarly, barring further delay, begin to be supplied to front-line units from 2021. SAP 2027 no doubt continues to support the acquisition and development of both, as it does the S-500.

Conclusion

The Aerospace Forces that entered the 2020s is a far smaller service than that of the 1990s, but it is more capable and has recent combat experience. While it fields only around 15% of the tactical combat strength of the air force and air-defence forces of the late 1980s, it has since around 2010 recovered from two decades of neglect and parlous underfunding. Upgraded types of combat aircraft and improved weapons are now in the inventory in reasonable numbers; for example, a production order for the Su-57 *Felon* has been placed, even if an interim engine will have to be used for longer than originally intended. A cadre of younger personnel has also gained from the experience of combat in Syria. Taken together, these changes have made the Aerospace Forces a more usable tool of military power, able to address the defensive and offensive roles with which it is tasked. It is a capability that, as involvement in Syria showed, the Russian government is willing to use when it deems it is in its interest.

Challenges for the service, however, include sustaining the progress made in the last decade, transitioning from aircraft designs and requirements originating in the late Soviet era, and ensuring the industrial base is adequate to design, develop and manufacture next-generation combat aircraft and weapons. Moreover, over-reach remains a risk, if the VKS tries to support too many acquisition programmes for aircraft and weapons, thereby diluting available funding.

Notes

1   The CIA Library holds some editions of the *Herald of the Air Fleet*. See, for example, *Herald of the Air Fleet*, no. 5, 1957, https://www.cia.gov/library/readingroom/docs/CIA-RDP81-01043R002000020002-1.pdf.

2   For the immediate impact of the dissolution of the Soviet Union on the Air Force, see Benjamin S. Lambeth, *Russia's Air Power at The Crossroads* (Santa Monica, CA: RAND, 1996), p. xiv.

3   *Ibid.*, pp. xiv–xvi.

4   Piotr Butowski, *Flashpoint Russia: Russia's Air Power: Capabilities and Structure* (Houston, TX: Harpia Publishing, 2019), p. 6; Fredrik Westerlund and Susanne Oxenstierna (eds), 'Russian Military Capability in a Ten-Year Perspective – 2019', FOI, December 2019, p. 17.

5   Douglas Barrie, 'Russian Aerospace Forces reform and its Syrian role: the view from Moscow', IISS Military Balance Blog, 6 December 2018, https://www.iiss.org/blogs/military-balance/2018/12/russian-aerospace-reform-syria.

6   Lambeth, *Russia's Air Power at The Crossroads*, p. xvi.

7   *Ibid.*, pp. 241–2.

8   Piotr Butowski, *Russia's Warplanes, Volume 1, Russian-made Military Aircraft and Helicopters Today* (Houston, TX: Harpia Publishing, 2015), p. 8.

9   The Embassy of the Russian Federation to the United Kingdom of Great Britain and Northern Ireland, 'The Military Doctrine of the Russian Federation', 25 December 2014, https://rusemb.org.uk/press/2029.

10 Lambeth, *Russia's Air Power at The Crossroads*, p. 59.

11 *Ibid.*, p. 75.

12 See, for example, 'Russia Military Power: Building a Military to Support Great Power Aspirations', US Defense Intelligence Agency, 2017, p. 46, https://www.dia.mil/Military-Power-Publications.

13 See, for example, Ekho Moskvy Radio, 'Defence Council Secretary Yuriy Baturin interviewed on Ekho Moskvy', BBC Monitoring, 17 July 1997, https://monitoring.bbc.co.uk/product/r002xj02.

14 Lambeth, *Russia's Air Power at The Crossroads*, pp. xiv, 78.

15 See, for example, Piotr Butowski, 'Russia's New Air Force Enters a Tight Manoeuvre', *Jane's Intelligence Review*, 1 May 1999, https://janes.ihs.com/Janes/Display/jir00234-jir-1999.

16 See, for example, Interfax, 'Russia's new Space Troops and commander profiled', BBC Monitoring, 29 March 2011, https://monitoring.bbc.co.uk/product/m111s1in.

17 See, for example, *Kommersant*, 'Paper details new Russian aerospace defence programme', BBC Monitoring, 17 August 2011, https://monitoring.bbc.co.uk/product/70156051; *Moskovskiy Komsomolets*, 'Russia: Article looks at failure of past attempts to create Aerospace Forces', BBC Monitoring, 17 August 2015, https://monitoring.bbc.co.uk/product/m1cl8q5x.

18 Butowski, *Flashpoint Russia: Russia's Air Power: Capabilities and Structure*, p. 13.

19 See, for example, Interfax-AVN, 'Russian Air Force working on bringing army avia-

tion into line', BBC Monitoring, 23 January 2003, https://monitoring.bbc.co.uk/product/m12uzpjl.

20 Peter Grier 'The Death of Korean Air Lines Flight 007', *Air Force Magazine*, 1 January 2013, https://www.airforcemag.com/article/0113korean; Tom Le Compte, 'The Notorious Flight of Mathias Rust', *Air & Space Magazine*, July 2005, https://www.airspacemag.com/history-of-flight/the-notorious-flight-of-mathias-rust-7101888.

21 Steven Lee Myers, 'Russia Punishes Commanders for Copter Crash That Killed 119', *New York Times*, 8 September 2002, https://www.nytimes.com/2002/09/08/world/russia-punishes-commanders-for-copter-crash-that-killed-119.html.

22 'Russian army's aviation service moved to air force', Interfax-AVN, 4 January 2003; Butowski, *Flashpoint Russia: Russia's Air Power: Capabilities and Structure*, p. 18.

23 See, for example, Ilya Kramnik, 'The Future of Russia's Naval Aviation', Russian International Affairs Council, 24 July 2014, https://russiancouncil.ru/en/analytics-and-comments/analytics/the-future-of-russia-s-naval-aviation.

24 Interfax, 'Russia's aerospace command comes into existence', BBC Monitoring, 16 June 2015, https://monitoring.bbc.co.uk/product/00042052.

25 See, for example, Roger McDermott, 'Russia Reforms Aerospace Defense Structures – Again', *Eurasia Daily Monitor*, vol. 12, no. 151, 11 August 2015, https://jamestown.org/program/russia-reforms-aerospace-defense-structures-again.

26 *Ibid.*

27 Butowski, *Flashpoint Russia: Russia's Air Power: Capabilities and Structure*, p. 13.

28 *Izvestia*, 'Russian trainee pilots to start flying year earlier', BBC Monitoring, 3 March 2020, https://monitoring.bbc.co.uk/product/c201i68g.

29 *Ibid.*

30 *Izvestia*, 'Russian air force facing jet trainer shortage', BBC Monitoring, 8 September 2019, https://monitoring.bbc.co.uk/product/c2012m2b.

31 *Ibid.*

32 See, for example, Mark Lambert (ed.), *Jane's All the World's Aircraft, 1993–94* (Coulsdon: Jane's Information Group, 1994), addenda, p. 696.

33 *Izvestia*, 'Russian trainee pilots to start flying year earlier', BBC Monitoring, 3 March 2020, https://monitoring.bbc.co.uk/product/c201i68g.

34 Interfax, 'Russia upgrading L-39 jet trainer', BBC Monitoring, 4 June 2020, https://monitoring.bbc.co.uk/product/c201s0li.

35 Zvezda TV, 'Russian defence minister announces overhaul of armed forces structure', BBC Monitoring, 14 October 2008, https://monitoring.bbc.co.uk/product/m16mdi3j.

36 *Moskovskiy Komsomolets*, 'New Russian defence minister Serdyukov profiled, gaps in biography questionened', BBC Monitoring, 8 March 2007, https://monitoring.bbc.co.uk/product/m158c2ut.

37 Carolina Vendil Pallin (ed.), 'Russian Military Capability in a Ten-Year Perspective – 2011', FOI, August 2012, p. 9.

38 *Ibid.*, pp. 44, 97.

39 See, for example, Ruslan Pukhov, 'Russia's Army Reform Enters New Stage', *Moscow Defense Brief*, no. 2, 2010, https://mdb.cast.ru/mdb/2-2010/item5/article1.

40 *Ibid.*

41 Vendil Pallin (ed.), 'Russian Military Capability in a Ten-Year Perspective – 2011', p. 112.

42 *Ibid.*, p. 113.

43 Mikhail Barabanov (ed.), *Russia's New Army*, CAST, 2011, p. 59, http://www.cast.ru/files/book/NewArmy_sm.pdf.

44 *Ibid.*, p. 56.

45 Butowski, *Flashpoint Russia: Russia's Air Power: Capabilities and Structure*, p. 14.

46 Barabanov (ed.), *Russia's New Army*, p. 59.

47 *Ibid.*, p. 56

48 *Ibid.*

49 Butowski, *Flashpoint Russia: Russia's Air Power: Capabilities and Structure*, p. 14.

50 Vendil Pallin (ed.), 'Russian Military Capability in a Ten-Year Perspective – 2011', p. 113.

51 See, for example 'Russian Defence Minister Anatoly Serdyukov fired by Putin', 6 November 2012, BBC News, https://www.bbc.co.uk/news/world-europe-20218216.

52 See, for example, *Komsomolskaya Pravda*, 'Russian defence minister interviewed on changed direction of the army reform', BBC Monitoring, 14 February 2013, https://monitoring.bbc.co.uk/product/70252750.

53 Butowski, *Flashpoint Russia: Russia's Air Power: Capabilities and Structure*, p. 15.

54 See, for example, Keith Crane, Olga Oliker and Brian Nichiporuk, 'Trends in Russia's Armed Forces: An Overview of Budgets and Capabilities', RAND Corporation, 2019, p. 56, https://www.rand.org/content/dam/rand/pubs/research_reports/RR2500/RR2573/RAND_RR2573.pdf.

55 Butowski, *Flashpoint Russia: Russia's Air Power: Capabilities and Structure*, p. 16.

56 *Ibid.*

57 See, for example, Julian Cooper, 'The Russian State Armament Programme, 2018–2027', NATO Defense College, May 2018, http://www.ndc.nato.int/news/news.php?icode=1167#.

58 REN TV, 'Russian TV examines reasons for failure of 2010 state defence order', BBC Monitoring, 27 March 2011, https://monitoring.bbc.co.uk/product/m19jt8z1.

59 Cooper, 'Russia's state armament programme to 2020: a quantitative assessment of implementation 2011–2015', FOI, March 2016, p. 20; President of the Russian Federation, 'Putin chairs meeting on air force armament programme – Kremlin transcript', BBC Monitoring, 15 June 2012, https://monitoring.bbc.co.uk/product/m1ah87r2.

60 Angela Monaghan and Julia Kollewe, 'Russia to fall into recession amid sanctions and plunging oil price', *Guardian*, 2 December 2014, https://www.theguardian.com/world/2014/dec/02/russia-warns-fall-into-recession-2015-sanctions-oil-price.

61 Inna Sidirkova, 'Borisov — RBC: Predpisanija po zakupke otechestvennogo oborudovanija budut', RBC, 3 December 2018, https://www.rbc.ru/politics/03/12/2018/5c0101a09a79477516bc7d72.

62 Butowski, *Flashpoint Russia: Russia's Air Power: Capabilities and Structure*, p. 6.

63 *Ibid.*

64 Richard Connolly and Mathieu Boulègue, 'Russia's New State Armament Programme: Implications for the Russian

Armed Forces and Military Capabilities to 2027', Chatham House, May 2018, p. 6, https://www.chathamhouse.org/sites/default/files/publications/research/2018-05-10-russia-state-armament-programme-connolly-boulegue-final.pdf.

65 Douglas Barrie and Henry Boyd, 'Russia's State Armament Programme 2027: a more measured course on procurement', IISS Military Balance Blog, 13 February 2018, https://www.iiss.org/blogs/military-balance/2018/02/russia-2027.

66 'Russian defense minister orders to consider restarting Tu-160 missile carrier production', TASS, 29 April 2015, https://tass.com/russia/792402.

67 'Putin inspects newly-built nuclear bomber, promises new contract', BBC Monitoring, 25 January 2018, https://monitoring.bbc.co.uk/product/c1d0qnh3.

68 President of the Russian Federation, 'Meeting with Deputy Prime Minister Dmitry Rogozin', 16 November 2017, http://en.kremlin.ru/events/president/news/56115.

69 Peter Dunai, 'Russia to resume NK-32 production', Jane's Defence Industry, 24 July 2014, http://janes.ihs.com/Janes/Display/jdin87829-jdin-2014.

70 Piotr Butowski, 'Modernised strategic bombers to debut in Victory Day parade over Moscow', Jane's Defence Weekly, 14 April 2016, https://janes.ihs.com/Janes/Display/jdw61579-jdw-2016.

71 IISS Military Balance+.

72 Interfax-AVN, 'Russian air force to get six upgraded Tu-95MS bombers this year', BBC Monitoring, 7 January 2020, https://monitoring.bbc.co.uk/product/c201d3xs.

73 Interfax-AVN, 'Russian minister outlines new military aviation projects'.

74 Interfax-AVN, 'Russia won't have next generation nuclear bomber until 2025 – source', BBC Monitoring, 3 March 2011, https://monitoring.bbc.co.uk/product/m19hoj66; Dmitry Sudakov, 'Russia develops new generation strategic bomber', Pravda, 2 May 2007, pravdareport.com/Russia/90775-russian_bomber; Interfax-AVN, 'Russian aircraft industry boss confirms Tupolev in charge of new bomber project', BBC Monitoring, 11 November 2014, https://monitoring.bbc.co.uk/product/f1c6pndu.

75 United Aircraft Corporation, 'Annual Report 2013', p. 8, https://www.uacrussia.ru/upload/iblock/b20/b206864d3b58721e-7a71b3d8e27f985f.pdf; 'Para slov o proyekte perspektivnogo bombardirovshchika PAK DA', BMPD, 9 February 2018, https://bmpd.livejournal.com/3088125.html.

76 Nikolai Novichkov, 'Russia's future PAK DA bomber to be delayed by Tu-160M2 production', Jane's Defence Weekly, 21 July 2015, http://janes.ihs.com/Janes/Display/jdw59269-jdw-2015.

77 'Tupolev nachnet proizvodstvo opytnykh obraztsov perspektivnogo dal'noboynogo aviatsionnogo kompleksa', Interfax, 28 February 2018, https://www.interfax.ru/russia/601823.

78 Interfax-AVN, 'Russian minister outlines new military aviation projects', BBC Monitoring, 29 August, https://monitoring.bbc.co.uk/product/c2011suy.

79 Ibid.

80 'Tu-22M3: long-range missile carrier bomber', Tupolev, https://www.tupolev.ru/en/planes/tu-22m3.

81 'Russia's Tu-22M3M bomber to enter service from 2021', Interfax, 16 August 2018.

82 See, for example, John W.R. Taylor (ed.), Jane's All the World's Aircraft, 1989–90 (Coulsdon: Jane's Information Group, 1989), p. 248.

83 See, for example, Yefim Gordon, Tu-160 (Moscow: Polygon Press, 2003).

84 See, for example, Mark Lambert (ed.), Jane's All the World's Aircraft, 1993–94 (Coulsdon: Jane's Information Group, 1993), p. 271; Taylor (ed.), Jane's All the World's Aircraft 1989–90, p. 252.

85 Vladimir Karnozov, 'Russia's Revived Il-76 Airlifter Now in Flight Test', AINonline, 22 March 2013, https://www.ainonline.com/aviation-news/defense/2013-03-22/russias-revived-il-76-airlifter-now-flight-test.

86 Douglas Barrie and Tom Waldwyn, 'Candid debate needed on Russian air-transport plan', IISS Military Balance Blog, 23 August 2018, https://www.iiss.org/blogs/military-balance/2018/08/candid-debate-russian-air-transport-plan.

87 'Russian defense firm to deliver 6 heavily upgraded IL-76 military transport planes in 2019', TASS, 22 March 2019, http://tass.com/defense/1050106.

88 'Kontrakt na postavku samoletov Il-76MD-90A perezaklyuchen', BMPD, 28 May 2020, https://bmpd.livejournal.com/4040738.html.

89 See, for example, IISS, The Military Balance 2020 (Abingdon: Routledge for the IISS, 2020), p. 201.

90 Ibid., pp. 199, 201.

91 Butowski, Russia's Warplanes, Volume 1, Russian-made Military Aircraft and Helicopters Today, p. 85.

92 Ibid., p. 204; Tim Ripley, 'Russia links maritime patrol aircraft to UAV', Jane's Navy International, 11 October 2019, https://janes.ihs.com/Janes/Display/FG_2413580-JNI.

93 See, for example, IISS, The Military Balance 2020, p. 201.

94 Butowski, Flashpoint Russia: Russia's Air Power: Capabilities and Structure, p. 129.

95 'Russian Defence Minister General of the Army Sergei Shoigu visits Irkutsk aviation plant to inspect manufacturing of Su-30SM multi-purpose fighter jet', Russian Aviation, 30 January 2019, https://www.ruaviation.com/news/2019/1/30/12853.

96 'Minoborony poluchit modernizirovannyy Su-34M po novomu kontraktu', RIA Novosti, 30 December 2019, https://ria.ru/20191230/1563005581.html.

97 Butowski, Russia's Warplanes, Volume 1, Russian-made Military Aircraft and Helicopters Today, p. 100.

98 'Krusheniye pervogo seriynogo istrebitelya Su-57', BMPD, 24 December 2019, https://bmpd.livejournal.com/3884284.html.

99 'Russia orders two more Su-57 stealth fighters', BBC Monitoring, 26 August 2018, https://monitoring.bbc.co.uk/product/c200640a.

100 'Contract to be signed for 13 Su-57 fifth-generation fighter jets in 2020 – source', TASS, 16 January 2019, https://tass.com/defense/1040167.

101 Butowski, Flashpoint Russia: Russia's Air Power: Capabilities and Structure, p. 132.

102 Butowski, Russia's Warplanes, Volume 1, Russian-made Military Aircraft and Helicopters Today, p. 100.

103 'Russian defence official sees "no need to push" for new fighter jet', BBC Monitoring, 30 July 2018, https://monitoring.bbc.co.uk/product/c2004h2o.

104 'Putin says Russia to buy 76 Su-57 stealth fighters', President of the Russian Federation website, 15 May 2019.

105 Ibid.

106 Vladimir Karnozov, 'Su-57 and MiG-35 Land Russian Orders During Army 2018', AINonline, 27 August 2018, https://www.ainonline.com/aviation-news/defense/2018-08-27/su-57-and-mig-35-land-russian-orders-during-army-2018.

107 'Ekipazhi rossiyskikh aerokosmicheskikh voysk zavershili prakticheskiy pusk kinzhala kompleksa "Kinzhal"', BMPD, 11 March, 2018, https://bmpd.livejournal.com/3118102.html.

108 Joel McGrath and Douglas Barrie, 'Russia's Victory Day Parade: Kinzhal makes its debut appearance', IISS Military Balance Blog, 25 May 2018, https://www.iiss.org/blogs/military-balance/2018/05/kinzhal-missile.

109 See, for example, Lambert (ed.) Jane's All the World's Aircraft, 1993–94, p. 287.

110 Butowski, Russia's Warplanes, Volume 1, Russian-made Military Aircraft and Helicopters Today, p. 35.

111 Ibid.

112 TASS, 'Former Russian air force boss discusses Moscow's air power', BBC Monitoring, 22 November 2017, https://monitoring.bbc.co.uk/product/c1dnm4l7.

113 Douglas Barrie and Piotr Butowski, 'Russia's high-speed air-to-air missile upgrade', IISS Military Balance Blog, 25 July 2019, https://www.iiss.org/blogs/military-balance/2019/07/russia-high-speed-air-to-air-missile-upgrade.

114 Piotr Butowski, Russia's Air-launched Weapons: Russian-made Aircraft Ordnance Today, (Houston, TX: Harpia Publishing, 2017), pp. 43–53. Soviet and Russian air-to-air missile projects use a 'K' designator – for example, as in K-30 – to denote a system in development. The missile is only given an 'R' designator once it is ready for entry into service.

115 Ibid., p. 47; Douglas Barrie, 'Russia's Foxhound finally gets its bite back', IISS Military Balance Blog, 30 April 2019, https://www.iiss.org/blogs/military-balance/2019/05/russia-Foxhound-upgrades.

116 Barrie and Butowski, 'Russia's high-speed air-to-air missile upgrade'; Butowski, Russia's Air-launched Weapons: Russian-made Aircraft Ordnance Today, p. 45.

117 Ibid., p. 47.

118 Barrie and Butowski, 'Russia's high-speed air-to-air missile upgrade'.

119 Ibid.

120 Pavel K. Baev, 'Russia's airpower in the Chechen War: Denial, punishment and defeat,' Journal of Slavic Military Studies, vol. 10, no. 2, June 1997, pp. 1–18; Marcel de Haas, 'The Use of Russian Airpower in the Second Chechen War', Conflict Studies Research Centre, January 2003, p. 15, https://www.files.ethz.ch/isn/96282/03_Jul_3.pdf; Ruslan Pukhov (ed.), The Tanks of August (Moscow: Centre for Analysis of Strategies and Technologies, 2010), p. 99, http://cast.ru/files/The_Tanks_of_August_sm_eng.pdf.

121 Samuel Charap, Elina Treyger and Edward Geist, 'Understanding Russia's Intervention in Syria', RAND Corporation, 2019, p. 1, https://www.rand.org/pubs/research_reports/RR3180.html; Valery Polovinkin (ed.), Russian Weapons in Syrian Conflict (Moscow: Status, 2016), p. 7.

122 Ibid., p. 22.

123 Ibid.

124 'Syria conflict: Russia's Putin orders "main part" of forces out', BBC News, 14 March 2016, https://www.bbc.co.uk/news/world-middle-east-35807689.

125 Anton Lavrov, 'The Russian Air Campaign in Syria, A Preliminary Analysis', CNA, June 2018, p. 11, https://www.cna.org/CNA_files/PDF/COP-2018-U-017903-Final.pdf.

126 Polovinkin (ed.), Russian Weapons in Syrian Conflict, p. 7.

127 Valery Polovinkin (ed.), Russian Weapons in Syria: Analysis, Results, Conclusions (Moscow: Status, 2018), p. 26.

128 Andrew Osborn, 'Putin, in Syria, says mission accomplished, orders partial Russian pull-out', Reuters, 11 December 2017, https://uk.reuters.com/article/uk-mideast-crisis-syria-russia-putin/putin-in-syria-says-mission-accomplished-orders-partial-russian-pull-out-idUKKBN1E50Z7.

129 Lavrov, 'The Russian Air Campaign in Syria, A Preliminary Analysis', p. 19, https://www.cna.org/CNA_files/PDF/COP-2018-U-017903-Final.pdf.

130 Polovinkin (ed.), Russian Weapons in Syrian Conflict, p. 7.

131 'Rossiyskaya aviatsionnaya gruppirovka na Aerome Khmeymi na 17 noyabrya', BMPD, https://bmpd.livejournal.com/2983563.html.

132 TASS, 'Russian defence minister says new fighter jet tested in Syria', BBC Monitoring, 1 March 2018, https://monitoring.bbc.co.uk/product/c1dow10y.

133 Interfax, 'Russia renews Su-57 fighter jet tests in Syria', BBC Monitoring, 18 December 2019, https://monitoring.bbc.co.uk/product/c201bkmn.

134 Thomas Newdick, 'MiG-31 "Foxhound" now in Syria?', Twitter ,14 November 2016, https://twitter.com/CombatAir/status/798268832213135362.

135 Lavrov, 'The Russian Air Campaign in Syria, A Preliminary Analysis', p. 24.

136 IISS, ISR & the Gulf: An Assessment (Abingdon: Routledge for the IISS, 2019), p. 75.

137 'Russia Tests Combat Drone in Syria', DefenseWorld.Net, 1 November 2019, https://www.defenseworld.net/news/25763/Russia_Tests_Combat_Drone_in_Syria#.Xl-XtRP7SHs.

138 Lavrov, 'The Russian Air Campaign in Syria, A Preliminary Analysis', p. 4.

139 See, for example, 'PTAB-1M submunitions documented in Syria', Armament Research Services, 2 March 2016, http://armamentresearch.com/tag/rbk-500.

140 Lavrov, 'The Russian Air Campaign in Syria, A Preliminary Analysis', p. 4.

141 Butowski, Russia's Air-launched Weapons: Russian-made Aircraft Ordnance Today, p. 67.

142 'Su-34 s protivokorabel'noy raketoy KH-35U v Sirii', BMPD, 12 February 2016, https://bmpd.livejournal.com/1732469.html.

143 Butowski, Russia's Air-launched Weapons: Russian-made Aircraft Ordnance Today, p. 30.

144 Interfax, 'Russian stealth jet fired new cruise missile in Syria – minister', BBC Monitoring, 25 May 2018, https://monitoring.bbc.co.uk/product/c1dpaoja.

145 Butowski, Russia's Air-launched Weapons: Russian-made Aircraft Ordnance Today, p. 37.

146 Ibid., p. 38

147 *Ibid.*, p. 16.

148 *Ibid.*, p. 15.

149 *Ibid.*, p. 16.

150 Douglas Barrie, 'Kh-101 test highlights bomber firepower', IISS Military Balance Blog, 8 February 2019, https://www.iiss. org/blogs/military-balance/2019/02/russian-bomber-firepower.

151 Lavrov, 'The Russian Air Campaign in Syria, A Preliminary Analysis', p. 23.

152 'Two thirds of Russian air force received in-theater experience in Syria', TASS, 11 August 2018, https://tass.com/defense/1016930.

153 'Voyennaya operatsiya VS RF v Siriyskoy Arabskoy Respublike – itogi v tsifrakh', 22 August 2018, https://www.youtube.com/watch?v=viCiwbJG5Pk.

154 *Ibid.*

155 Lavrov, 'The Russian Air Campaign in Syria, A Preliminary Analysis', p. 21.

156 *Ibid.*

157 Lucas Tomlinson, 'Russian attack helicopters destroyed in Syria; U.S. officials say "accident" to blame', Fox News, 25 May 2016, https://www.foxnews.com/world/russian-attack-helicopters-destroyed-in-syria-us-officials-say-accident-to-blame.

158 Lavrov, 'The Russian Air Campaign in Syria, A Preliminary Analysis', p. 21.

159 *Ibid.*

160 *Ibid.*

161 Interfax, 'Russia to maintain Mediterranean naval group as carrier goes home', BBC Monitoring, 6 January 2017, https://monitoring.bbc.co.uk/product/c1dbzgxd.

162 Lavrov, 'The Russian Air Campaign in Syria, A Preliminary Analysis', p. 21.

163 Interfax, 'General, 26 officers killed in Russian Syria plane crash', BBC Monitoring, 6 March 2018, https://monitoring.bbc.co.uk/product/c1dowsuo.

164 *Rossiya 24*, 'Russia blames Israel for Syria plane downing – full text', BBC Monitoring, 18 September 2018, https://monitoring.bbc.co.uk/product/c2007qj5.

165 See, for example, Robert Hewson (ed.), *Jane's Air-Launched Weapons: Issue Fifty-three* (Coulsdon: Jane's Information Group, 2009), p. 80.

166 Yefim Gordon, *Mikoyan MiG-31* (Hinckley: Midland Publishing, 2005), p. 89.

167 Butowski, *Russia's Warplanes, Volume 1, Russian-made Military Aircraft and Helicopters Today*, p. 35.

168 Douglas Barrie, 'Russia's *Foxhound* finally gets its bite back', IISS Military Balance Blog, 30 April 2019, https://www.iiss.org/blogs/military-balance/2019/05/russia-*Foxhound*-upgrades.

169 Butowski, *Russia's Air-launched Weapons: Russian-made Aircraft Ordnance Today*, p. 54.

170 See, for example, 'Chinese and Russian air-launched weapons: a test for Western air dominance', in IISS, *The Military Balance 2018* (Abingdon: Routledge for the IISS, 2018), pp. 7–9.

171 See, for example, Hewson (ed.), *Jane's Air-Launched Weapons: Issue Fifty-three*, p. 267.

172 See, for example, 'Emerging air-defence challenges', in IISS, *The Military Balance 2019* (Abingdon: Routledge for the IISS, 2019).

173 Robert Hewson, 'TMC unveils air-to-surface missiles at Moscow air show', *Jane's Defence Weekly*, 29 August 2007, https://janes.ihs.com/Janes/Display/jdw33997-jdw-2007.

174 'Air-Launched Short-Range Modular Missiles, Kh-38ME', Tactical Missile Corporation, http://eng.ktrv.ru/production/military_production/multipurpose_missiles/kh-38me.html.

175 'Russian Su-57 reportedly test fired cutting edge Kh-59MK2 cruise missile during tests in Syria', Russian Aviation, 29 May 2018, https://www.ruaviation.com/news/2018/5/29/11449.

176 Butowski, *Russia's Air-launched Weapons: Russian-made Aircraft Ordnance Today*, p. 20.

177 IISS, *The Military Balance 2020*, p. 194.

178 *Ibid.*

179 Russia, Ministry of Defence, 'Missiya v Siriyu', Russian Ministry of Defence Briefing, http://syria.mil.ru/news/more.htm?id=12070708@cmsArticle.

180 US National Air and Space Intelligence Center, 'Competing in Space', December 2018, pp. 20–1, https://media.defense.gov/2019/Jan/16/2002080386/-1/-1/1/190115-F-NV711-0002.PDF.

181 Bart Hendrickx, 'Russia develops co-orbital anti-satellite capability', *Jane's Intelligence Review*, 27 September 2018, https://janes.ihs.com/Janes/Display/FG_1076140-JIR.

182 'Russia may be conducting Nudol tests', Russian strategic nuclear forces, 30 June 2019, http://russianforces.org/blog/2019/06/russia_may_be_conducting_nudol.shtml.

183 Butowski, *Russia's Warplanes, Volume 1, Russian-made Military Aircraft and Helicopters Today*, p. 219.

184 'Russian President Vladimir Putin holds space and rocket development meeting', Parabolic Arc, 12 April 2020, http://www.parabolicarc.com/2020/04/12/russian-president-vladimir-putin-holds-space-rocket-development-meeting/.

185 'Fakel moves into AAM market', *Flight International*, 10 July 1996, https://www.flightglobal.com/fakel-moves-into-aam-market/6469.article.

186 Butowski, *Russia's Warplanes, Volume 1, Russian-made Military Aircraft and Helicopters Today*, p. 35.

187 Interfax-AVN, 'Russia merges Air Force, other troops to form Aerospace Forces', BBC Monitoring, 3 August 2015, https://monitoring.bbc.co.uk/product/m1ckjjqv.

188 *Ibid.*

189 See, for example, RIA Novosti, 'Russia sets conditions for including hypersonic weapons in US arms talks', BBC Monitoring, 17 April 2020, https://monitoring.bbc.co.uk/product/c201mf1x.

190 RIA Novosti, 'Russian Aerospace Defence Troops to receive new SAM systems, radars – commander', BBC Monitoring, 28 November 2013, https://monitoring.bbc.co.uk/product/m1bji2au.

191 Interfax-AVN, 'Russia touts new interceptor missile, tests SAM upgrade', BBC Monitoring, 23 June 2016, https://monitoring.bbc.co.uk/product/c1d39vcw; 'Moscow missile defense getting an upgrade?', Russian strategic nuclear forces, 14 December 2012, http://russianforces.org/blog/2012/12/moscow_missile_defense_is_gett.shtml; Interfax, 'Manager outlines production plans for new Russian missile system', BBC Monitoring, 22 January 2014, https://monitoring.bbc.co.uk/product/m1bn216u.

192 Interfax-AVN, 'Russian aerospace defence troops to complete acquisition of new arms

by 2020', BBC Monitoring, 25 January 2012, https://monitoring.bbc.co.uk/product/m1a7jt9p.

193 *Rossiyskaya Gazeta*, 'Russia: Air Force aides praise air defence system in Moscow region', BBC Monitoring, 19 February 2010, https://monitoring.bbc.co.uk/product/70124607.

194 RIA Novosti, 'Russian defence official says delivery of major weapons systems behind schedule', BBC Monitoring, 12 October 2011, https://monitoring.bbc.co.uk/product/m19znyix.

195 Ilya Kramnik, 'Deliveries of the S-400 Are Half as Fast as Planned: the Air Force Will Before 2015 Acquire No More Than 12 Battalions of the New Air-Defence System', *Izvestia*, 14 October 2011.

196 IISS, *The Military Balance 2020*, pp. 195, 201.

197 *Rossiyskaya Gazeta*, 'Putin article reviews Russian Armed Forces' progress, status, challenges', BBC Monitoring, 20 February 2012, https://monitoring.bbc.co.uk/product/70189770.

198 'First S-350 medium-range air defense system arrives for Russia's Aerospace Force', TASS, 26 February 2020, https://tass.com/defense/1124013.

199 *Kommersant-Vlast*, 'Russian air force, air defence, army aviation order of battle', BBC Monitoring, 23 November 2008, https://monitoring.bbc.co.uk/product/m16po83u.

200 Interfax-AVN, 'General discusses Russia's plans to boost defence research', BBC Monitoring, 24 April 2013, https://monitoring.bbc.co.uk/product/m1b3kc4t.

201 'Russia's latest S-500 anti-aircraft missile system at final stage of trials', TASS, 26 March 2020, https://tass.com/defense/1135819.

Russia's approach to military decision-making and joint operations

During the 1990s and into the early 2000s, the United States and, later, its NATO allies were starting to explore the implications of the digital-information revolution for the military realm. For Russia's armed forces, however, these post-Soviet years were about sustaining capability. Their focus was single service and based on survival, rather than developing joint operational concepts built on such digital architecture. However, this began to change with the New Look 2008 military-reform and -modernisation programme.

Indeed, developments in Russia's military decision-making process and its approach to command and control need to be viewed within the context of the impact of this reform programme, the conceptual shift that has attended resultant developments and the lessons of recent military campaigns. Until the New Look programme, the decision-making process was largely paper based. Over the past decade, the armed forces have focused on transitioning into the digital-information era and because of this, the development and adoption of more capable command, control, communications, computers, intelligence, surveillance and reconnaissance (C4ISR) has been a key element of the reform programme's modernisation drive.[1]

Elements of Russia's decision-making

Russia's military decision-making process does not simply mirror those of the US or NATO states. It is informed by the distinctive culture and military traditions of Russia's armed forces. Organisations within the defence and security establishment play an important role, while the personalities of key leaders and the abilities and competences of commanders in the field are also significant.

A revised framework for military decision-making has emerged over the past decade as a result of Moscow's widespread structural reorganisation of the armed forces and its command-and-control systems. This framework is designed to improve efficiency and speed in terms of decision-making and operational implementation, as well as positioning the armed forces to conduct operations in an information-driven environment.

CHAPTER SIX

Key takeaways

NEW LOOK IMPACT
The New Look programme spurred Russian interest in digital command and control as a core element of the reforms.

STRATEGIC COMMAND
Since being established in 2014, the National Defence Management Centre has played an increasingly central role in the decision-making process.

SYRIAN TESTS
Moscow's intervention in the Syrian civil war proved a vehicle to exercise the new command-and-control architecture.

TACTICAL TRIALS
Development of a tactical command-and-control system and supporting elements has proved difficult, taking almost two decades.

CONVENTIONAL BENEFITS
Russia's conventional military capability will, assuming continued investment, benefit further from the acquisition of improved C4ISR.

NATIONAL DEFENCE MANAGEMENT CENTRE
Russia's National Defence Management Centre operating remotely during the COVID-19 pandemic, April 2020. CREDIT: Alexei Yereshko/TASS/Getty Images

The defence ministry trialled a simplified command-and-control structure in June 2010, with a declared target of forming four new military districts by 1 December 2010. These function as military districts in peacetime and transition to joint strategic commands during military operations.

The new districts/commands were:

- **Western**: headquarters in St Petersburg, based on the former Moscow and Leningrad military districts and the Baltic and Northern fleets;
- **Eastern**: headquarters in Khabarovsk, comprising the former Far East Military District, the eastern part of Siberian Military District and the Pacific Fleet;
- **Central**: headquarters in Yekaterinburg, including the western part of the Siberian Military District and the Volga–Ural Military District;
- **Southern**: headquarters in Rostov-on-Don, merging the North Caucasus Military District and the Black Sea Fleet and the Caspian Flotilla.[2]

These command elements are essentially dual-roled, drawing on military forces from the Western, Southern, Central and Eastern military districts/joint strategic commands. On 15 December 2014, the fifth joint strategic command, based on the Northern Fleet, was formed. In June 2020, the Kremlin announced plans to create a corresponding fifth military district for the Northern Fleet, to be formed in January 2021.[3]

In addition, on 1 December 2014 the National Defence Management Centre (NDMC) (*Natsional'nyy tsentr upravleniya oboronoy*) started to operate in Moscow. The purpose of this was to create a national command centre at the strategic level connecting the political and military leadership and the wider defence and security command structures in near real time.[4] The national centre will eventually be fully connected to subordinate command centres, linking the strategic-operational and tactical levels; this will likely be implemented by 2027, with further technological refinements to follow. At the strategic-operational level, the centre will link via digital systems the joint strategic commands and army levels.[5]

At the tactical level, the Ground Forces are working to overcome problems with automated command-and-control systems while implementing network-centric capabilities through a range of technologies, including new tactical radios, military digital cell-phone and data systems, tactical laptops and tablets, and a secure military internet. This broadly fits the Ground Forces' procurement and modernisation priorities into Russia's broader network-centric framework.[6]

In terms of the changes made to the overarching command-and-control structure in 2010, the decision to drive joint decision-making has been of key importance. Operational control was removed from the single service chiefs and placed in the hands of the joint strategic command commanders, who would have control over all military and uniformed services (including non-defence-ministry forces) in their command, apart from strategic-level assets that remain under the aegis of the General Staff (the central organisational element of the armed forces, including the service chiefs), such as the Strategic Rocket Forces and the Airborne Forces. Assets in the region would come under the joint strategic command commander. For instance, in the Western Joint Strategic Command, this includes the 6th Combined Arms Army, 20th Combined Arms Army and the 1st Tank Army.[7] In addition, as part of the

RUSSIAN SECURITY COUNCIL
Russian President Vladimir Putin in conference with members of the Russian Security Council, July 2020. CREDIT: Alexei Druzhinin/TASS/Getty Images

goal of streamlining the command process, the number of stages an order had to pass though was reduced substantially.

The roles of the General Staff and the Russian Security Council in influencing, at times indirectly, the overall military decision-making architecture are outlined in the following excerpt, on how Russia might create a framework to conduct large-scale military operations:[8]

> In Russia the General Staff is responsible for operational-strategic level planning. The tactical, operational and strategic levels are differentiated by the scope of the task, not merely the scale of the unit or units involved. This can see a unit, such as a brigade, operate across more than one level. Strategic planning responsibility lies with the Security Council, which brings together top-level officials including the intelligence community. The chief of the General Staff is also a member of the Security Council.[9]

However, as the General Staff no longer has operational control over forces, in combat, war-fighting assets are under the control of the appropriate field commanders.[10] Indeed, the role of individual commanders in the Russian military decision-making process is more pronounced than in Western armed forces.

The National Defence Management Centre brings together many of the key military and security decision-makers to interact in near real time and oversee, guide and fine-tune military decision-making. This method is consistent with a network-enabled approach to combat operations, but Russia's digital systems architecture remains a work in progress and it will take time to fully integrate all the various nodes in the military system. The national centre is also likely intended to overcome the traditional stove-piping in the military decision-making system, whereby information could bypass elements of the military hierarchy, who would benefit from access.

Strategic, operational and tactical decision-making

The structural changes outlined above, combined with the revisions in approach to command and control, directly inform the Russian variant of the military decision-making process.

There is a close link between these structures and the significant roles of commanders across the strategic, operational and tactical levels. Russian military decision-making seems predicated on the competence and strong leadership skills of commanders, supported by relatively small staffs of officers. In this system and within the Russian variant of the military decision-making process, the personality of the commander in the field and at the joint strategic command level plays a significant part.

In addition, it is apparent that in future the National Defence Management Centre will play a central role in resolving some of the issues involved in automating

CHIEF OF THE GENERAL STAFF
Chief of the General Staff of the Russian Armed Forces General Valery Gerasimov. CREDIT: Mikhail Metzel/TASS/Getty Images

Russia's command-and-control system, and in streamlining the military decision-making process.

At the strategic level, the commander-in-chief will almost certainly play a critical and hands-on role in terms of command

Map 6.1: **Russia's military districts and joint strategic commands**

JOINT STRATEGIC COMMAND OF THE WESTERN MILITARY DISTRICT

St Petersburg

JOINT STRATEGIC COMMAND OF THE NORTHERN FLEET

JOINT STRATEGIC COMMAND OF THE EASTERN MILITARY DISTRICT

WESTERN MILITARY DISTRICT

NORTHERN FLEET

Rostov-on-Don

SOUTHERN MILITARY DISTRICT

EASTERN MILITARY DISTRICT

Yekaterinburg

JOINT STRATEGIC COMMAND OF THE SOUTHERN MILITARY DISTRICT

CENTRAL MILITARY DISTRICT

Khabarovsk

JOINT STRATEGIC COMMAND OF THE CENTRAL MILITARY DISTRICT

Source: IISS; *The Military Balance 2017*

● MILITARY DISTRICT HQ

and control. This might change in the post-Putin era, but it seems the system in which Russian military decision-making occurs is designed to be top heavy. An illustration of this was offered by Chief of the General Staff Army-General Valery Gerasimov when he noted that President Vladimir Putin had involved himself in the planning of military operations in Syria on a regular basis, as well as in setting operational aims:

I usually report to the Minister of Defence on a daily basis morning and evening on the state of affairs and the progress in mission performance, and he reports to the president. Once or twice a week the minister reports to the president in person, presenting the requisite documents, maps, and video materials. Sometimes the Supreme Commander-in-Chief himself comes to see me, sometimes the defense minister and I go to him to report. The president identifies the targets, the objectives, he is up to speed on the entire dynamic of the combat operations. And in each sector, moreover. And, of course, he sets the objectives for the future.[11]

Another work in progress is greater integration of C4ISR and automated command and control to produce a more cohesive approach toward the planning and coordination of military operations. A significant part in this is assigned to the National Defence Management Centre, which, as more technologies are introduced and stove-piping issues are resolved, will play an increasing role in overseeing operations in real time. Indeed, during operations the National Defence Management Centre will be the interface and central link between the national political leadership, General Staff, defence ministry and joint strategic commands down to mobile headquarters.

Exercising control

The recent history of Russia's operational-strategic exercises shows emphasis placed upon internal strategic mobility, and so it is probable that units would move from other joint strategic commands in any pre-war phase. For large-scale inter-state warfare, the desired ground-force structure may be based around divisions, regiments and brigades, rather than on independent battalion tactical groups (BTGs). Armies would employ divisions and brigades as the main elements of their tactical manoeuvre force. However, the continuing presence of whole battalions of one-year conscripts in almost all combat formations will cause serious problems for this approach; brigades and regiments will either have to backfill their missing battalions or BTGs with contract-manned units from other formations, or deploy understrength.

Vostok 2018

In referring to the annual operational-strategic exercise *Vostok* 2018, Chief of the General Staff Gerasimov used the phrase 'strategic manoeuvres' and said that Russia needed more of these kinds of exercises.[12] Whether Gerasimov simply used this language to reflect the participation of the Chinese People's Liberation Army (PLA) in *Vostok* 2018, or whether there was greater underlying significance in his choice of words, as of mid-2020 was uncertain.[13] Russia's General Staff does, however, appear to use such strategic-level exercises to assess, among other features, the speed and efficiency of the military decision-making process.

Vostok 2018 was held on 11–17 September 2018 and focused on five combined-arms and four air-defence training grounds in the Eastern and Central military districts, and in the Okhotsk and Bering seas. It also involved the Aerospace Forces, Airborne Forces and the Northern and Pacific fleets. Gerasimov provided an outline of the scenario for the exercise, with the first two days devoted to planning. The second active phase was staged over five days, and its novelty lay in extending the exercise from the Eastern into the Central military district, the inclusion of the Northern Fleet, and the participation, if limited, of the PLA.

Central MD commander Lieutenant-General Alexander Lapin noted the 'unprecedented' scale of the exercise, which entailed 'new forms and methods of combat' based on lessons drawn from

VOSTOK 2018
Heavy armour takes part in exercise *Vostok* 2018. CREDIT: Vadim Savitsky/TASS/Getty Images

Russia's operations in Syria. He made no mention of the rehearsal of large-scale inter-state warfare, though clearly it featured in the exercise.[14]

Highlighting the scale of the exercise, Gerasimov noted the presence of advanced weapons systems such as the 9K720 *Iskander*-M (SS-26 *Stone*) short-range ballistic-missile system and the 9M729 (SSC-7 *Southpaw*) land-attack cruise missile. He said that in the second active phase of the exercise, defeating a 'massive air strike' would be rehearsed, alongside nullifying cruise-missile attacks involving Aerospace Forces air-defence units and naval platforms in the Sea of Okhotsk and the northwestern Pacific Ocean. The rehearsal of offensive and defensive operations using land, air and sea power were also envisaged.

The joint operations conducted with the PLA and a small number of Mongolian troops at the Tsugol training ground included the rehearsal of combined-arms action against a hypothetical opponent. A complex range of targets reportedly allowed commanders to form a 'front' 24 kilometres long and 8 km deep.[15] On the basis of this detail, some analysts have concluded that *Vostok* 2018 was a rehearsal for large-scale warfare. Yet it also fits a series of conflict types built into an overall scenario to rehearse escalation control.

Such exercises help to illustrate Russia's approaches to the strategic, operational and tactical levels of combat operations, and afford insights into how the senior ranks seek to bring together these levels in accordance with the requirements of the exercise scenario vignettes.

Avoiding rigidity

While Russia's General Staff avoids applying models to its operational planning, as represented by its military exercises, it believes that the US and NATO conduct operations based upon templates. In general, the US and NATO overall approach is seen by Russian oper-

Figure 6.1: **Russia's military command systems**

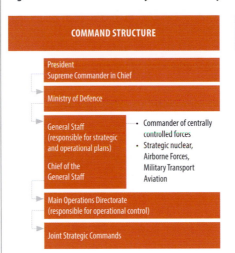

Sources: IISS; Russian Ministry of Defence

ational planners as constraining, as they are perceived to restrict thought, generally being evidenced in poor staff work. Gerasimov made this point when he said: 'It is unusually difficult to foresee the circumstances of a war … It is necessary to work out a particular line of strategic conduct for each war, and each war represents a partial case, requiring the establishment of its own peculiar logic, and not the application of some sort of model.'[16] From a Russian perspective, this may explain why the US has had tactical successes in Afghanistan, Iraq and Syria, but has failed to turn these into beneficial strategic outcomes.

In a similar vein, the General Staff views the United States' formal Military Decision Making Process as fixed and easy to predict in terms of its stages and possible weaknesses. This is evident in Russia's military coverage of NATO operations and the interest in countering a large-scale air campaign. This is factored into most Russian operational-strategic exercises, with an emphasis on countering cruise-missile attacks and responding to air sorties.[17]

Moreover, when the Russian Ground Forces and other arms and service branches train to fight, they have an adversary in mind. Unlike the US armed forces, which

SOUTHERN MILITARY DISTRICT EXERCISE
Hard-copy maps and boards and digital systems in use in a 2017 Southern Military District exercise. CREDIT: Vitaly Timkiv/TASS/Getty Images

is capability based, the Russian Ground Forces are combat trained to fight based on the General Staff's assessment of probable threats to the Russian state. This arguably could give the Russian Ground Forces a long-term training edge over their American and NATO counterparts, as well as imbuing them with the conviction that large-scale conflict will only occur close to Russia's borders.[18]

Following *Vostok* 2018, a command-staff exercise was held in October 2018 in the Southern Military District featuring large-scale force-on-force manoeuvres. The exercise included elements from the 8th, 49th and 58th combined-arms armies, the 22nd Army Corps, the Caspian Flotilla, the Black Sea Fleet, the 4th Air Force and the Air Defense Army, as well as military units subordinate to the Southern Joint Strategic Command and some Spetsnaz units.

As a rehearsal for large-scale force-on-force warfare, the exercise appeared to focus on rehearsing operations using divisions/regiments and brigades.[19]

Decision-making in state-on-state war

As noted, the General Staff has factored into operational-strategic military exercises the concept of fighting a large-scale inter-state war. But how does this differ from the Soviet approach involving multiple echeloned armies and fronts, and what might these differences mean for the armed forces, given the need for the General Staff to plan operations according to the specific demands of the local operational environment?

An influential volume published in 2017 by Major-General (retd.) Sergey Batyushkin offers an insight into Russian military thinking. Entitled 'Preparation and Conduct of Military Actions in Local Wars and Armed Conflicts', the writing provides detail on Russia's approaches to military planning.[20] The volume is notable in explaining the distinction between large-scale warfare and 'local wars and armed conflicts'.

Batyushkin states that the Soviet armed forces were trained and prepared to fight a conventional war in Europe using means and methods, including mass mobilisation, an approach that will now never be used. In distinguishing local wars and armed conflicts from large-scale inter-state warfare, Batyushkin's work importantly shows how Russia's armed forces would approach operations below the threshold of the latter type of war. It is likely that the military decision-making process would vary according to the scale, nature and mission goals of any particular combat operation.

Comments from senior Russian military officers in recent years make it clear that they have studied how the US approaches information-system-based command and control at what Russians would regard as theatre-level operations. A conference at the Academy of Military Sciences in January 2016 heard then Southern Military District commander Colonel-General Alexander Galkin discuss the challenges of command and control of integrated ('joint', in Western parlance) force groupings in a theatre of military operations. Galkin noted:

COMPUTER-BASED SYSTEMS
A battalion-level tank and motor-rifle unit exercise at the Kadamovsky firing range in 2019 makes use of computer-based systems. CREDIT: Valery Matytsin/TASS/Getty Images

The basis for C2 systems is the global information network of the US Department of Defense, which supports all types of communications. Characteristically, due to this advanced communication system, the command and control points were deployed at a significant distance from each other on the territories of various states (Jordan, Iraq, Bahrain, Qatar).[21]

In his view, such developments supported changing how the Russian General Staff should approach the conduct of operations.

Similar themes were addressed at the event by Major-General I.A. Fedotov, senior researcher at the Center for Military-Strategic Studies of the General Staff Academy. Despite the progress made since the New Look reforms began in restructuring the command-and-control system and introducing elements of automation, Fedotov was critical of the limited nature of actual integration of such systems into the armed forces and flagged the persistence of stove-piping.[22]

Network-centric New Look

Russia's view of the value of network-centric or net-enabled warfare is today broadly similar to those of Western states, covering the exploitation of digital information and communication systems in the realm of military operations.[23] How it sets about in detail exploiting the digital realm will, however, differ. An initial goal of this element of the New Look reform process was simply to get senior Russian military officers to begin to focus on network-centric-warfare concepts and to incentivise the domestic defence industry to develop the required digital systems. Initially used as a mechanism to promote reform and modernisation, the New Look process has now matured and moved into the implementation phase. Consideration is also now given to the

implications of network-centric warfare for future force development.[24]

The process triggered numerous practical experiments, advances in capability and the slow but important step of the development and acquisition of automated digital command, control and communications systems. There were also improvements in Russia's surveillance and reconnaissance systems, which are being combined with efforts to upgrade and innovate in terms of electronic-warfare capabilities. Russian defence planners reportedly see electronic warfare as being complementary to a network-centric military capability.

Some of these unifying features in Russia's ongoing military transformation provide pointers as to the likely shape and extent of its future conventional military capability. This is a capability that will prove useful for Russian military planners as a toolset to indirectly challenge the US and NATO or other powers on Russia's periphery. The General Staff will likely seek to use network-centric approaches to modern warfare to speed up the command-and-control process and to improve the overall efficiency of decision-making.[25]

While Russia's initial military intervention in Ukraine in 2014 revealed little that was network-centric in essence, the Syria campaign saw it experiment more with elements of net-enabled warfare. This included the use of precision strikes and uninhabited aerial vehicles (UAVs) for immediate post-attack battle-damage assessment. Most of Russia's operations in Syria, however, continued to rely on non-precision weapons, while network-centric-based experimentation constituted only a very small part of operational activities.[26]

Although it is difficult to gauge the extent of progress in this area, the general picture is of a greater adoption of digital-system-enabled warfare. This is consistent with progress in other areas such as command and control and electronic warfare, and the wider goal of embedding

information systems in the architecture of the armed forces. Observers anticipate continued progress in Russia's developing network-centric capability, as long as the state continues to provide sufficient financial investment to enable this.[27]

Sceptics and believers

During the formative period of Russian interest in and study of network-centric warfare, there were sceptics among the senior ranks of the armed forces and in the military-scientific community.

Russian military theorists writing in the post-1992 period can be divided loosely into three groups: traditionalists, modernists and revolutionaries. The traditionalists generally argued in favour of conservative approaches to warfare, stressing the continued need to study the Soviet experience of the Great Patriotic War, while trying to adapt this to modern conflict settings. Modernists favoured a modification of this approach that would allow a general updating of the doctrine, tactics, and weapons and equipment inventory to suit the conflicts Russia might face. The revolutionary school argued that new approaches were needed and was open to a complete overhaul of the armed forces.[28]

These areas could often overlap; chief among the traditionalists is the late Army-General Makhmut Gareev, recognised as one of Russia's major military theorists. Gareev was sceptical of US advances in network-centric warfare and argued against its adoption in Russia.[29] However, with the onset of the New Look reform in 2008, the modernisers and revolutionaries gained ascendency in the extent to which the defence ministry, senior officers and political leadership paid attention to the introduction of military digital systems and the development of a credible network-centric-warfare capability.[30] This has softened somewhat under Defence Minister Sergei Shoigu, who was appointed in November 2012, but the political-military leadership remains committed to building a network-centric-warfare capability and modernising the armed forces to make full use of C4ISR

However, there remain areas of contradiction that make outlining the longer-term shape of Russian military capability difficult to forecast.[31] Gareev, for example, frequently spoke or wrote against C4ISR, comments that still meet with varying degrees of approval from the political-military leadership. Although it is impossible to predict the detailed outcome of just how far Russia will go in adopting full-blown net-enabled command and control and its impact on Russia's conventional capability, there are indications that the defence ministry is willing to continue investing in the process of further modernising both forces and systems along information-based lines.

These efforts are sensitive to Russian military traditions and culture, and the transformation currently in progress has to be considered in this setting. Russia's network-centric capability is not about mirroring the US and leading NATO armed forces since it is unlikely to fit well within Russia's military system. Moreover, Russian military terminology does not mesh with Western terminology. Senior officers are, however, entertaining substantive changes that will eventually result in a capability level that as of mid-2020 was only embryonic.[32]

Different thinking

Russian thinking on C4ISR and other terms diverges somewhat from that of the US and NATO states. Since the 1990s, the key Russian developmental and conceptual C4ISR terms have been 'reconnaissance-strike complex' and 'reconnaissance-fire complex'. In the early 2000s, Russian military scientists added 'reconnaissance-strike system', 'reconnaissance-fire system' and 'reconnaissance-fire operation'. By 2009, two additional concepts were added: 'information-strike system' and

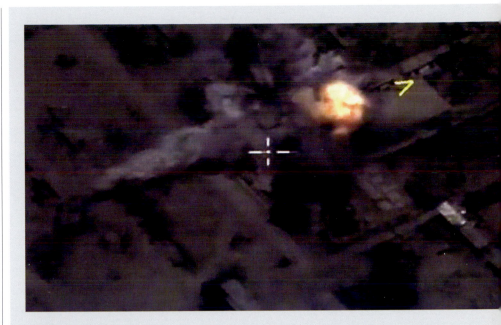

LAND-ATTACK CRUISE-MISSILE STRIKE
A 3M14 land-attack cruise-missile strike on a target near Palmyra, Syria, May 2017. CREDIT: Russian Defence Ministry Press Office/TASS/Getty Images

'information-strike operation'.[33] While these are variants of the C4ISR approach, there is in fact no Russian-language equivalent of network-centric warfare, and as such, when the term was used, it was first and foremost in reference to observing and analysing developments in the US and NATO states, in the context of China or, more recently, in grappling with its adoption in the Russian setting.

In the writings of Russian military scientists, there is understanding and a body of knowledge on Western approaches to network-centric warfare. These scientists tend to analyse operational experiences and draw conclusions concerning the relative strengths and weaknesses of such, approaches. Additionally, Russian specialists have also sought to study and draw lessons from examples of Western armed forces such as in Sweden that tried and later diluted efforts to introduce a network-centric-warfare capability, in order to avoid these pitfalls in Russia. Russian analysis of US and NATO network-centric warfare is also closely linked to how its officers follow, assess and understand the concept and the trends involved. Principal among these, clearly with permission to publish some of his analyses publicly, is GRU Colonel Aleksandr Kondratyev.[34]

Kondratyev's writings were most frequent in 2009–13. During this period, it became evident that although there was a clear understanding of network-centric warfare among Russian military scientists, there is in fact no equally elaborated Russian variant of the concept.[35] In other words, it remains unclear in the work of the country's leading specialists in this area as to how precisely the concept is adopted, adapted and applied in the Russian context.[36]

Despite these issues, the idea of network-centric warfare has been preserved as one of the key drivers in Russia's conventional military-modernisation process.[37] For senior officers and defence planners, this means a reliance on 'learning by doing', and therefore paying closer attention to the limited experimental use of networked operations in the Syrian theatre. This is to better understand how such networks may be furthered in future defence planning and the subsequent shaping of the internal military structures and modernisation priorities.

Recent work by Russian military theorists acknowledges that the adoption of a network-centric capability in the armed forces will involve a change in the outlook of the military leadership at all

Figure 6.2: The development of Russia's tactical command-and-control system

INDUSTRY LEAD SELECTED
(GROUP OF ENTERPRISES
KNOWN AS SOZVEZDIYE)

INITIAL TESTING OF
YeSU-TZ ELEMENTS

BRIGADE-LEVEL TESTING
EXPOSES YeSU-TZ OPERATING
AND OPERATOR ISSUES

YeSU-TZ PERFORMANCE
IN *KAVKAZ* EXERCISE
DEEMED SUCCESSFUL

TSENTR EXERCISE
INCLUDES USE OF
YeSU-TZ ELEMENTS

| 2000 | 2001 | 2002 | 2003 | 2004 | 2005 | 2006 | 2007 | 2008 | 2009 | 2010 | 2011 | 2012 | 2013 | 2014 | 2015 | 2016 | 2017 | 2018 | 2019 | 2020 | |

PRESIDENTIAL APPROVAL GIVEN TO
DEVELOP A UNIFIED TACTICAL COMMAND-
AND-CONTROL SYSTEM (YeSU-TZ)

ANALYSIS OF WAR WITH
GEORGIA REINFORCES THE
SYSTEM REQUIREMENT

KAVKAZ EXERCISE EXPOSES FURTHER
PROBLEMS – CANCELLATION
OPTION CONSIDERED

PROCUREMENT CONTRACT
ANNOUNCED

Sources: IISS; Russian Ministry of Defence

levels. This will include establishing an automated infrastructure, operating in a single information space, further developing modern means of surveillance and reconnaissance, the information from which can be transmitted across telecommunications networks, and populating the armed forces with a 'sufficient number of high-precision weapons'.[38] Clearly, this involves long-term and systemic work on the part of Russian defence planners, in order to integrate combat platforms into such an information network, and make such changes as are necessary to personnel and training.

Following several years of experimentation with network-centric approaches and what this means for force structure, education, training and operational tactics, Russian senior officers and theorists seem in broad agreement that this concept may be used to inspire, shape and drive the defence industry's work to modernise the country's armed forces. However, possessing a mature network-centric-warfare capability is not an end in itself, but rather is a combat enabler.[39]

Tactical automated command and control

Russia's military decision-making architecture and its approaches to decision-making at the strategic, operational and tactical levels are tied into the development in recent years of increasingly automated command-and-control systems and wider efforts as part

of the military-modernisation process to transition into the information era.

The unifying theme in these efforts to streamline the command-and-control system and introduce automated systems is the focus on speed in decision-making and speed of action in military conflict. The Soviet Union, followed by Russia, attempted to field computer-based command-and-control systems, though the lack of technical means for implementation resulted in many delays. This situation has changed in the last few years as Russia's information-systems sector has improved and military industries are now developing and fielding the requisite technologies. As previously noted, at the heart of this effort is the National Defense Management Centre, which will increasingly connect to subordinate command centres at the joint strategic command and army levels.[40]

Tactical trials

In 2000, President Putin ordered Russia's defence industry to design and develop YeSU-TZ. Since then, work on this system has been carried out by Sozvezdiye Concern, which oversees the domestic companies working on the project.[41] The development process intensified following the Russia–Georgia war in August 2008 and ensuing military reforms. These reforms transitioned the Ground Forces to a brigade-based structure and the General Staff concentrated on enhancing the speed of military decision-making, which would be facilitated by the planned tactical control system, and grappled

with network-centric approaches tied to improving speed in other areas, including strategic and tactical mobility. So far the process has not provided overall a fully integrated system, or arguably system of systems. Efforts continue to try to fix this.[42]

Discussion among Russian military theorists, specialists in network-centric warfare and senior military officers in 2008–12 focused largely on the need to improve on the time needed to generate orders for the conduct of an operation.[43] They saw the YeSU-TZ tactical command system as a means to close the gap in this regard with leading NATO armed forces. One of the main points of the General Staff's lessons-learned analysis of the Russia–Georgia conflict was the ineffective nature of the existing command, control and communications system.[44]

Tactical problems

Despite high-level support for such an ambitious technological transformation and clear understanding within the General Staff concerning the overall importance of both digitising communications and fielding an integrated network-enabled command, control and communications system, in practical terms the defence industry struggled to meet this challenge. Problems with the tactical command-and-control system stemmed from the failure of senior officers, commanders, the defence ministry and defense industry to work together to coordinate these efforts. There were consequent issues linked to the design and technical parameters of the system.

The YeSU-TZ system was repeatedly tested at brigade level in Alabino, Moscow oblast, and was used experimentally in the annual operational-strategic exercises, during which its failures and numerous system-related issues were identified. In 2010, for example, tests in military exercises (and at brigade level) exposed the complex and overly detailed nature of the graphic displays in the hand held and laptop devices used by officers and troops, who complained that this rendered the system too difficult to use. The defence ministry and General Staff realised that part of the wider problem with system testing related to the need to train officers and contract personnel concerning the use and exploitation of the system.[45]

Kavkaz 2012 was a critical test for YeSU-TZ. Unfortunately, the system's numerous weaknesses were exposed during the exercise, and a report was submitted to the General Staff elaborating more than 200 flaws. The General Staff recommended that the defence ministry terminate the contract and instead opt for an alternative, which was still in its early design phase. Minister Rogozin succeeded in preserving the existing arrangements by providing the defence industry with time to resolve these problems.

Among the issues identified during *Kavkaz* 2012, 160 were attributed to human error, while the remaining, technical issues had to be resolved by Sozvezdiye Concern. The large number of human-error issues led to the re-prioritisation of training and education in the use of the system. Progress in this area has proved to be marked, and this will likely continue over the next few years as the numbers of contract personnel in the armed forces further increase. The target date at that time for the defence industry to resolve the remaining technical issues and begin supplying the system to the armed forces was 2015.[46]

The effort to introduce this automated tactical command-and-control system into the Russian armed forces is now well advanced, but the 'brigade sets' are expensive, such that the cost of introducing YeSU-TZ into one brigade is estimated to be 8 billion roubles (US\$123 million).[47] There is currently the capacity to equip three brigades per year. In terms of integrating the system into the armed forces, an additional issue is that some services and arms already use other automated systems, tailored to meet their operational needs. For example, the Airborne Forces has the 'Andromeda-D', which is understood to enable command and control of the future *Armata*-based land-vehicle platforms.[48]

The Ground Forces, Aerospace Forces and Naval Infantry also have different automated tactical command-and-control systems, which presents an ongoing challenge in terms of linking these to new or modernised equipment platforms and digitised communications systems. Although critics point to issues, *Kavkaz* 2016 was deemed a success. Despite issues, integration in the 2025–30 time frame seems feasible.

An integrated communications model is now gradually becoming a reality in the Russian armed forces, with all fixed command posts already digitised and plans in place to digitise mobile command posts over the next few years. In late 2016, the signals command referred to the overall command-and-control system as containing 13 subsystems and called for further sustained work to improve the functionality of the overall automated system.[49] These advances facilitate the functioning of the overall military decision-making architecture.

While the defence ministry and defence industry struggled with the numerous issues involved in developing and introducing an automated command-and-control system for the armed forces, the complex nature of operating such a system in the information space has presented many other problems and challenges. In professional Russian military publications, two such areas that stand out are the problems of interoperability and 'information conflict'. These issues are frequently presented as being closely interconnected with the pursuit and adoption of a network-centric-warfare capability. Indeed, interoperability is an issue that weighs heavily in Russian military thinking and planning. Russia has no equivalent to NATO's military-interoperability standards.[50] This lack of standardisation to create a unified set of hardware, software and interface requirements has implications for Russian military command and control and will need to be adequately addressed if the armed forces are to benefit fully from digitisation.

URALVAGONZAVOD MANUFACTURING PLANT
T-72B3 main battle tanks on the range at Alabino, the site of numerous YeSU-TZ tactical command-and-control system tests. CREDIT: Sergei Bobylev/TASS/Getty Images

Conclusion

Russia's armed forces have undergone considerable change since the New Look programme began in 2008. A central component in this process has been to improve the speed and efficiency of command and control at the strategic and tactical levels by streamlining organisational structures and adopting new technologies. At the strategic level, the National Defence Management Centre is crucial, while at the tactical level, it is the YeSU-TZ that is central. In terms of structures, the strategic, operational and tactical levels are being increasingly integrated by the establishment of the National Defence Management Centre and the wider adoption of C4ISR.

Russia's evolving military decision-making architecture appears more able to address the armed forces' large-scale-warfare requirements, with its primary focus on high-speed decision-making in the context of manoeuvre warfare and rapidly developing situations that provide little opportunity for lengthy planning. The Russian personnel system was built to support the manoeuvre-warfare system, with an emphasis on battle drills for junior officers and enlisted soldiers, while more senior officers focus on the study of tactics and their historical employment. However, this system is not well suited to staff-centric war-fighting command and control, with large numbers of headquarters personnel, as practised by the US and other NATO states. Russia's system is instead more like a flow chart or computer algorithm, with staff simply inputting variables. In the past, this planning process was conducted on paper by the use of nomograms, but with the adoption of digital technology the Russian armed forces are moving to rapidly expedite staff estimates for force and operational requirements through automated command and control.

These automated systems, such as YeSU-TZ, use this information to war game potential courses of action, provide options for improvement and eventually disseminate orders. As such, although more rigid than those utilised in Western states, they significantly enhance arguably the greatest potential advantage Russia's military decision-making architecture has over the US and NATO – that of speed. All this is, however, dependent on the continuing success of developing and integrating the National Defence Management Centre with the other elements of the emerging digital command network, from the tactical level up.

Notes

1   Andrey Garavskiy, 'Svyaz reshaet vse', *Krasnaya Zvezda*, 22 May 2010, http://old.redstar.ru/2010/05/22_05/1_01.html; Boris Cheltsov, Iskander Zamaltdinov and Sergey Volkov, 'NATO and western countries' work on "network-centric" warfare and Russia's slowness in this area', *Vozdushno kosmicheskaya oborona*, 21 June 2009.

2   Grigoriy Maslov, 'They Will Divide the Russian Armed Forces by the Compass', www.infox.ru, 30 April 2010, https://www.infox.ru/news/23/47587-rossijskuu-armiu-podelat-po-kompasu.

3   President of Russia, 'Decree of the President of the Russian Federation dated 05.06.2020 No. 374: On the military-administrative division of the Russian Federation', 5 June 2020, http://kremlin.ru/acts/bank/45591; Ministry of Defence of the Russian Federation, 'The Joint Strategic Command of the Northern Fleet celebrates the fourth anniversary of its foundation', 15 December 2018, https://function.mil.ru/news_page/country/more.htm?id=12208252@egNews.

4   Ministry of Defence of the Russian Federation, 'Na boevoe dezhurstvo zastupila operativnaja dezhurnaja smena Nacional'nogo centra upravlenija oboronoj Rossii', 1 December 2014, https://function.mil.ru/news_page/world/more.htm?id=12002205@egNews.

5   E.O. Ostroovskiy and A.S. Sizov, 'Podkhod k modelirovaniyu kognitivnoy sfery ob'yektov operativnoy razvedki', *Voyennaya Mysl*, no. 2, 2016.

6   'Ukazatel Statey Opublikovannykh V Zhurnale "Morskoi' Sbornik"', *Morskoi' Sbornik*, no. 12, 2015.

7   Oleg Vladykin, '"Zapad-2017" natselen na zashchitu Vostoka', *Nezavisimoye Voyennoye Obozreniye*, 15 September 2017, http://nvo.ng.ru/realty/2017-09-15/1_965_west2017.html; 'Pochemu "Zapad-2017" vyzval isteriyu na Zapade', *Nezavisimoye Voyennoye Obozreniye*, 8 September 2017, http://nvo.ng.ru/gpolit/2017-09-08/2_964_nvored.html; Ivan Dragomirov, 'Soldatam – udachi!', *Voyenno-Promyshlennyy Kuryer*, 19 September 2017, https://www.vpk-news.ru/articles/39002; 'Sily PVO Zapadnogo voyennogo okruga razvernulis' v novykh rayonakh na ucheniyakh Zapad-2017', TASS, 16 September 2017, http://tass.ru/armiya-i-opk/4567491; 'Baltic Fleet corvettes destroy air, sea and coastal targets during Zapad-2017 drills', TASS, 17 September 2017, https://tass.com/defense/966015.

8   In Russian usage, the term 'large-scale warfare' refers to warfare on the scale of the First and Second world wars. When describing conflicts on a lesser scale, the term 'local wars and armed conflicts' [*lokalnykh voynakh i vooruzhennykh konfliktakh*] is regularly used. This term has been used in a wide variety of conflicts to include the Korean War; the five Arab–Israeli wars; the Vietnam War; the Iran–Iraq War; the First and Second gulf wars; the Afghanistan wars; and the Chechen wars. Given this view, the Russian definition of 'local wars and armed conflicts' encompasses military activities from the level of what would be considered counter-insurgency operations through the level of state-on-state conflict, up to and including much-discussed Western notional

scenarios where Russia and NATO become engaged in some sort of limited armed conflict regarding the Baltics. For purposes of clarity, in this dossier a more Western definition of 'large-scale warfare', which can roughly be defined as any state-on-state military conflict, has been used.

9   Charles K. Bartles, 'Russian Force Structure for the Conduct of Large-Scale Combat Operations', *Military Intelligence Professional Bulletin*, vol. 45, no. 1, January/March 2019, p. 56, https://fas.org/irp/agency/army/mipb/2019_01.pdf.

10 *Ibid.*

11 Viktor Baranets, 'Nachal'nik Genshtaba Vooruzhennykh sil Rossii general armii Valeriy Gerasimov: "My perelomili khrebet udarnym silam terrorizma"', *Komsomolskaya Pravda*, 26 December 2017, https://www.kp.ru/daily/26775/3808693.

12 The terms *operativno-strategicheskikh ucheniy* (operational-strategic exercise) and *strategicheskiye komandno-shtabnyye* (strategic command staff [exercise]) are frequently used interchangeably in Russian military literature, though the latter implies fewer forces used or deployed for the exercise.

13 'V Rossii podoshla ochered' provodit' strategicheskiye manevry, zayavil Gerasimov', RIA Novosti, 6 September 2018, https://ria.ru/defense_safety/20180906/1527948289.html.

14 'V masshtabnom uchenii Vostok-2018 budut zadeystvovany osnovnyye sily Tsentral'nogo voyennogo okruga', Rambler.ru, 30 August 2018, https://news.rambler.ru/middleeast/40685993-v-masshtabnom-uchenii-vostok-2018-budut-zadeystvovany-osnovnye-sily-tsentralnogo-voennogo-okruga; Dmitriy Sergeyev, '"Vostok-2018": kakova tsel' samykh masshtabnykh za postsovetskiye gody manevrov voysk', Tvzvezda.ru, 21 August 2018, https://tvzvezda.ru/news/forces/content/201808210722-xsmd.htm.

15 Ivan Dragomirov, '"Vostok" – delo gromkoye: Bol'shiye vostochnyye manevry proshli ot Zabaykal'skogo kraya do beregov Severnogo Ledovitogo okeana i tikhookeanskogo poberezh'ya Rossii', Voyenno-Promyshlennyy Kuryer, 18 September 2018, https://www.vpk-news.ru/articles/45052; Ilya Kramnik, 'Vostok s oglyadkoy na zapad: chem interesny ucheniya Vostok-2018 Dlya chego nuzhny samyye krupnyye s sovetskikh vremen manevry', *Izvestia*, 17 September 2018, https://iz.ru/789818/ilia-kramnik/vostok-s-ogliadkoi-na-zapad.

16 General Valery Gerasimov, 'Tsennost' nauki v predvidenii: Novyye vyzovy trebuyut pereosmyslit' formy i sposoby vedeniya boyevykh deystviy', *Voyenno-Promyshlennyy Kuryer*, 26 February 2013, http://vpk-news.ru/articles/14632.

17 Oleg Vladykin, '"Zapad-2017" natselen na zashchitu Vostoka', *Nezavisimoye Voyennoye Obozreniye*, 15 September 2017, http://nvo.ng.ru/realty/2017-09-15/1_965_west2017.html; 'Pochemu "Zapad-2017" vyzval isteriyu na Zapade', *Nezavisimoye Voyennoye Obozreniye*, 8 September 2017, http://nvo.ng.ru/gpolit/2017-09-08/2_964_nvored.html; Dragomirov, 'Soldatam – udachi!'.

18 Vladislav Morenkov and Andrey Tezikov, 'Istoricheskiy aspekt razvitiya ASU PVO', *Vozdushno-Kosmicheskaya Oborona*, no. 1, 7 February 2015, http://www.vko.ru/oruzhie/istoricheskiy-aspekt-razvitiya-asu-pvo; Igor M. Kuptsov, 'Bor'ba s giperzvukovymi letatelnami apparatami (GZLA): Novaya Zadacha i trebovaniya k sisteme vozdushno-kosmicheskoy oborony (VKO)', *Voyennaya Mysl'*, no. 1, January 2011, pp. 10–17; Anton Balagin, 'Ispytaniya zenitnoy sistemy S-500 nachnutsya do kontsa goda', *Russkoye Oruzhiye*, 1 February 2016, http://rg.ru/2016/02/01/s500-site-anons.html; 'S-500 Prometheus', Missile Threat, http://missilethreat.com/defense-systems/s-500; 'S-500 budet sposobna odnovremenno porazhat' 10 ballisticheskikh tseley s pochti pervoy kosmicheskoy skorost'yu – glavkom VVS', TASS, 24 December 2012, http://tass.ru/politika/654566; Alexander Lemansky, Igor Ashurbeyli and Nikolai Nenartovich, 'ZRK S-400 "Triumf": obnaruzheniye – dal'neye, soprovozhdeniye – tochnoye, pusk – porazhayushchiy', *Vozdushno-Kosmicheskaya Oborona*, 3 June 2008, http://www.vko.ru/oruzhie/zrs-s-400-triumf-obnaruzhenie-dalnee-soprovozhdenie-tochnoe-pusk-porazhayushchiy.

19 'Soyedineniya armii Yuzhnogo voyennogo okruga (YuVO), dislotsirovannyye v Volgogradskoy i Rostovskoy oblastyakh prinimayut uchastiye v dvukhstoronnem komandno-shtabnom uchenii', 1 October 2018, Tvzvezda.ru, https://tvzvezda.ru/news/forces/content/201810011602-mil-ruj6tgf.html; Ministry of Defence of the Russian Federation, 'Chetyre divizionnykh i brigadnykh takticheskikh ucheniya proydut v ramkakh KSHU sgruppirovkami voysk YuVO', 18 September 2018, https://function.mil.ru/news_page/country/more.htm?id=12195952@egNews.

20 Major-General (retd.) Sergey Batyushkin graduated from the Frunze Military Academy (now called the Combined Arms Academy of the Armed Forces of the Russian Federation) with a prestigious 'gold medal' for academic excellence and was later an instructor at the institution. He is also a Doctor of Military Sciences and a member of the Russian Academy of Military Science.

21 Galkin, 'Forms of the Application of Military Force and the Organization of Command and Control of Integrated Armed Force Groupings in the Theater of Military Activity', pp. 51–4.

22 I.A. Fedotov, 'Trends in the Development of the Operational-Strategic Command of the Military District at the Present Stage of Developing the Structure of the Armed Forces of the Russian Federation', *Vestnik*, vol. 4, no. 57, 2016, pp. 65–9.

23 N. Tyutyunnikov, *Voyennaya mysl' v terminakh i opredeleniyakh: v trekh*, vol. 3 (Moscow: Pero, 2018), p. 160.

24 See, for example, V.I. Korchmit-Matyushov, *Teoriya voyn* (Moscow: Slovo, 2001); S.A. Parshin, Yury Yevgeni Gorbachov and Yury A. Kozhano, *Sovremennyye tendentsii razvitiya teorii i praktiki upravleniya v vooruzhonnykh silakh SShA* (Moscow: Lenand, 2009); 'Khochesh' mira, pobedi myatezhevoynu! Tvorcheskoye naslediye', *Ye.E. Messnera/russkiy voyennyy sbornik*, no. 21, 2005; V.I. Slipchenko, *Voyny novogo pokoleniya: distantsionnyye i beskontaktnyye* (Moscow: OLMA-Press, 2004); M.A. Gareyev and V.I. Slipchenko, *Budushchaya voyna* (Moscow: OGI, 2005); General Staff of the Armed Forces of the Russian Federation,

'Setetsentricheskaya voyna. Daydzhest po materialam otkrytykh izdaniy i SMI', Moscow, 2010.

25 V.D. Dobykin et al., *Radioelektronnaya bor'ba. Silovoye porazheniye radioelektronnykh system* (Moscow: Vuzovskaya kniga, 2007); A.I. Paliy, *Ocherki istorii radioelektronnoy bor'by* (Moscow: Vuzovskaya kniga, 2006); *Sovremennaya radioelektronnaya bor'ba. Voprosy metodologii* (Moscow: Radiotekhnika, 2006); V.V. Tsvetnov, V.P. Demin and A.I. Kupriyanov, *Radioelektronnaya bor'ba. Radiomaskirovka i pomekhozashchita* (Moscow: MAI, 1999); V.V. Tsvetnov, V. Demin and A.I. Kupriyanov, *Radioelektronnaya bor'ba. Radiorazvedka i radioprotivodeystviye* (Moscow: MAI, 1998); V.N. Chernavin, *Voyenno-morskoy slovar* (Moscow: Voyenizdat, 1990); *Entsiklopediya 'Oruzhiye i tekhnologii Rossii. XXI vek'*, 'Sistemy upravleniya, svyazi i radioelektronnoy bor'by' (Moscow: Arms and Technologies Publishing House, 2006).

26 O.V. Tikhanychev, 'O roli sistematicheskogo ognevogo vozdei'stviia v sovremennykh operatsiiakh', *Voyennaya Mysl'*, no. 11, November 2016, pp. 16–20.

27 Author interviews with Russian SMEs, December 2016.

28 Tor Bukkvoll, 'Iron Cannot Fight – The Role of Technology in Current Russian Military Theory,' *Journal of Strategic Studies*, vol. 34, no. 5, 2011.

29 M. Gareev, 'For the army of the 21st Century: a local war is first of all a war', *Krasnaya Zvezda*, 31 October 2010; M. Gareev, 'Opyt pobeditelei v velikoi voine ne mozhet ustaret', *Nezavisimoye Voyennoye Obozreniye*, 12 March 2010.

30 Y. Gavrilov, 'Interview with General Staff Chief Makarov', *Rossiyskaya Gazeta*, 23 March 2010.

31 S.P. Stolyarevskiy and D.V. Sivoplyasov, 'Problemy realizatsii federal'nykh gosudarstvennykh obrazovatel'nykh standartov vysshego obrazovaniya v podgotovke ofitserskikh kadrov', *Voyennaya Mysl'*, no. 3, 2016.

32 S. Melkov and O. Zabuzov, 'Initiativa v onlaine i offlaine. Virtualnie voini i realnie problem', *Nezavisimoye Voyennoye Obozreniye*, 16 July 2010.

33 S.N. Razin'kov, Ye. A. Reshetnyak and A.M. Chernyy, 'Radioelektronno-informatsionnoye obespecheniye voysk

radioelektronnoy bor'by Vooruzhennykh Sil Rossiyskoy Federatsii', *Voyennaya Mysl'*, no. 12, 2015; Andrey Yevdokimov et al., 'Strelyayem Moshchno. No Chasto Mimo', *Zashchita i bezopasnost'*, 30 June 2016; Sergey Osipov, Aleksandr Kolesnichenko and Vitaliy Tseplyyayev, 'Nam Yest' Chem Gordit'sya!', *Argumenty i fakty*, 13 May 2015.

34 J.W. Kipp, 'Promoting the New Look for the Russian Armed Forces: the Contribution of Lieutenant-Colonel Aleksandr Kondratyev', *Eurasia Daily Monitor*, vol. 7, no. 113, 11 June 2010.

35 A. Kondratyev, 'Problemy organizatsii aviatsionnoi podderzhki operatsii sukhoputnykh voysk SShA', *Zarubezhnoe Voyennoe Obozrenye*, no. 9, November 2009; A. Kondratyev and A. Medin, 'Doroga SShA k novomu obliku sukhoputnykh voysk', *Voyenno Promyshlennyy Kuryer*, 14 October 2009; A. Kondratyev, 'Edinaya razvedka evrosyuza: byt ili ne byt?', *Voyenno Promyshlennyy Kuryer*, 25 February 2009.

36 A. Kondratyev, 'Problemnye voprosy issledovaniya novykh setetsentricheskikh kontseptii vooruzhennykh sil vedushchikh zarubezhnykh stran', *Voyennaya Mysl'*, no. 11, November 2009, pp. 1–74; V.V. Kvochkov and Y.A. Martsenyuk, 'On the character of wars and armed conflicts with the participation of the Russian Federation', *Voyennaya Mysl*, no. 2, 2002.

37 Yu.Ye. Donskov, S.V. Golubev and A.V. Mogilev, 'Model' podgotovki spetsialistov radioelektronnoy bor'by k vypolneniyu zadach po informatsionnomu obespecheniyu voyennykh (boyevykh) deystviy', *Voyennaya Mysl'*, no. 4, 2015.

38 'Iranskiy BLA, Khamashekh vpervyye prinyal uchastiye v uchebnykh manevrakh KSIR', *Voyenno-tekhnicheskoe sotrudnichestvo*, April 2016; Dmitriy Litovkin, 'Armiya perekhodit na elektronnyye pasporta', *Izvestia*, 26 July 2016, https://iz.ru/news/623819.

39 V. Kovalov, G. Malinetskii and Y. Matviyenko, 'Kontseptsiya 'setetsentricheskoy' voyny dlya armii Rossii: 'mnozhitel' sily' ili mental'naya lovushka?', *Vestnik, Akademii Voyennykh Nauk*, no. 1 (50), 2015.

40 E.O. Ostrovskiy and A.S. Sizov, 'Podkhod k modelirovaniyu kognitivnoy sfery ob'yektov operativnoy razvedki', *Voyennaya Mysl'*, no. 2, 2016.

41 G.I. Metlitsky and U.E. Zaitsev, 'Sovershenstvovanye sistemy upravleniya voinskimi chastyami', *Voyennaya Mysl'*, 4 April 2008, pp. 18–22, http://www.mil.ru/files/vm4_2008.pdf; E.A. Perov and A.V. Pereverzev, 'O perspektivnoy tsifrovoy sisteme svyazi Vooruzhennikh Sil Rossiyskoy Federacii', *Voyennaya Mysl'*, no. 3, March 2008.

42 Author's emphasis. See Dmitry Kandaurov, 'Komp'yuteru davno pora priyti na smenu karandashu v rukakh shtabnogo ofitsera', *Nezavisimoye Voyennoye Obozreniye*, 12 November 2010, http://nvo.ng.ru/armament/2010-11-12/10_computer.html; Dmitry Kandaurov, 'Glavnyye resursy v rasporyazhenii ASUV – informatsiya i vremya', *Nezavisimoye Voyennoye Obozreniye*, 8 October 2010, http://nvo.ng.ru/concepts/2010-10-08/6_asuv.html. A valuable insight into characteristic flaws in Russian defence planning can be found in Carolina Vendil, *Russian Military Reform: A Failed Exercise in Defense Decision Making* (London: Routledge, 2009).

43 V.I. Vladimorov and V.I Stuchinskiy, 'Obosnovaniye boyevogo primeneniya aviatsionnykh nositeley sredstv radioelektronnoy bor'by v operativnoy glubine dlya zavoyevaniya informatsionnogo prevoskhodstva', *Voyennaya Mysl'*, no. 5, 2016.

44 'Interview with CGS Makarov', *Voyenno-Promyshlennyy Kuryer*, 1 February 2011; Oleg Falichev, 'Preobrazovaniya zakoncheny, razvitiye prodolzhayetsya', *Voyenno-Promyshlennyy Kuryer*, 31 January 2011, http://vpk-news.ru/articles/7058; General Aleksandr Postnikov, 'Vremya "avtomatizirovannykh" voyn', *Nezavisimoye Voyennoye Obozreniye*, 14 January 2011, http://nvo.ng.ru/realty/2011-01-14/1_automate.html.

45 Dmitry Kandaurov, 'ASUV v Alabino: zhelayemoye i deystvitelnoye', *Nezavisimoye Voyennoye Obozreniye*, 19 November 2010, http://nvo.ng.ru/armament/2010-11-19/1_asuv.html.

46 Author discussions with Russian SMEs, December 2016.

47 Author interviews with Russian military specialists, Moscow, December 2018.

48 Alexey Ramm, 'Airborne Forces will be able to control "Armata" online', Izvestia,

23 August 2016, https://iz.ru/news/628366; Ministry of Defence of the Russian Federation, 'V reshenii zadach vnezapnoj proverki boegotovnosti desantniki Novorossijskogo gvardejskogo gornogo

soedinenija VDV ispol'zujut vozmozh-nosti ASU "Andromeda-D"', 18 June 2020, https://function.mil.ru/news_page/country/more.htm?id=12302741@egNews.

49 Author interview.

50 A.Ya. Oleynikov and I.I. Chusov, 'Voyenno-organizatsionnoye: razvitiye Problema vzaimodeystviya v Vooruzhennykh Silakh Rossiyskoy Federatsii', *Vestnik, Akademii Voyennykh Nauk*, no. 1 (61), 2017, pp. 61–8.

Economics and industry

Four distinct periods can be identified in the trajectory of Russian defence spending since 1992. The first, in the years immediately following the end of communism, saw a sharp decline in expenditure. The second, during the 2000s, saw the beginning of a recovery, although procurement goals remained out of reach. In the third, from 2011 to 2015, there were stronger increases in funding, enabling Moscow to achieve procurement targets. And during the fourth, since 2016, the aim has been to sustain this progress, but annual increases in spending have been more modest. The former Soviet Union's sprawling defence industry has generally followed a similar trajectory to that of military expenditure, with swingeing cuts and then significant increases taking effect on production after a time lag of a couple of years.

Defence in the Russian budget

Almost all Russian military spending is financed through the federal budget, the only exception being occasional modest additions from regional budgets to support conscript recruitment. Since 2008 there has been a rolling three-year federal budget, updated annually, which sets out spending for the year ahead and provisional outlays for the following two years. The federal budget consists of 14 chapters, the second of which is titled 'National Defence' and covers military spending. It is divided into subchapters covering areas such as personnel, operations and maintenance, investment, weapons procurement and support equipment, and military-related research and development (R&D). There is also a subchapter on nuclear-weapons-related funding, which is overseen by the state-owned corporation for the nuclear industry, Rosatom.

When decisions are being taken on the volume of defence spending, discussion focuses only on the lines of funding included in this chapter of the federal budget. The information it contains is therefore sufficient to provide a guide to spending patterns, although its scope is not as broad as the standard definition of military spending employed by NATO. The IISS's *Military Balance* reflects this by giving separate figures for the Russian defence budget and for total Russian defence expenditure.[1]

Key takeaways

DEFENCE FUNDING
Significant increases in investment in military equipment were maintained between 2011 and 2015, as a key element of the 2020 State Armament Programme.

INVESTMENT IMPACT
Modernisation goals are close to achievement but progress within SAP 2020 was uneven across the domains.

SPENDING HORIZON
The short-term outlook for defence spending is subdued by low oil prices and economic challenges.

AEROSPACE AND AIR DEFENCE
The aerospace and air-defence sectors benefit from domestic support and export success.

NEXT-GENERATION SYSTEMS
Shifting to the production of next-generation weapons and systems remains a challenge.

R&D INVESTMENT
Sustained research and development investment is needed in order to provide the technology base required for advanced weapons.

POLITICAL IMPORTANCE
The defence-manufacturing sector continues to be politically important for Russia, as a significant source of employment and national prestige.

Figure 7.1: Russian federal budget: subchapters in the 'National Defence' chapter (since 2005)

SUBCHAPTER	TITLE	DETAILS
2.01	Armed forces of the Russian Federation	Includes personnel, operations and maintenance, investment, and the procurement of weapons and other military hardware
2.02	Modernisation of the armed forces	Budget line not used
2.03	Mobilisation and training of reserves	Covers the costs of mobilising personnel for the armed forces
2.04	Mobilisation preparation of economy	Funding for the management of economic preparations for mobilisation
2.05	Preparation for and participation in collective security and peacekeeping operations	No funding allocated since 2013
2.06	Nuclear-weapons complex	Procurement of nuclear devices produced by Rosatom
2.07	International obligations in military-technical cooperation	Fulfilment of international state-level obligations in the sphere of military-technical cooperation, including the export of armaments and the provision of military services, training and aid
2.08	Applied R&D in field of national defence	Funding for defence R&D
2.09	Other issues in field of national defence	Includes funding of Ministry of Defence investment in facilities, and some funding for the development of the defence industry and for the agency that oversees arms exports, the Federal Service for Military-Technical Cooperation

Source: Russian Ministry of Finance, annual budget documentation

Figure 7.2: Defence in the 2019 Russian federal budget: implementation of spending

LINE OF FUNDING (BUDGET CHAPTER/SUBCHAPTER)		VOLUME OF SPENDING (MILLION ROUBLES)
'NATIONAL DEFENCE' (Chapter 2 of federal budget)		
• Armed forces of the Russian Federation (2.01)		2,216,945
• Mobilisation and training of reserves (2.03)		7,717
• Mobilisation preparation of economy (2.04)		3,144
• Nuclear-weapons complex (2.06)		46,020
• International obligations in military-technical cooperation (2.07)		9,900
• Applied R&D in field of national defence (2.08)		303,456
• Other issues in field of national defence (2.09)		410,997
'NATIONAL DEFENCE' (minus past debt payments)	TOTAL	2,998,179
ARMS RECYCLING		3,244
'NATIONAL DEFENCE' minus arms recycling and mobilisation preparation of economy*	TOTAL	2,991,791
OTHER MILITARY EXPENDITURE** Other Ministry of Defence expenditure:		
• Economy (Chapter 4)		35
• Housing (5)		105,646
• Environment (6)		2,838
• Education (7)		86,094
• Health (9)		76,720
• Culture and cinematography (8)		4,155
• Physical culture and sport (11)		3,964
• Mass media (12)		2,823
• Pensions (10)		347,293
• Social support (10)		197,451
• Fees to international agencies (1)		8
PARAMILITARY FORCES		
• Troops of National Guard (Rosgvard) (3.03)		242,066
• Border Service of Federal Security Service (3.07)		138,727
Support for closed cities of the MoD and Rosatom (14)		8,849
Support for Baikonur space centre (14)		2,287
OTHER MILITARY EXPENDITURE	TOTAL	1,218,956
MILITARY EXPENDITURE	TOTAL	4,210,747
BUDGET EXPENDITURE	TOTAL	18,220,235
'NATIONAL DEFENCE' as % of total expenditure		16.42
MILITARY EXPENDITURE as % of total expenditure	TOTAL	23.11
GROSS DOMESTIC PRODUCT (GDP)		109,361,524
'NATIONAL DEFENCE' as % of GDP		2.74
MILITARY EXPENDITURE as % of GDP	TOTAL	3.85

*Excluded because not part of the standard NATO definition of military spending. **Number in parentheses indicates the budget chapter that funding is sourced from.

Source: Russian Ministry of Finance, annual budget documentation

Reconciling Russia's stated military budget with the more widely accepted definition requires two lines of funding to be removed and certain items to be added. The former are the funding of economic preparations for mobilisation and the costs associated with the disposal and recycling of weapons that have been retired. The items to be added, which appear in other chapters of the federal budget, include Ministry of Defence spending on housing, education, health, culture, physical fitness and sport, mass media, pensions and some social support for service personnel and their families.

Paramilitary forces would also be included in the more conventional calculation of military expenditure, along with the National Guard (formerly the troops of the Ministry of the Interior) and the Federal Security Service's Border Guards. The other items that should be added are the financing of military facilities such as closed cities, for example those associated with nuclear-weapons R&D and production, and the Baikonur space centre in Kazakhstan, leased to Russia mainly for military purposes. Baikonur and the closed cities are included in the 'Inter-budget Transfers' chapter.

There is a significant disparity – 1.2 trillion roubles, or more than 1% of Russia's GDP – between total defence spending calculated using the Russian methodology and the figure derived from the more broadly recognised approach (see figures 7.2 and 7.3).

Post-Soviet expenditure

While the annual laws on budget implementation provide a way of looking at Russia's military expenditure since the break-up of the Soviet Union, the figures derived can only be approximate. This is in part due to occasional changes in the way expenditure is classified and because during the upheaval of the 1990s the reporting of budget implementation was patchy. But even with these caveats, the distinct periods in the post-Soviet history of Russian military expenditure can still be seen.

The first period, immediately following the break-up of the Soviet Union, saw a sharp decline in Russian defence spending, exacerbated by the country's financial crisis during the third quarter of 1998. The government was trying to move rapidly from a command to a market economy, which included the privatisation of state-owned industries, but the result was a sharp contraction in economic output combined with inflation. The defence budget came under severe pressure and spending plummeted to its lowest level, as a proportion of GDP, during the entire post-communist period.

The mismatch between economic performance and military needs was stark. The armed forces had inherited the very large personnel numbers of the Soviet era along with the organisational challenges resulting from the dissolution of the USSR, which included trying to deal with those elements of its nuclear arsenal that now lay outside its borders.

In the early 1990s the defence ministry's share of GDP was maintained at a sizeable 6%, although economic contractions at the time somewhat distort the figures and weapons acquisition was cut by two-thirds. Defence expenditure began to fall as a proportion of GDP from 1995, dropping to less than 3% during the 1998 crisis.

The economy began to recover in 1999, marking the start of nearly a decade of growth. The earlier economic reforms finally brought benefits and, with rising oil prices and increased output of oil and natural gas providing a further boost, an average annual rate of GDP growth of about 7%, combined with only a modest rate of inflation, was maintained until the global financial crisis of 2008.

Against this more positive economic backdrop, the second distinct period in the post-Soviet history of Russian defence expenditure ran approximately from 2000 to 2010. Military spending hovered at

3.4–3.6% of GDP throughout the decade, but investment in new weapons remained limited. The country's defence industry, ravaged by the cuts of the 1990s, began to show signs of recovery in the mid-2000s. Just how badly the military had fared in the post-Soviet era, however, was made apparent in its lacklustre performance in Russia's brief war with Georgia in 2008.

In February 2007 a new defence minister, Anatoly Serdyukov, was appointed with the task of overhauling the military and recapitalising platform and weapon inventories. The New Look reform programme was launched in October 2008. But then came the global financial crisis, with Russian GDP declining by 7.8% between 2008 and 2009, the sharpest contraction of any G20 country. That was followed, however, by an equally quick recovery, which in 2010 allowed the government to sign into law the most ambitious military-modernisation programme since the collapse of the USSR, the *Gosudarstvennaya programma vooruzheniya* (State Armament Programme, SAP) 2020.[2]

The years 2011–15 mark the third period, characterised by significant increases in spending. There was a determined effort to quickly modernise the armed forces' hardware, along with financial support for R&D for the creation of new weapon systems. Though the level of military expenditure in 2011 reflected an economy still in recovery, it began to increase in 2012 and peaked in 2015 at just under 5% of GDP before dropping back to 4% in 2017.

The key aim of SAP 2020 was to address the armed forces' ageing equipment inventory and to increase the share of what the defence ministry deemed to be modern hardware, including both upgraded and new-build weapons and platforms. Modern equipment accounted for only 10% of the overall inventory in 2010, and for active-service units the goal was to reach 70% by 2020. Senior officials gave annual updates as the defence ministry progressed towards its target. In May 2019,

Figure 7.3: Russia's military spending, 1992 to 2019 (billion roubles, current prices)

YEAR	'NATIONAL DEFENCE'	'NATIONAL DEFENCE' AS % OF GDP	TOTAL MILITARY EXPENDITURE	TOTAL MILITARY EXPENDITURE AS % OF GDP
2019	2,998	2.74	4,211	3.85
2018	2,826	2.72	3,850	3.71
2017	2,666*	2.90	3,704	4.02
2016	2,983*	3.47	3,831	4.45
2015	3,181	3.83	4,026	4.85
2014	2,479	3.14	3,224	4.08
2013	2,104	2.88	2,787	3.81
2012	1,812	2.66	2,505	3.67
2011	1,516	2.51	2,029	3.37
2010	1,276	2.76	1,698	3.67
2009	1,188	3.06	1,580	4.07
2008	1,041	2.52	1,385	3.36
2007	832	2.50	1,105	3.32
2006	682	2.53	910	3.38
2005	581	2.69	773	3.58
2004	430	2.53	571	3.35
2003	356	2.70	473	3.58
2002	295	2.72	392	3.62
2001	248	2.77	330	3.69
2000	192	2.63	255	3.49
1999	116	2.40	154	3.19
1998	56.7	2.16	75	2.85
1997	79.7	3.40	106	4.33
1996	63.9	3.18	85.0	4.23
1995	47.6	3.33	63.3	4.43
1994	28.0	4.59	37.2	6.10
1993	7.2	4.20	9.6	5.60
1992	0.9	4.50	1.1	6.00

*Annual laws on the implementation of the federal budget. Note that the data for the early years is not very precise. For years prior to 2005 it has been necessary to estimate the additional volume of spending over and above 'National Defence'. Note that the methodology employed by the Russian statistical agency, now known as the Federal Service of State Statistics (Rosstat), has been updated a number of times without revision of the entire series. A new method for calculating GDP has been used since 2011.

Source: IISS

Figure 7.4: Russian federal budget, 2010–19: share of classified spending in the 'National Defence' chapter

2010	2011	2012	2013	2014	2015	2016	2017	2018	2019
46.5%	45.4%	47.5%	50.4%	56.0%	65.4%	70.5%	63.9%	65.1%	64.2%

Sources: 2010–18 data from Zatsepin (2019), p. 607. 2019 data based on non-classified spending figures from Federal'nyi zakon ot 02.12.2019 No389-FZ 'O vnesenii izmeneniy v federal'nyi zakon 'O federal'nom byudzhete na 2019 god i na planovyi period 2020 i 2021 godov', http://publication.pravo.gov.ru/Document/View/0001201912020075

according to the ministry's own metric, the goal had been met and surpassed in the cases of strategic and aerospace forces. Equipment modernisation for the land forces had been slower, languishing at around 50% in 2019, according to official figures.[3] However, in April 2020, Minister of Defence Sergei Shoigu stated that the target for active-service units was close to being achieved, with 68% of their total inventory consisting of 'modern' systems.[4]

The fourth period, since 2016, has seen a transition to a more steady-state annual renewal of weapons. This will make it possible to moderate the rate of growth of defence spending and to reduce its share of GDP. Total expenditure fell from a high of 4.9% of GDP in 2015 to 3.9% in 2019, and the three-year budget indicates that a further marginal decrease to 3.6% is

RUSSIAN FORCES IN GEORGIA
The performance of Russia's armed forces in the war with Georgia in 2008 was considered to be substandard.
CREDIT: Alexander Popov/TASS/PA Images

likely by 2022. President Vladimir Putin has been urging defence companies to diversify product portfolios by developing competitive high-technology civilian goods capable of meeting domestic and export demands. The success or otherwise of such an approach has yet to be seen. The defence industry's debt burden has also limited its ability to invest to support diversification, while the impact of the COVID-19 pandemic on the Russian economy may well put further pressure on defence expenditure in the short term.

The structure of military spending

The limited transparency of the defence budget makes analysis of the structure of Russian military spending a challenge. During the Soviet era the defence budget was shrouded in secrecy and significant categories of expenditure were omitted, notably procurement and R&D. This changed in the second half of the 1980s when Mikhail Gorbachev was leader, with a more realistic and transparent defence budget appearing for the first time in 1989. This increased openness carried over into the post-Soviet Russian defence budget in the early 1990s, even if considerable secrecy remained. Since the late 1990s, however, detailed information has again become increasingly restricted.

There is an important systemic factor promoting the maintenance and even extension of such secrecy. In government agencies, including the ministries of defence and finance, personnel who handle classified data receive additional pay, and this financial reward was increased in 2006. In these circumstances, especially while Russia is subject to external sanctions, the

defence budget is unlikely to become more transparent in the foreseeable future.

Related to this is a lack of public accountability. The fact that so much of the defence budget is classified means that even in parliament – the Federal Assembly with its two chambers, the State Duma and the Council of the Federation – only the few deputies with the appropriate security clearance are able to see the full federal budget with its classified appendices. Detailed examination of the defence budget is undertaken by the Duma's Defence Committee, most of the members of which have a military or security-services background. The secrecy also means that there are hardly any independent academics with expert knowledge of the defence budget, and only a handful of journalists familiar with issues of military spending.

Classified elements of the budget include weapons acquisition, the repair and modernisation of existing equipment, and military R&D. Much of the spending aimed at supporting the defence industry is also shielded from scrutiny, including the funding allocated in May 2016 to sustain the industry's development.

This funding supports a range of activities, including investment in new facilities; substitution of components that used to be imported but since 2014 have been subject to sanctions imposed by the US, NATO members and some other countries; items previously supplied by Ukraine but now unobtainable by Russia; and measures to train the labour force. Total funding under the programme when originally adopted was reported as 1,067bn roubles, but only 35bn roubles was non-classified.[5]

Unsurprisingly, all spending under the nuclear subchapter is classified, as is all spending on mobilisation preparation of the economy. Finally, since 2014, some of the expenditure on 'military-technical cooperation' has also been classified – apparently the part relating to military aid of a politically sensitive nature during the period in which Russia has been subject to sanctions.

Procurement and R&D funding

Since the mid-1980s there have been two key elements of Russian arms procurements: the previously mentioned SAP and the State Defence Order (SDO) (*Gosudarstevennyi oboronnyi zakaz*, GOZ). The latter is approved by government decree and has legal force. A classified document, it sets out the annual funding allocation for new weapons and the acquisition of other military hardware, the modernisation and repair of in-service hardware, and military-related R&D. SDO contracts used to be drawn up between the defence ministry and the relevant industry partners on an annual basis, but recently there has been a shift to a multi-year approach. The intention is to move eventually to life-cycle contracts covering all stages from initial research to the final withdrawal of the system from service.

The SAP differs from the SDO in that although it is approved by the president, it has no legal force. Like the SDO, it is covered by a high degree of classification. The SAP is normally a rolling ten-year document, renewed every five years. It sets out the volume of armaments to be procured by each service arm, by type of system, and details new weapons to be developed over the following ten years, with schedules in each case for R&D and entry into serial production.

The SAP is very detailed regarding the first five years but less defined for the later five. It establishes the total volume of funding over the ten-year period and the proportion to be allocated to the first five years, providing guidance for the scale of the annually determined SDO. The programme is often amended but details are not made public.

There are several performance indicators included in the SAP but the most important is the share of modern systems in the inventory of each service branch and the armed forces as a whole. This modernisation drive has focused on the equipment of active-service units rather than the entire stock held by the Russian armed forces. The SAP also contains details regarding

PRESIDENT VLADIMIR PUTIN
Shaking hands with Minister of Defence Sergei Shoigu during discussions on the next State Armament Plan, May 2017. CREDIT: Mikhail Metzel/ TASS/Getty Images

procurement and R&D for other agencies with armed forces, in particular the National Guard and the Federal Security Service's Border Guards.

The target volume of funding within the annual SDO is stated in an appendix of the federal budget that was published during the years 1992–97 and 2004–05 but has otherwise been classified. The funding target is rarely met, if ever, and details of implementation only become available if revealed by Putin or a top official involved in defence matters. However, it is possible to assemble some details for recent years – Figure 7.5 indicates the implementation of the SDO from 1997 to 2017 based on the work of a leading independent specialist on Russian defence procurement.

The data indicates the high priority given to R&D during the SAP to 2010, given that many of the equipment-procurement goals could not yet be met. There is little doubt that this was helpful in the implementation of the subsequent SAP to 2020, which prioritised acquisition.

Analysis of Russia's spending on nuclear weapons indicates that the development and production of nuclear devices, and the equipment and maintenance of the nuclear triad, account for approximately 15% of the country's total military expenditure.[6]

A comparative view of military spending

How does Russia's military spending compare to that of other major powers? The usual method of calculation is the one adopted by the the IISS, and indeed most other defence economic institutions, namely that of converting the volume of spending in roubles into US dollars using the market exchange rate in any given year. According to IISS data, Russia rose in the military-spending ranking from fifth position in 2010 to fourth in 2015 and 2016, before falling back to fifth in 2017 and then sixth in 2018, where it remained in 2019.

The use of market exchange rates is not without limitations. Consideration is not given to countries' varying levels of development or to the differing cost of inputs – principally personnel, equipment and investment – that determine a country's military capabilities. Converting figures from local currency to US dollars at market rates masks the fact that these input costs will be lower in some countries and therefore understates the resource commitment to defence in countries such as China and Russia. An alternative approach would be to make conversions using purchasing power parity (PPP) exchange rates, which would at least partially take into account these cost differentials. However,

Figure 7.5: The implementation of the State Defence Order (SDO), 1997–2017 (billion roubles, current prices)

YEAR	TOTAL SDO*	PROCUREMENT BILLION ROUBLES	REPAIRS/ MODERNISATION %	RESEARCH AND DEVELOPMENT BILLION ROUBLES	%	BILLION ROUBLES	%
2017	1,400	910	65.0	144	10.3	346	24.7
2016	1,600	(1,050)	65.6	(230)	14.4	(320)	20.0
2015	1,800	1,188	66.0	360	20.0	252	14.0
2014	1,450	942	65.0	290	20.0	218	15.0
2013	894	550	61.5	178	19.9	166	18.6
2012	677	447	66.0	108	16.0	122	18.0
2011	575	368	64.0	92	16.0	115	20.0
2010	487**	317	65.1	63	12.9	107	22.0
2009	485**	272	56.1	76	15.7	137	28.2
2008	365	201	55.1	73	20.0	91	24.9
2007	303	145	47.9	60	19.8	98	32.3
2006	237	116	48.9	48	20.3	73	30.8
2005	187	112	60.0	12	0.6	63	56.3
2004	138	64	46.4	22	15.9	52	37.7
2003	125	67	53.6	11	8.8	47	37.6
2002	79	46	58.2	***		33	41.8
2001	52	29	55.8	***		23	44.2
2000	48	37	77.1	***		11	22.9
1999	39	21	53.8	6	15.4	12	30.8
1998	28	13	46.4	8	25.6	7	25.0

Note: All numbers in parentheses are estimates. *For some years after 2011 the figure consists of budget funding plus state-guaranteed credits. **Planned. ***Included in procurement.

Sources: 2013–17: Frolov (2018), p. 12. Frolov is explicit that the breakdown is estimated on the basis of limited available data. 2016 breakdown is estimated. 2011–12: http://cast.ru/projects/proekt-tsifry-vooruzheniy.html (Frolov's data). 2010: Frolov (2010a). 2009: plan, http://www.vpk.ru/cgi-bin/uis/w3.cgi/CMS/Item/2540032, accessed 8 July 2010. Website no longer exists. 2005–08: Frolov (2010), p. 32. The 2005 breakdown is suspect. 2001–02: data from TS VPK, 30 June 2014. The website ts.vpk.ru no longer exists. 1997–2000: data from TS VPK, 11 June 2000. The website ww.vpk.ru no longer exists

Figure 7.6: Countries with the highest military spending in constant (2015) US$ billion, 2010, 2015 and 2017–19

2010		2015		2017		2018		2019	
US	755.7	US	597.5	US	581.6	US	589.6	US	637.8
China	99.8	China	145.9	China	163.7	China	173.9	China	185.3
UK	74.1	Saudi Arabia	81.9	Saudi Arabia	85.4	Saudi Arabia	74.3	Saudi Arabia	68.2
France	45.6	Russia	65.7	UK	59.5	UK	60.3	UK	61.5
Russia*	44.1	UK	58.4	Russia	55.6	India	55.4	India	57.0
Saudi Arabia**	43.6	France	46.6	India	53.3	Russia	52.4	Russia	52.9
Japan	40.0	India	44.8	France	47.4	France	49.1	France	50.2
Germany	38.4	Japan	41.1	Japan	42.3	Japan	42.9	Germany	45.2
India	37.0	Germany	36.6	Germany	40.2	Germany	41.2	Japan	43.2
South Korea	28.2	South Korea	33.2	South Korea	34.4	South Korea	36.4	South Korea	39.8

*IISS figure for total defence expenditure – one-off debt repayments to defence industry removed as not relevant to current resource commitment to defence. **IISS figure includes security expenditure.

Sources: *The Military Balance* (2010, 2015, 2017, 2018 and 2019 editions)

---

the appropriateness of PPP conversions depends on the extent to which a country is self-sufficient in developing and producing the armaments required by its armed forces. For Russia and China they are appropriate, as imported systems play almost no role in Russia's case and only a small and decreasing one in China's.

Adopting PPP conversion rates would elevate Russian defence expenditure in 2017 and 2018 to US$125–135bn (PPP international $), while Chinese expenditure would increase to US$320–340bn (PPP international $). Russia would therefore probably have a higher position in the defence-expenditure ranking. However, while the measure is appropriate for China and Russia, it is less suitable when assessing the spending of countries such as India and Saudi Arabia, which rely heavily on imports of military equipment from relatively high-cost producers. For those countries it would be necessary to adopt a hybrid approach to determine defence expenditure in dollars, with the market exchange rate used for converting defence procurement and the PPP conversion rate applied to all other defence expenditure (personnel, operations, etc.).

Looking to the future

Even prior to the COVID-19 pandemic and the consequent economic contraction – Russia's real GDP is projected to decrease by 6.6% during 2020[7] – the official outlook for Russian defence spending was already subdued, with lower oil prices throughout 2019 constraining Russian state finances. Combined with Shoigu's assessment in April 2020 that the target of modernising 70% of the equipment of active-service units was close to being achieved,[8] this has resulted in a stagnant defence-budget outlook. Prior to the COVID-19 outbreak the 2020–22 Russian federal budget[9] suggested little growth in defence spending in real terms over the next couple of years. As of July 2020, as part of measures to offset the worst of the impact, the finance ministry was seeking three successive cuts of 5% to the annual defence-procurement between 2021 and 2023.

A further complicating factor for the defence industry is the very significant burden of debt that has accumulated over the past few years, an unforeseen legacy of SAP 2020 that may also have implications for the defence budget. Without a meaningful recovery in oil prices, the short-term outlook for Russian defence spending is likely to deteriorate further, although there is probably a level below which Russia will be reluctant to allow spending to fall. Indeed, as a share of GDP, military spending is likely to remain high by international standards, reflecting the fact that Russia is a major nuclear power with a vast land mass and an extremely long border necessitating the maintenance of sizeable armed forces in terms of personnel.

Russia's defence industry

The Russian defence industry has undergone enormous change over the past three decades. After functioning as the core of the Soviet Union's militarised economy, it subsequently shrank to a fraction of its former size during the turbulent shift from a planned to a market economy in the 1990s. But it remains a very important source of employment, directly or indirectly sustaining approximately 2.5 million jobs, largely in cities and regions that focus on defence production.[10] The defence industry is also the source of a large proportion of Russia's technology-intensive production, with Putin having once declared that it could 'serve as fuel to feed the engines of modernisation in [the Russian] economy'.[11] But the industry's most valuable contribution is in endowing Russia with well-equipped armed forces – a key component in the country's status on the world stage.[12]

It was for these reasons that the decision was made to embark on the ambitious programme of rearmament embodied by the ten-year SAP 2020 programme

MILITARY INDUSTRIAL COMMISSION
President Vladimir Putin chairing a session of the commission, the top-level body that manages relations between the armed forces and industry, September 2017. CREDIT: Alexei Nikolsky/TASS/Getty Images

approved at the end of 2010 by then-president Dmitry Medvedev.[13] A total of 20.7trn roubles (about US$700bn at the average 2011 exchange rate) was reported to have been assigned to fulfil SAP 2020 and to revitalise the wider defence-industrial base.[14] SAP 2020 is now concluding after running concurrently with its replacement, SAP 2027, since 2018, but it continues to shape the fortunes of Russia's defence industry.

Trends in structure and ownership

After enjoying priority status for decades, the defence industry experienced a period of enormous and often traumatic transformation following the disintegration of the Soviet Union. The defence budget of newly independent Russia was significantly smaller than that of the USSR, with spending on procurement and R&D drastically reduced. By 1997 the volume of military output of the defence industry had collapsed to less than 10% of its 1991 level.[15] The brutal reduction in spending on defence-industrial production was accompanied – and compounded – by institutional and organisational fragmentation as the production associations and research-production associations that characterised the Soviet defence industry were disbanded in anticipation of privatisation. Initially it was hoped that privatisation would result in a smaller number of more efficient enterprises. However, because of resistance from defence-industry directors, only a quarter of companies had been fully privatised by the end of the 1990s, and the anticipated efficiency gains were not achieved. Indeed, at the turn of the millennium there were still many loss-making defence manufacturers in Russia.

In the years following Putin's accession to the presidency in 2000, against a backdrop of rapid economic growth, a concerted effort was made to bring order to the defence industry. This was essentially focused on merging the numerous producers into so-called 'integrated structures' or holding companies. Consolidation, it was hoped, would allow vertical management structures to make the companies more efficient and competitive. Industrial behemoths emerged, including United Aircraft Corporation (UAC), a holding company created by presidential decree in 2006, which encompasses military and civil fixed-wing aircraft production; United Shipbuilding Corporation (USC), which brings together most of the country's shipyards; and Rostec, which oversees 13 holding companies and nearly 700 military and/or civilian manufacturers. By the end of 2013 it was estimated that around three-quarters of Russian defence-industrial production took place within these structures.[16]

Map 7.1: **Selected aerospace and guided-weapons companies, Moscow and Moscow region**

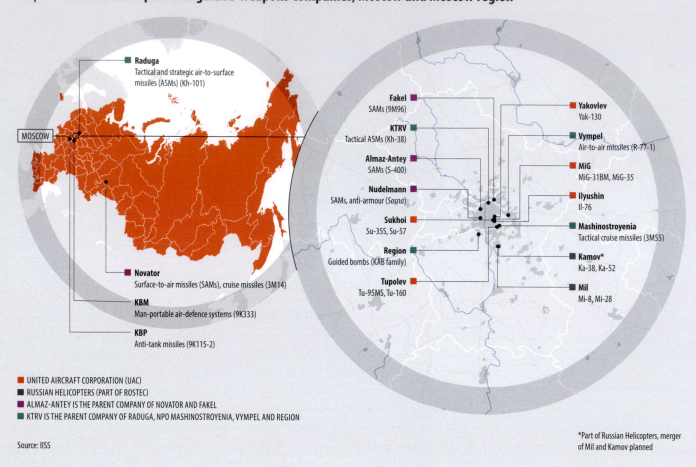

Raduga
Tactical and strategic air-to-surface missiles (ASMs) (Kh-101)

MOSCOW

Novator
Surface-to-air missiles (SAMs), cruise missiles (3M14)

KBM
Man-portable air-defence systems (9K333)

KBP
Anti-tank missiles (9K115-2)

Fakel
SAMs (9M96)

KTRV
Tactical ASMs (Kh-38)

Almaz-Antey
SAMs (S-400)

Nudelmann
SAMs, anti-armour (*Sosna*)

Sukhoi
Su-35S, Su-57

Region
Guided bombs (KAB family)

Tupolev
Tu-95MS, Tu-160

Yakovlev
Yak-130

Vympel
Air-to-air missiles (R-77-1)

MiG
MiG-31BM, MiG-35

Ilyushin
Il-76

Mashinostroyenia
Tactical cruise missiles (3M55)

Kamov*
Ka-38, Ka-52

Mil
Mi-8, Mi-28

■ UNITED AIRCRAFT CORPORATION (UAC)
■ RUSSIAN HELICOPTERS (PART OF ROSTEC)
■ ALMAZ-ANTEY IS THE PARENT COMPANY OF NOVATOR AND FAKEL
■ KTRV IS THE PARENT COMPANY OF RADUGA, NPO MASHINOSTROYENIA, VYMPEL AND REGION

Source: IISS

*Part of Russian Helicopters, merger of Mil and Kamov planned

Today, most of Russia's defence manufacturers are owned by the state, either entirely or through equity stakes. These stakes are administered by different government ministries, with the Ministry of Industry and Trade holding the largest number. It is often the case that the state shares ownership with minority private investors and local governments. Sporadic efforts have been made over the years to raise private participation and to reduce state holdings in certain areas of the defence industry, but so far with only limited success.

Even before the imposition of Western and Ukrainian sanctions in 2014, foreign firms and technology played only a minor role in the Russian defence industry and were concentrated in only a few areas of the production cycle. Most of the cooperation was with companies in ex-Soviet republics such as Ukraine and Belarus, where integrated supply chains were a legacy of Soviet-era production. In many cases they manufactured crucial intermediate components for Soviet materiel – such as helicopter engines, vehicles designed to transport ballistic missiles, guidance systems for certain missiles and power units for large warships – and those production networks continued to function after the planned economy started to unravel from the end of 1991.

Close relationships like these have only rarely developed with companies outside the former Soviet Union. Although Western and Chinese components – especially electronic components – have sometimes been used in the production of Russian military equipment, imports from outside the former Soviet space have tended to be off-the-shelf purchases and not part of any closely integrated production network. Russia did import a significant amount of components in the post-Soviet years but avoided purchasing complete weapons systems until Serdyukov became defence minister in 2007. Wanting to expose domestic producers to greater competition, he decided that several types of weapons systems should be imported from Western countries. These efforts would ultimately fail, however, because Serdyukov was removed from office at the end of 2012 and then the imposition of Western and Ukrainian sanctions in 2014 prompted Russian officials to focus on raising the level of self-sufficiency in defence-industrial production. Since 2014, Russia has invested significant funds in the production of components that were previously imported and is now virtually self-sufficient in a number of key areas of production, for example cruise-missile and helicopter engines.[17] Slower progress has been made towards self-sufficiency in the production of electronic components and advanced machine tools.

Figure 7.7: **Rostec: selected subsidiaries, 2020**

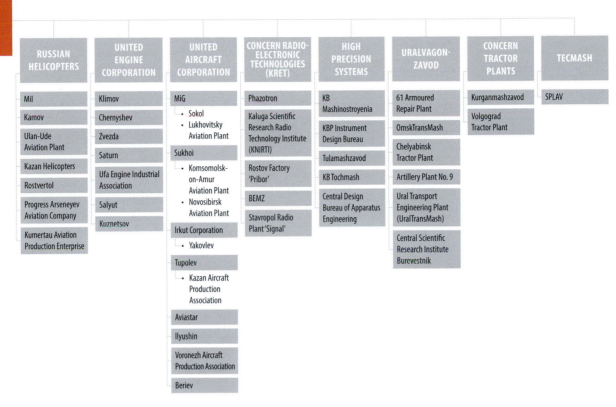

Sources: IISS; Rostec

The aerospace sector

Most of the production cycle for Russia's fixed-wing-aircraft industry, including R&D, manufacturing and support services, takes place under the aegis of the UAC holding company, which has consolidated control over the most important aerospace companies (such as Ilyushin, MiG, Sukhoi and Tupolev), manufacturers (such as Irkut and Komsomolsk-on-Amur Aircraft Plant) and design bureaus. UAC has around 100,000 employees and is able to produce a full range of aircraft, including training, transport and combat aircraft of different sizes.

In the rotary-wing aerospace sector, Russia's main helicopter design, production and services companies are consolidated under Russian Helicopters (*Vertolety Rossii*), which in turn is controlled by Rostec. Employing almost 50,000 people, it controls the Mil and Kamov design bureaus as well as the main production units, the Ulan-Ude Aviation and Kazan manufacturing plants. Russian Helicopters exhibits a high degree of vertical integration and comprises enterprises responsible for the production of a wide range of components, such as the Vpered Moscow Machine Building Plant (tail rotors and blades for Mil helicopters) and RET Kronshtadt (navigation systems). It also produces a wide range of training, transport and combat helicopters.

Russian capabilities in the sphere of uninhabited aerial vehicles (UAVs) are less advanced. The 2008 war with Georgia highlighted deficiencies in this area, prompting investment in developing new domestic systems, albeit based on the integration of imported Israeli technology. To date, most progress has been made in developing smaller UAVs for reconnaissance and electronic-warfare purposes (e.g., *Orlan*-3M and *Orlan*-10), although heavier strike systems, such as the *Okhotnik* and *Korsar*, are being developed.[18] UAVs are designed and produced by a range of enterprises, including ENICS (a producer of tactical and surveillance UAVs) and STC in St Petersburg (the manufacturer of the *Orlan* surveillance-UAV family), and the Izhevsk-based Zala Aero (part of the Kalashnikov concern, in turn owned by Rostec).

In 2011, the original SAP 2020 schedule envisaged the procurement of more than 600 fixed-wing aircraft, including 60 new fifth-generation multi-role fighter aircraft now known as the Su-57 *Felon* (previously the T-50), around 180 advanced fourth-generation (4++) fighter aircraft and 90 Su-34 *Fullback* strike aircraft. Substantial numbers of the Yak-130 *Mitten* advanced jet trainer, as well as a variety of light, medium and heavy transport aircraft, were also to be acquired. Delays to the Su-57 programme meant the combat-aircraft programme had to be revised, with serial production of the Su-57 delayed until the early 2020s.[19]

The aerospace sector has enjoyed most success in the continued development of designs originating in the 1970s, particularly that of the Sukhoi Su-27 *Flanker* family. The Su-35S *Flanker* M, now the most capable multi-role fighter in the air-force inventory, was the second attempt at a deep modernisation of the single-seat Su-27 *Flanker* B. Efforts in the 1980s to develop what was originally known as the Su-27M were shelved in the mid-1990s after 12 prototypes and three initial production standard aircraft had been built. Likewise, the Su-34 *Fullback* was originally known as the Su-27IB (Fighter Bomber) and had its origins in the 1980s. The Su-30SM *Flanker* H can also be traced back to the late 1980s. The importance of these types can be gauged by the fact that, of the three, only the Su-34 was in service at the beginning of SAP 2020, in small numbers, but by 2020 the core of the Air Force included 90 Su-35, 122 Su-34 and 91 Su-30SM. The Su-30SM and the Su-35 had their genesis in the export market. A version of the former was first produced at the Irkutsk Aviation Plant as the Su-30MKI, which was delivered to India, from 2002, while the Su-35 was originally aimed at the export market rather than the Russian Air Force.

While there have been development issues and delays with the Su-34 and Su-35, it is in the development of new models of combat aircraft that most problems have arisen. This is particularly evident with the Su-57 programme, where there have been difficulties in the production of the new *Izdeliye* 30 engine and in keeping costs at an acceptable level. By March 2016, Russian media reports indicated that the Aerospace Forces would be lucky to receive more than 12 Su-57 *Felons* by 2020.[20] However, Putin's announcement in 2019 that the air force would procure 76 of the aircraft by 2027 (i.e., by the end of the current SAP), with cost reductions the primary reason for expanding the order,[21] put the programme on a better footing.

MiG has fared less well than Sukhoi in the post-Soviet era. Efforts to introduce a much-improved version of the MiG-29 *Fulcrum*, known as the MiG-35, have encountered problems. The defence ministry postponed the original plans to order at least 28 MiG-35 aircraft due to persistent technical and industrial obstacles.[22] An interim order was made for 16 MiG-29SMT aircraft, a model developed in the late 1990s.[23]

In addition to the procurement of new combat aircraft, a programme for the modernisation of Russia's existing fleet is also under way. This includes the MiG-31 *Foxhound*, Su-24 *Fencer* and Su-25 *Frogfoot*. Attention has also been paid to the modernisation of the strategic bomber fleet. Between 2011 and 2019, small numbers of Tu-95MS *Bear* Hs and Tu-160 *Blackjack*s were modernised each year. A new-build and updated version of the Tu-160, the Tu-160M, is also in development. As of 2020, ten were on order, but the initial ambition was that a considerably larger number would eventually be produced.[24]

The procurement of modern transport aircraft has been least successful. In 2011 it was envisaged that 175 new aircraft would be delivered by 2020, an objective subsequently revised up to almost 300 due to the needs of the Russian armed forces.[25] By the end of 2017, however, only 37 new aircraft had been delivered. Most of the problems in this sphere were due to the breakdown of defence-industrial relations with Ukraine, which affected plans to acquire the Antonov An-70 (jointly developed), An-124 and An-140 aircraft from the Ukraine-based producer. Although programmes are under way to deliver the Il-112 and Il-76MD-90A (or Il-476) transport aircraft, the former remains in development and the latter only began to enter service from 2017.[26]

Rotary-wing aircraft

While production of fixed-wing aircraft has been patchy, progress in delivering

IL-112V LIGHT TRANSPORT
The much-delayed aircraft finally being flown for the first time, March 2019. -
CREDIT: Armen Gasparyan/Ilyushin Press Office/TASS/Getty Images

helicopters to the Russian military has been more consistent. This is a sector of the aerospace industry that appears to have adjusted better to the breakdown of defence-industrial relations with Ukraine.[27]

Russian Helicopters has delivered a substantial number of helicopters during SAP 2020, although in the case of combat helicopters it again appears that initial targets have not been met fully.

Orders for additional Ka-52 *Hokum* and Mi-28 *Havoc* helicopters, including systems upgrades based on the experience gained by Russia's armed forces in Syria that exposed the need for improved performance from some onboard systems, have been placed, with deliveries beginning in the early 2020s.

Naval systems: organisation

Most of Russia's military- and civilian-shipbuilding enterprises – for construction of both surface and sub-surface vessels – were consolidated within the state-owned USC in 2007. As with UAC, USC encompasses the full production cycle, including R&D, construction and repair, maintenance and conversion. Employing over 80,000 people, USC's network of facilities spans the whole country, from Kaliningrad and St Petersburg in the west to Khabarovsk in the east, and from Severodvinsk in the north to Astrakhan in the south. Notable smaller shipyards that are not owned by USC include Pella (St Petersburg) and Zelenodolsk (Tatarstan), both of which build Project 22800 *Karakurt*-class corvettes, as well as the 'Zvezda' complex in Bolshoi Kamen near Vladivostok. USC is able to design and build a wide range of vessels, with only the very largest of warships (e.g., cruisers and aircraft carriers) currently beyond their capabilities. After the breakdown of defence-industrial relations with Ukraine in 2014, it became more self-sufficient in the construction of components, most notably power units for large surface vessels.

Figure 7.8: Russian 2020 State Armament Programme aims and outcomes: aircraft and helicopters

SELECTED SAP 2020 GOALS		ESTIMATED DELIVERIES, 2012–19*	
AIRCRAFT		**AIRCRAFT**	
Su-34 *Fullback*	90	Su-34 *Fullback*	108
Su-35S *Flanker* M (plus 2009 order for 48)	50	Su-35S *Flanker* M	90
Su-30SM *Flanker* H	120	Su-30SM *Flanker* H	113
Su-30M2 *Flanker* G	16	Su-30M2 *Flanker* G	16
Su-57 *Felon* A	60	Su-57 *Felon* A	0
MiG-29KR (for navy)	20	MiG-29KR	20
MiG-35	28	MiG-35	2
Yak-130	65	Yak-130 *Mitten*	101
Il-76MD-90A *Candid*	30	Il-76MD-90A *Candid*	6
BOMBER UPGRADES		**BOMBER UPGRADES**	
Tu-160 *Blackjack* mod	14	Tu-160 *Blackjack* mod	6
Tu-95MS *Bear* mod (MSM)	30	Tu-95MS *Bear* mod (MSM)	16
Tu-22M3 *Backfire* (M3M)	30	Tu-22M3 *Backfire* (M3M)	0
HELICOPTERS		**HELICOPTERS**	
Mi-28N *Havoc* B	150	Mi-28N/UB *Havoc* B	70
Ka-52A *Hokum* B (including 40 for navy)	180	Ka-52A *Hokum* B	120
Mi-35 *Hind*	49	Mi-35 *Hind*	65

*Under 'estimated deliveries' some deliveries likely carried over from SAP 2015.

Source: IISS

Naval systems: performance

The navy was reported to have been allocated the largest share of funding under SAP 2020, for the construction of up to 15 frigates, 25 corvettes and 24 submarines (including ballistic-missile and diesel-electric submarines).[28] This would be complemented by the modernisation of up to 15 late-Soviet-era surface combatants and up to 20 submarines. However, progress has been much slower than initially envisaged due to delays in the development of newer models, the imposition of Western sanctions in the aftermath of Russia's annexation of Crimea in 2014, and the breaking of ties with Ukrainian companies that produced important components used in military shipbuilding.

MIL MI-28 *HAVOC* ATTACK HELICOPTER
This benefited from renewed R&D and production-funding investment in the 2020 State Armament Programme. CREDIT: Valery Matytsin/TASS/Getty Images

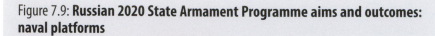

Figure 7.9: **Russian 2020 State Armament Programme aims and outcomes: naval platforms**

SELECTED SAP 2020 GOALS		ESTIMATED DELIVERIES, 2012–19	
Project 955 *Borey*-class SSBN	8	Project 955 *Borey*-class SSBN	3
Project 885/08851 *Yasen/Yasen*-M SSGN	8	Project 885 *Yasen*-class SSGN	1
Project 636/06363/Project 677 SSK	8+	Project 06363 *Varshavyanka*-class SSK	7
		Project 677 *Lada*-class SSK	1
Frigates:	15	Frigates:	
• Project 20380 *Steregushchiy* class FFGHM		• Project 20380 *Steregushchiy*-class FFGHM	7
• Project 20385 *Gremyashchiy* class FFGHM		• Project 20385 *Gremyashchiy*-class FFGHM	1
Corvettes:	25	Corvettes:	
Buyan/Buyan-M/*Karakurt* FSM/FSGM/FSG		• *Buyan* FSM	1
		• *Buyan*-M FSGM	8
		• *Karakurt* FSG	2
Mistral-class LHD	4	*Mistral*-class LHD	0
Project 1144 *Orlan*-class CGHMN	4 upgraded	Project 1144 *Orlan*-class CGHMN	0 upgraded

Source: IISS

Submarines

Some progress has been made in modernising Russia's fleet of nuclear-powered ballistic- missile submarines (SSBNs). Three *Borey*-class (Project 955) SSBNs are already in service, but the commissioning of a fourth – the first of the Project 955A vessels – was delayed repeatedly. Initially expected to be delivered in 2017, the first *Borey*-A was only handed over in June 2020.

Production of new multi-role nuclear-powered submarines has been even slower than that of the *Borey*s. Only one of the *Yasen*-class (Project 885) submarines has been delivered to date. The first of the Project 08851 submarines, the *Kazan*, was due to be transferred to the navy in 2019, but problems with the design, detected during sea trials, have caused USC to state that it may not be delivered until after 2020.[29] It is clear, therefore, that the orig-inal objective of acquiring eight *Yasen*-class submarines by 2020 will not be met.

Modernisation of the submarine fleet has come mostly through overhaul and upgrade work on existing boats, such as variants of the Project 971/09711 *Schuka*-B class (*Akula* I/Akula II), and production of the *Varshavyanka*-class (Project 06363, or 'Improved *Kilo*') submarines, which are based on well-established technology and production techniques. Six of the latter were built and delivered to the Black Sea Fleet, and a further six are under construction for use in the Pacific Fleet. Development of the newer *Lada*-class (Project 677) submarines, which began in the late 1990s, suffered setbacks, principally concerning their air-independent propulsion system. However, the lead vessel, the *Sankt Peterburg*, is in service with the Northern Fleet; the second, the *Kronshtadt*, was scheduled to enter service in 2019 but as of July 2020 had not been handed over; and a third is close to completion. In a sign that the development problems may have been ironed out, a further two could be ordered for delivery under SAP 2027.[30]

VOLKHOV IMPROVED-*KILO*-CLASS SUBMARINE
Prior to launch at the Admiralty Shipyard in St Petersburg, December 2019.
CREDIT: Alexander Demianchuk/TASS/Getty Images

Surface vessels

Procurement of larger surface vessels has proceeded only slowly. The *Admiral Gorshkov*-class (Project 22350) and *Admiral Grigorovich*-class (Project 11356) frigates have not been delivered on schedule. The defence ministry originally planned to acquire six of each type. However, the gas-turbine engines used for both types of ship were produced in Ukraine by Zorya-Mashproekt and the outbreak of conflict in 2014 brought supply to an abrupt end, which delayed the overall production process.[31] One *Admiral Gorshkov*-class and three *Admiral Grigorovich*-class vessels were delivered by the end of 2017. A second *Gorshkov*-class frigate, the *Admiral Kasatonov*, was due to be transferred to the Northern Fleet in 2019 but was only accepted into service in July 2020. A further six are under construction, and there are reports that a further ten *Admiral Gorshkov*-class vessels could be built to an augmented design over the next decade.[32]

Western sanctions affected the supply of German-made engines for the *Gremyashchiy*-class corvettes (Project 20385), which were intended to form the backbone of a modernised corvette fleet. As a result, the Ministry of Defence initiated an import-substitution programme to produce the engines in Russia and has also increased orders of *Steregushchiy*-class (Project 20380) corvettes. A number of other corvettes (Project 22800 and Project 20856) have been ordered to make up for the delays, and several small missile ships and patrol vessels have been delivered, with more under construction. Sanctions also led to the cancellation of the purchase of French-made *Mistral* amphibious-assault ships. Smaller landing, artillery, minesweeping, intelligence and other auxiliary ships have been delivered in greater quantities.[33]

Land systems: organisation

Production of systems for Russia's land forces is more dispersed than in the aerospace and naval sectors. For most of the post-Soviet period, a relatively large number of state and privately owned enterprises and conglomerates have designed and produced the full spectrum of vehicles, including main battle tanks (MBTs), infantry fighting vehicles (IFVs), armoured personnel carriers (APCs), artillery systems, utility vehicles and logistics vehicles. Only recently, with the transfer of Uralvagonzavod to Rostec, have signs of industry consolidation of the type observed in the naval and aerospace sectors emerged. It is also notable that many of the enterprises active in this sector also manufacture vehicles for the civilian market.

Uralvagonzavod, now owned by Rostec, employs more than 35,000 people and is responsible for production of the T-14 *Armata*, T-72 and T-90 MBTs. It also produces a number of other combat vehicles such as the BMPT (*'Terminator'*), which recently entered production. Kurganmashzavod supplies the BMP family of IFVs, while the Volgograd Machine Building Plant (VGTZ) supplies the BMD family of tracked IFVs. Both are part of the Russian Tractor Plants Concern, which employs more 45,000 people and produces a range of other defence and civilian products. The sole shareholder is a state-owned bank, Vnesheconombank. Kamaz, which is partly owned by Rostec and employs over 35,000 people, is the primary supplier of logistics vehicles to the Russian military. Military Industrial Company (VPK), which forms part of the privately owned Basic Elements group, supplies armoured vehicles, including the BTR family of wheeled APCs.

Land systems: performance

SAP 2020 envisaged the purchase of new command-and-control systems, modern infantry combat systems (such as *Ratnik*), thousands of new armoured vehicles, tens of thousands of trucks and automobiles, and new artillery systems. While there was some ambiguity over precise objectives for procurement of armoured vehicles for the ground forces, it is clear that production of the most high-profile system, the T-14 *Armata* tank (and its associated vehicles), has not kept pace with expectations. Orders for the *Armata* family so far only stand at around 132, and there remains ambiguity with regard to this number.[34] Instead, hundreds of modernised T-72 and T-80 tanks, as well as new T-90s, have been delivered to the army. There has been more success in producing upgrades based on older models of multi-role vehicles such as the BMP-3 and the BTR-82A, both of which entered/re-entered serial production under SAP 2020.

Missile systems: organisation

Russia's defence industry as a whole is highly self-sufficient in comparison with those of most other countries, and its most self-sufficient sector is for the production of intercontinental ballistic missiles (ICBMs). The principal design enterprises are the Makeyev State Rocket Centre (which produces the RS-28 *Sarmat* (SS-X-29), R-29RMU *Sineva* (SS-N-23 *Skiff*) and R-29RMU.2.1 *Layner* (SS-N-23 *Skiff*) ICBMs) and the Moscow Thermal Institute (*Buluva*, *Yars*), with production respectively taking place at Votkinsk (in the Udmurt Republic) and Krasmash (in Krasnoyarsk). The production of shorter-range tactical missiles, including ballistic, cruise and other types of missile, takes place primarily at Almaz-Antey and Tactical Missiles Corporation, both of which are vertically integrated conglomerates comprising a wide range of enterprises responsible for different stages of the production cycle. Almaz-Antey, which produces the S-350 (SA-28) and S-400 (SA-21 *Growler*) air-defence systems, employs almost 100,000 people, while Tactical Missiles Corporation (KTRV), which produces a wide range of missile systems and other defence products, including the 3M55 *Oniks* (SS-N-26 *Strobile*) and 3M24 *Uran* (SS-N-25 *Switchblade*) anti-ship missile systems, is estimated to have around 50,000 employees.

Missile systems: performance

Strategic missiles

Deliveries of strategic missiles under SAP 2020 have largely taken place on schedule. The R&D and testing phases for the RS-12M2 *Topol*-M and RS-24 *Yars* ICBMs, and the 3M30 *Bulava* (SS-N-32) submarine-launched ballistic missile (SLBM), began under previous SAPs. The development of additional strategic weapons systems continues, with plans to deploy the RS-28 *Sarmat* (SS-X-29), a liquid-fuelled heavy ICBM equipped with countermeasures to evade anti-missile systems, in the near future.

Tactical missile systems

Deliveries of other advanced missile systems have also proceeded smoothly. The objective of delivering ten 9K720 *Iskander*-M (SS-26 *Stone*) brigade sets by 2020 was achieved. The targets set for deliveries of the S-400 (SA-21 *Growler*) system and other shorter-range air-defence systems appear to be within reach by the end of 2020. In the case of the S-400, however, it has been necessary initially to acquire the system without some of its primary missiles, notably the 40N6 long-range missile.

The S-350 (SA-28) and S-500 have taken longer than anticipated to develop. However, the former began to enter service in 2020 and the latter may do so in the next few years.

Innovation in the defence industry

Problems such as those with the Su-57, the T-14 and the *Admiral Gorshkov*-class frigates make it clear that the Russian defence industry has not performed as well as the country's leaders would have liked. One explanation for the setbacks in the development of newer weapons systems lies in the structure of the defence-industrial innovation system. There are deficiencies when it comes to innovation in manufacturing as a whole, which constrain the growth of knowledge-intensive sectors across the country, and also in the defence industry specifically.[35] Russia inherited an innovation system from the Soviet Union that was arguably ill-suited to the modern global economy. As a result, broad-based innovation has been stymied by numerous structural obstacles, such as the state-dominated R&D system, a relatively small proportion of higher-education institutions engaged in R&D, ageing and under-skilled researchers, a weak governance system that fails to reduce overlapping and top-down implementation strategies by public bodies, and poorly developed linkages between sectors and regions.[36] Russia also scores badly in measures of the degree of competition within the economy. Large and important sections of the economy are dominated by uncompetitive producers that are often protected by either the federal or local government. Furthermore, in recent years, many of the most high-profile attempts to stimulate high-technology growth have been state-led, which has often exacerbated rather than solved these weaknesses.[37]

Within the defence industry itself, it is evident that many Russian defence companies' production processes remain more labour-intensive than those of their foreign peers.[38] Despite efforts to upgrade the

URALVAGONZAVOD MANUFACTURING PLANT
Located in Nizhny Tagil, a key producer of heavy armour for Russia's army.
CREDIT: Donat Sorokin/TASS/Getty Images

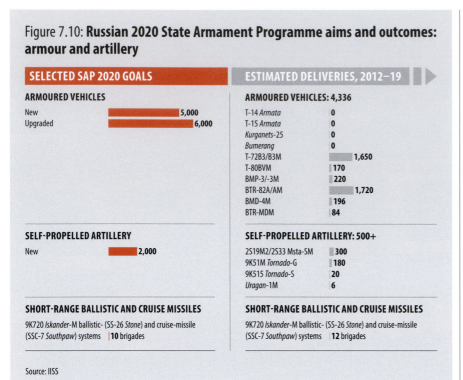

Figure 7.10: Russian 2020 State Armament Programme aims and outcomes: armour and artillery

SELECTED SAP 2020 GOALS	ESTIMATED DELIVERIES, 2012–19

ARMOURED VEHICLES

New	5,000
Upgraded	6,000

ARMOURED VEHICLES: 4,336

T-14 *Armata*	0
T-15 *Armata*	0
Kurganets-25	0
Bumerang	0
T-72B3/B3M	1,650
T-80BVM	170
BMP-3/-3M	220
BTR-82A/AM	1,720
BMD-4M	196
BTR-MDM	84

SELF-PROPELLED ARTILLERY

New	2,000

SELF-PROPELLED ARTILLERY: 500+

2S19M2/2S33 Msta-SM	300
9K51M *Tornado*-G	180
9K515 *Tornado*-S	20
Uragan-1M	6

SHORT-RANGE BALLISTIC AND CRUISE MISSILES

9K720 *Iskander*-M ballistic- (SS-26 *Stone*) and cruise-missile (SSC-7 *Southpaw*) systems | **10** brigades

SHORT-RANGE BALLISTIC AND CRUISE MISSILES

9K720 *Iskander*-M ballistic- (SS-26 *Stone*) and cruise-missile (SSC-7 *Southpaw*) systems | **12** brigades

Source: IISS

physical-capital stock (i.e., machinery, facilities, infrastructure), most of it is relatively old. This weakness is exacerbated by an ageing R&D workforce and fragile links between higher education, R&D organisations and defence companies.[39] Also, the defence industry is only weakly integrated with international production chains. After a brief opening to international markets between 2010 and 2012, the conflict in Ukraine in 2014 and the subsequent imposition of Western and Ukrainian sanctions intensified Russia's focus on bolstering its self-sufficiency in arms production. Although this may reduce Russia's vulnerability to arms embargoes in the future, it also has the potential to narrow the scope for defence-industrial technological development through cooperation.[40]

These factors have led some commentators to suggest that the Russian defence industry might not be well placed to develop the next generation of weapons systems.[41] But it remains the case that Russia is one of the very few countries capable of producing the full spectrum of military equipment, and as a result it is the world's second-largest exporter of weaponry. Moreover, while in some ways Russia's defence-industrial output may appear less technologically advanced than that of its peers, this does not necessarily mean an inferior product under combat conditions.

Russia's defence industry: potential futures

It is possible to sketch out three basic scenarios for the future development of the Russian defence industry, based on several key variables including the volume of state spending on defence-industrial equipment, the volume of demand from abroad for Russian armaments, the level of investment in the industry's capital stock (both human and physical) and the degree to which defence-industrial firms are able to switch focus from military to civilian output.

A positive scenario would see increases both in government procurement and in purchases by foreign customers. A modest rate of real (i.e., adjusted for inflation) annual growth in orders would be sufficient for Russian manufacturers to maintain production lines and develop new systems for the future. Companies would be able to reinvest part of their profits in upgrading their production capabilities, which in turn might facilitate the expansion of non-military output; they could provide a more varied range of goods and services while remaining competitive in the international armaments market. Russia would continue to be self-sufficient in the production of a wide range of effective weapons systems.

In what one might call an inertia scenario, demand from both the Russian government and foreign customers would stay at current levels in nominal terms, but the value of those sales would be gradually eroded by inflation. This would reduce the funds available for reinvestment in productive capacity, limiting the prospects for shifting production to non-military output. The Russian defence industry would be characterised to an even greater degree by uneven capabilities. Those firms that are globally competitive would be able to reinvest profits in new production facilities and maintain their positions as leaders in their respective sub-sectors; those with lower-quality output would become increasingly uncompetitive and would survive only through state orders.

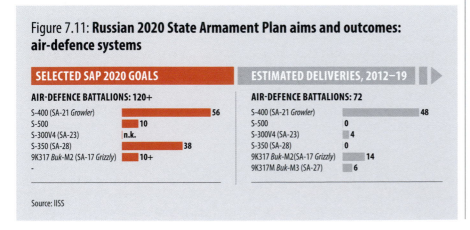

Figure 7.11: Russian 2020 State Armament Plan aims and outcomes: air-defence systems

SELECTED SAP 2020 GOALS	ESTIMATED DELIVERIES, 2012–19

AIR-DEFENCE BATTALIONS: 120+

S-400 (SA-21 *Growler*)	56
S-500	10
S-300V4 (SA-23)	n.k.
S-350 (SA-28)	38
9K317 *Buk*-M2 (SA-17 *Grizzly*)	10+
-	

AIR-DEFENCE BATTALIONS: 72

S-400 (SA-21 *Growler*)	48
S-500	0
S-300V4 (SA-23)	4
S-350 (SA-28)	0
9K317 *Buk*-M2(SA-17 *Grizzly*)	14
9K317M *Buk*-M3 (SA-27)	6

Source: IISS

Only modest progress would be made in expanding non-military production.

In a negative scenario, domestic defence spending would suffer cuts in both real and nominal terms, and Russian exporters would see orders diminish in the face of increasing competition from China and sanctions from the US. Profits would fall, leaving little scope for investment in production capabilities, and in turn reducing the quality of output and throttling any further expansion into civilian production. Russian enterprises would not become more efficient and innovation would be restricted to just a few high-priority areas, such as missiles and the nuclear industry.

Conclusion

It is evident that the increase in spending on defence-industrial production that began in 2011 has resulted in a significant recovery of output and in the re-equipment of the Russian armed forces. It is true that progress has been uneven and that some areas of development and production (e.g., helicopters, ballistic missiles, tactical and cruise missiles, and air-defence systems) have generally proceeded with fewer difficulties than others (e.g., surface warships, advanced fighter aircraft and transport aircraft). Nevertheless, the Russian defence industry has now largely recovered from the debilitating contractions of the 1990s. Large swathes of the capital stock have been updated, the workforce's conditions and morale have improved, and production lines are delivering sizeable quantities of equipment. Though the industry certainly has its weaknesses, it is also true that Russia is one of only three countries (alongside the US and China) capable of producing the full spectrum of military equipment. This maintains Russia's position as a key defence-industrial power. The challenge will be to sustain this recovery, and to shift from the production of platforms and systems that have their genesis in the late Soviet era to the successful design, development and manufacture of a new generation of weapons.

Notes

[1] See, for example, IISS, *The Military Balance 2020* (Abingdon: Routledge for the IISS, 2020), p. 194.

[2] Julian Cooper, 'Russia's State Armament Programme to 2020: a quantitative assessment of implementation 2011–2015', FOI, 2016, https://www.foi.se/rapportsammanfattning?reportNo=FOI-R--4239--SE.

[3] 'Soveshchanie s rukovodstvom Ministerstva oborony i predpriyatii OPK', President of Russia, 13 May 2019, http://kremlin.ru/events/president/news/60512.

[4] Roger McDermott, 'Shoigu Reflects on Military Modernization Amid COVID-19 Crisis', *Eurasia Daily Monitor*, vol. 17, no. 51, April 2020, https://jamestown.org/program/shoigu-reflects-on-military-modernization-amid-covid-19-crisis/.

[5] Julian Cooper, 'The Russian State Armament Programme, 2018–2027', *Russian Studies*, NATO Defence College, 01/18 – May 2018, http://www.ndc.nato.int/news/news.php?icode=1167.

[6] See Julian Cooper, 'Russia's Spending on Nuclear Weapons in a Comparative Perspective', Changing Character of War Centre, Pembroke College, University of Oxford, October 2018, http://www.ccw.ox.ac.uk/blog/2018/10/19/russian-military-expenditure-by-julian-cooper.

[7] International Monetary Fund, *World Economic Outlook Update, June 2020* (Washington DC: International Monetary Fund, 2020), https://www.imf.org/en/Publications/WEO/Issues/2020/06/24/WEOUpdateJune2020.

[8] Kirill Ryabov, 'Boleye polutora trillionov na oruzhnie. Perevooruzheniye armii RF v 2019 godu', *Military Review*, 17 December 2019, https://topwar.ru/165839-perevooruzhenie-v-2019-godu.html.

[9] Federal'nyi zakon ot 02.12.2919 No389-FZ 'O vnesenii izmenenii v federal'nyi zakon "O federal'nom byudzhete na 2019 god i na planovyi period 2020 i 2021 godov", 12 February 2019, http://publication.pravo.gov.ru/Document/View/0001201912020075.

[10] Julian Cooper, 'From USSR to Russia: The Military Economy', in Paul Hare and Gerard Turley (eds), *Handbook of the Economics and Political Economy of Transition* (London: Routledge, 2013).

[11] 'Ukaz o realizatsii planov razvitiya Vooruzhennykh Sil i modernizatsii OPK', President of Russia, 7 May 2012, http://kremlin.ru/news/15242; 'Byudzhetnoe poslanie Prezidenta RF o byudzhetnoi politike v 2013–2015 godakh', President of Russia, 28 June 2012, http://www.kremlin.ru/acts/15786.

[12] See, for example, Bettina Renz, *Russia's Military Revival* (Cambridge: Polity Press, 2017).

[13] Cooper, 'Russia's State Armament Programme to 2020: A Quantitative Assessment of Implementation 2011–2015'.

[14] Oleg Falichev, 'Den'gi vydelyayutsya zhdem kachestvennykh izdeliy', *Voyenno-Promyshlennyy Kur'yer*, 19 October 2011, http://vpk-news.ru/articles/8250.

[15] Cooper, 'From USSR to Russia: The Military Economy'.

[16] Ivan Karavaev, 'Osnovnye itogi realizatsii gosudarstvennoi politiki v OPK Rossii v 2012 godu i zadachi na blizhaishuiu perspektivu', in *Federalnyi spravochnik: Oboronno-promyshlennyiy kompleks Rossii* (Moscow: Federalnyi spravochnik, 2013), pp. 205–12.

[17] Richard Connolly, *Russia's Response to Sanctions: How Western Economic Statecraft is Reshaping Political Economy in Russia* (Cambridge: Cambridge University Press, 2018).

[18] 'Russian heavy strike drone Okhotnik makes first flight', TASS, 3 August 2019, https://tass.com/defense/1071784.

19 'Putin says 76 Su-57 jets to be purchased before 2028', TASS, 15 May 2019, https://tass.com/defense/1058494.

20 Sergey Sargsyants and Alexey Khazbiev, 'Sekvestr pyatogo pokoleniya', Expert Online, 31 May 2016, http://expert.ru/2015/03/26/sekvestr-pyatogo-pokoleniya.

21 'Putin says 76 Su-57 jets to be purchased before 2028', TASS.

22 'Minoborony i "MiG" podpishut kontrakt na postavku MiG-35 do kontsa goda', RIA Novosti, 5 February 2016, http://ria.ru/defense_safety/20160205/1370354093.html.

23 'Minoborony kupilo 16 istrebiteley MiG-29SMT', Lenta, 15 April 2014, https://lenta.ru/news/2014/04/15/mig29smt.

24 'Putin made decision to revive production of Tu-160M strategic bomber – Air Force commander', TASS, 28 May 2015, http://tass.ru/en/russia/797164.

25 'Primernyy kolichestvennyy sostav VVS RF k 2020 godu', VPK, 12 March 2013, http://vpk.name/news/85870_primernyii_kolichestven-nyii_sostav_vvs_rf_k_2020_godu.html.

26 'VKS RF poluchil vtoroy voyenno-trans-portnyy samolet Il-76MD-90A', Weapons of Russia, 17 May 2019, https://www.arms-expo.ru/news/armed-forces/vozdu-shno-kosmicheskie-sily-rf-poluchili-vtoroy-voenno-transportnyy-samolet-il-76md-90a.

27 Helicopter engines were previously supplied by the Ukrainian company Motor Sich.

28 'Rossiyskiy flot poluchit 24 podvodnyye lodki i 54 korablya do 2020 goda', RIA Novosti, 29 February 2020, https://ria.ru/20130311/926659011.html.

29 'Istochnik: atomnaya podvodnaya lodka Kazani ne budet sdana flotu v 2019 godu', TASS, 17 May 2019, http://tass.ru/armiya-i-opk/6441111.

30 'V Rossii prodolzhat stroitel'stvo serii neatomnykh podlodok "Lada", RIA Novosti, 28 March 2019, https://ria.ru/20190328/1552182854.html.

31 'Razrabotchik fregatov proyekta 11356 rassmatrivayet dva varianta zameny ukrainskikh dvigateley', VPK, 16 October 2014, http://vpk.name/news/119510_razrabotchik_fregatov_proekta_11356_rassmatrivaet_dva_vari-anta_zamenyi_ukrainskih_dvigatelei.html.

32 'Rossiya planiruyet postroit' 12 modern-izirovannykh fregatov proyekta 22350M', TASS, 9 May 2019, https://tass.ru/armiya-i-opk/6415468.

33 Maxim Shepavalenko, 'Predvaritel'nyye itogi SAP-2020 v chasti voyennogo kora-blestroyeniya', Eksport vooruzheniy, no. 1, January–February 2018, pp. 9–15.

34 'Russian commentator says fifth-genera-tion weapons only good for exhibitions', Regnum News Agency via BBC Monitoring, 27 February 2019, https://monitoring.bbc.co.uk/product/c200narc.

35 Organisation for Economic Co-operation and Development, Review of Innovation Policy: Russian Federation (Paris: OECD, 2011); Loren Graham, Lonely Ideas: Can Russia Compete? (Cambridge, MA: MIT Press, 2018); Roger Roffey, 'Russian Science and Technology is Still Having Problems – Implications for Defense Research', Journal of Slavic Military Studies, vol. 26, no. 2, 2013, pp. 162–88; Dimitry Adamsky, 'Defense Innovation in Russia: The Current State and Prospects for Revival', IGCC Defense Innovation Briefs, January 2014, https://escholarship.org/uc/item/0s99052x.

36 Leonid Gokhberg and Vitaly Roud, 'The Russian Federation: A New Innovation Policy for Sustainable Growth', in Soumitra Dutta (ed.), The Global Innovation Index 2012: Stronger Innovation Linkages for Global Growth (Fontainebleau: INSEAD, 2012), pp. 121–30.

37 Richard Connolly, 'State Industrial Policy in Russia: The Nanotechnology Industry', Post-Soviet Affairs, vol. 29, no. 1, 2013, pp. 1–30.

38 See Richard Connolly and Cecilie Sendstad, 'Russian Rearmament: An Assessment of Defense-Industrial Performance', in Problems of Post-Communism, vol. 65, no. 3, 2018, p. 156.

39 Sergey Matyushkin, 'Martyshkin GOZ – chast' I'[[Martyshkin State Defence Order – Part 1], VPK, 17 May 2016, http://www.vpk-news.ru/articles/30670.

40 'Importozameshcheniye – "blesk i nishcheta" rossiyskogo oboronno-promyshlennogo kompleksa', VPK, 20 January 2016, http://vpk.name/news/147993_importozamesh-enie__blesk_i_nisheta_rossiiskogo_oboron-nopromyishlennogo_kompleksa.html.

41 Vladimir Dvorkin, 'Trebuyetsya Innovatsionnyy Proryv', Voyenno-Promyshlennyy Kur'yer, 19 February 2014, http://www.vpk-news.ru/articles/19190; Andrey Frolov, 'Opasnosti na gorizonte', Russia in Global Affairs, 11 December 2015, http://ni.globalaffairs.ru/opasnosti-na-gorizonte.

Conclusion

The Soviet Union was a global military power. As of 2020, Russia is a capable continental military power, with intercontinental-range nuclear weapons. To its west it sees an enlarged NATO as a 'threat' and to its east it shares a land mass with the emerging global power of China.[1] Moscow entered this century with conventional armed forces incapable of carrying out important defence tasks required by the state and was therefore overly reliant on nuclear forces. Two decades on, following almost 15 years of sustained investment, Russia now has conventional military forces more commensurate with its defence and security goals.

Then-defence minister Anatoly Serdyukov's overarching aim for the 2008 'New Look' reform programme was to move beyond Soviet-era mass mobilisation and establish a modern, high-readiness force. This has been achieved, even if most of the New Look's organisational changes have subsequently been revised or abandoned. What this modernisation process has not delivered is a force of the capability and scale to match the United States and NATO in a sustained all-out conventional war, but this was likely never the aim. Rather, Moscow now has armed forces that provide it with the ability to rapidly mount a sizeable operation where it would have conventional superiority for a limited period. In a European context, the challenge to NATO would instead be maintaining alliance cohesion and managing the risk of escalation.

Equipment and defence spending

The New Look was underpinned by increased defence expenditure. This, alongside much-improved combat readiness, is a further legacy of the programme. All of Russia's armed forces have benefited from increased funding, though some elements arguably more than others.[2] Strategic forces and the Aerospace Forces have profited the most from re-equipment programmes, while the Navy has struggled, for example, to meet surface-ship ambitions. Procurement goals for the Ground Forces have also failed to be met in some key areas, such as heavy armour.

Faced with development delays and often woefully optimistic entry-into-service dates, Moscow has been forced to turn to upgrades of in-service designs as interim solutions to capability needs, for which it has the industrial capacity.[3] This approach has for the most part been successful, while not fulfilling completely the armed forces' long-term equipment goals.

The modernisation programme was supported and for the most part delivered, albeit with occasionally lowered ambition, by the 2020 State Armament Programme (SAP). Several of the equipment aims of SAP 2020 had been rolled over from SAP 2015, which had proved less successful in meeting targets. Although funding was made available as part of SAP 2015, the maturity of some of the systems and Russia's industrial capacity lagged behind. Instead it was SAP 2020 that was to prove to be the vehicle that delivered more than any previous armament programme in terms of Russia's modernisation aims.[4] Similarly, some of the missed goals of SAP 2020 have since been rolled into SAP 2027, while others have been placed in abeyance.[5]

Combat experience

The armed forces are also gaining from combat experience, and the less tangible but nonetheless valuable morale boost of militarily successful interventions in Crimea, eastern Ukraine and Syria. The last operation showed Russia's capacity to conduct a sustained intervention at distance beyond its immediate neighbourhood. Even though the force deployed to Syria was relatively small, this operation represented a gamble in terms of the ability to support the deployment, the performance of the personnel and equipment, and the risk that irrespective of the Russian presence the Syrian regime might lose the civil war. President Vladimir Putin in his December 2015 address to the Federal Assembly noted:

> The Russian Army and Navy have convincingly demonstrated their combat readiness and their increased capabilities. Modern Russian weapons have proved to be effective, and the invaluable practice of using them in combat conditions is being analysed and will be used to further improve our weapons and military equipment.[6]

Securing a professional personnel core on which to base high-readiness units has been a central element of the army's modernisation programme. The Airborne Forces position as a strategic reserve and a repository of highly trained troops and the establishment of the Special Forces have also improved the quality and utility of the armed forces. Their use in the annexation of Crimea, in the wider war in Ukraine and in Syria has underscored their worth and provided them with valuable combat experience.

Strategic forces

Russia's strategic nuclear arsenal was better insulated from the economic chaos of the 1990s and under-financing of the early 2000s than its conventional armed forces. However, related strategic programmes were far from unaffected by the country's wider economic misfortunes, with significant equipment delays a regular feature.

Even so, the Strategic Rocket Forces will by the end of this decade have a recapitalised missile inventory, operating the RS-12M1 *Topol*-M (SS-27 mod. 1), RS-24 *Yars* (SS-27 mod. 2), *Yars*-S and *Sarmat* (SS-X-29). The navy's nuclear-powered ballistic-missile-submarine fleet will by the mid-2030s consist of the *Borey* and *Borey*-A designs, while the air force will from the mid-2020s field the improved Tu-160M *Blackjack* bomber. There is less certainty in the role of Russia's 'novel' nuclear systems, and in some cases, such as the *Burevestnik* (SSC-X-9 *Skyfall*) nuclear-powered ground-launched cruise missile, whether the technology can be made to work reliably. What can be assumed is that Moscow will continue to look for ways to counter US missile defences, and these will likely consist of a mix of established and novel systems.

Conventional forces

Ground Forces

There has been less success in recapitalising elements of the Ground Forces' equipment inventory, especially its armoured vehicles. The new *Armata* family of main battle tank and heavy infantry fighting vehicle platforms is badly behind schedule.[7] Intended to be introduced into the inventory in significant numbers during SAP 2020, the *Armata* has now been delayed to SAP 2027. There

VOSTOK 2018 EXERCISE
Russia has increasingly held large-scale exercises, such as this one, September 2018. CREDIT: Vadim Savitsky/TASS/Getty Images

also remains a question as to how many of the main-battle-tank version of the *Armata* will eventually be acquired. Relatively small acquisition numbers, because of cost, could be supplemented by further purchases of the T-90M and continued modernisation of older T-72 models.

However, the 2020 SAP was more successful in delivering the replacement for the 9K79 *Tochka* (SS-21 *Scarab*) short-range ballistic missile. All of the army's ballistic-missile brigades have now been re-equipped with the 9K720 *Iskander*-M (SS-26 *Stone*).[8] This offers around three times the range of the longest-range version of the 9K79 and can also be used with the 9M728 (SSC-7 *Southpaw*) land-attack cruise missile. The army is also beginning to re-equip with the *Tornado*-S precision-guided multiple-launch rocket system.[9]

Navy

Russian naval ambition and outcomes have diverged over the course of Moscow's military-modernisation process. While some in the navy continued to harbour ambitions of a blue-water capability and carrier-borne air power, surface-ship and submarine build programmes have fallen far behind schedule. Nonetheless, the navy has gained key capabilities, among them the capacity to engage land targets at ranges of up to 2,500 kilometres using conventionally armed cruise missiles. The 3M14 (SS-N-30A *Sagaris*) is now deployed widely on ships and submarines. State trials of a high-speed cruise missile, *Tsirkon*, are also under way.[10]

The *Yasen/Yasen*-M cruise-missile-armed nuclear-powered submarine build programme, while badly behind schedule, is key to the navy's offensive sub-surface role. However, its larger surface-fleet build goals have fared less well. The *Lider*-class destroyer did not appear to be funded as part of SAP 2027.[11] Similarly, there is little indication of funding being allocated for the development of a replacement to the *Admiral Kuznetsov* aircraft carrier.[12] The *Kuznetsov*, with all its limitations, may have to be kept in service into the 2030s

if the navy is to remain even a marginal operator of carrier-borne aviation.

Aerospace Forces

The Aerospace Forces, like the navy, has had to watch key developments delayed. Unlike the navy, however, it has been better placed to pursue interim options. While the introduction of the Su-57 *Felon* combat aircraft, a main goal of SAP 2020, was not met, it was able to rely on a back-up, the Su-35S *Flanker* M. Although not a low-observable design, the Su-35S has provided the air force with a capable multi-role fighter for the air-superiority role. As of mid-2020, three regiments of the Su-57 were meant to be in service by the end of 2027, and together with the Su-35S and Su-30SM *Flanker* H these designs will be at the centre of Russian tactical air-power throughout the 2030s.[13] Meanwhile, the Su-34 *Fullback* derivative of the Su-27 is replacing the Su-24 *Fencer* in the fighter/ground-attack, electronic-warfare and reconnaissance roles.

Long-range aviation is benefiting from continuing investment in the Tu-160 *Blackjack* and Tu-95MS *Bear* H bombers. Work is continuing on a new bomber design to meet the PAK-DA requirement, although this project has, like the Su-57, suffered from delays. And like the Su-57, the air force has turned to an already existing design, the Tu-160, as a stopgap. The programme will return the *Blackjack* to production after a gap of three decades. But whether Russia has the financial or industrial heft to run the Tu-160M and the new design in parallel remains to be seen.[14]

In air-defence terms, progress on the S-500 surface-to-air missile system has also been slower than intended. By comparison, the goal with regard to S-400 unit numbers has been met. The focus now may shift to the S-500 and increasing the S-350 production rate.

The space element of the Aerospace Forces has also benefited from the renewed investment in space-based surveillance systems. Counter-space-systems development has also gained from improved funding, with direct-ascent, air-launched, directed-energy and co-orbital capabilities as of 2020 all in the latter stages of development and testing.

While the air force was the main participant in and beneficiary of Russia's Syrian intervention, the effects were wider. It provided Moscow with the opportunity to flex elements of its command-and-control architecture, including the National Defence Management Centre, in a joint operational environment. Joint operational doctrine, and the command-and-control structures to support this at all levels of command, is a growing focus for Russia's armed forces.

TU-160 *BLACKJACK* BOMBER
Pictured at Engels air base, which remains home to the only Tu-160 squadron yet in service with the Aerospace Forces, August 2017.
CREDIT: Marina Lystseva/TASS/Getty Images

Budgetary and industrial risks

Even before the finance ministry's July 2020 pitch to reduce near-term defence spending as a result of the impact of the COVID-19 pandemic, Putin had put Russia's defence industry on notice over SAP 2027 and the scale of procurement.[15] He indicated acquisition levels would not be the same as in the 2010–20 period, and industry would have to adapt accordingly. The finance ministry is reported to have proposed cutting 5% from the planned procurement budget from 2021 to 2023 to help alleviate the worst of the economic downturn.[16] Should the recommendation be adopted, the defence ministry will be faced with either spreading cuts or delays across multiple projects, or selecting a smaller number to deliver the savings, but with greater impact on these programmes.

While Russia's defence industry delivered on many of the programmes funded by SAP 2020, it was not able to produce some key new equipment types, suggesting that structural issues, and challenges for the defence-technology base, have yet to be resolved fully. Concluding development of the Su-57, the *Armata* family and the S-500, for example, and then producing them at a reasonable annual rate and to cost within SAP 2027 will be indicative of the wider health, or otherwise, of the defence-technology and manufacturing sector. There is also the requirement to sustain research and development (R&D) funding. Moscow may be forced to choose whether to prioritise the production of the new systems at the expense of some of the emphasis on R&D.

Outlook

While it is likely that not all the percentage targets of Russia's modernisation programme (that the inventory should consist of 70% modern equipment by 2020) will be met by the end of the year, it has succeeded more than it has failed. A review by Moscow of these modernisation goals may be accompanied by the renewal of several key classified texts on Russia's Arctic, maritime and military doctrines, as well as the latest update of the National Security Strategy. Some or all of these could be concluded by late 2020 or early 2021. Together, these will offer further insight into the medium- to long-term goals for Russia's armed forces.

From the collapse of the Soviet Union and Russia's military decline in the 1990s to the interventions under Vladimir Putin, the arc of Soviet and Russian military development has on occasion caught Western analysts by surprise. Indeed, the trajectory of Russia's military modernisation and the use Moscow will make of its forces in future remain uncertain, dependent perhaps on the economy as well as politics. However, what is apparent is the effect that Russia's sustained period of military reform and recapitalisation has had, and continues to have, on its conventional and nuclear capabilities.

Russia's political leaders now have at their disposal well-equipped conventional armed forces built around professional rather than conscript personnel. These forces are held at higher readiness and are able to be used, or their potential use signalled, at very short notice. Combined with a more assertive foreign policy, these forces constitute a capability that should not be ignored.

Notes

1 President of Russia, 'Military Doctrine of the Russian Federation', 25 December 2014, clause 12, https://rusemb.org.uk/press/2029.

2 See, for example, Michael Kofman, 'The Durability of Russian Military Power: Moscow's Prospects for Sustaining Direct Competition', Russia Military Analysis, 25 May 2018, https://russianmilitaryanalysis.wordpress.com/tag/state-armament-program.

3 Regnum News Agency, 'Russian commentator says fifth-generation weapons only good for expos', BBC Monitoring, 15 February 2019, https://monitoring.bbc.co.uk/product/c200narc.

4 See, for example, *Kommersant*, 'Russia's leading missile maker blames structural innovations for problems', BBC Monitoring, 13 July 2011, https://monitoring.bbc.co.uk/product/70152703.

5 'Avangard hypersonic missiles replace Rubezh ICBMs in Russia's armament plan through 2027', TASS, 22 March 2018, https://tass.com/defense/995628.

6 President of Russia, 'Presidential Address to the Federal Assembly', 3 December 2015, http://en.kremlin.ru/events/president/news/50864.

7 *Rossiyskaya Gazeta*, 'Russia begins designing new tank to substitute for aborted T-95 – paper', BBC Monitoring, 15 May 2011, https://monitoring.bbc.co.uk/product/70147790.

8 See, for example, IISS, *The Military Balance 2020* (Abingdon: Routledge for the IISS, 2020), p. 195

9 *Ibid.*, p. 196.

10 'Russia to hold about 10 more test launches of hypersonic Tsirkon missile – source', TASS, 23 April 2020, https://tass.com/defense/1148571.

11 Douglas Barrie and Henry Boyd, 'Russia's State Armament Programme 2027: A more measured course on procurement', IISS Military Balance Blog, 13 February 2018, https://www.iiss.org/blogs/military-balance/2018/02/russia-2027.

12 *Ibid.*

13 *Rossiyskaya Gazeta*, 'Paper looks at the future role of Russia's Su-35, Su-57 jets', BBC Monitoring, 15 July 2020, https://monitoring.bbc.co.uk/product/c201wrzh.

14 Pavel Podvig, 'Russia ambitious plans for strategic bombers', Russian strategic nuclear forces, 10 May 2017, http://russianforces.org/blog/2017/05/russias_ambitious_plans_for_st.shtml.

15 'Russia, hit by coronavirus crisis, considers military spending cuts', Reuters, 21 July 2020, https://www.reuters.com/article/us-russia-economy-military/russia-hit-by-coronavirus-crisis-considers-military-spending-cuts-idUSKCN24M1IF.

16 *Ibid.*

Index